CRIMINAL INVESTIGATION

BASIC PERSPECTIVES

TENTH EDITION

PAUL B. WESTON
(Deceased)

CHARLES LUSHBAUGH

Retired Lieutenant, Sacramento County Sheriff's Department
Sacramento, California

Lecturer of Criminal Justice
California State University
Sacramento, California

FBI National Academy, 185th Session

PEARSON
Prentice
Hall

Upper Saddle River, New Jersey 07458

Library of Congress Cataloging-in-Publication Data

Lushbaugh, Charles.
  Criminal investigation : basic perspectives / Charles Lushbaugh.—10th ed.
    p. cm.
  Rev. ed. of: Criminal investigation / Paul B. Weston, Charles Lushbaugh. 9th ed. c2003.
  Includes bibliographical references and index.
  ISBN 0-13-118859-3
  1. Criminal investigation—United States.   I. Weston, Paul B. Criminal investigation.
II. Title.

  HV8073.W44 2006
  363.25'0973—dc21   2004030495

Executive Editor: Frank Mortimer, Jr.
Associate Editor: Sarah Holle
Production Liaison: Brian Hyland
Production Coordination: *The GTS Companies/*York, PA Campus
Managing Editor: Mary Carnis
Director of Production & Manufacturing: Bruce Johnson
Manufacturing Buyer: Cathleen Petersen
Design Director: Cheryl Asherman
Senior Design Coordinator: Miguel Ortiz
Cover Design: Marianne Frasco
Cover Photo: Stephane Ruet/CORBIS SYGMA

This book was set in Janson Text by *The GTS Companies/*York, PA Campus. It was printed and bound by R.R. Donnelley. The cover was printed by Phoenix Color.

Pearson Education LTD.   Pearson Education Canada, Ltd.
Pearson Education Australia PTY, Limited   Pearson Educación de Mexico, S. A. de C.V.
Pearson Education Singapore, Pte. Ltd.   Pearson Education—Japan
Pearson Education North Asia Ltd.   Pearson Education Malaysia, Pte. Ltd.

10 9 8 7 6 5 4 3 2 1
ISBN: 0-13-118859-3

Paul B. Weston (1910–2003)

"Men who have never met him profess to know him. They repeat his theories and ideals as if they were their own. No man could ask more."*

Raised in New York City during the Depression in the tough district of Harlem. Trained as a gunsmith and self-taught marksman, he was issued two patents for gun-related inventions by age 25.

1936	Joined the New York City Police Department (NYPD).
1941	Joined the U.S. Navy during World War II as a chief petty officer and taught gunnery while stationed in Hawaii.
1948	The youngest officer to be promoted to the rank of captain.
1956	Promoted to deputy chief, the highest civil service rank in the NYPD.
1958	Retired to devote his time to writing.
1958	Joined the faculty at the California State University at Sacramento to teach police science courses.
1963	Became the chief of the California State Police.
1968	Rejoined the faculty at the California State University at Sacramento to become the chairman of the Criminal Justice Department.
1977	Named outstanding criminal justice instructor of the year.
1980	Retired from teaching to concentrate on his writing.

Forty-four years of public service. The author of twenty-nine books and four theatrical plays. A true mentor and friend to students and peers.

---

*Written by A. Robert Matt, Assistant Director for the Center for Police Training at Indiana University in 1978 for the book jacket of *Combat Shooting for Police.*

CONTENTS

Chapter 13   Arson, Bombings, and Hate Crimes   251

Chapter 14   Property Crimes   271

PREFACE

The tenth edition of *Criminal Investigation: Basic Perspectives* was written to reflect changes in the field of criminal investigation. Chapter 7, Interviewing and the Detection of Deception, and Chapter 8, Interrogation of Suspects, were extensively rewritten. The changes to these chapters highlight new insights in these areas of criminal investigation. In addition, new segments were added to three chapters:

Motivating witnesses, separating witnesses, obtaining a commitment from a witness, and using gunshot residue examinations (Chapter 2, Direct and Circumstantial Evidence)

Using computer databases (Chapter 5, Basic Investigative Leads and Informants)

Implementing search warrants (Chapter 6, Major Investigative Techniques)

Reviewing federally controlled substances law (Appendix B)

Two new case studies, (Chapters 2 and 16), designed to enhance the learning process, were also added to this edition. The case study method of instruction facilitates learning by linking case content to textbook topics and by encouraging the exchange of opinions and viewpoints among students during discussion sessions. The case studies in this book are designed to contribute to this type of learning process. Each case provides factual information likely to promote analysis and discussion and thus aid in developing the student's ability to analyze, evaluate, and reason. The topic of discussion focuses on the facts of each case study, but only the range of student opinions and ideas limits the scope of the discussion.

Some cases are presented in straight, narrative style, whereas others are written in dialogue form as the best means of joining the personalities and the situations of the case study. Each case presents a real-life situation or episode experienced some time in the past. No "doctoring" has been done to develop points, theories, or problems. However, names, dates, and locations have been altered in some instances to avoid embarrassing any persons or their families.

A note of thanks to the reviewers of the last edition: Steven Egger, University of Houston–Clearlake, Houston, TX; David Lashley, Faulkner University, Montgomery, AL; and Donald Alsdurf, Kansas City Kansas Community College, Kansas City, KS.

PART I ELEMENTS OF INVESTIGATION

1

THE INITIAL INVESTIGATION

Criminal investigation is a lawful search for people and items useful in reconstructing an illegal act or **omission** and analysis of the mental state of the person committing the act or omission. It is a probing from the known to the unknown, backward in time. The objective of criminal investigation is to determine truth as far as it can be discovered in any inquiry. Successful investigations are based not only on fidelity, accuracy, and sincerity in lawfully searching for the facts, but also on an equal faithfulness, exactness, and probity in reporting the results.[1]

The marriage of science and traditional criminal investigation techniques has offered new horizons of efficiency in criminal investigation. New perspectives in investigation reject a total or major reliance on informers and custodial interrogation, and instead increasingly advocate skilled scanning of the crime scene for physical evidence and searching for as many witnesses as possible. Mute evidence tells its own story in court, either by its demonstrativeness or through the testimony of an expert witness involved in its scientific testing. Such evidence may serve in lieu of, or as a corroboration of, informant information, custodial interrogation results, and testimonial evidence of witnesses found and interviewed by police. Through this marriage of science and investigation, an increasing certainty of solving crimes is possible, which will contribute to the major deterrent of crime: the certainty that the criminal will be discovered, arrested, prosecuted, and convicted.

Hans Gross (1847–1915) was the earliest advocate of criminal investigation as a science. Gross was a native of Austria, born in Graz. Educated in law, he became interested in investigation while serving as an examining magistrate. He became a professor of criminology at the University of Vienna. Perhaps his legal training, or his education in rational theory joined with the study of law, made Magistrate Gross unhappy with the lack of science in police investigation. In any event, he deserves credit for developing a system of investigation. His *System der Kriminalistik (Criminal Investigation)*, translated into English and published in 1906, is a classic text in this field.

Gross strongly supported scrupulous accuracy and strict ethics in criminal investigation. His greatest contribution to the introduction of science in criminal investigation was advocacy of a parallel system of inquiry based on the crime scene.

THE LEGAL SIGNIFICANCE OF EVIDENCE

Evidence is the only means of convincing the triers of fact (judge or jury) of the truth or untruth of allegations and accusations made by the parties in their pleadings. Inasmuch as investigators must collect all the evidence, and prosecutors and the court must weigh the significance of any evidence in relation to its possible presentation in court, the first item of importance is whether the evidence will be admissible in court. Admissibility usually depends on whether the evidence is relevant, material, and competent.

The legal significance of evidence rests in its influence on the judge or jury. Once evidence passes the test of admissibility and is part of the court record, it may influence the outcome of the trial. Any piece of evidence, either alone or in combination with other evidence, must be persuasive to the triers of fact. Such persuasiveness is the impact energy of an item of evidence.

Investigators must learn the difference between evidence and facts to avoid confusion in evaluating evidence in its role as proof. Evidence is not synonymous with fact. Evidence may be ambiguous—that is, subject to different interpretations. It may be false, exaggerated, planted, or perjured. It may be modified by forgetfulness, inattention, or silence. Conversely, a fact is the truth—insofar as the truth can be determined by the triers of fact in a criminal trial. A fact in this sense of the term is the effect of evidence, and it depends on evidence. A fact is established from a personal evaluation, by the trier of fact, of the evidence presented in a particular case. Evidence may tend to prove a fact, may be sufficiently strong to compel a conclusion of fact, or may be just strong enough to create a reasonable doubt.

In the U.S. justice system, the defendant is presumed to be innocent and the prosecution is required to prove the case against the defendant beyond a reasonable doubt—to a moral certainty. These legal principles of the adversary system of justice have a simple reality factor: accusations of crime must be supported in court by legally significant evidence.

Knowledge of evidence and its legal significance is essential to an investigator's success. The investigator must know what evidence is required on the issue of guilt or innocence; whether such evidence indicates guilt or innocence; and, when guilt is apparent, whether such evidence—in total—is likely to prove guilt beyond a reasonable doubt. In the final analysis, the success of an investigation depends on the evidence collected and its legal significance.

COORDINATION OF THE CRIME SCENE

The crime scene is the focus of the preliminary investigation. En route to the scene, the assigned investigator plans his or her action upon arrival and reviews the problems usually connected with any crime scene.

The initial response should include a notation of any persons or vehicles leaving the scene. Upon arrival, the investigator should scan the area to determine whether the crime is ongoing and whether the suspect is still at the scene. The first responder's responsibility is to neutralize the crime scene and thus make it safe for other personnel to enter the area. Neutralization of the crime scene includes arresting any suspects and eliminating any hazards that might present a threat.

The investigator's next responsibility is to ensure that medical attention is provided, if it is required, and that this attention is administered with as little impact on the crime scene as possible. The best way to minimize this impact is to work with the medical personnel so that they know the importance of limiting the number of persons who enter the area and respect the need to minimize the possible destruction of evidence. The investigator, however, must be mindful that the possibility of saving a life supersedes the possible destruction of evidence.

The first step in processing a crime scene for clues and evidence is to accurately survey the surroundings and carefully evaluate the situation—that is, to take "a long, hard look." Deliberate action at this time guards against false moves and mistakes. The impact of the overall picture of the scene on an experienced investigator will provide guidelines for modifying a base plan of action. The assigned investigator must ascertain as soon as possible where the crime happened. Usually the crime scene is readily discernible.

A search for evidence starts with effective protection of the crime scene. The searcher must be certain that nothing has been removed from or added to the scene since the arrival of responding police—in short, that the scene is intact. Posting "freeze" signs ("Keep Out—Crime Scene Search in Progress") and stretching barrier tape aids in delineating the crime scene area. Guards posted at the perimeter will also prevent the entry of unauthorized persons. Crime scene boundaries should be established beyond the initial scope of the crime scene with the understanding that the boundaries can be reduced if necessary but cannot be easily expanded.[2]

The main purpose of a search—to look for clues and for evidence of what happened during the crime—must always be foremost in the investigator's mind. A search is not a random groping but rather a selective looking for objects and materials. The investigator's expertise, acquired by training and experience, should indicate what items are to be found at the scenes of different types of crimes. For a search to be successful, its main purpose must be aligned with some particularity in knowing what to look for. Otherwise, the search lacks necessary professional direction.

The preliminary investigator's work concentrates on three basic elements of investigation: searching the crime scene, collecting and preserving evidence found at the scene, and locating and interviewing available witnesses at or near the crime scene. When crimes are not witnessed or when a reliable witness cannot be located at this stage of the investigation, the investigative leads likely to produce a solution to the crime will originate with physical evidence found at the crime scene.

The chain of command at a crime scene is often hectic. Most law enforcement agencies specify that the "first officer" on the scene is in charge until a patrol sergeant arrives. This sergeant (or officer of higher rank) is in command until he or she is relieved by a detective or an officer of higher rank. At the scene of a minor crime, the sergeant may relinquish command by calling the dispatcher, reporting that he or she is leaving the scene, and reporting the name of the officer now in charge. At the scene of a more serious crime, the sergeant waits for the detective's arrival, briefs him or her about what the police at the scene have learned about the circumstances of the crime, and turns over command of the investigation to the detective. However, the sergeant will remain at the scene, in command of the uniformed personnel guarding the limits of the scene, monitoring new arrivals, and performing similar duties.

At the scene of a more serious crime, particularly a homicide, larger police units field a so-called mobile crime laboratory with detectives trained in forensic science or crime laboratory forensic scientists to process the crime scene. At this point, determining who is in charge becomes even more difficult. Despite this identification problem, most police units have men and women who are self-starters and work together to prepare for the search of a crime scene.[3]

SYSTEMATIC SEARCH PROCEDURES

The methodology of searching depends on the case and the scene. Staffing problems in police units and problems associated with proffering evidence in court have resulted in the **single-officer search**. Associates of this officer often assist in locating evidence, but they do not disturb it or collect it. The goal is to limit the number of officers in possession of crime scene evidence to only the officer searching the scene. The use of double coverage in searching crime scenes is valuable as a double check for evidence, but it frequently results in conflicting testimony by searching officers.

When the search must cover a wide area, the available investigators should be assigned to teams. One member of each team serves as the single officer collecting evidence, and each team is assigned responsibility for searching a specified segment of the crime scene. A designated investigator or a superior officer commands the entire search operation.

A crime scene is the place of the crime, including any adjoining entry or exit areas. Therefore, prior to a search, the assigned investigator surveys the scene, noting its dimensions and the existence of any adjoining entry (approach) and exit (flight) areas. This evaluation forms the basis for setting limits on the search area, for determining how to organize the search procedure, and for ascertaining what assistance is needed.

Traditionally, systematic searching has involved the following four methods (Figure 1–1):

1. A **point-to-point movement** following a chain of objects that are obviously evidence.

Ever-Widening Circle

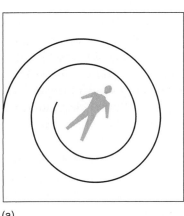

(a)

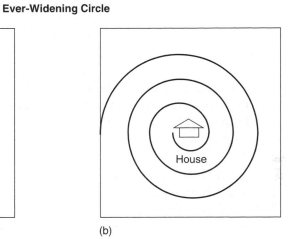

(b)

Zone or Sector

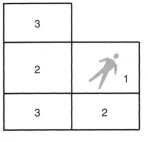

(c)

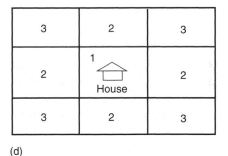

(d)

Strip

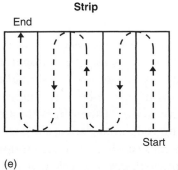

(e)

Grid

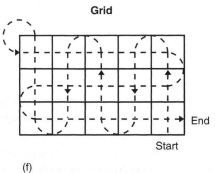

(f)

FIGURE 1–1   Search methods: (a) indoors, (b) outdoors, (c) immediate area, (d) extended area, (e) strip search of large area, (f) grid search of large area.

2. An **ever-widening circle**, in which the searching officer starts at the focal point of the scene or the center of the security area and works outward by circling in a clockwise or counterclockwise direction until the fringes of the protected area are reached. The **ever-narrowing circle** technique reverses this procedure: the searching officer starts at the outskirts of the crime scene and works toward its focal point.
3. A **zone or sector search**, in which the scene is divided into segments and each zone or sector is searched as an individual unit.
4. A strip or grid search for outdoor areas. In the *strip* **search**, the area to be searched is plotted like a football field. Searching starts at a sideline and moves across the field to the other sideline. Searchers work back and forth across the field until the entire area is searched. The *grid* **search** starts with a strip search and then covers the same area in a similar manner but at right angles to the strip search pattern. Metal or wood stakes and heavy cord are used to direct and control outdoor searches.

Some experienced investigators dislike describing any search method by name because doing so emphasizes technique rather than purpose and has often led to criticism during cross-examination. When queried on the witness stand about searching the crime scene, investigators should state that they began the search by looking around, moved generally in a clockwise direction (if this was the technique), and made field notes as items of evidence were discovered. The field notes should therefore support the fact that the search was a systematic examination of the scene.

A search of deceased persons, when suspicion exists that a criminal act was involved in the death, is often assigned to field representatives of the coroner's or medical examiner's office. In some jurisdictions, the coroner or medical examiner will permit body searches by the police upon request. In any event, the search must be methodical and thorough. Regulations in many police units require the investigator to delay such a search until it can be made in the presence of a disinterested witness and to record the name of such a witness in his or her field notes. A complete list of all property found on the deceased victim and where it was found (e.g., right side pocket of trousers, hidden in bra) are made part of the officer's notes.

The ability to discover and recognize evidence is a prerequisite to successful searching. As the investigator surveys the crime scene before searching it, he or she develops some concept of the type and nature of evidence that should be the objective of the crime scene search. Physical evidence can be anything from massive objects to microscopic traces. The nature of the crime offers the first clue: weapons are used in assaults; premises are entered in burglaries; a fire is set in arson cases. The victim, the offender's **modus operandi**, and other circumstances that can be observed during this survey may suggest possible clues.

Where to search for physical evidence is particularized by the type of evidence the investigator is seeking. In an assault or a homicide case, the injuries the victim sustained suggest a weapon and orient the search toward it. In a burglary case, the means used to gain access to the premises and the place of entrance indicate the possible location of tool marks. Tabletops, glassware, and other smooth surfaces guide the search for imprints. Soft earth, mud, and dust are known sites for foot and tire impressions.

When searching a crime scene, the investigator should be mindful of **Locard's exchange principle**. Edmond Locard, the founder of the Institute of Criminalistics, in Lyon, France, believed that suspects will bring items of evidence into the crime scene and will take items with them when they leave. This exchange of trace evidence involves such items as hairs, fibers, dirt, dust, blood, body fluids, skin cells, and other microscopic materials.[4]

Initially, the investigator must identify the type of evidence he or she wants to find and its likely area of discovery, then make a systematic search, and finally recognize the evidence when it is found. The experienced investigator is always alert for evidence that may seem unimportant but is, in fact, material and relevant.

Collecting Evidence

Investigators should not rush to pick up evidence since its significance may be destroyed in the process. The investigator's field notes should include a record of the discovery and recognition. In addition, photographs and accurate measurements are necessary to show the original position and the nature of the evidence. When searching for evidence at crime scenes, the investigator should never alter the position of, pick up, or touch any object before it has been minutely described in an official note and a photograph of it has been taken.

The integrity of evidence is maintained by keeping it in its original state. No alterations should be made to any item that is or may be evidence. Blood, rust, grease, and dirt should not be removed from objects, nor should the investigator add his or her fingerprints to the evidence or smear or wipe off any such clues. An item of physical evidence important in and of itself may have another important item of evidence on or attached to it. This item can range from a fingerprint on a fragment of glass to blood and fibers on weapons.

Evidence likely to be found at crime scenes and amenable to scientific analysis is divided into seven major groups: (a) weapons; (b) blood; (c) imprints and impressions (traces of a person or a vehicle); (d) marks of tools used to gain access to locked premises or containers; (e) dust, dirt, and other traces; (f) questioned documents; and (g) miscellaneous trace or transfer evidence. Such evidence is discussed in more detail in Chapter 2.

Marking Evidence

Marking evidence identifies it. Marking must not impair the value of evidence or restrict the number and kind of examinations to which it might be

Crime scene being processed with items of evidence identified with numbered tags.

subjected by criminalists and other experts. Consideration should also be given to the monetary value of the item of evidence and whether the item will be returned to the rightful owner when it is no longer needed. Will marking the evidence destroy or diminish the value of the item? If so, another means of marking the item should be considered. Tamperproof evidence tags and bags might suffice, as well as the use of correction fluid, which can be applied to the item of evidence, written on, and later removed without causing permanent damage.

Traditional marking of objects includes the investigator's initials, the date, and the report number if ample space is available. Counterfeit money should have a dual marking. The name of the person last in possession should be signed across a corner of the bill, or the person should be asked to scratch his or her initials on a coin. In addition, the investigator should place his or her mark of identification on the money. When currency is mutilated by marking it with a tracing powder or dye, it should not be cleaned but should be placed immediately in a sealed envelope and handled with care. Later, when no longer required as evidence, this mutilated currency should not be returned to general circulation but should be redeemed at a local bank with a statement that it contains stained material added to develop it as evidence.

The factor of overriding importance in identifying evidence exhibits in court is how the investigator knows this exhibit is the object he or she found. On direct examination, questions usually have the following format:

Q: Officer, I show you this revolver, now marked as people's exhibit no. 7. Do you recognize it? (Officer takes the revolver, looks for his mark, finds it, and answers.)

A: Yes, I do.

Q: How do you recognize it?

A: By my mark here on the butt. (Pointing to rear and bottom of revolver.)

Q: Where and under what circumstances did you first see this revolver?

The witness proceeds with the testimony; the identification serves as a foundation for the remainder of the testimony.

Establishing the Chain of Possession

Continuity of possession—the **chain of possession**—must be established when evidence is proffered in court as an exhibit. Whenever possible, if the officer locating the evidence is not the investigator assigned responsibility for the case, the evidence should not be disturbed until its location and nature can be brought to the attention of the responsible investigator, nor should it be moved until its location and description have been noted, photographs have been taken, and measurements have been made to place it.

Adherence to standard and required procedures in every case is the best guarantee that the collection and possession of physical evidence will stand a court test of what happened, or could have happened, to it from the time of its finding to its presentation in court. Any deviation from standard procedures in processing physical evidence can affect its credibility and contribute to a reasonable suspicion in the minds of the triers of fact about the entire police investigation.

In narcotics cases in many areas, investigators seal the evidence in manila envelopes, initial the sealing, and drop the envelopes through a slot into a locked box at local headquarters. The chemist who will make the examination has the only key to this box. He or she removes the evidence by cutting the sealed envelope open, examines the evidence, replaces it in the original manila envelope, reseals the envelope with gummed tape, initials the sealing, and places the envelope in a locked box.

An idea of the ritual used to prove the continuity of the possession of evidence is illustrated by the questions and responses recorded during a grand jury hearing in a case of possession and sale of narcotics. The testimony, on direct examination of the finding investigator, relative to this evidence was as follows:

Q: I believe you found a large quantity of what you believe to be drugs in the house?

A: Yes, sir.

Q: Do you recognize this plastic bag as containing the quantity you discovered?

A: Yes, sir.

Q: Where were the drugs taken?

A: They were brought to the station.

Q: Where were they put?

A: In the interrogation room and locked up.

Q: The next day, did you take the drugs from the interrogation room to the Bureau of Narcotics Enforcement?

A: Yes, sir. I did.

Q: In the Bureau of Narcotics Enforcement, were they put in a locker?

A: Yes.

Q: Was this locker locked?

A: Yes.

Q: Did you have a key to open it again?

A: No, sir.

Q: Where is this locker located?

A: The chemist's office.

The chemist was then sworn in and questioned:

Q: Do you recall having seen that plastic bag (indicating bag identified by previous witness) and the contents of it?

A: Yes, I do.

Q: Did you bring it with you today?

A: Yes, I did.

Q: When did you first come into contact with that particular bag?

A: On December 28th of last year.

Q: Where did you find it?

A: It was removed by me from a locked locker at the Narcotics Bureau, an evidence locker in my office that is used to submit evidence for analysis when I am not present to take it personally and to which I have the only key.

Q: Now, did you subsequently examine the drugs in this bag?

A: Yes, I did.

Since the basic legal integrity of the evidence was shown, the witness continued his testimony about his examination of the contents of the plastic bag.

Packaging Physical Evidence

Evidence must be packaged to avoid breakage, loss, or contamination in transit. Tweezers, forceps, and similar tools are used to collect and place trace evidence and small items in their containers. Latex gloves are suggested for handling some physical evidence.

An evidence box or board can be used for transporting evidence short distances. An evidence box with Peg-Board sides allows small and medium-sized objects to be tied or wired in place. A series of drilled holes and appropriately sized dowel rods can serve the same purpose. Items of evidence that will undergo comparison analysis for possible relationships should be packaged in separate containers to obviate any allegation of cross-contamination. No wet or soiled materials or boxes or bottles should be used. Thoroughly clean and dry containers, wrapping paper, corrugated paper, boxes, and sealing tape are the basic safeguards for physical evidence in transport.

Documentary evidence is first placed in a transparent envelope without folding or bending. Then, this envelope is placed between two pieces of firm, corrugated cardboard, all of which is then put in a manila envelope or another wrapper.

Plastic pill bottles or film containers with pressure lids are unbreakable, can be easily sealed with tape, and are excellent containers for hair, fibers, and other small articles. They are ideal for spent bullets, empty cartridge cases, and cartridges because they can be packed with cotton gauze to minimize movement of such evidence.

Plastic envelopes and bags are available in various shapes and sizes and are easily sealed. However, when they are used for transporting soil, debris, or clothing that may contain bloodstains, bacterial action can easily contaminate the blood sample. Plastic containers should be used with caution. To an unusual degree, they can act as greenhouses for the cultivation of mold, which can destroy the integrity and identity of some types of evidence.

For blood samples and swatches used to collect bloodstains, only the tubes or vials with stoppers found in the blood collection kit should be used. Directions on the kit for refrigeration and other care should be followed.

If the stain is on a solid object that can be moved, such as a firearm or another weapon, the object should be transported with the area of the stain protected or the object completely enclosed in a package if the object is small. If the stain is on clothing, the garments should be wrapped separately in paper, marked appropriately, and packaged. This procedure is superior to any technique for removing a sample of the stain for analysis.

Articles of clothing, tablecloths, and similar evidence should be folded as little as possible and without pressure. If the areas of the fabric to be examined are known, they should be protected from friction with wrapping paper or other containers.

A soil-stained or mud-soaked object should be taken to the laboratory intact. No attempt should be made to remove and transport the soil or mud as a separate item. When such traces are picked up as individual items of evidence, every precaution must be taken to keep the evidence in separate sealed containers to avoid any accidental loss or mixing in transit.

Charred wood, carpet, and drapery material from the scene of a suspicious fire may be wrapped in metal foil and sealed in an airtight container. Smaller objects, such as paper and rags, or solid samples should be sealed in the container in which they were found or placed in airtight bottles or cans. Doing so protects the fire accelerant and its residues from evaporation.

Pills and other noncaustic substances should be left in their original containers for transport to the laboratory. Such containers often provide useful information. The investigator should count the number of pills or capsules or accurately determine the bulk quantity of fluids or powders and should include these data in his or her field notes.

Caustic poison should not be transported until the investigator has ensured that the container in which it was found (or placed after its recovery from a sink, a bathtub, or another place) is safe for a period equal to at least twice the likely transport time.

Food, body substances, and fluids should be placed in as many separate moisture-proof bottles or containers as necessary to avoid any contamination of evidence. Food or other substances suspected of containing or known to contain poison should be plainly labeled as suspected or known samples of poison.

If a weapon is suspected of containing hair, blood, or fragments of flesh, it should be packaged in a sealed container of appropriate size.

Microscopic traces, hair, and fibers should be sealed in folded paper or placed in a clean, sealed envelope or box of appropriate size.

Matching Physical Evidence with Known Standards

Criminalistics includes identifying physical evidence and determining its origin. This individualization of evidence often requires that physical evidence collected at a crime scene be matched with a **known standard of evidence** or a control. Known standards may be collected at the crime scene, from the victim, from a suspect, or from other sources and must be collected in exactly the same manner as any other evidence because they have equal evidential value. Just as with other evidence, known standards must be recognized, possessed legally, and marked for identity. The integrity of the sample must be preserved, and its acquisition reported accurately.

Locating a known standard of fingerprints may require no more than a search of records for a suspect's fingerprints. Shoe prints may require collection of a known standard of soil from the area near a footprint or heel print for comparison with soil traces on a suspect's shoes. Collection of a hair sample is often required, as is the search for and the recovery of a coat or sweater or another garment that may be a known standard for fibers recovered at the crime scene.

Known samples of blood start with the victim. Samples can be secured only by a medical practitioner upon the investigator's request. Since *Schmerber v. California*, investigators may lawfully take a sample from an arrested person charged with a crime in which blood collected as evidence requires a known sample for comparison analysis.[5]

The self-incrimination clause of the Fifth Amendment to the U.S. Constitution protects against compelling a person or suspect to communicate or testify to matters that may incriminate him or her. However, the Fifth Amendment does not protect a person or suspect from being compelled to be the source of "real or physical evidence." The recovery of blood, clothing, and hair without consent is not prohibited by the Fifth Amendment because all these items are considered "real or physical evidence" and thus are subject to the controls of the right-to-privacy and search-and-seizure clauses of the Fourth Amendment, rather than to the self-incrimination clause of the Fifth.

Handwriting analysis requires exemplars, or samples, as well as proof of authorship. These known standards are classed as either *requested* (by the investigator) or *regular course of business*. In death cases in which a suicide note is found, the only exemplar possible is some regular-course-of-business handwriting found on the victim or at the scene, or secured from relatives and associates, and identified by a responsible person as the victim's handwriting. In other cases, such exemplars may be available at the crime scene, at the place of employment, or in the public record. Requested exemplars are often less reliable because of attempts to disguise the normal writing style or distortions due to nervousness.[6]

Investigators obtaining handwriting samples from a suspect should supply him or her with paper and a pen or pencil similar to those used to create the questioned writing, dictate the material to be written or printed, and allow the suspect to spell words as he or she would usually spell them. Misspelled words can contribute to the physical **match** between sample and questioned writing.[7] In addition, the suspect should be asked to write out and sign a statement verifying the validity and source of the sample or samples.

Requiring a suspect to give handwritten exemplars is also not considered a request for communications that fall within Fifth Amendment protection. The Fifth Amendment prohibits only the compulsion of communicative or testimonial evidence from a defendant. In producing the exemplar by writing for identification, the defendant is no more than the source of identification. Handwriting exemplars have been specifically held to be such an identifying physical characteristic.[8]

As with obtaining handwriting exemplars, compelling the accused to utter words spoken by an alleged thief is not within the scope of the Fifth Amendment privilege against self-incrimination. However, voice identification is subject to the Sixth Amendment right-to-representation-by-an-attorney clause and is regarded as part of a critical stage of the proceedings against a suspect.[9]

U.S. Supreme Court justices have expressed a minority viewpoint that handwriting exemplars and voice identification are within the scope of constitutional protection. Therefore, compelling these two types of evidence against a person's will is at least questionable if either is the key evidence in the case. A better policy would be to obtain handwriting exemplars and speech for identification by consent and not by force. If the investigation is beyond the general inquiry stage and has focused on a suspect, the *Miranda v. Arizona** admonishment should be given to inform the person of his or her constitutional protection against self-incrimination.

Many paint and glass manufacturers provide scientific laboratories with known standards of their products, and criminalistics laboratories maintain many reference files of known standards. However, the investigator should not assume such standards are on file and should seek them until he or she is informed they are not required.

Because the legal significance of physical evidence is often based on comparison with a known standard, physical evidence and its collection must be viewed as a dual process of collecting and preserving the basic physical evidence and of collecting and preserving the known standards of such evidence.

Transporting Evidence

Transporting physical evidence to a laboratory, to a place of storage, or to the prosecutor's office or the courtroom is the responsibility of the investigator who found the evidence. Such evidence is usually delivered personally, but when distance is a problem, it may be shipped by registered mail, insured parcel post, or express. When food or physiological fluids or substances are collected, temperature control is a primary precaution. Refrigeration without freezing will prevent deterioration, and containers with insulating qualities are now available for transporting such material. Evidence should be shipped by the fastest available route. Local delivery should be made by the finding investigator in person or by authorized personnel of his or her employing agency.

When physical evidence is sent to a laboratory for scientific examination, it must be accompanied by an informative report. The report must, in effect, bring the crime scene into the laboratory. This report must be on the official letterhead of the law enforcement agency with jurisdiction in the case and should contain the following eight elements:

1. Name and address of the agency submitting the evidence
2. Crime classification of the case by type and grade of offense
3. Case number of the agency submitting the evidence
4. Copy of the offense report, the report of the preliminary investigation, or a brief history of the case
5. List of evidence, consecutively numbered by item, with a brief description of each item and a notation as to (a) when and where it was found, (b) whether the item is a known standard for comparison, and (c) whether any change has taken place in the evidence either through accidental mishandling or because a sample is being submitted rather than the full amount of evidence collected
6. List of suggested scientific examinations

---

*See Appendix A, case study of *Miranda v. Arizona*, 384 U.S. 436 (1966).

7. Brief statement of the problems in the case
8. Name and address of the investigator to whom the exhibits should be returned upon completion of the examination

Packages in which physical evidence is to be shipped to a laboratory should be marked "Evidence for Examination," and the written request for an examination should be pasted securely to the outside of the package with the notation "Letter" or "Invoice" indicating its location. The criminalist receiving the package can read the request letter and have some idea of the nature of the evidence before opening the package.

Packages containing blood or other body fluids suspected of being contaminated by a person with AIDS, hepatitis B, or tuberculosis should be marked "CAUTION," followed by the name of the disease suspected. The technician in charge at the crime laboratory should be consulted before this type of evidence is submitted.

Laboratory technicians must carefully mark, tag, and otherwise identify all items of evidence while the evidence is in their custody. Such careful handling will preserve the integrity of the evidence. Upon return of the evidence to the investigator, the laboratory expert's report is integrated with other information collected during the investigation. At no time should an investigator return any part of the evidence to its rightful claimant without the prosecutor's authority. If the prosecutor believes the evidence is not required at the offender's trial, he or she has the authority to return it to the rightful owner or to store it until it is disposed of according to law. When the case is complete, the prosecutor has the authority to release the evidence.

Handling Infected Evidence

AIDS, hepatitis B, and tuberculosis are potentially lethal infectious diseases more likely to be encountered at crime scenes now than in the past. The scenes of violent crimes involving victims with one of these diseases will likely contain blood and may contain other infectious body fluids. Therefore, investigators should take all possible precautions against infection by such diseases.

Investigators arriving at the crime scene should question other officers about the possibility that the victim has a lethal infectious disease. High-risk groups of victims include users of injectable drugs and possibly prostitutes (male and female). A quick survey of the crime scene may indicate some warning signals, such as the victim's condition and the presence of prescription or nonprescription drugs.

The first line of defense against infectious diseases is to wear disposable gloves. A surgical mask and protective eyewear may also be appropriate if any likelihood exists that liquid or dried blood will come into contact with the investigator's or crime scene technician's face. The second line of defense is to avoid cutting or puncturing a finger or another portion of the body while the crime scene is searched and evidence collected. A collateral line of defense is for the investigator to seek medical assistance immediately if he or she does sustain an accidental cut or another wound or believes particles of possibly infected blood may have come into contact with his or her mouth or eyes.[10]

To protect others, investigators should place any evidence suspected of contamination in clearly marked plastic bags and seal them. However, these bags should not be forwarded to the crime laboratory until the investigator ascertains that the laboratory will accept this type of evidence.

Because of the epidemic spread of AIDS, investigators are urged to meet with local health officials to discuss how to best protect all concerned. Health personnel should be able to outline signs at crime scenes that might indicate a victim has an infectious disease, to explain the proper procedure for disposing of latex gloves after their use at such a crime scene, and to denote the best procedure to follow from the time an investigator or technician believes he or she has been in contact with potentially infected blood or body fluids to the time medical assistance will be available.

Identifying Physical Changes at the Scene

Investigators search for and collect evidence of any observable damage to objects at the scene—items bent, broken, dented, or scratched, and furniture turned over, broken, or moved from its normal location at the scene. Disarrangement, damage, and theft may be useful in determining what happened and who did it.

A crime scene can be well defined by using barrier tape or barricades.

A fight or struggle of some kind is indicated by overturned and broken furniture. Damage may indicate the direction of force. Photographs of the scene preserve the "as is" quality of the change or disarrangement.

Not only may articles taken from the scene lead to a major suspect, but they may also supply incriminating evidence when recovered from the suspect's possession or control at the time of arrest. The responsible investigator includes a description of the stolen property in the alarm broadcast. Even articles of little value, such as snapshots or ashtrays, have potential value as evidence when recovered.

Conducting a Final Survey of the Scene

The officer in charge should conduct a final survey of the scene before relinquishing control of the crime scene area. This final survey ensures that all the evidence has been identified and collected and that the scene has been properly processed prior to release. This review of the crime scene also ensures that equipment and materials generated by the investigation are not inadvertently left behind. Investigators should keep in mind that returning to the scene for follow-up crime scene work because items were inadvertently overlooked may require a search warrant, since once the area is released, it no longer carries the legal status of a crime scene.[11]

A crime scene can be anywhere, even in the middle of nowhere.

MEDIA RELATIONS

Most crime scenes will not attract the media's attention. However, the media's need for law enforcement is obvious: crime and the police make news. In some studies, for example, crime reporting made up one-third of all the coverage in local television newscasts. Newspaper, radio, and television reporters have a real hunger for news about crime and the police. This relationship is reciprocal: law enforcement also needs the media. The media is essential for publicizing information on wanted suspects and for alerting residents to crime trends. In addition, the news media can be a valuable tool for advertising various activities that build public support for the agency's mission.[12]

This symbiotic relationship between the media and law enforcement should be used to develop a long-term professional working relationship. The best way to accomplish this goal is to work with the media honestly and to provide information that can be released in a timely manner.

Usually, the following information can be released to the media:

- The type of crime committed, including a brief description of what happened, where, and when.
- The victim's identity, unless the victim is dead. Then, this information should not be released until after notification of the next of kin. In cases of sexual assault, the victim's identity should also be withheld.
- Facts concerning the arrest of the suspect or suspects, including name, age, and circumstances of the arrest, such as time, place, amount of resistance, and any weapons involved.

Information that should *not* be released to the media includes the following:[13]

- Prior criminal charges and convictions against the suspect or comments about the suspect's reputation, character, guilt, or innocence
- Identification of any juvenile suspects
- Comments on any admission or confession or the fact that an admission or confession has or has not been made
- The identity of any possible witnesses
- A precise description of the amount of money or other items taken

CHAPTER REVIEW

CASE STUDY

Incredible Evidence

Late Sunday afternoon on June 12, 1994, Nicole Brown Simpson, the former wife of football great O. J. Simpson, attended her daughter's dance recital in West Los Angeles. Also in attendance was her former husband, who is the father of her two children. When the recital ended, Nicole, her children, and her other family members dined at the Mezzaluna restaurant near her home in Brentwood. She arrived home at approximately 8:30 p.m. and called the restaurant to inquire about her prescription sunglasses she had left behind. A waiter friend, Ron Goldman, found the glasses and offered to bring them to her on his way home from work. Goldman left the restaurant at about 9:45 p.m.

At approximately 10:45 p.m., a limousine driver arrived at O. J. Simpson's estate to pick him up and take him to the airport. The driver noted that his passenger was "agitated and sweaty." At 11:45 p.m., Simpson's plane left for Chicago. At this time, an acquaintance noted that Simpson appeared composed and talkative about playing golf the next day in Chicago.

On Monday morning, June 13, at about 12:10 a.m., a neighbor found Nicole's dog wandering around the neighborhood. He returned the dog to Nicole's townhouse and discovered the bodies of Nicole Brown Simpson and Ron Goldman outside the front entrance to Nicole's home. Both victims had been stabbed, and their throats had been slashed.

The police were notified and quickly responded to the scene. The first officer on the scene located the victims and searched the interior of the townhouse, finding Nicole's two children unharmed, asleep in their beds. The area was cordoned off and the crime scene technicians and homicide detectives were requested to respond. During the initial search for evidence at the crime scene, a bloody leather glove was found at the feet of victim Ron Goldman.

By 5:00 a.m., the detectives assigned to the case had determined the victims' identities and decided to go to the Simpson estate a few miles away to notify him of his ex-wife's death. Upon arrival at the estate, the detectives noticed what appeared to be blood on the driver-side door handle of Simpson's Ford Bronco, which was parked on the street outside the estate. A string of what could have been blood droplets led from the Bronco to the front entrance of the residence. The detectives received no response at the gate intercom or to follow-up phone calls to the residence. Believing the safety of O. J. Simpson and other family members was at risk, one detective scaled a 5-foot wall surrounding the estate and opened the gate, which allowed the other detectives to enter.

The detectives entered the residence, but O. J. Simpson was not there. The detectives found two navy blue socks on the floor of the master bedroom. A search of the grounds led to the discovery of a bloody leather glove, similar to the one found at the crime scene, on the rear walkway on the south side of the estate. The detectives seized these items and the Ford Bronco as possible items of evidence. These items of evidence were eventually forwarded to the crime laboratory for processing.

O. J. Simpson's whereabouts in Chicago were then determined. He was contacted by telephone in the early morning hours and informed of his ex-wife's death. Simpson arranged to catch the next flight back to Los Angeles. Upon arrival in California, Simpson was taken to police headquarters, questioned by the homicide detectives, and later released.

On June 17, Simpson was charged with two counts of murder and a warrant was issued for his arrest. On June 20, Simpson entered a plea of not guilty, and his trial was scheduled to begin on January 24, 1995. During his 8-month-long trial, Simpson did not take the witness stand in his defense, and the prosecution did not use any portion of his statement given to the police on June 13. There were no eyewitnesses to the crime, so the prosecution relied primarily on the physical evidence to make its case against the defendant, which included the following:

Simpson's Ford Bronco. A crime scene technician collected blood samples from the interior of the vehicle 2 days after the murders. The **DNA** test results of the samples indicated these bloodstains matched the blood of both victims as well as that of the defendant. On cross-examination, the crime scene technician who collected the samples admitted that she had used the same cotton swab on different bloodstains, which was contrary to her training, and this unapproved method of collection could have led to possible contamination of the samples.

Blood at the Crime Scene.   In addition to finding the victims' blood, investigators found bloodstains that matched the defendant's blood. About 3 weeks after the crime was committed, a drop of Simpson's blood was also found on the rear gate at the crime scene. The prosecution maintained that Simpson cut himself while attacking his two victims. The defense countered that the 3-week delay in finding this evidence would have given the police ample time to plant the evidence.

Navy Blue Socks.   DNA tests revealed that the socks found in Simpson's master bedroom contained bloodstains that matched the blood of victim Nicole Brown Simpson as well as that of the defendant.

Leather Gloves.   DNA tests indicated that the bloodstains on the glove found at the crime scene and the glove found at the Simpson estate matched the blood of both victims and the defendant. The defense countered by suggesting that one of the gloves had been transported by the police from the crime scene and was then planted on the estate's rear walkway.

Simpson's Blood Sample.   The defendant supplied a blood sample at police headquarters shortly after being questioned by the homicide detectives. Detective Vannatter then took the sample from police headquarters to the Simpson estate. Detective Vannatter gave the sample to the crime scene technicians who were still collecting evidence. The defense argued that this act was contrary to established standard procedure. The detective should have booked the blood sample at police headquarters. In addition, the defense maintained that a small quantity of this sample, 1.5 milliliters, was unaccounted for by the crime laboratory. The defense suggested that the police used the missing blood to plant the defendant's blood samples at the crime scene and on various pieces of evidence.

EDTA.   The defense, in their analysis of blood evidence, found minute quantities of a preservative known as *EDTA*. Such a finding could suggest that the blood attributed to the defendant had come from Simpson's sample. The prosecution adamantly refuted this contention.

After 8 months of trial testimony, most experts expected the jury to deliberate for days, if not weeks, before reaching a verdict. However, within only a few hours, the jury completed deliberations and reached a unanimous verdict of not guilty. Juror Brenda Morgan, interviewed after the verdict was announced, told the press that the jury found Detective Vannatter's decision to carry Simpson's blood sample around with him for several hours "suspicious because it gave him the opportunity to plant evidence." Another juror said this: "[It was] not a conspiracy with all the police officers, but maybe with some."

Source: Adapted from Vincent Bugliosi, *Outrage: The Five Reasons Why O. J. Simpson Got Away with Murder* (New York: Norton, 1996), 291–97.

DISCUSSION QUESTIONS

1. Trace the growth in the use of physical evidence in criminal proceedings.
2. Will physical evidence actually establish a case for or against a suspect? Does it have real legal significance?
3. Describe standard procedures for collecting and preserving evidence.

4. Can any single rule of evidence gathering be identified as of primary importance?

5. Explain when and why known standards of evidence should be collected.

6. Why are blood samples exempt from the scope of the Fifth Amendment privilege against self-incrimination?

7. What other types of identification samples, in which a defendant is the source, are exempt from Fifth Amendment protection?

8. Regarding the case study, discuss how a deviation from standard operating procedures in handling physical evidence can affect the outcome of a criminal trial.

9. Regarding the case study, is the *perception* of wrongdoing as persuasive to a jury as *actual* wrongdoing?

LIBRARY ASSIGNMENT

Search available literature on police rules and prepare a list of at least five references that describe standard procedures for collecting and preserving physical evidence.

WORKBOOK PROJECT

Search for material on the suggested procedure for processing "suspect" crime scenes (likely to have blood and other body fluids of persons with infectious diseases), and summarize the precautions recommended and their source (library reference, local or nearby police unit, or other source).

RELATED WEB SITES

To find out more about crime scene investigation, visit the National Criminal Justice Reference Service Web site at *www.ncjrs.org*.

To learn more about the role of the public information officer (PIO) and media relations, visit the National Information Officers Association Web site at *www.nioa.org*.

New technologies are constantly being developed to help investigators find evidence and solve crimes. Learn more about these emerging technologies at *www.officer.com*.

Interested in being a crime scene investigator? If so, information from the International Crime Scene Investigators Association can be found at *www.icsia.com*.

NOTES

1. HANS G. A. GROSS, *Criminal Investigation*, 5th ed., trans. John Adam and J. Collyer Adam, rev. R. L. Jackson (London: Sweet & Maxwell, 1962).

2. U.S. DEPARTMENT OF JUSTICE, NATIONAL INSTITUTE OF JUSTICE, OFFICE OF JUSTICE PROGRAMS, *Crime Scene Investigation: A Guide for Law Enforcement* (Washington, DC: Government Printing Office, 2000), 11–14.

3. H. J. WALLS, "Evidence Technicians Are Called Scenes-of-Crime Officers in England," in *Forensic Science: An Introduction to Scientific Crime Detection* (New York: Praeger, 1968), 4.

4. VERNON GEBERTH, "Physical Evidence in Sex-Related Death Investigations," *Law and Order*, July 2003, 106.

5. *Schmerber v. California*, 384 U.S. 757 (1966).

6. JAMES V. P. CONWAY, *Evidential Documents* (Springfield, IL: Charles C Thomas, 1959), 73–83.

7. CLAUDE W. COOK, *A Practical Guide to the Basics of Physical Evidence* (Springfield, IL: Charles C Thomas, 1984), 10–12.

8. *Gilbert v. California*, 388 U.S. 263 (1967); *United States v. Blount*, 315 F. Supp. 1321 (1970).

9. *United States v. Wade*, 388 U.S. 218 (1967). See also *United States v. Ash*, 413 U.S. 300 (1973), and *Kirby v. Illinois*, 406 U.S. 682 (1972).

10. PAUL D. BIGBEE, "Collecting and Handling Evidence Infected with Human Disease-Causing Organisms," *FBI Law Enforcement Bulletin* 18, no. 9 (1991): 66–70.

11. U.S. DEPARTMENT OF JUSTICE, *Crime Scene Investigation*, 30.

12. BILL TOOHEY, "Tips from the Trenches: Advice from a PIO." *Police Chief*, April 2001, 43.

13. D. P. BLARICOM, "The Media: Enemies or Allies?" *Police Chief*, April 2001, 52.

2

Direct and Circumstantial Evidence

During a criminal trial, two kinds of proof are used to answer the question of guilt or innocence: direct evidence and circumstantial evidence. **Direct evidence** involves eyewitnesses who have, through one or more of their five senses, experienced something relative to the crime in question or its circumstances. Willing witnesses are often found at the crime scene. However, unwilling witnesses must often be located by revisiting the crime scene, canvassing the neighborhood, and issuing pleas for public cooperation. In contrast, **circumstantial evidence** is defined as evidence from which an inference can be drawn and includes items such as **physical evidence**. The major types of circumstantial evidence include weapons; blood; imprints and impressions; tool marks; dust, dirt, and other traces; questioned documents; and miscellaneous trace or transfer evidence.

DIRECT EVIDENCE

Locating Witnesses at the Crime Scene

Witnesses at the crime scene include individuals discovered in the **view area** and neighborhood. The duty of the first officer at the scene of a suspected crime is to "contain" it. Standard regulations require responding officers to detain witnesses and other persons at the scene. These officers procure adequate information about the identities of all persons found at a crime scene: their names, addresses, telephone numbers, and employers' names and business addresses. The perpetrator is arrested if he or she is at the scene and so identified, but, at this time, the major concern with regard to witnesses is to locate them, secure a description of the perpetrator and the facts of the crime, and record their identities and where they can be located.

The degree of difficulty involved in locating a particular witness is directly related to the willingness of that person to be a witness and whether the person knows he or she *is* a witness to a crime. A **willing witness** may wait at the crime scene until the police arrive or contact the police to supply information. Many willing witnesses are motivated by a sense of civic responsibility. Others may be motivated to assist the police to eliminate business competitors. For instance, a drug dealer will often inform on another drug dealer whose territory he or she covets.

Relatives, spouses, and lovers may also provide the authorities with information about the location of wanted loved ones. Their motivation is the hope that the offenders will get needed treatment or learn the lesson that crime does not pay.

Perhaps one of the most powerful motivations for cooperating is revenge. People whom the suspect has wronged in one way or another may cooperate with investigators to get even.

The **unwilling witness** does not want to cooperate with the investigation and will usually disappear from a crime scene when the police arrive. The motivations of these witnesses vary. The person may simply dislike authority, may have outstanding warrants, or may be a crime suspect. Many other unwilling witnesses say they don't want to get involved. The basis for such unwillingness may be selfishness or a genuine concern for the loss of income or another inconvenience that may result from being required to testify at a lengthy criminal trial.

Other potential witnesses may be unaware that they are witnesses to a crime or its circumstances. For instance, a witness may have observed the arrival or departure of the suspect from the crime scene, but not the crime. Although the nature of the crime may be unknown, this witness is potentially important because he or she can place the suspect at the crime scene.

Once potential witnesses are identified at the crime scene, investigators should separate them and get some type of commitment from them.

Separate Witnesses.   The crime scene is the one place where a number of witnesses will be together at the same time. The first officer on the scene should identify potential witnesses and separate them as soon as possible.[1] Witnesses should not be allowed to discuss the crime among themselves because the investigator wants only the information the witness independently observed or experienced. In fact, when interviewing a witness, investigators often use a nonsuggestive structure, asking open-ended questions, so that the witness's response is unadulterated by suggestion (Figure 2–1). When a witness discusses the crime or overhears others talking about the crime, he or she may unconsciously incorporate some of this information as his or hers or alter recollections to fit with those of other witnesses. This process is normal and is known as **retroactive interference**.[2]

Get a Commitment.   When trying to identify potential witnesses, the officers at the crime scene will encounter people who are uncooperative or who state that they have no knowledge of the crime. This situation is not unusual. However, as soon as the officers determine that these persons were in a position to be

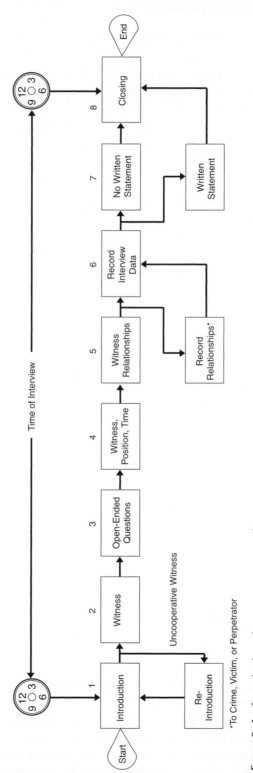

FIGURE 2-1 Interviewing witnesses—nonsuggestive structure.

27

witnesses to the crime, they should be identified and their refusal to give information or their statement of ignorance should be properly recorded in the police report. This process makes a record of the fact that these potential witnesses were given the opportunity to assist the investigation shortly after the crime occurred. The statement of a potential witness that indicates he or she refused to cooperate or had no knowledge of the crime can be used to impeach the witness when, at trial, the person appears as the star defense witness.

Revisiting the Crime Scene

Revisiting the crime scene area has been effective for locating witnesses. Motorists and pedestrians who do not live or work in the area but who travel the area at about the same time daily or weekly are often witnesses; however, they leave the scene before the responding officers arrive, sometimes not even knowing the event they witnessed was a police case.

The technique of revisiting a crime scene area to search for witnesses was adapted from the investigation of hit-and-run crimes. The solution of cases of motorists who are involved in an accident and flee the scene usually requires locating the vehicle involved. Investigators can use only the identification potential of the physical evidence found at the scene and, when the suspect vehicle is located, the damage to the suspect car. For this reason, witnesses who can provide some clue to the identity of the vehicle and its operator must be discovered. When the initial inquiry at the scene does not produce witnesses, investigators revisit the scene for an hour or more each day, spanning the time of the accident, for a week or two, then revisit on the same day of the week for 3 or 4 weeks. Traffic accident investigation units have used this technique for years to find witnesses and collect information about the identity of a hit-and-run vehicle. In some cases, key witnesses have been located as long as a month after an accident. The procedure involves two steps:[3]

1. Revisit the accident scene daily for no less than a week and weekly on the day of the week of the accident for no less than a month at the same time of day that the accident occurred.
2. Question motorists and pedestrians, paying particular attention to schoolchildren and service personnel, such as operators of delivery vehicles.

Canvassing the View Area

An inquiry in, or a **canvass** of, the view area of the crime scene is also standard practice. When a crime is committed within a building, as in an office or apartment, the universe of possible witnesses may be small. However, when the crime is committed in a store or in the street, a large group of people might have witnessed it. This situation requires a search for persons who may have been witnesses but who have not been so identified. Officers visit places of business, apartments, and residences near the scene. Customers and employees of markets, taverns, and service stations, as well as residents at home and their visitors, are all questioned. Such solicitation is for information about the crime and anyone who might have seen the event, witnessed suspicious persons in the area before the crime, viewed the perpetrator's flight from the scene, heard anything unusual, or know of someone who has or might have information.

Canvassing the Neighborhood

Superior officers supervising the criminal investigation often assign additional personnel to an extensive **neighborhood canvass** to find a witness. The plan used in such a canvass may be based on the approach and flight route of the perpetrator, the travels of witnesses, or the path of a bullet in sniper cases. The pattern for canvassing witnesses in the neighborhood of the crime starts with revisiting persons residing or employed in the view area of the crime scene and extends to establishing contacts with employees of delivery service firms and public utilities. This canvass expands to nearby areas, bus stops, and public transit stations beyond the crime scene but within a convenient distance of it. Such a canvass involves the traditional task of ringing doorbells. Often, the assignment, appears to be hopeless yet time and again an investigator canvassing an area finds a witness or, equally important, a person who knows a witness's identity.

This knocking on doors and asking questions is a productive source of evidence in homicide cases. The seriousness of the crime impresses most people, and they usually respond meaningfully when questioned. In these cases, investigators are seeking information about the victim as well as the killer or killers.[4]

Attempting to locate witnesses by canvassing a neighborhood involves the following:

- Friends and immediate relatives of the victim who are living in the neighborhood are located and interviewed.
- A house-to-house, apartment-to-apartment, door-to-door canvass of the following people is conducted:
    Residents and shopkeepers and their employees
    Delivery persons, utility personnel, and other service personnel
    Bus and taxi drivers

Supermarkets, which are isolated within the moats of their immense parking lots, have created problems for investigators trying to locate witnesses. The problem is not that the viewing area is curtailed; people are still in and around this area. However, they are transients in the view area. They do not reside in it, nor is it their place of employment. They walk or drive to a view area, then leave it and return to their homes or places of business. Thus, the tremendous population of people and vehicles in and around shopping centers complicates the problem of locating witnesses to crimes and has led to the concept of the **shopping area canvass** for witnesses (Figure 2–2). Unlike the neighborhood canvass developed by

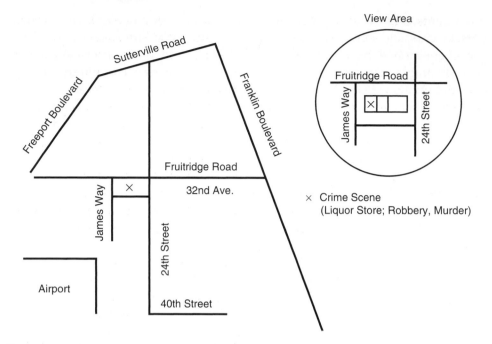

FIGURE 2–2   Shopping area canvass for witnesses.

detectives in large urban central cities, the shopping area canvass can be geo-graphically extensive. The canvass in urban centers encompasses the area in which the *perpetrator* may have traveled to and from the crime scene; the shopping area canvass encompasses the area in which *witnesses* travel to and from the crime scene.

During such canvasses, many individuals who otherwise cooperate with the police often reject any semblance of the informer role. These persons be-lieve that revealing a witness's name or whereabouts is not in the same category as revealing the identity of a person who might have committed the crime.

Investigators successful in locating witnesses through informants are skilled at establishing liaisons with persons likely to have information and at maintaining contact with such individuals until their cooperation is needed. This procedure cannot usually be developed for a specific investigation. The contacts must be established first. Then, when a crime occurs and this type of cooperation is needed, the investigator has available sources of information.

Issuing Pleas for Public Cooperation

In serious felony cases receiving unusual publicity, the police receive numerous investigative leads from community members. These offers of help proliferate when the crime is child molestation, a series of murders or rapes, or robberies or thefts of large sums of money or immensely valuable jewelry. Unfortunately, most of these calls are from persons justly classified as "cranks." Most of the leads are useless, and the time spent making inquiries is lost entirely. An investigator cannot afford to verify every offer of information from such sources. Selectivity must be exercised, and techniques for auditing these unsought messages should be developed. In the audit, all messages containing the name and address or other identifying data of a potential witness are separated from letters and calls presenting theories of the crime or suspicious persons. A prompt follow-up inquiry is made on the witness leads, and the remainder are set aside for later analysis.

Police officials, in attempting to locate witnesses to important crimes, use all the communications media: newspapers, radio, local television outlets, and the Internet. In New York, Chicago, San Francisco, Miami, and other large cities, the standard plea to the public is for people to contribute any information about the case to police by using a special telephone number. In some cases, posting a reward hastens the response to these pleas for public cooperation. However, this mercenary inducement for help should be avoided unless it is deemed necessary because some persons seeking gain may supply false or meaningless information solely in the hope of making a future claim. Silent Witness programs seek the same help but offer rewards and confidentiality.

Another public plea technique has been developed with the aid of local television stations: a telecast of clues about an unsolved and recent crime. This **clue-in** offers the viewers a minimum of facts about the case, and the core of the program is a request for listeners to call the local station if they believe they may have witnessed any of the suspected offenders' travels. Several radio stations across the United States have cooperated with police in a similar fashion. Listeners in either instance are accustomed to calling the station to enter contests and participate in opinion polls held by the station, so they are likely to feel more comfortable with this method of responding to police pleas.

In both the information wire and the multimedia programming of clue-ins, the emphasis is not on finding people with theories about the crime or ideas of techniques the police should use in searching for the offender, but on locating witnesses. Listeners and viewers are asked to call a specific, easily remembered telephone number under any of the following conditions: if they witnessed any segment of the crime, any act concerned with its preparation, any of the postcrime travels, or other activities of the criminal or his or her associates; if they know the identity of the criminal or his or her associates from other sources of information; or if they know the identity of any other person who might have been a witness or who might know the identity of the offender and his or her associates.

One problem U.S. police have is securing the public's cooperation in solving crimes. However, when the crime is widely recognized as vicious and hurtful, the potential for community support is excellent. Persons who would not normally cooperate will do so when the atrocity of a crime inspires their sympathy for the victim and the public appeal for information orients them to the police. The public appeal technique has optimum potential because everyone in the community is exposed to multimedia.

CIRCUMSTANTIAL EVIDENCE

Evidence likely to be found at crime scenes and amenable to scientific analysis is divided into seven major groups: (a) weapons; (b) blood; (c) imprints and impressions (traces of a person or a vehicle); (d) marks of tools used to gain access to locked premises or containers; (e) dust, dirt, and other traces; (f) questioned documents; and (g) miscellaneous trace or transfer evidence.

Weapons

Firearms should be handled to preserve ballistic identity. **Ballistics** is the study and identification of firearms, bullets, cartridges, and shotgun shells. **Interior ballistics** refers to the functioning of firearms through the firing cycle, and **exterior ballistics** is the study of projectiles in flight. In ballistics, the inside of the barrel (the bore with its "lands" and "grooves"), the firing pin, the breech face in which the firing pin hole is located, the chamber, and the ejector and extractor are used as primary sources of identification.[5]

Investigators reject such techniques for picking up firearms as inserting a pencil into the barrel of a handgun and instead follow procedures that will not change the portions of the weapon commonly used for ballistics comparison and identification. Firearms should be picked up by their rough or checkered wooden portions, if possible, or any external metal portion except the trigger guard and trigger area and promptly placed in a container or tied to a board or

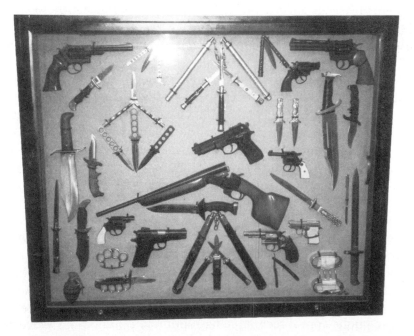

A collection of weapons commonly encountered by investigators.

strong piece of cardboard. Firearms should not be handled unnecessarily, nor should the mechanism be actuated repeatedly. Safety is of paramount importance. However, unloading a firearm should be held to the minimum procedure for emptying the gun. No attempt must be made to fire a gun, to dismantle it, or to interfere with the mechanism in any way.

A description of a firearm should start with the name of the manufacturer and the serial number. These data are necessary for tracing the weapon. All names and numbers stamped on the firearm, along with their location on the gun, should be recorded. Some numbers are part numbers, and one- or two-digit numbers are usually model numbers. Some marks may indicate the maker, others proof testing. (Emblems and symbols are **proof marks**, which indicate tests performed to prove the chamber strength of a firearm by actual firing with maximum loads.) All these marks help identify the gun. Sometimes a number has been obliterated by grinding, filing, or center punching. The investigator should describe the damage and its location and request laboratory services to restore the number. (Restoring a number is difficult when it has been center punched, but restoration may be possible, and even a fragment of the number may be helpful.)

The caliber of the weapon or the gauge (if a shotgun) is also an identifying characteristic. It is often marked on the firearm in a stamping associated with the manufacturer's name or the model number. If the caliber is not marked, the investigator should qualify any estimate of the caliber by writing "Unknown" in his or her field notes and noting a measurement across the bore of the weapon in fractions of an inch. This procedure is in line with the requirement of accuracy in collecting evidence. A defense attorney can raise doubt about testimony in relation to firearms (and possibly doubt about the entire police case) by questioning police failure to make accurate notations about the caliber of a weapon. Professional conduct requires an investigator to qualify any lack of knowledge, and writing "Unknown" is more desirable than specifying an approximate caliber and later finding it to be grossly incorrect.

Fired (empty) and unfired cartridge cases, shotgun shells, and spent bullets should also be handled with particular attention to the portions used in ballistics identification: that is, the base and the rim just above the base of the case, and the side of the cartridge or the shell immediately above the base (extractor marks). When empty cartridge cases or shotgun shells are picked up, the location where they were found should be pinpointed by measurements for future reference. Because some firearms throw out, or eject, the cases with some distinctiveness as to direction and force, the exact location of the cases indicates the position of the person firing the gun, sometimes as each shot was fired.

Spent bullets are excellent clues to the firearm used in the crime. They must be carefully removed from their point of impact, and the location where they were found must be recorded accurately in the investigator's field notes. Investigators must search for bullets embedded in walls and furniture at crime scenes. A spent bullet can be ruined by being dug out with a pocketknife. Care must be taken so that the drill or cutting instrument used in this operation does not ruin identifying characteristics on a bullet by coming into contact with the softer metal. Bullets should also be handled as little as possible and packaged to prevent movement and to protect the side portions used in ballistics comparison and identification. When the victim is dead and an autopsy is performed, one of the **postmortem forensic science** procedures is removal of spent bullets without damage to their original condition. In the United States, physicians and surgeons are very conscious of the evidential value of spent bullets (Figure 2–3).

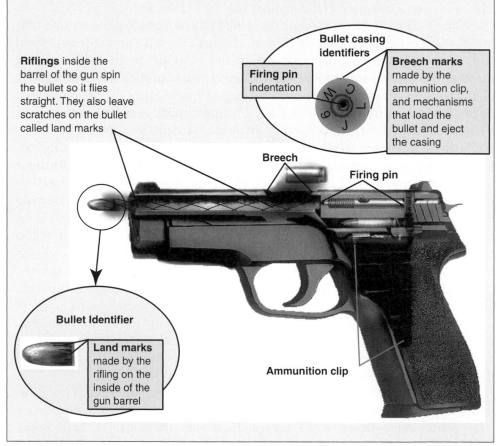

Fingerprinting a gun

A gun can be identified through several distinctive markings it leaves on bullets and casings. Just like human fingerprints, each gun leaves its own unique markings as identification. The Bureau of Alcohol, Tobacco and Firearms wants to take fingerprints of new guns to create a national database prior to their sale. These images along with ones of gun fingerprints from crime scenes can then be searched for matches. If a match is found in the database, the gun that created the match can be traced to other crimes and back to where and to whom it was sold.

Riflings inside the barrel of the gun spin the bullet so it flies straight. They also leave scratches on the bullet called land marks

Bullet casing identifiers

Firing pin indentation

Breech marks made by the ammunition clip, and mechanisms that load the bullet and eject the casing

Breech

Firing pin

Bullet Identifier

Land marks made by the rifling on the inside of the gun barrel

Ammunition clip

FIGURE 2–3   Interior ballistics identification.

Because establishing the position of a person in crimes involving a shooting is sometimes necessary, the investigator at the crime scene should look closely for places the bullet has struck in its flight.[6] These marks or holes are items of evidence and are correlated with other positioning factors such as the location of ejected cartridge cases found at the scene and the path of a bullet in the victim's body.

One question that must be answered concerns whether a suicide victim or a homicide suspect recently fired a weapon. This question can be answered through a **gunshot residue (GSR) examination**. This test starts with applying adhesive tapes to the person's hands. After these tapes are removed, they are sent to the **crime laboratory**, where they are examined by using a scanning electron microscope interfaced with energy-dispersive X-ray.[7] This examination is conducted to search for the presence of the major components in a center-fire cartridge, which are antimony sulfide, barium nitrate, and lead styphnate, as well as supporting metallic particles of zinc, copper, or nickel. These compounds and elements are deposited on a person's hands when he or she fires a weapon. These components undergo an intense **exothermic reaction**: a rapid increase in temperature followed by a sharp decrease. This supercooling phenomenon leads to a unique spheroidal formation not generally observed in the natural environment.[8]

Other weapons police investigators commonly encounter are knives and various blunt instruments. Accuracy in describing such evidence may depend on a general description. The presence of serial numbers is uncommon, and clubs and similar weapons are not stamped with the maker's name. However, the length of a knife blade and the length of the handle are easily determined without excessive handling, as are the length and other dimensions of clubs and bludgeons. Distinctive features of the object should be noted in the investigator's field notes. The greatest possibility of error in connection with these weapons results from the tendency of investigators, when searching the crime scene, to ignore common items of furniture or equipment as suspect weapons. In one case, the bludgeon used in a killing was a piece of 2-inch by 4-inch lumber about 3.5 feet long. The crime scene was a lumberyard. In another case, an apparently innocuous empty soft drink bottle was collected; later, the autopsy report cited a depressed skull fracture as the victim's cause of death, and laboratory tests revealed blood traces on the bottle.

Blood

Blood is a trace that can divulge a great deal of information about the criminal, the victim, and the happenings during a crime. Police first to arrive at the scene of assaults are often smeared with blood in their efforts to help a victim. In some cases, walking around the scene without stepping into some trace of blood and then transporting it around the scene is almost impossible. Conversely,

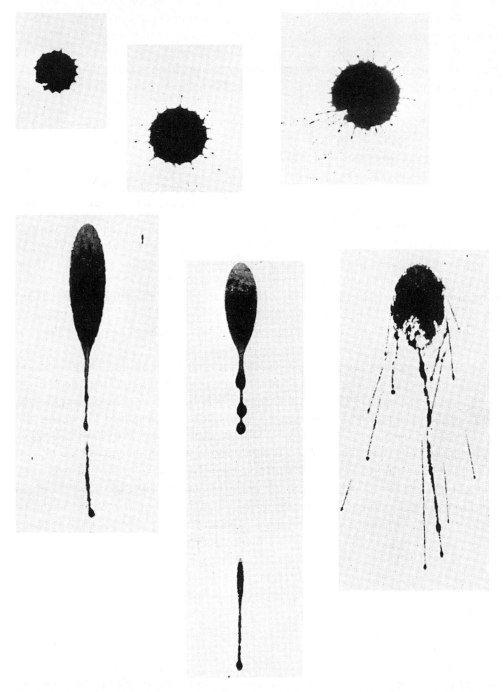

The hydrodynamics of blood drops and splashes—drop size increases with the distance of the fall; the tails, or pointed ends, indicate the direction of movement, and the rounded edges face the source of bleeding.

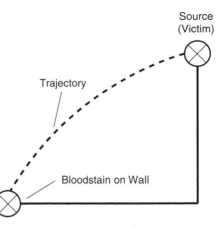

FIGURE 2–4   Blood trajectory—wall stains.

investigators often fail to recognize bloodstains on clothing and other objects and, therefore, fail to collect valuable evidence. To complicate the problem of blood and its stains and residues as evidence, frequently this residue is a mixture at crime scenes when both the victim and the offender have been wounded. In addition, the evidence may have an animal as well as a human source, or a common liquid may dilute the blood.

Despite some of the problems associated with this type of human trace, blood drops and splashes help narrow the size of the suspect group, support identity when a suspect is located, and plot the victim's and the assailant's movements (Figure 2–4). Information that can be discovered through careful bloodstain pattern analysis includes the angle of the impact, the nature of the force involved in the bloodshed and the direction from which that force was applied, the nature of any object used in applying the force, the approximate number of blows struck during the incident, and the relative position of the suspect, the victim, or other related objects during the incident.[9]

Imprints and Impressions

Personal imprints and impressions found at crime scenes identify or tend to identify a person or vehicle as having been at the crime scene. These traces offer promising areas of inquiry, although they usually require a suspect or a suspect vehicle before their evidential value can be realized.

Imprints are markings on a surface left by protruding parts of a person or vehicle. Imprints found at a crime scene include bloody handprints or footprints, or the tire tread mark left after a tire is contaminated with oil or mud. Such evidence is first photographed and then maybe lifted by dusting it with a contrasting powder; applying clean, sticky, transparent tape to the dusted area to pick up the markings; and then pressing the tape to a clean card to preserve the evidence. Sometimes, the object with the imprint can be transported to the laboratory instead.

Impressions are made by a person or an object in a material softer than the item of evidence making the impression. Impressions include tire tracks or footprints left in snow or soft dirt. A trail of shoe prints or footprints offers some clues to the size or weight of the person making them, the speed of movement, and any abnormal "walking picture." Impressions are collected as evidence by first photographing and then casting the impression with plaster of paris or dental plaster. Vehicle tire marks are highly individualistic. When suspects are identified and located, vehicles used by such persons can be processed for comparison with the tire marks found at the scene. Moreover, tire marks can be clues that aid in solving a crime inasmuch as the type of vehicle used may indicate fruitful lines of investigation. Knowing, for example, that the vehicle was a large late-model, high-priced car or a 10-year-old automobile can be helpful. Shoe or heel prints and footprints in soft earth or other material that will take and hold a likeness are excellent to use for matching after a suspect is located.

Fingerprints can be found at crime scenes as either imprints or impressions. Bloody fingerprints left on weapons or at the crime scene are called **contaminated fingerprints**. These types of prints are observable with the naked eye and are collected by first photographing and then dusting and lifting them with transparent tape. Fingerprints are also found as impressions that a burglar might leave behind when his or her fingers come into contact with soft glazier's putty around window edges. These impressions are called **plastic fingerprints** and are collected by first photographing them and then casting them with dental plaster. These prints can also be observed with the naked eye.

Other fingerprints are called **latent fingerprints**. Such prints cannot usually be seen with the naked eye and thus need to be developed to be seen. These fingerprints are caused by the transfer of body perspiration or oils present in finger ridges to the surface of an object. Latent prints found on smooth, nonporous surfaces, such as glass, can be developed by dusting with a powder, the color of which should contrast with that of the surface on which the print is found. Latent fingerprints on porous surfaces, such as paper, are developed in the laboratory through an iodine fuming process or a ninhydrin process. The iodine fumes or the ninhydrin reacts with the amino acids in the print, which appears purple when developed. Prints left on smooth, slippery surfaces, such as plastic bags, which are resistant to dusting, can be developed by using the cyanoacrylate fuming process. Cyanoacrylate, a common glue product, is heated in a covered tank, and the resulting fumes settle on the fingerprint, which becomes observable and can then be photographed.[10]

Traditionally, fingerprints have been taken from persons by inking their fingertips and then rolling the contaminated print onto a card. These cards

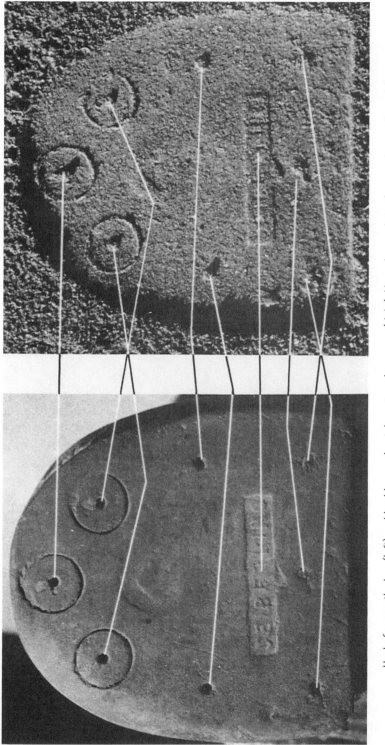

Heel of suspect's shoe (left) and heel impression taken at a crime scene (right). Lines show points of comparison—a "match."

Computers are now being used to fingerprint and electronically transmit the prints to a database.

would then be sent to the Federal Bureau of Investigation (FBI) or to a state agency to be read and classified. This process would take weeks or months to complete. Unclassifiable cards were returned, and often the person who supplied the prints was no longer available to supply another set of prints and an opportunity to have this person's prints on file was lost.

Computer technology now allows a person's fingerprints to be captured electronically. The person's hand is placed on a platen, and a scanner reads and records the person's fingerprints digitally. The machine reads the print and indicates, while the person is still at the machine, whether a classifiable set of prints has been obtained. With a touch of a button, the set of prints is electronically sent to the FBI's database, which contains 41 million sets of prints. This automated system has reduced the FBI's criminal ten-print processing time from 45 days with the inked card system to less than 2 hours.[11]

Tool Marks

Just as a weapon is likely to be found at the scene of an assault or a homicide, tool marks are likely to be found at the scene of a burglary or another crime in which the offender forced entry into the premises or forced open locked containers. The criminal must gain access by force. Windows, doors, and skylights are the traditional means of ingress for such criminals. Roofs and walls have been cut and pounded in to provide entry. In some cases, criminals exit from another area of the building. The modus operandi of many burglars is multiple entry through rows of offices or commercial establishments: the burglars burrow through interior walls in a molelike progress from store to store. The entry or exit points and all the locked desks and cabinets forced open along the way will bear some mark of the tools used. Safes, unless found open or opened with a combination or a key, also bear traces of prying, ripping, or battering. Scientific laboratory procedures can individualize these marks and impressions. When suspect tools are discovered, laboratory technicians can make comparison analyses.

The initial procedure for collecting the marks of tools used to gain access is to accurately locate the impression at the scene and to record the general description and measurements. Accuracy, again, is the keynote. The impressions must be measured with an accurate rule and the dimensions recorded in the investigator's field notes. The impressions should also be photographed. If feasible, the substance bearing the mark should be transported to the laboratory. Sometimes a cast impression of the mark can be made, and this casting will be an effective trial exhibit. Inasmuch as the mark is small, a material more costly than plaster of paris can be used to form the impression. Various dental waxes and molding materials can be pressed into the imprint and allowed to harden. The overriding factor in reporting and collecting tool impressions at the crime scene is preservation of the impression, or its reproduction, for future comparison with a suspect tool.

Often, an investigator finds a tool that might have made an impression at the crime scene and visually attempts to match the tool with the impression by fitting it to the mark. This second contact of the tool to the impression ruins the evidence. Prevailing philosophy suggests that the best procedure is to treat any likely tool as suspect and to collect it for laboratory comparison by an expert.

Tools found on a suspect or under his or her control at the time of arrest (or traced to the suspect) become incriminating evidence when laboratory examinations show that the particularities of the suspect tool relate to the tool impressions found at the crime scene.

Dust, Dirt, and Other Traces

Traces have value as associated evidence when laboratory examination can establish their identity and origin and can connect a suspect with a crime. The evidence potential of soil and mud, the debris from the underside of a vehicle, and dust in various forms, particularly on persons and their clothing, is excellent. Minute samples of glass and paint recognized as evidence may be processed to demonstrate similarities or differences in identity and origin. Larger samples of glass may be matched physically, and chips of paint at crime scenes can now be matched layer by layer with a suspect sample. Laboratory analysis has developed an amazing range of methods of identification for comparing these substances and tracing their origins to the crime scene, the victim, or the perpetrator.

Potential evidence in arson cases exists when the nature of the trace can be identified as a flammable fluid or its residue. Traces of volatile fluids of suspicious origin are lost if not searched for promptly and retrieved without delay. Precautions should be taken primarily to avoid loss by evaporation.

Explosives residue should be handled similarly. The primary requirement is to find and collect as much of the bomb as possible. Fragments of the container and timing mechanism of the bomb, if any, are loaded with residues, as are the objects close to the center of the explosion.

A direction-of-force potential is also inherent in arson cases and crimes involving explosives. The survey of the fire scene may indicate fire trails resulting from the natural downward flow of liquid fire accelerants; laboratory tests may indicate the origin and spread of the fire by revealing the depth of charring in burnt wood collected at the scene. The expansion of gases in an explosion is discernible in a visual examination at the scene and can indicate the type of explosive and its placement. Distinctive damage at explosion sites can indicate the amount and type of explosive used in the blast.

The direction of force can be determined and some data on the force used can be gained by studying glass and its fragments found at crime scenes. Glass

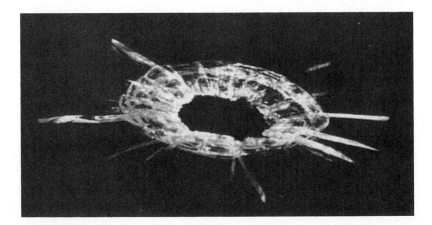

"Cratering" of a bullet hole in a glass window indicates the direction of travel. The bullet enters from the bottom, or small side of the crater and exits from the top, or large side.

breaks first on the side opposite of where the force is applied. When bullets penetrate a glass window, the projectile blasts out a cone-shaped hole on the side of the glass away from the shooter. The shape of this exit crater gives some indication of the direction or angle at which the bullet struck the glass.

Questioned Documents

In cases involving checks, the check is a **questioned document** and an important item of evidence. In apparent suicides, the victim may leave a note. This note is an evidence item, and when found, it is often processed as a questioned document.

Documents that have been destroyed or partially destroyed by fire can sometimes be restored by laboratory technicians. Charred paper must be sprayed with a preservative and requires special packaging and transport to the place of examination. This process is critical and time consuming, but the potential of charred paper as evidence is worth the work involved in its recovery.

The general style of a typewritten document, margins, separation of words at the end of the typed lines, spelling errors, paragraphing, and other indentation may all contribute to identification of the person who typed it.[12] Chances of matching a suspect typewriter, printer, or copying machine through a comparison of the exemplars taken from the machine and the document under suspicion are excellent.

Indented or embossed writing is sometimes found on telephone pads, blotters, and other impressionable surfaces even if the original paper on which the note was written was removed.

Other Evidence

Hair and fibers have excellent potential for identification. The primary problem with this type of evidence is finding it. When laboratory examination indicates that hair or fibers found on the victim or on the victim's clothing are not the victim's, the possibility exists for future identification when a suspect is located. In addition, examination of the suspect for such traces may uncover hair or fibers belonging to the victim.

Seminal fluid stains are a trace found in sex crimes. The presence of such stains is often meaningful to the investigation. They are useful for and, at times, vital to showing the commission of a crime when the victim is too young to testify or to remember having been molested or when the sexual attack is part of a homicide.

In narcotics and dangerous drug cases (possession and sale of drugs), the evidence must be identified as a drug in violation of the law. The examination need only identify the drug as illegal.

Drugs and poisons may be either the means of attack in homicides and assaults or the fatal substance in suicides and, as such, must be searched for and collected. When the victim becomes ill in a suspected poisoning case or is given an emetic to bring up a poisonous fluid or substance, the investigator must collect all material vomited. Urine specimens should also be collected if the victim is still alive. In poison cases, precautions must be taken primarily to prevent loss, contamination, or deterioration of the substance in transit. The collected physical evidence, as well as any witnesses' stories about the circumstances of death, should be recorded in the officer's field notes. Such data help the medicolegal experts prepare a clinical history of the death.

Cigars and cigarettes, butts, and ashes have an evidence potential. Unique brands, lipstick smears, and chewed ends may be of particular value. Wooden matchsticks and a distinguishable method of breaking them have been rewarding to searchers in some cases. Paper matches, torn from a book of matches, are evidence at the scene likely to reward a searcher if the book from which the matches were torn can be located and traced to a known suspect.

CHAPTER REVIEW

CASE STUDY

Revenge

His plan was simple yet effective. He would get up around noon and on the days he needed money, he would leave the apartment around three in the afternoon. He would go to one of the supermarkets in the area and throw a few items into a cart. He would walk around the store in search of a victim. He was looking for a woman who put her purse in the grocery cart, usually in the child seat. When he found his potential victim, he would follow at a discrete distance, and when she turned away from the cart to select a cut of meat or handle produce, he would approach her cart. If she was still occupied, he would grab the purse, conceal it under his jacket, and calmly walk out of the market.

On his return to the apartment, he would get comfortable at the kitchen table, where he would spread out the contents of the purse on the table. Any money he found was pure profit, but what he really wanted was the ATM cards. Once they were located, his real search began. He didn't find many personal identification numbers (PINs) in these purses, but he did make note of any four-digit numbers. He would write down the person's address, telephone number, and birth date, and the last four numbers of the person's Social Security number. Armed with these numbers, he would venture out again around eleven at night. He would go to the ATM; he preferred local banks because he thought the security was not as tight as at the bigger banks. He was dressed in a hooded sweatshirt and dark sunglasses. He would insert the stolen card and begin using the list of possible PINs he compiled from the victim's personal information. He would try a few numbers before midnight and a few after. Once gaining access to the victim's account, he would take out as much money as he could before the machine cut him off.

I first heard of this case from a call I received from a local bank manager. The banks were assisting us in putting our Community-Oriented Policing neighborhood office online, and they had the telephone number for my direct line. I sent one of my detectives to the bank to make contact, and I called our robbery detail to get the initial police reports. My detective returned with a series of photos of the suspect. The robber had hit four times, and the ATM cameras had captured great photos of a male suspect wearing a hooded sweatshirt and dark glasses. We didn't have much to work with, so the detectives conducted a neighborhood canvass, a modus operandi check, and even surveillance—with negative results. We worked the case for the next 6 weeks, learning little for our efforts, although the suspect kept hitting the bank regularly.

I sensed that my team of detectives were becoming frustrated by the lack of results, so I invited them out to lunch. One detective was not hungry, so he declined and stayed behind to watch the office. While we were gone, a woman came to the office to have a domestic violence report taken and to obtain a restraining order. The detective invited her to sit at his desk so that he could take the report. As she sat down, she noticed the photos of our hooded thief and said, "I see you already know my boyfriend." She then gave a complete statement about her knowledge of the suspect's activities and later took the detectives to her apartment, where the hooded sweatshirt and several of the victims' purses were recovered. She even gave us the address of his new girlfriend's apartment, where he was arrested shortly before five that night without incident.

DISCUSSION QUESTIONS

1. Describe the various methods investigators use to locate potential witnesses.
2. Discuss the need to separate witnesses at a crime scene and the group dynamics involved.
3. Discuss the motivation of the woman involved in the case study. Can you think of other cases that have been solved in this or a similar manner?
4. Explain the difference between internal and external ballistics as it relates to firearms examinations.
5. Describe the three types of fingerprints likely to be found at a crime scene. How are these various types of prints processed?
6. Explain the advantages of capturing a person's fingerprints electronically rather than using the traditional ink-and-paper system.

LIBRARY ASSIGNMENT

Review the available literature on direct evidence. Prepare a list of books and articles on this subject.

WORKBOOK PROJECT

Review the differences between direct and circumstantial evidence. Determine which is the most reliable form of evidence and outline the reasons for your choice.

RELATED WEB SITES

To learn more about firearms, visit the University of Utah Health Sciences Center Web site, where you can refer to a tutorial on the anatomy of firearms, ballistics, laboratory methods, and gunshot residue testing: *http://medlib.med. utah.edu/WebPath/TUTORIAL/GUNS/GUNINTRO.html.*

Tour a virtual comparison microscope used in firearms identification at *www.firearmsid.com/new_index.htm.*

For more information about the history of fingerprints, fingerprint examinations, and the legal challenges to fingerprints, visit *www.onin.com/fp.*

NOTES

1. U.S. DEPARTMENT OF JUSTICE, NATIONAL INSTITUTE OF JUSTICE, OFFICER OF JUSTICE PROGRAMS, *Eyewitness Evidence: A Guide for Law Enforcement* (Washington, DC: Government Printing Office, 1999), 15.
2. LARRY DANAHER, "The Investigative Paradigm," *Law and Order,* June 2003, 134.
3. J. STANNARD BAKER, *Traffic Accident Investigator's Manual for Police,* 4th ed. (Evanston, IL: Traffic Institute, Northwestern University, 1963).
4. BARBARA GELB, *On the Track of Murder: Behind the Scenes with a Homicide Commando Squad* (New York: Morrow, 1975), 26.
5. JURGEN THORNWALD, *Century of the Detective,* trans. Richard Winston and Clara Winston (New York: Harcourt Brace Jovanovich, 1965), 434.
6. J. S. HATCHER, FRANK J. JURY, and JOE WELLER, *Firearms Identification and Evidence* (Harrisburg, PA: Stackpole Books, 1957), 286.
7. NICOLE LUNDRIGAN, "Gunshot Residue Technology," *Law and Order,* May 2004, 66.
8. TERRENCE MCGINN, "The Forgotten Evidence," *Law and Order,* November 2002, 30.
9. MICHAEL DELEO, "Bloodstain Pattern Analysis," *Law and Order,* November 2002, 43.
10. RICHARD SAFERSTEIN, *Criminalistics: An Introduction to Forensic Science,* 5th ed. (Upper Saddle River, NJ: Prentice Hall, 1995), 424–32. See also J. B. Wallace, "In Defense of Traditional Technology in a High-Tech World," *Journal of Forensic Identification* 4, no. 4 (July/August 1993): 378–85.
11. "Unsolved Case Fingerprint Matching," *FBI Law Enforcement Bulletin* 69, no. 12 (2000): 12–13.
12. WILSON R. HARRISON, *Forgery Detection* (New York: Praeger, 1964), 209–12.

3

RECORDS OF THE CRIME SCENE

Field notes made during the search of a crime scene are the basic record of the search and the evidence discovered. Photography and sketching offer opportunities to portray the scene and the evidence located during the search graphically. The investigator's preliminary report is prepared from his or her field notes. The notes and report both become permanent records in the case and have the inherent integrity of records prepared during the performance of official duties. Photographs must be taken and sketches made with care so that they represent the subjects accurately.

Sketches and photographs are usually offered into evidence as exhibits that are more realistic than words or that can assist the jurors in understanding the case or both. These records must withstand the basic tests of relevancy and materiality. Graphic representations are not automatically presumed to be correct. Their accuracy is verified by the person who made them or by any witness with sufficient knowledge of the subject to confirm that the sketch or photograph is a faithful representation of the subject.

Maps and diagrams were used to illustrate testimony long before photographs were first offered into evidence. As early as 1857, in a Maine case, one doctor's nonphotographic drawings illustrating the microscopic appearance of blood were admitted into evidence as exhibits to clarify a medical witness's oral description. When a drawing is admitted into evidence, its ability to clarify testimony and to orient evidence to the crime scene enhances such testimony and evidence.

Videotaping is the most recent addition to the use of graphics at the crime scene. Its pictorial storytelling provides substantial benefits for investigators. Likewise, the videotape may be equally useful to defense attorneys in court.

FIELD NOTES

Field notes are memoranda the investigator records during an investigation. The investigator begins recording field notes when he or she is assigned to the case and arrives at the scene, and he or she continues recording then until the case is closed. The portion of field notes in which the search for evidence at a crime scene is recorded usually includes the time the search started, the names of assisting personnel, a description of the weather and lighting conditions, a description of the area searched as the investigator proceeds, a note of any special equipment used, and an accurate note of the discovery of every significant item of evidence—when and where it was found, who found it, and what it looks like. Any measurements that place the evidence are recorded at this time, as is the disposition of the evidence. Sketches and diagrams drawn at the crime scene are field notes that, by their graphic portrayal of the crime scene, supplement the measurements and other data recorded.

In addition, the searching officer must record in his or her field notes any damage to objects at the scene or any disturbance of furniture and other objects. Anything unusual or foreign to the scene is also noted. Moreover, failure to locate an item of evidence commonly found at the scene of similar crimes is noted. These factual reports may be important as clues or as evidence against defense claims about the theory of the crime and its reconstruction.

PRELIMINARY INVESTIGATIVE REPORT

The place and time to obtain data for a **preliminary investigative report** are at the crime scene during the initial investigation. Anything omitted or overlooked is either lost or must be ascertained later, which is usually difficult and time consuming. Information about each item of importance must be collected if an investigation is to be comprehensive; the reports required of the officer processing the crime scene are incomplete without such information. The ten data included in the preliminary investigative report are as follows:

1. Victim's name, sex, age, occupation, residence and business addresses, and telephone numbers
2. Where the event occurred
3. Time of occurrence
4. Who reported the event, if other than the victim, and personal data about this person
5. Date and time reported, and sometimes how reported—in person, by mail, or by telephone
6. Time the reporting officer arrived at the crime scene
7. Full information on witnesses, along with their personal data
8. Name of arrestee, if any, and personal data available on him or her
9. Names and descriptions of suspects and personal data available on them
10. Name of reporting officer

While at the crime scene, the reporting officer must determine the perpetrator's method of operation and collect data about this phase of the crime. These data are the modus operandi data, and they have a stylized form because data storage and retrieval are based on major segments of a criminal's technique (Figure 3–1). The officer processing the crime scene must pay attention to all

| DIST. | SECT | SUB. | ☐ CUSTODY   ☐ PEND.
☐ CITATION   ☐ CLEARED ADULT
☐ FURTHER INVEST. ☐ CLEARED JUV. | **CRIME REPORT** | | **REPORT NUMBER** |

LOCATION OF OCCURRENCE

| REPORT DATE | DAY | TIME | EVENT NO. |

| OCC. DATE FROM | DAY | TIME | OCC. DATE TO | DAY | TIME | CONNECTED REPORT(S) — NUMBER AND TYPE |

CODE SECTION	F	M	CRIME TITLE
		A	
		B	
		C	
		D	

SPECIAL CRIME CATEGORIES EXIST? ☐ NO ☐ YES — CATEGORY FROM REVERSE _____

V NAME (LAST, FIRST, MIDDLE) | RES. PHONE | BUS. PHONE

RESIDENCE ADDRESS | CITY | STATE | ZIP | BUSINESS ADDRESS (SCHOOL IF JUVENILE) | CITY | STATE | ZIP

DOB | AGE | SEX | RACE | VICTIM'S VEHICLE (YR., MAKE, MODEL, LIC. NO.) | A | B | C | D | E |
| | | | | | F | G | H | I | J |

V/R NAME (LAST, FIRST, MIDDLE) | RES. PHONE | BUS. PHONE

RESIDENCE ADDRESS | CITY | STATE | ZIP | BUSINESS ADDRESS (SCHOOL IF JUVENILE) | CITY | STATE | ZIP

DOB | AGE | SEX | RACE | VICTIM'S VEHICLE (YR., MAKE, MODEL, LIC. NO.) | A | B | C | D | E |
| | | | | | F | G | H | I | J |

A. PLACE of CRIME
1 ☐ STRUCTURE 4 ☐ STREET/ALLEY 7 ☐ OTHER _____
2 ☐ VEHICLE 5 ☐ LOT/PARK
3 ☐ RES./YARD 6 ☐ BUS/STORAGE

B. DESCRIPTION OF SURROUNDINGS
1 ☐ RESIDENTIAL 4 ☐ RECREATIONAL 7 ☐ OPEN SPACE
2 ☐ BUSINESS 5 ☐ INSTITUTIONAL 8 ☐ OTHER
3 ☐ INDUSTRIAL 6 ☐ CONST. SITE

| TYPE OF STRUCTURE | ☐ N/A | G POINT OF ENTRY | J METHOD OF ENTRY | INVESTIGATIVE NOTATIONS |

C NON-RESIDENTIAL
☐ 1 CONVENIENCE
☐ 2 FAST FOOD
☐ 3 RESTAURANT/BAR
☐ 4 DRUG/MEDICAL
☐ 5 GAS STATION
☐ 6 RETAIL
☐ 7 SCHOOL
☐ 8 FINANCIAL INST.
☐ 9 ENTERTAIN/REC.
☐ 10 PUBLIC BLDG.
☐ 11 OTHER _____

D TARGET(S)
☐ 1 SHOP
☐ 2 CASH REG/DRAWER
☐ 3 OFFICE
☐ 4 SAFE/BOX
☐ 5 VENDING MACHINE
☐ 6 DISPLAY ITEMS
☐ 7 CLASS ROOM
☐ 8 OTHER _____

E RESIDENTIAL
☐ 1 SINGLE FAMILY
☐ 2 APT/CONDO
☐ 3 DUPLEX/TOWN
☐ 4 MOTEL/HOTEL
☐ 5 MOBILE HOME
☐ 6 OTHER _____

F TARGET(S)
☐ 1 STORAGE BLDG.
☐ 2 CLOSET
☐ 3 BATHROOM
☐ 4 DEN
☐ 5 FAMILY ROOM
☐ 6 GARAGE/CARPORT
☐ 7 KITCHEN
☐ 8 LIVING ROOM
☐ 9 STORAGE ROOM
☐ 10 BEDROOM
☐ 11 DINING
☐ 12 OTHER _____

G POINT OF ENTRY
1 ☐ N/A 4 ☐ SIDE
2 ☐ FRONT 5 ☐ GR LEV.
3 ☐ REAR 6 ☐ UP LEV.

H
☐ 1 UNKNOWN
☐ 2 DOOR
☐ 3 WINDOW
☐ 4 SLIDE GLASS
☐ 5 DUCT/VENT
☐ 6 ADJ. BLDG.
☐ 7 ROOF/FLOOR
☐ 8 WALL
☐ 9 BASEMENT
☐ 10 OTHER _____

I ALARM SYSTEMS
☐ 1 YES ☐ 2 NO
SET OFF
☐ 3 YES ☐ 4 NO

J METHOD OF ENTRY
☐ N/A
☐ 1 ATTEMPT ONLY
☐ 2 NO FORCE
☐ 3 KEY/SLIP
☐ 4 BODY/FORCE
☐ 5 SAW/DRILL
☐ 6 HID IN BLDG.
☐ 7 CHANNEL LOCK
☐ 8 PRY TOOL _____
☐ 9 LIFT OUT
☐ 10 BRICK/ROCK
☐ 11 BOLT CUTTERS/PLIERS
☐ 12 WINDOW SMASH
☐ 13 TAPE/WIRE
☐ 14 DOOR PUNCH
☐ 15 DOOR KICK
☐ 16 OTHER _____

INVESTIGATIVE NOTATIONS
SUSPECT INFO PAGE
(NUMBER SUSP _____) _____YES_____NO
PHYSICAL EVIDENCE
GATHERED BY R/O _____YES_____NO
CSI REQUESTED _____YES_____NO
IDENTIFIABLE PROPERTY _____YES_____NO
ADDITIONAL VICTIMS/
WITNESSES _____YES_____NO
NEIGHBORHOOD CANV _____YES_____NO
PROPERTY LOSS _____YES_____NO
PROPERTY LIST ATTACHED _____YES_____NO
INVESTIGATIVE DIV. PERS. NOTIFIED
_____

K SUSPECT'S ACTION ☐ N/A
☐ 1 ENTERED OCCUPIED BLDG.
☐ 2 ENTERED UNOCCUPIED BLDG.
☐ 3 VACANT RES./BLDG.
☐ 4 VANDALIZED/RANSACKED
☐ 5 USED MATCHES/SMOKED AT SCENE
☐ 6 DISABLED ALARM
☐ 7 ATE/DRANK ON PREMISES
☐ 8 VEHICLES NEEDED FOR LOOT
☐ 9 USED VICTIM'S TOOLS
☐ 10 KNEW LOCATION OF HIDDEN CASH
☐ 11 SELECTIVE IN LOOT
☐ 12 USED LOOKOUT DRIVER
☐ 13 BOUND/GAGGED VICTIM
☐ 14 RIPPED/CUT CLOTHING
☐ 15 MOLESTED VICTIM
☐ 16 FORCED VICTIM TO MOVE
☐ 17 DISABLED PHONE/ELECTRIC
☐ 18 INJURED VICTIM
☐ 19 THREATENED VICTIM
☐ 20 MASTURBATED
☐ 21 DISROBED FULLY/PARTIALLY
☐ 22 FIRED WEAPON
☐ 23 SUSPECT ARMED
☐ 24 OTHER _____

L PROPERTY TAKEN ☐ N/A
☐ 1 LARGE LOSS VALUE
☐ 2 TOOK CHECKS/CREDIT CARDS
☐ 3 CONSUMABLE GOOD
☐ 4 OFFICE EQUIPMENT
☐ 5 CAMERA
☐ 6 POWER TOOLS/LAWN EQUIP.
☐ 7 FIREARMS
☐ 8 SILVERWARE
☐ 9 FINE JEWELRY
☐ 10 MONEY
☐ 21 OTHER _____
☐ 11 LARGE APPLIANCES
☐ 12 SMALL APPLIANCES
☐ 13 CLOTHING/FURS
☐ 14 DRUGS
☐ 15 CONSTRUCTION MATERIALS
☐ 16 AUTO PARTS/ACCESSORIES
☐ 17 TOOLS/CARP./MECH./ELECT.
☐ 18 GOLD/SILVER COINS
☐ 19 TV/STEREO/VIDEO
☐ 20 NO LOSS

SYNOPSIS OF CRIME

| INVESTIGATING OFFICER | BADGE | DIVISION | SUPERVISOR |

PAGE _____ OF _____

FIGURE 3–1 Crime report—information called for on this printed form is the primary record of the circumstances of a crime.

ORIGINAL REPORT USE ONLY

THIS PORTION OF THE REPORT IS REQUIRED BY LAW. REFER TO UNIFORM CRIME REPORTING STANDARDS FOUND IN THE REPORT WRITING MANUAL. IT IS **NOT** TO BE FILLED OUT ACCORDING TO CALIFORNIA PENAL CODE STANDARDS. IF YOUR CRIME CLASSIFICATION INVOLVES A BURGLARY, ROBBERY, THEFT, HOMICIDE, ASSAULT OR RAPE, BE CERTAIN TO CIRCLE WHATEVER CATEGORY BELOW IS APPROPRIATE. CODE ONLY THE TYPE AND VALUE OF PROPERTY STOLEN AS INDICATED BELOW. RECOVERED PROPERTY IS TO BE CODED DIRECTLY ON THE RECOVERED PROPERTY REPORT, UNLESS RECOVERED SIMULTANEOUSLY AT THE TIME OF THE CRIME REPORT.

PROPERTY	Stolen Value	Recovered Value	BURGLARY	ROBBERY	THEFT
			VEHICLE AND SHOPLIFT	TYPE	TYPE
A CURRENCY, NOTES, ETC.	$	$	BURGLARIES ARE TO BE	031 FIREARM	0610 PICKPOCKET
B JEWELRY, PRECIOUS			CODED UNDER THEFT	032 KNIFE	0620 PURSE SNATCH
METALS	$	$	ENTRY	033 OTHER WEAPON	0630 SHOPLIFT
C CLOTHING, FURS	$	$	051 FORCIBLE	034 STRONGARM	0640 FROM VEHICLE
E OFFICE EQUIPMENT	$	$	052 UNLAWFUL	LOCATION	0650 AUTO PARTS &
F TV, CAMERA, STEREOS	$	$	053 ATTEMPT FORCIBLE	1 HIGHWAY	ACCESSORIES
G FIREARMS	$	$	STRUCTURE	2 COMMERCIAL HOUSE	0670 FROM BUILDING
H HOUSEHOLD GOODS	$	$	1 RESIDENCE	3 SERVICE STATION	0680 COIN-OPERATED
I CONSUMABLE GOODS	$	$	2 NON-RESIDENCE	4 CONVENIENCE STORE	MACHINE
J LIVESTOCK	$	$	(CLOSED)	5 RESIDENCE	0690 ALL OTHER
K MISCELLANEOUS	$	$		6 BANK	
				7 OTHER	ATTEMPT VEHICLE THEFT
TOTAL	$	$			

REPORTED DATE _____
REPORTED TIME _____

DATE OCC. _____
TIME OCC. _____

FROM	TO

0710 AUTO	
0720 TRUCK/BUS	A
0730 OTHER VEHICLE	

SPECIAL CRIME CATEGORY		NUMBER OF VICTIMS HOMICIDE		NUMBER OF VICTIMS ASSAULTS	
A CRIMES AGAINST CHILDREN	0110	MURDER NON-NEG	0410	GUN	0440 HANDS/FEET
01 NEGLECT/ABUSE		MANSLAUGHTER	0420	KNIFE	(SERIOUS INJURY)
02 SEXUAL	0120	MANSLAUGHTER	0430	OTHER	0450 HANDS/FEET
B CRIMES AGAINST ELDERLY		BY NEGLIGENCE		DANGEROUS	(MINOR OR
C DOMESTIC VIOLENCE				WEAPON	NO INJURY)
D GANG AFFILIATION					
E CRIMES MOTIVATED BY:		NUMBER OF VICTIMS		RAPE	
01 RACE					
02 RELIGION					
03 SEXUAL PREFERENCE		0210 FORCIBLE	0220	ATTEMPT FORCIBLE	

ARSON				
PROPERTY CLASSIFICATION		INHABITED	UNINHABITED	TOTAL ARSON $ DAMAGE
091 SINGLE OCCUPANCY RESIDENTIAL (House, Townhouse, Duplexes, etc.)		1	2	$
092 OTHER RESIDENTIAL (Apartments, Tenements, Flats, Hotels, Motels, Inns, Dormitories, Boarding Houses, etc.)		1	2	$
093 STORAGE (Barns, Garages, Warehouses, etc.)		1	2	$
094 INDUSTRIAL MANUFACTURING		1	2	$
095 OTHER COMMERCIAL (Stores, Restaurants, Offices, etc.)		1	2	$
096 COMMUNITY/PUBLIC (Church, Jails, Schools, Colleges, Hospitals, etc.)		1	2	$
097 ALL OTHER STRUCTURE (Out Buildings, Monuments, Buildings under Construction, etc.)		1	2	$

0981 MOTOR VEHICLES (Automobiles, Trucks, Buses, Motorcycles, etc.)				
0982 OTHER MOBILE PROPERTY (Trailers, Recreational Vehicles, Airplanes, Boats, etc.)				
0990 OTHER (Crops, Timber, Fences, Signs, etc.)				

FIGURE 3-1   Continued.

these elements to ensure thorough reporting of the technique used in the crime. The nine modus operandi elements are as follows:

1. Type of crime
2. Person attacked
3. How attacked
4. Means of attack
5. Trademark of perpetrator (peculiarities)
6. Words spoken (or the written note used)
7. Vehicle used
8. Property stolen
9. Name or physical description of suspect

Investigators must collect pertinent data for each element. For this reason, a checklist should be prepared as a reminder of the data to be collected about various crimes. Crimes can be grouped for this purpose as crimes against property, crimes against persons, and other crimes. Finally, investigators must report the details of the crime. This segment of the crime or offense report should be structured to tell the story of the circumstances of the crime to supplement the facts contained in the primary information or the modus operandi segments of the crime report. Many police departments suggest the following sixfold organization for this segment of the preliminary investigation:

1. **Suspect.**   Additional information describing the suspect or suspects, from aliases (the designation **a.k.a.,** "also known as," is used to indicate aliases) and nicknames to physical oddities and dress, including any data on employment or schools attended.
2. **Property Taken.**   For thefts, additional descriptive data on the property stolen, including the value set by the victim, the approximate date of original purchase or acquisition by other means ("age" of article), and the original purchase price or estimated value at the time.
3. **Physical Evidence.**   Detailed descriptions of all items of evidence, including traces, tool marks, and other imprints or impressions, along with full information about when and where such evidence was found and who found it, handled it, and disposed of it.
4. **Victims' Statements.**   The victim or victims who make statements are identified by name, address, age, and employment (or school attended), and the essential facts of the victim's story are stated.
5. **Statement of Witnesses.**   Identification of each witness making a statement and the essential facts of the story told by the witness. In addition, this segment of the report should include (a) data about the location of the witness at the time of observation, (b) the lighting conditions, and (c) any relationship between the witness and the victim or suspects.
6. **Observations by Reporting Officer.**   Facts that are not evidence, such as weather, conditions at the scene, and sobriety of persons contacted. Opinions based on observations are permissible in this segment, but both the opinion and its objective base should be reported (opinions not based on objective facts do not belong in a crime report).

Offense or crime reports originate at the operational level. Their basic purpose is to record and transmit information. Such reports inform interested persons of the action taken at a crime scene by the reporting officer. They place the data reported in the possession of others who can take appropriate action and ensure the continuity of an investigation with little or no need to backtrack or duplicate the preliminary investigator's work.

Primary data, modus operandi information, and the "details" or narrative of the crime and its circumstances must be written legibly and in clear and simple language. They must be complete in that all available and related facts are included, but they must also be brief. In addition, they must be accurate; all facts must be reported as they are known to the reporting officer, and opinions clearly noted and differentiated from the factual content of the narrative report.

PHOTOGRAPHY

An investigator should not disturb the crime scene or any objects at the scene before photographing the scene. So that the scene can be shown in its original condition, it must be preserved until photographs are taken.

Crime scene photography provides a permanent record of the facts at the crime scene. Photography is one means of recording facts for future use so that they can be used to reconstruct the crime scene and sometimes the crime. However, photography is not a substitute for field notes, accurate measurements, and sketches of the scene. Pictures supplement the other forms of recording the facts of a crime scene, and they are often the best way of recording and illustrating the details of a crime scene and its evidence. Sometimes, photos are the only feasible means of recording and illustrating certain features of a crime and the scene.

Photographing a crime scene serves the following purposes: it provides a pictorial representation of the appearance and position of objects at the scene, and it serves as evidence to support the investigator's testimony about what he or she found at the scene and its location, nature, and condition.[1]

If a photo-processing laboratory is not available within the limits of the chain of possession of evidence, daylight tanks for instantly developing negatives and almost-automatic contact printing apparatus are available. If such film developing is too complex or time consuming, the Polaroid camera system, with its brief routine from picture taking to finished print, may be useful. The finished print is ready in seconds, and if it is out of focus or did not picture the subject adequately, another photograph can be taken immediately and reviewed for quality. This 60-second trial-and-error system is excellent for instruction, and investigators soon learn to take high-quality photographs with Polaroid cameras.

Color photography outperforms the black-and-white process in showing evidence as it is. When projected on a large screen in court, color transparencies appear to be superior to prints for focusing the attention of the triers of fact. The quality of life-size reproduction and natural color in this type of photograph goes far beyond what can be achieved by any black-and-white enlarged print. The use of color slides was pioneered by experts in criminalistics, spread to medicolegal experts for autopsy photographs, and is being adopted for on-the-scene photography in many police agencies.

Investigators who do not take their own photographs should be on the crime scene ready to supervise the photographer's work. As a general rule, police photographers working crime scenes are responsive to instructions from an assigned investigator because they realize the investigator is responsible for the adequacy of the photographs taken.

The camera positions and the range at which photographs are taken should take advantage of the natural composition at the scene. The story of the scene is to be told graphically, and coherence requires an orderly progression in picture taking. In this type of camera work, objects cannot be moved to gain better composition, but the camera is mobile and its mobility should be used to the best advantage.

In general, the subject matter of crime scene photography should move from the general to the specific. Long-range views should tell a story of what happened at the crime scene and serve as a backdrop to locating the subjects of close-up photographs of items of physical evidence. The long-range photos may show the locale, the approach route, the means of ingress to the scene or its premises, a hallway, two connected rooms, or a view of the scene from the normal entrance. Midrange photographs (10 to 20 feet) pinpoint a specific object of evidence or a significant segment of the crime scene. Close-up photographs are used for recording evidence in position and detail—the location, nature, and condition.

Aerial photographs are excellent for studying crimes in series to ascertain whether the locations of past crimes suggest a pattern of criminal behavior from which the location of the next crime in the series can be projected. Such photographs are also excellent for locating outdoor crime scenes or controlling search patterns when large areas must be searched for evidence.

Proving the **corpus delicti**—the essential elements of the crime—requires a close-up crime scene photograph. This graphic exposition of the full story of the crime, insofar as it can be revealed from any mute viewing of the place of occurrence and its evidence, may be extremely important in preparing the case for presentation in court. The photographic composition must vary with the crime—a full-length picture of the homicide victim to show the position of the body or the location of a wound or wounds, the place of forced entry in a burglary, or the point of origin of the fire in a suspicious blaze. Close-ups include views of the weapon and wounds in a homicide, tool marks at the site of forced entrance, and a fire-setting contrivance or the distinctive charring along the fire trails of the accelerant often used in arson.

Photographs can also be used to trace the modus operandi of the criminal and the continuity of crimes occurring in a series. Photographs of tool impressions record the characteristics of the tool used. Enlargements can be made and the prints cut in half for comparison. Often a **jimmy**, or pry bar, can be traced from crime to crime. Linking the impressions sometimes offers a basic lead for an investigator and often provides multiple evidence when a matching tool is found in a crime suspect's possession.

Photography of evidence at crime scenes can be used to reveal blood and hair on weapons, the trajectory of flying objects from marks on floors and walls, the location and characteristics of imprints and impressions, and the full extent of injuries and wounds. Important details can be revealed by close-up photography. When a close-up view does not indicate the entire item of evidence, the photographer should show a progression from one end or side of the object to the other side, in a series of sectional views. Sectional photography reassures the triers of fact that the entire surface of the item of evidence was examined. Thus, the number of photographs taken of any single item of evidence depends on the dimensions of the evidence and the need for photographic detail.

Measurements and measurement markers have always been a problem in crime scene photography because they intrude on the photographer's reproduction of the scene as he or she found it. One acceptable procedure is to take a photograph without any change (as is) and then to take another picture with the measurement marker (a flat ruler, or the beginning section of a steel tape stretched out flat) placed in position.

Identification cards or markers are used in some photographs to record the date, time, location, photographer, and agency involved. However, they are not placed on the evidence, and they are positioned so that they do not conceal any part of the major subject of the photograph.

The series of photographs of a crime scene are dated and numbered consecutively (starting with *1*) or identified by a series of film file numbers. Information that will supply data that can be written on each photographic print should be linked with these numbers in the photographer's field notes. Pertinent data consist of the case number and subject of the picture, the crime classification, the date and time taken, the photographer's name, the location of the camera, the direction in which the camera was aimed, and the distance (in feet) to the subject of the picture. Most photographers also enter into their field notes such vital professional information as the illumination, lens setting, shutter speed, and ASA (American Standards Association) rating (film speed).

SKETCHES

The basic reason for sketching a crime scene is to provide an in-depth understanding of the circumstances of the crime beyond the level of comprehension attained solely by reading a written report or studying photographs. A sketch is

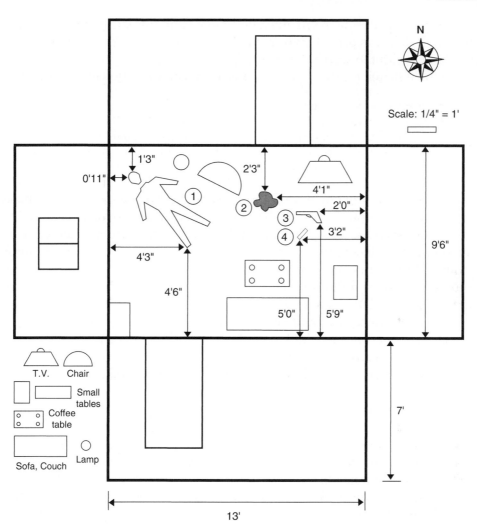

FIGURE 3-2   Floor-plan sketch showing walls of room and location of (1) body, (2) blood, (3) gun, and (4) empty cartridge cases.

better than a written report and not as good as a photograph with regard to depicting a crime scene. However, because of its unique virtues, it can supplement both reports and photographs. The advantage of a sketch is that unnecessary detail can be eliminated, whereas it cannot be eliminated from a photograph and is eliminated from a report only with difficulty. Sketching a plan (e.g., a floor plan) or diagramming the scene in the regular course of police business records the facts available to the viewer (sketcher) so that at any time in the future the assigned investigator and the triers of fact both have access to graphic representation of the crime scene (Figure 3-2).

Sketching a crime scene must be timely. The investigator must include the rough sketch as part of his or her field notes; both the sketch and the notes are aligned with the search of the scene.

A field sketch is marked for identification with the following information:

- Investigator's full name
- Time, date, case number, and crime classification
- Full name of any person assisting in taking measurements
- Orientation—Address; position in building; location adjacent to building; landmarks and compass direction, if outdoors

A common error committed during scene sketching is to attempt to make an architectural reproduction of the scene or to include too many details. The crime scene sketch is not unlike the diagram of a traffic accident. Items that do not aid in reproducing the accident should not be shown.[2] Standard symbols are used to indicate characteristics of a sketch, such as roads, walks, fences, common items of furniture, and evidence frequently encountered at crime scenes (Figure 3–3). A sketch shows and locates important objects at the scene; unimportant objects are omitted for simplicity. No one except the sketcher should mark or correct a field sketch in any way. This document is the first permanent graphic record of the investigation. It is kept for years, beyond any possible need in court, and a photocopy is attached to the investigator's report of the case.

When a graphic illustration is meant to clarify a written report, accurate measurements are needed. Steel tapes are the approved means of measuring distances in criminal investigation. The so-called measuring wheel is an accurate device, but the investigator must show that he or she knows how to use it and did use it in a manner that produced an accurate measurement. The investigator should test it against a known distance measured with a steel tape to verify its accuracy before use. One of the worst mistakes an investigator can make is to record an erroneous measurement on a drawing or in his or her field notes of a crime, for in such a case, no matter how many persons subsequently certify the correct measurement, a question will always remain about the initial recording and why it was erroneous.

In general, measurements are made of the area searched. They are made, first, with the eye: the investigator surveys the crime scene and decides what to measure and where to start. Second, the distance lines of the sketch plan are drawn. Last, the actual measurements are made and recorded on the plan. Measurements should extend along and from fixed and identifiable points. Any distance measurement with a **floating base**—that is, a reference point that may be moved or cannot be located with accuracy—should be avoided. Angular measurements can serve as coordinates to locate a point on the sketch only if the angle is broad and has two reference measurements from identifiable fixed points or objects.

Distance (Measurement) Line

Items of Evidence   1, 2, 3, etc.

Light Pole

Traffic Signal

Gun

Knife

Road or Driveway

Fence

Railroad

Tree

Hedge, Low Shrubbery

Footpath, Walkway

Vehicle   ▷ Front

Bicycle or Motorcycle   ▷ Front

Camera (Position)

Blood

Body (Victim)

Chair

Sofa, Couch, Daybed

Table (Coffee or Large)

Table (Small)

Table (Round)

Lamp

Television

Bed

Dresser

Bath (Tub)

Shower (Stall)

Toilet Bowl

Stove (Range) (Circles Indicate Number of Burners)

Refrigerator   ◀── Door

Sink   One Bowl   Two Bowl

Built-Ins (Place Open Side Against Wall)

Counter (Island in Kitchen, Merchandise in Store or Showroom)

Cash Register   CR

Safe   S

Door   (Indicates Direction of Opening)

Double Doors

Sliding Door

Folding Door   (Hinge or Fastened Side)

Wall (Building, Interior or Exterior)

Casement Window (Drawn in Extension of Wall)

Stairs (Arrow Indicates Up)

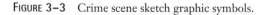

FIGURE 3–3   Crime scene sketch graphic symbols.

If possible, nothing should be moved during measurement because moving the objects changes the scene. The sketcher can claim that an object was returned to the same spot, but any such movement can taint the officer's testimony.

A **crime scene area diagram** can supplement a crime scene diagram. It is warranted when one or more of the basic facts in the case lies beyond the

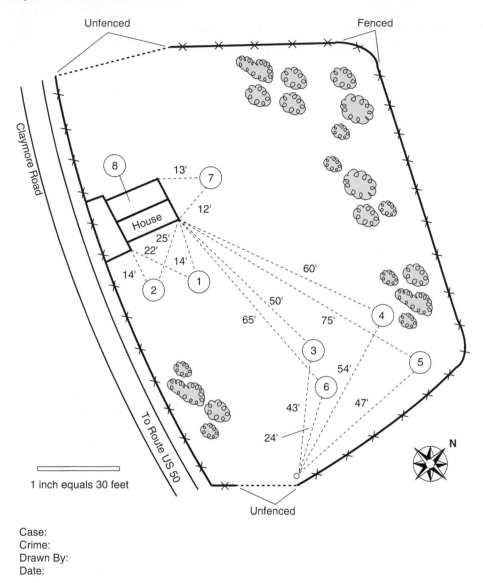

FIGURE 3–4   Crime scene area diagram. Each numbered location represents an item of physical evidence.

crime scene. These sketches pinpoint the location of shoe prints, tire tracks, weapons, and similar evidence linked to the crime scene (Figure 3–4).

Erasures may be made on such drawings. In fact, the drawings are usually completed in pencil, then inked in with permanent ink, and the pencil marks erased after the ink has dried completely. The drawings are identified in the same way as the crime scene sketch, and similar symbols may be used and annotated as necessary. Colors may be used for special effects, and overlays of semitransparent paper may be used to diagram the travels of participants in the crime. Schematic diagrams are often used to show the travels (paths) of the victim, offenders, bullets, and other moving objects.

Many graphic illustrations are drawn to scale by using the investigator's rough sketch and measurements. Recommended scales range from 1/8 inch equals 1 foot (1:96) for indoor scenes to 1 inch equals 20 feet (1:240) for larger outdoor areas. These scales usually permit the work to be presented on an 8.5-by-11-inch sheet of paper. Ideally, the investigator should select a scale that permits reproduction of the scene without completely filling the 8.5-by-11-inch paper so that space is allowed for a key or legend and necessary identification.

Individuals with special training professionally assist in preparing an investigator's sketches and diagrams for use in court. These items may be enlarged (blown up) but will be to a scale noted on the drawing. They are usually endorsed or certified by the investigator as being a reproduction of his or her original crime scene sketch. However, software is now available that will allow an investigator to prepare his or her own sketches. These 3-D applications are user friendly, and the investigator can begin creating diagrams after just a few lessons.[3]

Traditionally, the crime scene sketch has been used as a single-purpose tool merely to indicate the position of physical evidence at the crime scene. Its major purpose has been to place various items of physical evidence at the crime scene rather than to serve as a complete graphic report. Basically, the objective of crime scene sketching should be the graphic presentation of the crime scene in a manner that will permit reconstruction of the crime from the sketch details. Thus, an ability to draw must be ranked high among an investigator's necessary skills.

For years, sketching has been particularly effective for representing vehicular traffic accidents. However, it is a standard investigative technique for pictorial recording in all types of investigations.

VIDEOTAPES

Videotaping is pictorial storytelling, and it offers compelling reasons for investigators to use it. First, the videotaper is not limited by photograph borders or the camera lens. Second, videotaping has several other advantages over photography: (a) it provides immediate results without the need to develop film, (b) a tape can be reused by recording over images on it, (c) visual movement allows the viewer to perceive the scene as it is shown, and (d) sound may be used.[4] Third, the low cost of camcorders, their portability, their user-friendly sophistication, their high-quality image, and the ease with which the tape can be moved from camcorder to tabletop or large-screen monitors for viewing are all sound reasons for police departments to adopt this graphic system and adapt it to their needs.

However, when using the video camera to record the graphics of a crime scene record, the videographer should be extremely aware of the story that it could tell and carefully record the scene. Although prosecutors have used videotaping to their advantage at trial to show jurors meaningful views of a crime scene, defense attorneys have also used videotaping to destroy an investigator's credibility by using select segments of the video to contradict the investigator's court testimony. The segment may show only a minor oversight on the officer's part, but it may be sufficient to destroy the police case by casting suspicion on police crime scene conduct.

In crime investigation, videotaping has been used successfully for clandestine observation of suspicious places and persons and the transactions in "sting" operations. It is now being used more extensively to record interviews with witnesses, and the built-in "statement" feature has been helpful to investigators when a witness attempts to change or deny his or her initial version of the circumstances of a crime. Videotaping at crime scenes has also become more commonplace. Along with prosecutors, local judiciary, and defense attorneys, investigators participate in decisions to use videotaping.[5]

PROGRESS REPORTS

Progress reports are made either to inform the commanding officer of a new development in an investigation or at specified intervals—daily when a lot of progress is occurring, or every 5 days while the case is still "active." The purpose and scope of progress reports prepared during a continuing investigation depend on the investigator's assignment. If the assignment is limited—to check out one of the basic leads in a case or to interview a witness—the scope of the report is limited to this assignment, and the purpose is to collect data on a possible lead or a witness's story. However, if the investigator is assigned to complete a continuing investigation, as many reports must be made as necessary to record the work done, the data collected, and the status of the investigation.

Reports made during a continuing investigation have four primary objectives:

1. To inform persons reading the report of the findings resulting from an assigned investigation, including both information and the precise source of the information
2. To facilitate understanding of the entire investigation to date
3. To foreshadow the uncompleted portion of the investigation, if any
4. To fulfill the duties of the assignment (basic lead, witness interview, etc.)

A frequent and successful arrangement is to structure these reports according to the classic queries of news reports—when, where, who, what, how, and why. These queries, and segments of the report responsive to them, need not be in this order, but such queries are reminders to report writers to tell the entire story within the scope of their assignment.

Because a major segment of the work done in the continuing investigation is interviewing, investigators should develop a standard method for reporting interviews. This method should not extend to the content of the interviews, but should include listing such standard items of information as the time and date of the interview, the name of and other identification data on the interviewee, any relationship to other individuals who are involved, and the place of the interview.

This standard method can be extended to another major segment of the continuing investigation: physical evidence. The item of physical evidence is identified, then whatever facts are to be reported in connection with it are supplied.

DISCOVERY

Discovery is the term used for a request by the defense counsel for the prosecutor to disclose the police case against the defendant before the trial. The objective of discovery is to aid in ensuring that the defendant receives a fair trial. Detectives have become accustomed to disclosing the fruits of their investigations, knowing that when the defense counsel makes a discovery request in local courts, prosecutors must provide all crime reports, photographs, sketches, and other pertinent materials. Consequently, the importance of accurately recording the crime scene—regardless of the methods used—should always be foremost in the investigator's mind.

CHAPTER REVIEW

CASE STUDY

The Lucky Market Case

Police reports summarize the armed robbery of a supermarket, the subsequent investigation, and its results:

Details of Crime

On July 23, officers received a call at 1854 hours regarding a 211 P.C. at the Lucky Market, 56th and Broadway. Upon arrival, officers were met by the holdup victim, Edith Sheridan, who stated she was checking out at a cash register for customers. The next person in line was Suspect No. 1, and he left the groceries in the cart and didn't unload them, so victim started to take them out and Suspect No. 1 said, "Leave them alone." Suspect No. 1 took a gun from his belt with his right hand and said, "Empty the till and hurry up!" Victim took the money from the till and Suspect No. 1 said, "What's underneath?" Victim said, "Nothing but checks." Suspect came around and looked for himself, taking out the drawer. Suspect then said to the victim, "Go to the next till and pull out the cash." Victim asked if he wanted the coins and Suspect No. 1 said, "No, I don't want them." Victim went to the next till and Suspect No. 1 said, "Hurry up; you're not going fast enough." Suspect said he wanted all the coins in this till. Victim told Suspect No. 1, "There's no money in the last two tills," and Suspect No. 1 said, "Open them anyway," which the victim did.

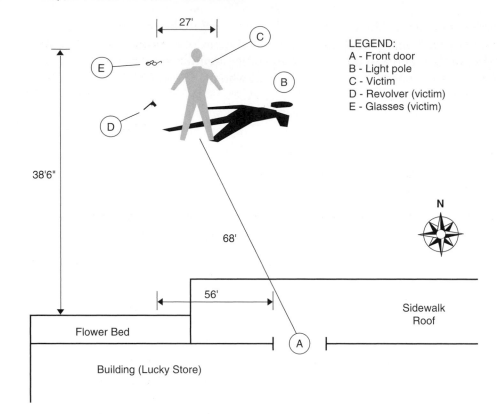

27'

LEGEND:
A - Front door
B - Light pole
C - Victim
D - Revolver (victim)
E - Glasses (victim)

38'6"

68'

N

56'

Sidewalk
Roof

Flower Bed

Building (Lucky Store)

FIGURE 3–5   Crime scene diagram—Lucky Market case study.

Suspect told victim to "stay put," and then the two suspects went out the front door separately, the short man in front.

John Cox, off-duty Sacramento Police Officer, Badge #178, at this time was standing at the checkout counter waiting in line and knowing the holdup was in progress. When the suspects left the front door, Cox pulled his gun on the way to the front door and caught up with Suspect No. 2 and told Suspect No. 1, who was seated in the car, to "hold it right there."

Suspect No. 2 at this time was standing beside Cox. Suspect No. 2 wheeled behind Cox and pinned his arms and pushed him down. Cox then went down and Suspect No. 2 pulled his gun from his belt and shot Cox in the neck. The next thing the victim saw was Cox lying on the pavement (Figure 3–5). Victim stated she heard no shot.

Victim stated Suspect No. 2 was possibly standing behind her in the store. She did not get a good look at him.

Victim also stated she felt that if she didn't obey Suspect No. 1's commands, she would be shot.

Victim also stated that the bag boy walked back to unload suspect's basket of groceries as they were at the counter, and Suspect No. 1 said, "Hey, stay right there." This incident happened at No. 1 check stand.

The amount of cash taken is not known at this time. Victim will advise.

Officers: Joseph Bals, #196/George Maloney, #189

Casualty Report

On July 23, police officer John Cox, age 38, white male, off duty, was shot by one of two holdup men, during a robbery at Lucky Market, 56th Street and Broadway. Victim taken by Superior Ambulance to Sutter Hospital, Unit 50 following ambulance, and reporting officer was present in Sutter Hospital emergency room when Dr. Meehan pronounced victim DOA [dead on arrival] at 1912 hours. Victim had been shot in the neck.

Officer: Edward Leonard (Unit #50)

Supplementary (Progress) Investigative Reports

On July 23–24, 2015 to 0115 hours: I took the following photographs at the Lucky Market, 56th Street and Broadway:

1. The front of the store: bloodstains in the parking lot in front of the NW corner of the store (color).
2. The check stand area from four (4) different angles (black and white).
3. A wire basket with grocery items in it. This basket was located in front of the store office, NW corner of the store (black and white).

I checked the following items found in the wire basket for fingerprints:

1. A potato bag
2. A paper bag of ice
3. A carton (six pack) of Busch Bavarian beer
4. A box of Lucky detergent (giant size; 1 lb. 15 oz.) (On the face of the box of detergent, I found two partial tips of fingerprints; latents protected with an Ace tab lift. No other latents of value found.)

I took color photographs of the deceased police officer, John Cox, at the coroner's morgue. These show the powder-burned area and a bullet hole in the left side of the officer's neck, a small black-and-blue spot on the right side of the officer's neck, a photograph of the officer's face, and a photograph of the officer, showing his gun holster strapped to his belt on the left side of his body. (All photographs in color, and taken at f/8 and 1/50th of a second.)

I checked a red Cadillac convertible with a black top, bearing California license MYY-625, for fingerprints in the police yard. Numerous partial latent fingerprints were found.

Officer: Joseph Green

On July 23, at 1854 hours: Mr. LeRoy Kennedy, a clerk in the market, stated he was standing alongside Aisle 31 in the Lucky store when an unidentified man tapped him on the shoulder and said, "There's a holdup going on." Kennedy walked to the cash register at the front of the store and observed two male subjects with a female clerk, Edith Sheridan (615 Crown Road, 675-6404), as she removed money from various cash registers at the direction of a suspect wearing an orange-colored, nylon, shell-type jacket, who will be designated as Suspect No. 1.

His accomplice, Suspect No. 2, wearing a blue jacket of somewhat the same type, was standing by. Kennedy further stated that he could see that Suspect No. 1 had some bulky object in the waistband at the front of his trousers, and he (Kennedy) concluded that it was a gun.

When the clerk (Edith Sheridan) had emptied several registers, Suspect No. 1 took the bag and left the store. Suspect No. 1 went to a vehicle parked to the west of the front doors in the parking area and got behind the wheel as Suspect No. 2 left the store, walking toward the vehicle.

Mr. Kennedy stated that he then observed a customer (later identified as off-duty Officer John Cox), pursuing the suspects from inside the store and approaching them at their vehicle. Cox had a gun in his hand and turned slightly away from Suspect No. 2 as he pointed the gun at Suspect No. 1, seated in the vehicle.

At this point, Suspect No. 2 wheeled around behind Cox, appeared to pin Cox's left arm behind him, and then pushed down on Cox's shoulder or head with his left hand, while pulling a gun from his waistband, shoving it tight against Cox's neck, and firing once. Cox fell to the asphalt; his gun fell from his hand.

Suspect No. 2 then entered the vehicle and both suspects left, driving east on Broadway and then south on 59th Street out of sight.

Physical descriptions of suspects:

Suspect No. 1—WMA [white male adult], taller than Suspect No. 2, possibly 6' 0", 165 lb., dark skin, medium build, wearing orange-colored nylon windbreaker-type zipper jacket, same age group as Suspect No. 2.

Suspect No. 2—WMA, 5' 8", 165 lb., mid-20s to early 30s, wearing faded-blue nylon windbreaker and hunting-type cap with bill, dark in color.

Officer: George Maloney, #189

On July 23, at 1910 hours: This officer received a call by radio that a police officer had been shot and that the subjects were last seen in a late-model Cad headed possibly E/B [eastbound] on U.S. 50 beyond the Elvis Freeway. This unit responded and rolled to the intersection of Watt Ave. and U.S. 50, and upon arrival at the Watt Ave. on-ramp E/B, observed the late-model Cad E/B in the No. 1 lane with one man at the wheel. The vehicle was a late-model Cad, black top over red bottom, convertible, license number MYY-625 California. The subject was ordered to the curb with the red light, and the vehicle stopped. The driver alighted and stood by the rear of his vehicle. This officer was out with gun in hand and ordered the driver to lie on the ground spread eagled, and then the rear of the Cad was approached and the car was seen to move as if someone was still in it. This officer then poked his gun into the Cad's interior, and the subject hiding in the rear came out from under several coats and trousers and surrendered. Subject driving was Harry W. Burrell, and the passenger was James Brainard. Brainard was the man hiding in the rear seat area.

The subjects were taken out of the car and lain on the ground on their stomachs, head to head, with each man's hands cuffed together. The subjects offered no resistance and were handcuffed without incident. The driver, Harry Burrell, stated as he watched this officer poke his gun into the car, "Come on out Brainard, looks like they have got us."

The subjects were transported from the scene to the county jail.

Note: Two Colt .38 Police Positive revolvers, No. 1 loaded with four rounds and No. 2 loaded with five rounds, were found together in the front seat of the car when it was stopped.

Officer: John Gayne, #111

On July 23, at 1920 hours: Upon my arrival at the scene (outbound U.S. 50, near Watt Ave.), Officer John Gayne had two suspects on the ground on the shoulder of the freeway, handcuffed. I observed two handguns in a red 1970 Cad convertible. The guns were on the right front seat of Cad. Subjects transported to county jail in my unit, number 245.

While en route to county jail, subject Brainard stated that he had shot the policeman. He stated he did not know that the man was a police officer until he [the police officer] pulled his gun on the two subjects. Subject Brainard stated he told the police officer to drop the gun, and when the officer moved, the subject's gun went off, and the officer fell.

Officer: Walter Morris, #622

On July 23, at 2330 hours: Following the arrest of the two subjects, Brainard and Burrell, the two weapons were brought into the Detective Bureau and examined by Harkness of the State CII (Criminal Investigation and Identification) Division and myself:

1. One .38-caliber revolver, serial no. 325597, was found to contain five live rounds of .38-caliber ammunition. This gun marked and turned over to Harkness, CII.
2. One .38-caliber revolver, serial no. 333563, was found to contain four live rounds of .38-caliber ammunition and one spent .38-caliber casing. This gun marked and turned over to Harkness of CII.
3. Both guns received by Harkness of CII at 2340 this date.

Officer: John Gayne, #111

On July 23, at 2355 hours: As shown on attached diagram, following articles removed from Cad 2-dr convertible bearing California license MYY-625 in county jail yard:

1. Paper bag containing a receipt from Grants dated July 23rd, one light socket, and one jar of hand cream
2. Paper bag, brown, containing $1,370.51 in currency and coin
3. Paper bag, empty
4. Cigarette package, opened, Marlboros
5. Dark glasses, bubble type
6. Dark glasses, flat
7. Hat, green with white webbing in front, bearing new price tag
8. Bag, empty, between seat and door, on floor
9. Hat, green with white webbing in front, bearing new price tag; identical to item 7
10. Glove, brown cotton
11. Man's Naugahyde jacket, pile lining
12. Dark glasses, flat
13. Shirt, khaki tan, cotton
14. Shirt, orange colored with several buttons missing
15. Jacket, rain repellant, dark color with white lining
16. One glove, dark color identical to glove item 10 and found wrapped in item 13
17. Bag, small size, found wrapped in shirt, item 13
18. Watch, Timex
19. One green metal toolbox containing:
    a. Empty brown paper bag
    b. Cloth glove similar to items 10 and 16
    c. Jar, Cover Girl makeup
    d. Tube lipstick, lavender color
    e. One box .38-caliber ammunition containing 33 Peters cartridges
20. One man's green hat, soft
21. One white coverall, J. C. Penney, Big Mac brand with light-colored paint over all
22. Boots, brown, medium high with light-colored paint on same
23. Two buttons, four-hole, pearl color

Regarding articles from the Cad (MYY-625):

1. Items 1 and 3 to 23 inclusive turned over to Allen Harkness, State CII.
2. Item 2 booked with jail sergeant.
3. Brown paper bag, item 2, containing $1,370.51 in currency and coin consisted of the following:

CURRENCY

25 held together by paper clip	$ 1.00 bills	$ 25.00
Loose	$ 1.00 bills	208.00
Loose	$ 5.00 bills	535.00
Loose	$10.00 bills	350.00
Loose	$20.00 bills	220.00
	Currency, total:	$1,338.00

COINS

1 roll 25-cent pieces	$10.00
3 rolls 10-cent pieces	15.00
3 rolls 5-cent pieces	6.00
3 rolls 1-cent pieces	1.50
1 loose penny	.01
Coins, total:	$32.51

Officer: John Gayne, #111

On July 24, at 0830 hours: The officer listed below was sent to the county morgue to pick up the cartridge belt and the clothing of Officer Cox.

Officer was present when Dr. Prisinzano removed the bullet or slug from the mouth of Officer Cox. I witnessed the doctor mark same, and he then handed the slug to me and I then marked same and placed in envelope. This envelope was later turned over to Allen Harkness of the CII at approximately 2230 hours.

The slug entered the neck of Officer Cox on the left side, approx. 5" below and 1" to the rear of the ear. It then passed through the neck and then lodged itself in the lower jaw on the right side.

This slug appears to be that of a .38 cal., and it is badly damaged, having smashed against the jawbone.

Deputy Shiner of the Coroner's Office advised that he will dry the shirt and other items of clothing and will then turn same over to Allen Harkness, CII, in the morning.

Joseph Green of our B of I took colored photos of the deceased, showing close-ups of the wounds, including the powder burns. Dr. Prisinzano removed a large section of flesh from around the wound, showing the powder burns, and this will be preserved and turned over to the CII by the Coroner's Office.

Officer: Harry Wells, #233

DISCUSSION QUESTIONS

1. What is the meaning of the *inherent integrity* of records prepared in the performance of official duties? Can this designation be applied to field notes of a crime scene search? To photographs at a crime scene? To sketches?
2. Explain why a photograph or a sketch must be a faithful representation of the item shown.
3. Relate the purposes of photographing a crime scene to the need for planned picture taking.
4. What are the advantages of a floor-plan sketch?
5. Who is responsible for the adequacy of crime scene photography? Why? Discuss.
6. What are the primary objectives of reports made during a continuing investigation?
7. What is the most appropriate form or structure of investigative reports?
8. What is meant by *chronological order* in the preparation of reports of a continuing investigation?
9. What are the six classic reporters' queries useful in guarding against omission of details in an investigative report?

LIBRARY ASSIGNMENT

Research the field of crime scene investigation. Prepare a bibliography of at least five references, books, and articles in this field, and cite the page numbers containing material about how to prepare a crime scene sketch.

WORKBOOK PROJECT

List the equipment and material you believe necessary for sketching a crime scene.

RELATED WEB SITES

To learn more about crime scene photographing and sketching, visit the following Web sites:

www.crime-scene-investigator.net
www.feinc.net/cs-proc.htm

NOTES

1. EASTMAN KODAK COMPANY, *Basic Police Photography*, 2nd ed. (Rochester, NY: Eastman Kodak, 1968), 16–22.

2. PAUL B. WESTON, *The Police Traffic Control Function*, 2nd ed. (Springfield, IL: Charles C Thomas, 1968), 196–99.

3. BOB DAVIS, "The CAD Zone: Law Enforcement Drawing Software," *Police*, March 2004, 86.

4. LARRY L. MILLER, *Sansone's Police Photography*, 3rd ed. (Cincinnati, OH: Anderson, 1993), 111–13.

5. KENNETH M. WELLS and PAUL B. WESTON, *Criminal Procedure and Trial Practice* (Upper Saddle River, NJ: Prentice Hall, 1977), 29–34.

4

LABORATORY AND TECHNICAL SERVICES

An expert's trustworthiness is important to the net worth of the entire investigation. Any suspicion of an expert's subjectivity or dishonesty destroys the legal significance of evidence because the average trier of fact often views such conduct as affecting the credibility of the entire investigation. An example of this type of reaction is illustrated by an unusual case in which the U.S. Supreme Court justices voted unanimously to reverse an Illinois murder conviction. The case was *Miller v. Pate*:

> Lloyd Eldon Miller, Jr., was convicted of murder in an Illinois state court in a prosecution for the death of a girl that resulted from a sexual attack. A piece of compelling evidence against Miller was a pair of reddish-brown stained men's shorts found in an abandoned building, known as *Van Buren's Flats*, a mile away from the crime scene.
>
> The prosecution theorized that the stains on the shorts were human blood and that the petitioner had been wearing these shorts when he committed the crime. The judgment of conviction was affirmed on appeal by the Supreme Court of Illinois (13 Ill. 2d 84, 148 N. E. 2d 455). On receiving an application for a writ of **habeas corpus**, the U.S. District Court for the Northern District of Illinois granted the writ (226 F. Supp. 541), but the Court of Appeals for the Seventh Circuit reversed it (342 F. 2d 646). In the federal habeas corpus proceeding, the reddish-brown stains on the shorts in question were established to be not blood, but paint, and counsel for the prosecution was found to have known at the time of the trial that the shorts were stained with paint.

Using words of unusual bluntness, the Supreme Court justices stated the following unanimous opinion:[1]

> More than 30 years ago this Court held that the Fourteenth Amendment cannot tolerate a state criminal conviction obtained by the knowing use of false evidence. There has been no deviation from that established principle. There can be no retreat from that principle here. The judgment of the Court of Appeals is reversed, and the case is remanded for further proceedings consistent with this opinion. (p. 7)

CRIMINALISTICS: FORENSIC SCIENCE

The crime laboratory in which physical evidence obtained by police during an investigation is examined is now often known as a **forensic science laboratory**, and the laboratory technicians as **forensic scientists**. However, the professional group in this field still identifies with the terms *criminalistics* and **criminalists**. Criminalistics is the profession and scientific discipline directed toward recognizing, identifying, individualizing, and evaluating physical evidence by applying the natural sciences in matters of law and science.[2]

Identification in criminalistics is aligned with the logic of **set theory**: all objects can be divided and subdivided into various sets on the basis of their properties. Identification in relation to physical evidence and its analysis is defined as the determination of some set to which an object or a substance belongs, or the determination as to whether an object or a substance belongs to a given set. Fingerprints, tool marks, blood, hair, glass, paint, and other types of evidence can be so classified. In addition, criminalistics is concerned with identity or origin: given a bloodstain found and collected at a crime scene, the criminalist is asked to determine from whom it originated; given a spent bullet recovered from a human body, the criminalist is asked to decide whether a particular firearm fired the bullet. In reaching a decision about identification, the criminalist is also asked to individualize the identification by specifying how individual or unique the item of evidence is within the set of its origin.

The crime laboratory is staffed by technicians educated and trained in the forensic science that is criminalistics. It is a subsystem in the administration of justice in which the effect of a criminal on a crime scene (and other sites of criminal activity) is studied, and vice versa. The informational output of a crime laboratory depends on its input: the physical evidence collected at crime scenes and forwarded to the laboratory for examination. Whether to develop information from physical evidence within a laboratory operation is the decision-making responsibility of the forensic science staff. Depending on the circumstances of the case, the general strategy is to order the analyses so that the maximum amount of information is secured.[3]

When scientific findings are interpreted, the criminalist who is reconstructing the event and the person or persons associated with this reconstruction cannot make deductions with certainty and usually make them with prudence. Criminalists offer the *most probable* reconstruction on the basis of reasonable criteria and do not assign mathematical probabilities to the possibility that two materials from different sources (two items of evidence, or one item of evidence and one known standard) have a common origin. Even the most sophisticated and specific analysis techniques do not, as a general rule, offer an opportunity for a criminalist to evaluate identification in terms of mathematical probability.

The effect of identification and individualization of evidence on an accused person and his or her legal counsel is considerable. Associative evidence placing a suspect at the crime scene ruins a not guilty pleading based on a general denial of presence at the crime scene or of contact with the victim at any time, and it seriously damages a defense based on an alibi. Tracing an item of evidence found at the crime scene to the accused person or an item found on the suspect to the scene has serious implications for any successful defense unless a reasonable explanation is forthcoming. The effect is not necessarily an inducement to confess, but it can function in this fashion by influencing the defendant and his or her legal adviser.

DNA "FINGERPRINTING"

DNA testing has become an established part of criminal justice procedure. Despite early controversies and challenges by defense attorneys, the admissibility of DNA test results in the courtroom has become routine. Understanding the importance of DNA typing to criminal investigations requires knowledge of some fundamental biological facts.

Each molecule of DNA, the primary carrier of genetic information in living organisms, consists of a long, spiral structure that has been likened to a "twisted ladder." The "handrails" of the ladder string together the ladder "rungs." Each rung consists of a **base pair**, two of four varieties of nucleic acids. The sequence of these base pairs constitutes the genetic coding of DNA.

DNA in humans is found in all cells that contain a nucleus—except red blood cells. Each nucleated cell (except sperm and eggs cells) usually contains the full complement of an individual's DNA, called the **genome**, which is unvarying from cell to cell. The genome consists of approximately 3 billion base pairs, of which about 3 million actually differ from person to person. However, the base pairs that vary represent a virtually incalculable number of possible combinations. Person-to-person differences within a particular segment of a DNA sequence are referred to as **alleles**.

DNA typing focuses on identifying and isolating discrete fragments of these alleles in a sample (Figure 4–1) and comparing one sample with another. For example, a forensic scientist might compare a semen sample retrieved from a rape victim with a DNA sample taken from a suspect. If identical fragments appear in both samples, a match is declared. To determine the likelihood that a match is mere coincidence, the criminalist must compare a particular combination of alleles with the frequency with which the combination appears in the statistical population.

Many of the specimens frequently encountered at crime scenes are either contaminated, degraded, or in small quantity. These problems are surmounted by **polymerase chain reaction (PCR) analysis**. This technique involves

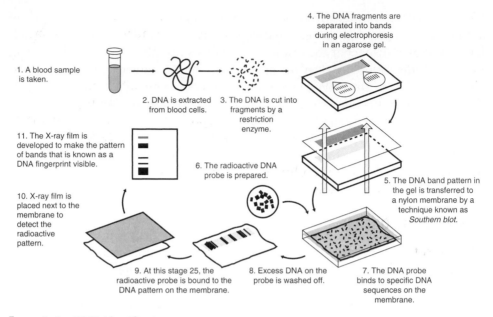

1. A blood sample is taken.

2. DNA is extracted from blood cells.

3. The DNA is cut into fragments by a restriction enzyme.

4. The DNA fragments are separated into bands during electrophoresis in an agarose gel.

5. The DNA band pattern in the gel is transferred to a nylon membrane by a technique known as *Southern blot*.

6. The radioactive DNA probe is prepared.

7. The DNA probe binds to specific DNA sequences on the membrane.

8. Excess DNA on the probe is washed off.

9. At this stage 25, the radioactive probe is bound to the DNA pattern on the membrane.

10. X-ray film is placed next to the membrane to detect the radioactive pattern.

11. The X-ray film is developed to make the pattern of bands that is known as a DNA fingerprint visible.

FIGURE 4–1   DNA identification process.

extracting DNA from a small evidence sample and then replicating it through a complex operation of repeated heating and cooling cycles and exposure to an enzyme. Because each cycle doubles the quantity of DNA, the original extraction can be replicated several million times within a short period. Examining several *locations (loci)* where variation occurs allows a typing profile to be produced. The Federal Bureau of Investigation (FBI) has selected 13 **short tandem repeat (STR)** loci to serve as a standard battery of core loci, each of which contains a short sequence of DNA, normally two to five base pairs long, that is repeated a different number of times in different people. Samples identified by a radioactively labeled, allele-specific probe are blotted onto a membrane, according to standard PCR protocol. Each dark spot that appears can be read as "yes" or "no" to the question of whether a particular individual possesses a given allele. When DNA samples from known individuals are compared with evidence samples, a difference of a single allele can exclude someone as the donor of that evidence sample. The more locations that show the same allele pattern, the stronger the evidence that the two samples came from the same individual.[4]

DNA is found in all body tissues and fluids. Thus, saliva, skin cells, bone, teeth, tissue, urine, feces, and a host of other biological specimens, all of which may be found at crime scenes, are sources of DNA. Saliva may be found in chewing gum and on cigarette butts, envelopes, and possibly drinking cups. Fingernail scrapings from an assault victim or a broken fingernail left at the scene by the perpetrator may also be useful DNA evidentiary specimens. Even hatbands and other articles of clothing may yield DNA. Because the DNA molecule is long lived, it is likely to be detectable for many years in bones or body fluid stains from older criminal cases in which questions of identity remain unresolved.

Almost all states have legislation related to DNA data banking, most of which focuses on collecting and testing DNA from individuals convicted of sexual assaults or homicides. The FBI supports this effort by linking these state databases to form a national database known as **CODIS (Combined DNA Index System)**. This system networks to link the typing results from unsolved criminal cases in multiple jurisdictions and by alerting investigators to similarities among unsolved crimes.[5]

LABORATORY DETERMINATIONS

After scientifically examining physical evidence, laboratory personnel report their findings. Their determinations for past cases lead field investigators to have a certain set of expectations for other cases. However, meeting these expectations is not always possible for a specific case. As a result, the field investigator may be disappointed, and, perhaps, become reluctant to request such technical or laboratory assistance in the future. Thus, having an optimistic but realistic view of the determinations possible through scientific aid is necessary and should encourage field investigators to use technical and laboratory services more extensively.

Following is a list of findings that may result from a scientific examination of physical evidence. The list is organized, for ready reference, according to the nineteen basic types of evidence common to police cases:

1. *Weapons*—Firearms
   a. Identification of bullets, shells, or cartridge cases with a specific gun
   b. Operating condition of the firearm; functioning of the safety and the trigger pull
   c. Distance at which the gun was fired
   d. Shooter's position at the time of firing
   e. Ownership trace
   f. Restoration of obliterated serial number
   g. Development of imprints (latent fingerprints), impressions, or transfer evidence
   h. Use in other crimes

2. *Weapons*—Knives and Bludgeons
   a. Description of cutting, stabbing, or striking surfaces
   b. Comparison with wounds
   c. Ownership trace
   d. Development of imprints, impressions, or transfer evidence
   e. Use in other crimes

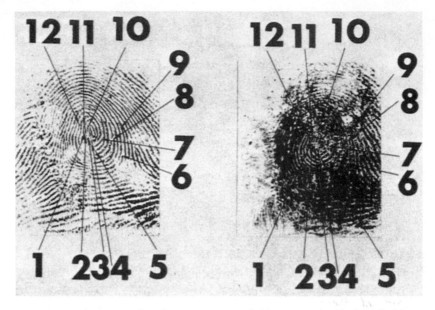

FIGURE 4–2   Latent fingerprint found at a crime scene (left), compared with the rolled fingerprint of the suspect (right). Twelve points of identity indicate a match.

    f. Direction of force
    g. Assailant's position
    h. Identity of assailant; sex, strength, and which hand held weapon

3. ***Drugs and Poisons***

    a. Analysis by type (name)
    b. Determination of quantity of fatal dose
    c. Origin (purchase, manufacturer, growth)
    d. Comparison with effect—wounds, body functions
    e. Use in other crimes

4. ***Imprints and Impressions***

    a. Nature of object making imprint or impression
    b. Identity by manufacturer or group
    c. Individual identity—comparison (imprint or impression made by or not made by submitted suspect object)
    d. Individual identity—fingerprints (Figure 4–2)
    e. Individual identity—footprints[6]
    f. Direction of movement
    g. Development of transfer evidence

5. ***Tool Marks***

    a. Nature of tool
    b. Identity by manufacturer or group
    c. Identity—for search
    d. Origin (purchase)

   e. Individual identity (mark made or not made by submitted suspect tool)
   f. Development of transfer evidence
   g. Use in other crimes

6. *Traces of Identity*—Blood

   a. Identification as blood
   b. Determination (human or animal, grouping, direction, and velocity of drops and splashes)[7]
   c. Direction of force
   d. Assailant's position
   e. Individual identity (blood of victim or defendant)
   f. Same blood found at other crime scenes
   g. Development of transfer evidence[8]

7. *Blood (test)*

   a. Blood alcohol level (percentage)
   b. Interpretation of percentage as to degree of intoxication

8. *Hair and Fibers*

   a. Origin (human, head, body, pubic; animal; clothing)
   b. Identity (sex, race—a broad grouping)
   c. Individual identity—comparison of known standards of victim's hair with defendant's hair; comparison of fibers from clothing of victim (or found at scene) with material found on suspect
   d. Dog hair (victim's pet to clothing of suspect; suspect's pet to crime scene or victim)

9. *Dust, Dirt, and Debris*

   a. Origin (locale, occupation)
   b. Identity (group)
   c. Development of individual identity or transfer evidence

10. *Flammable Fluids*—Fire and Explosive Residue

   a. Identity by physical properties
   b. Origin (purchase, manufacturer)
   c. Direction of force (flow)
   d. Use in other crimes

11. *Glass*

   a. Identity and comparisons
   b. Direction of force
   c. Development of transfer evidence
   d. Similar damage at other crime scenes

12. *Paint*

   a. Identity (group)
   b. Origin (purchase, use, manufacturer)

    c. Individual identity—the same as or similar to submitted sample

    d. Development of transfer evidence

13. *Semen Stains*

    a. Identity of stain as semen

    b. Location and extent of stain

    c. Origin—individual identity in relation to blood or other body substances or fluids of a suspect in custody[9]

14. *Wood*

    a. Identity (type, group, name)

    b. Origin (purchase, production, growth)

    c. Identity—same as or similar to submitted suspect sample

15. *Suspected Poisoned Food*

    a. Isolation and identity of noxious or poisoned substance

    b. Origin (source, process)

16. *Documents*

    a. Authenticity of document or signature or both

    b. Authorship (handwriting); authorship (typewriter); identity— "trademarks" of writer (form, spelling, vocabulary, etc.); fraudulent check "trademark"

    c. Age (date written)

    d. Nature of alteration or erasure

    e. Copy traces, carbon paper, embossed writing, typewriter ribbons

    f. Development of transfer evidence

    g. Dating of ink and paper[10]

    h. Use in other crimes

17. *Feces.*   Comparison with samples taken from other crime scenes; undigested food residues possible and informative

18. *Vomit.*   When suspect is located, comparison of vomit at crime scene with traces on suspect's clothing; in suspected poison cases, analysis for content and identification of poison, if present

19. *Urine.*   Analysis of submitted specimens (alcohol level in blood), and analysis in suspected poisoning cases

LABORATORY EQUIPMENT

The criminalist's work involves the use of physical and biological science laboratories, examination of substances involved with crime and suspects, and the use of selected equipment normally associated with scientific techniques in such disciplines. Equipment designed especially for identification of firearms and examination of questioned documents is part of the inventory of a criminalistics laboratory.

Major items of equipment, other than the basic assortment of test tubes, retorts, burners, and the like, that may be found in a modern laboratory of considerable size range from optical equipment through X-ray and spectrographic devices to machines and measuring devices that use the latest space-age technology. Microscopes usually span the range of magnification from low-power instruments of comparatively low cost to high-power instruments of high cost. The comparison microscope, designed for work in the identification of firearms, and photographic equipment necessary for microphotography are common optical tools in these laboratories.

Equipment for spectrographic analysis has been a part of the criminalistics scene for many years. In spectrography, the radiation from an incandescent gas or vapor is concentrated in certain discrete wavelengths. Such wavelengths are characteristic of the emitting elements in the gas. Each element emits a unique and characteristic pattern of wavelengths, or **spectrum**. A spectrograph has a narrow slit to admit the radiation, a prism or grating to distribute the radiation, and a system of lenses to focus the wavelength pattern on a photographic plate. The pattern is recorded photographically as a series of short lines, each line being an image of the slit formed by the radiation of one wavelength. In analysis, the evidence sample is vaporized to incandescence by flame, arc, or spark, and the radiation is recorded. Evidence samples are normally composites. Therefore, spectra of all the elements composing the evidence sample are recorded simultaneously, and the criminalist analyzes the composition of the sample by sorting the recorded lines, their widths, and their positions in the spectrum. Spectra of known standards and charts of the standard wavelengths of various elements are used for identification. A medium-size quartz prism instrument with a range into the ultraviolet region disperses incident light on a 10-inch photographic plate. The spectrograph is an all-purpose instrument for criminalistics that will produce a complete elementary analysis of evidence samples containing mineral and other inorganic compounds.[11]

Chromatography is a method of separating compounds to identify the components. Modern chromatography equipment can identify compounds. Gas or vapor chromatography uses a columnar device in which the evidence sample is injected into the system at the beginning of the column and carried along by a stream of carrier gas. Each constituent of the sample being tested is separated, emerges at a definite time from the time of injecting the sample (retention time), and is fed into a recorder. The recorder provides a trace in which the peaks and their position on a time axis (the retention time) identify each component of the sample. Gas chromatographs are valuable analytic tools because with them microsamples of complex compositions such as gasoline, fuel oil, perfumes, hair dressings, and paint thinners can be separated and identified from their constituents—a difficult task with other scientific techniques when only minute quantities of evidence are available.[12]

X-ray crystallography is useful for identifying any crystalline solid or compound from which a crystalline-solid derivative can be made. X-ray diffraction is also of use in processing extremely small samples, in examining samples with noncrystalline impurities, and in identifying inorganic and mineral substances. X-ray spectra are used for analysis and identification. Equipment is based on standard X-ray devices adapted to testing and recording X-ray spectra and diffraction patterns.

The newest piece of laboratory equipment is a type of nuclear reactor used for **neutron activation analysis (NAA)**—a technique that can analyze samples 100 times too small for ordinary spectrographic techniques. Such equipment cannot be easily purchased for a local laboratory, but a centrally located radiochemistry laboratory can make this new technique available to any local criminalistics laboratory.

NAA is an extremely sensitive method of analyzing a sample for the elements in its composition. This method involves bombarding the sample with neutrons in a nuclear reactor, which causes the different elements in the sample to become radioactive and thus makes identifying the different radioactive elements and determining the quantity of each possible. The great sensitivity of this method allows the detection of mini-micro elements. The research reactor is much smaller and simpler than a nuclear power reactor. In operation, it produces vast numbers of neutrons by uranium fission chain reaction, but under precise control. When an evidence sample is inserted into this intense field of neutrons, the various elements in the sample undergo a nuclear reaction that causes some of the elements to become appreciably radioactive. After the irradiation, the activated sample is removed for counting. The different radioactive elements that are then present emit radiations of different energy levels and decay at different rates. Some die out within seconds, some die out within minutes or hours, and some require days, weeks, or even longer. A sophisticated apparatus, the **gamma-ray spectrometer**, is used to measure the distinctive radioactive gamma-ray emissions and thus to identify the elements from which the rays originate. The data are printed on paper tape and displayed on the face of an oscilloscope. As the number of elements found at the same concentrations in two samples increases, matching the two samples becomes increasingly positive.[13]

The NAA technique and its application in the study of gunshot residues has returned a potential item of evidence to investigators. Testing for gunshot traces had fallen into disuse when the old "paraffin test" was found to react to urine and a few similar substances as well as to gunshot residues. Now paraffin-lifting kits are used on a suspect's hands, and NAA measurements for the presence of antimony and barium, common gunshot residues, have indicated a new and useful discrimination and particularity. Distinctive "signatures" of handguns, tools, and other metal objects are available to investigators through another innovative technique—the **trace metal detection technique (TMDT)**—which makes the patterns of these objects visible on the skin or clothing of suspects when the skin or clothing is treated with a test solution and examined under ultraviolet light.[14]

Ultrasonic cavitation is an etching method that may replace chemical, electrolytic, and magnetic particle methods of restoring obliterated serial numbers on firearms and other metal objects. Cavitation is similar to boiling liquids; vapor bubbles form in a liquid agitated by a vibrator. An ultrasonic generating system is used for inducing cavitation. The high-energy bubbles produced have the effect of etching a metal surface. This method is rapid and effective for serial number recovery.[15]

Lasers (argon-ion or copper-vapor) are widely used in the detection of latent fingerprints. Laser examination of questioned documents has been useful in some cases of alteration or obliteration. Laser examination can reveal information unattainable by any conventional nondestructive means.[16]

The equipment found in crime laboratories is extensive. Basic cameras, microscopes, spectrographs, and fluoroscopes are being supplemented by computers and space-age devices. As new equipment is obtained and used by laboratory technicians, the director of the laboratory informs local police managers of the additional services available. Investigators should be alert to such changes in the availability of services and use the new services whenever doing so is in the best interest of an investigation.

VOICEPRINT IDENTIFICATION

Voiceprinting is the graphic identification of voices. Voiceprints are an innovative concept for personal identification and are fast becoming useful tools in criminal investigation. Their use is limited only by the adaptation of this technique to the many areas of oral communication encountered in an investigation.

Voiceprint identification is based on the physical characteristics of each person's vocal cavities (the throat, mouth, nose, and sinuses) and the manner of manipulating the lips, teeth, tongue, soft palate, and jaw muscles. This technique of personal identification may challenge fingerprints as the most positive means of personal identification. The chance that any two individuals have precisely the same size of vocal cavities and have learned to use their articulators in the same manner is remote. To date, this premise has survived thousands of attempts to disprove it. Efforts to disguise the voice or to imitate the voice of another individual have been easily discerned. Whispering, muffling, nose holding, and even filling the mouth with marbles can be detected.

Suspect voices are recorded on a good-quality tape recorder. Known standards for comparison are also tape-recorded. Tape recordings are fed into a specially designed spectrograph that reacts to the sound of the recorded voice and produces a voiceprint in much the same way as the polygraph produces a chart.

The voice spectrograph reacts to voice frequency, to volume, and to the timing of a person's speech. Voiceprint techniques of identification are particularly applicable to the identification of voices involved in kidnappings, obscene-language telephone calls, and telephoned threats.

Automatic methods of voice identification are under development. They involve machine-aided speaker recognition: naming the speaker, identifying the speaker, or distinguishing the speaker who has produced a given voice sample from other speakers. These methods are a mechanized, computerized extension of people's ability to recognize voices. Speech samples will be processed for their unique features and categorized by these extracted features. Recognition will be automatic and will be based on digital computer technology rather than on the skill of a technician, a "user," or an operator.[17]

CRYPTOGRAPHY

The use of simple ciphers and codes to protect the security of messages—**cryptography**—is increasing in the world of crime. It is common in unlawful gambling cases, in which records of customers' wagers must be kept. It is used by organized crime personnel because written communications have been found to be less susceptible to investigative examination than have telephone conversations. It is also likely used for communications among extremist groups planning crimes, as well as by various types of offenders who want to protect the security of personal telephone and memo books.

Cryptography also involves deciphering such cryptograms to reveal their underlying messages. Investigators encounter and must decode several types of ciphers that criminals use.

The most common cipher in use by criminals is a simple **substitution cipher**, in which a symbol, letter, or digit stands for another symbol, letter, or digit. Many criminals' simplistic thinking confines the substitution to some simple order, such as *1* represents *A*, *2* represents *B*, *3* represents *C*, and so on. **Transposition ciphers** are characterized by a change in the order of the enciphered material. Investigators find them used fairly often for recording telephone numbers: a **reversal transposition** may be used, in which, for example, the telephone number 445-1769 becomes 967-1544; or **split combination** may be used—for example, 445-1769 becomes 176-4459, 769-4451, or 544-1769; and so on. Investigators are aided by the fact that most criminals are amateur encipherers, and solving their ciphers is simple. A criminal does not have access to the few sources of information available about ciphers, and when he or she sits down to create a cipher, no one is there to tell the person that his or her invention is, in truth, hundreds of years old.[18]

Federal agents successfully solved a stolen bonds fraud case involving Mafia members in a typical national crime syndicate operation with international overtones when a key to a code was found hidden in one gang member's wallet. The code had been used in cable communications between gang members in New York and those in London to communicate secretly the denominations of stolen bonds available for sale and the asking prices. Court action by the Federal District Attorney brought the records of these communications into court, and the knowledge of the code key made their content intelligible to the trial jury and showed the joint action of the conspiracy.

Investigators can learn to solve simple substitution or transposition ciphers by running down the alphabet with the first eight or ten letters of the message and then testing for substitution. This process requires substituting letters one further on in the alphabet in the first run-through, then two further on in the second testing, and so on: trying *b* for *a*, then *c* for *a*, and so on. Julius Caesar is said to have used a cipher based on the simple substitution of a letter three letters further on in the alphabet. Simple transposition ciphers can be solved by trial and error when the enciphered work or numerical prefix in telephone numbers in known or suspected. Telephone and memo book codes are usually solved by using the local telephone exchange prefix of three numbers to break the method of transposition by trial and error. A frequency distribution study will solve more complex ciphers, but such a study requires the work of experts with tables of letter and word frequencies. However, an investigator may break a complex cipher or code if he or she has some preknowledge or can guess that a certain word is likely to appear in the message and then looks for this word.[19]

When the use of a cipher or code is suspected, the investigator should attempt to collect as much of the suspected writing as possible and to ascertain the languages and skills with which the defendant is familiar. Knowing the suspect's language fluency and whether he or she has any particular skill, such as stenography, printing, piano playing, or the like, may be helpful in deciphering the communication, because these areas of skill or experience often form the base of the cipher or code scheme. When expert assistance is required, the enciphered material should be forwarded to the police laboratory in the same manner as other questioned documents, with the data just mentioned noted under the details of the case along with some of the possible words likely to be used frequently in the enciphered communications.

CHAPTER REVIEW

CASE STUDY

Child Abduction

Twelve-year-old Courtney left home around 2 p.m. to go to the local convenience store two blocks away. She was reportedly seen there at about 2:15 p.m., talking to a man who was seated in a dark-colored BMW. At about 7:00 p.m., when she did not return home, her parents reported her missing. More than 20 officers and volunteers began a neighborhood search, knocking on doors in the area in an effort to find her.

Unknown to the searchers was that Courtney's body had already been found in an adjoining county about 25 miles away. At about 5:30 p.m., some fishermen approached a spot on the river by boat, which was near the highway. As they approached, they noticed a subject running away from the beach, leaving behind a dead body. The beach where the body was found is a popular spot to fish, drink beer, fire guns, and dump bodies. The beach averages two to three bodies a year. A search of the crime scene disclosed some key pieces of evidence: a sun visor, boxer shorts, and sunglasses that the suspect had left behind.

Eight months after Courtney was slain, an arrest was made. More than 1,200 possible suspects were considered and subsequently eliminated. Investigators traced the sun visor lot number to its source and were able to determine that twenty of these visors had been sold in the area. Detectives then began tracking down the buyers through credit card receipts and by asking for DNA samples. One visor purchase, which had been made near the time of the abduction and slaying, was particularly interesting. This purchaser was already under investigation for allegedly advertising in Internet chat rooms that he had child pornography to trade. When investigators went to his residence to talk to him, they determined that he had left town and was somewhere in New Mexico.

Investigators posted a "Be on the lookout" notice for this subject on the National Crime Information Computer (NCIC) system. When the subject, a 20-year-old male, was arrested a few days later for walking out of a restaurant without paying for his meal, the arresting officers ran his name through NCIC and were alerted to the notice and contacted the case investigators.

Two detectives flew to Albuquerque to question the suspect and to obtain a DNA sample. This sample was later matched to the DNA materials found at the scene where Courtney was sexually assaulted and strangled. At the time of his arrest, the suspect was driving a dark-colored BMW. The vehicle was searched, and three newspaper stories on Courtney's death were found. The search also revealed an adult magazine that had faces of young girls pasted over those of the nude adult models. Investigators stated that no evidence existed to indicate that the suspect knew the victim prior to her death and speculated that she may have been abducted at random.

Source: Adapted from Ted Bell, Gwendolyn Crump, and Sam Stanton, "Suspect Arrested in Killing of Girl, 12," *Sacramento Bee,* July 20, 2001, A1.

DISCUSSION QUESTIONS

1. Are laboratory personnel handicapped by the legal precept that the admissibility of any scientific process in relation to evidence must be tested against acceptance of the scientific principle involved?

2. Does any difference exist between the terms *forensic science* and *criminalistics?*

3. Who decides the best strategy (or strategies) for the forensic science examination of physical evidence?

4. Describe spectrographic analysis, the trace metal detection technique, and ultrasonic cavitation.

5. Are criminalists' determinations truly scientifically objective? Why or why not?

6. Discuss the concept of voiceprinting in criminal investigation.

7. Explain the meaning of one word or phrase criminalists use to describe comparison analysis determinations.

8. What was the role of DNA analysis in the case study?

LIBRARY ASSIGNMENT

Compile a selected bibliography of at least three references on cryptography and its use in crime or among criminals.

WORKBOOK PROJECT

Prepare a 500-word theme paper on trace evidence and discuss the value of this type of evidence in criminal investigations.

RELATED WEB SITES

To learn more about crime laboratory services, consult the FBI lab home page at *www.fbi.gov/hq/lab/labhome.htm*.

Interested in becoming a criminalist? The American Academy of Forensic Science lists employment opportunities on its Web site: *www.aafs.org*.

Answers to the most frequently asked questions about cryptography can be found at this Web site: *www.faqs.org/faqs/cryptography-faq*.

NOTES

1. *Miller v. Pate*, 386 U.S. 1 (1967).

2. JAMES W. OSTERBERG, "What Problems Must Criminalistics Solve?" in *Law Enforcement Science and Technology*, ed. I. S. A. Yefsky, 297–303 (Chicago: Thompson Book Co., 1967). The term *forensic science* is commonly used to describe criminalistics. See Richard Saferstern, *Criminalistics: An Introduction to Forensic Science*, 5th ed. (Upper Saddle River, NJ: Prentice Hall, 1994).

3. BRIAN PARKER and JOSEPH PETERSON, "Physical Evidence Utilization in the Administration of Criminal Justice," in *Sourcebook in Criminalistics*, 50–58 ed. Carroll R. Hormachea, Reston, VA: Reston, 1974).

4. HOLLY HAMMOND and C. THOMAS CASKEY, *Automated DNA Typing: Method of the Future* (Washington, DC: U.S. Department of Justice, National Institute of Justice), 1–2.

5. VICTOR WALTER WEEDN and JOHN W. HICKS, *The Unrealized Potential of DNA Testing*, (Washington, DC: U.S. Department of Justice, National Institute of Justice), 1–8.

6. LOUISE M. ROBBINS, *Footprints—Collection, Analysis, and Interpretation* (Springfield, IL: Charles C Thomas, 1985), 183–207.

7. HERBERT L. MACDONELL, *Flight Characteristics of Stain Patterns of Human Blood* (Washington, DC: U.S. Department of Justice, National Institute of Law Enforcement Assistance Administration, Superintendent of Documents, Stock No. 2700-0079, 1971), 1–29.

8. "Examination of Biological Fluids," *FBI Law Enforcement Bulletin* 41, no. 6 (1972): 12–15, 30.

9. Ibid., 15, 30.

10. RICHARD L. BRU BELLE and ROBERT W. REED, *Forensic Examination of Ink and Paper* (Springfield, IL: Charles C Thomas, 1984), 6–8.

11. H. J. WALLS, *Forensic Science* (New York: Praeger, 1968), 60–61.

12. Ibid., 49–55.

13. DONALD E. BRYAN et al., "High-Flux Neutron Activation Analysis as an Investigative Tool in the Field of Criminalistics," in *Law Enforcement Science and Technology*, ed. I. S. A. Yefsky, 371–77 (Chicago: Thompson Book Co., 1967).

14. U.S. DEPARTMENT OF JUSTICE, NATIONAL INSTITUTE OF LAW ENFORCEMENT AND CRIMINAL JUSTICE, LAW ENFORCEMENT ASSISTANCE ADMINISTRATION, *Trace Metal Detection Technique in Law Enforcement* (Washington, DC: U.S. Department of Justice, National Institute of Law Enforcement and Criminal Justice, Law Enforcement Assistance Administration, 1970), 1–16.

15. RICHARD S. TREPTOW, *Handbook of Methods for the Restoration of Obliterated Serial Numbers* (Cleveland, OH: Lewis Research Center, prepared for the National Aeronautics and Space Administration, 1978), 73–82.

16. RONALD E. BLACKLOCK, "The Laser: A Tool for Questioned Document Examination," *Journal of Police Science and Administration* 15, no. 2 (July 1987): 125–26.

17. R. W. BECKER et al., *A Semiautomatic Speaker Recognition System* (Washington, DC: U.S. Department of Justice, Law Enforcement Assistance Administration, 1973), 1–26.

18. PARKER HITT, *Manual for the Solution of Military Ciphers* (Fort Leavenworth, KS: Press of the Army Service Schools, 1966), vii; David Kahn, *The Code-Breakers* (New York: Macmillan, 1966), passim.

19. DAN TYLER MOORE and MARTHA WALLER, *Cloak and Cipher* (Indianapolis, IN: Bobbs-Merrill, 1962), 17–19, 98–112.

5

Basic Investigative Leads and Informants

The problem of "who did it" is simple when the offender is caught in the act or apprehended in flight from the scene shortly after the crime. However, when the perpetrator is not promptly arrested, the direction of the investigation varies according to whether the case falls into one of two categories: known identity or unknown identity. In the case of **known identity**, the perpetrator is known and has been named by the victim or witnesses. All other cases are cases of **unknown identity**. Cases involving named suspects are a high percentage of the cases cleared by arrest in any police agency. In these cases, the victim or witnesses have provided the principal lead to the perpetrator's identity. The challenge to any investigator's skill is the case without a named suspect. In such cases, the investigator must develop the basic investigative leads to reveal the perpetrator's identity.

Motive and opportunity (or presence) are broad areas of investigation basic to any crime. The people and things involved in a crime offer leads to the identity, motive, and opportunity of any perpetrator, known or unknown.

BASIC LEADS

The victim offers the initial basic lead. The victim's background furnishes data, as do his or her activities just before the crime. A group of suspects can be developed from inquiries about who would benefit from the crime and who had the requisite knowledge about the target—the object of the crime. Field contact reports of interviews by patrol officers at and around the time and place of the crime can also offer data about suspects and sometimes about vehicles. When motor vehicles or weapons are involved in a crime, inquiries often link these material items to their owners or users. Latent fingerprints and other trace evidence found at a crime scene can confirm that a suspect has been at the scene and can indicate opportunity. Another trace of a presence at the crime scene is the manner in which the crime was committed—the modus operandi. Sometimes, recovered stolen property can be traced to the thief. Police records of previously

FIGURE 5–1 This composite sketch resulted in prompt identification of the shooter in a double homicide committed outside Central Intelligence Agency (CIA) headquarters in Virginia. From Fairfax County Police Department, Fairfax, VA, in *Bureau of Alcohol, Tobacco & Firearms Handling of Suspect Lead in Langley/CLA Headquarters Shooting Incident* (Washington, DC: U.S. Government Accounting Office, April 1994), 10.

arrested persons contain photographs that witnesses can view when investigators suspect the perpetrator's identity. When photographs are not available, composite drawings may be used instead (Figure 5–1). Finally, injuries characteristic of certain crimes furnish leads that often help link a suspect to a crime.

Experienced investigators dislike associating the development of investigative leads with any intuitive process; they believe using hunches is inappropriate when dealing with people. Instead, developing leads involves a combination of know-how, the cognitive process, and an ability to work rapidly. Time is of the essence in criminal investigation and has an effect on witnesses and the investigator. Time gives the criminal an opportunity to dispose of evidence, to develop defenses against the shock of being arrested, or to get farther away if he or she is in flight. No time should be lost before inquiries indicated by the basic leads of a case are made.

In cases of known identity, the objective is to corroborate the eyewitness's story. The investigator follows the basic investigative leads, but particular effort is also made to corroborate the eyewitness's story. In addition, parallel inquiries are pursued to avoid error in identity and to make the case compelling rather than subject to doubt.

In cases of unknown identity, the objective is to develop a list of suspects by following the basic investigative leads with the goal of identifying the perpetrator. The action is oriented to expanding the universe of suspects, to identifying prime suspects, and to finding the guilty person or persons among the prime suspects.

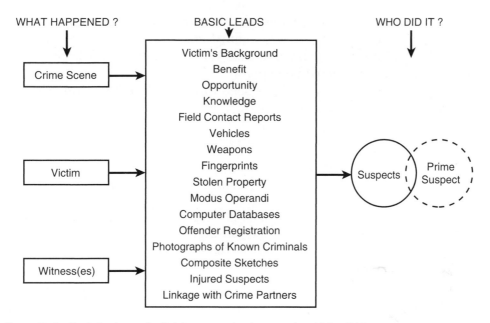

FIGURE 5-2   Basic leads are the link between what happened and who did it.

Determining who committed the crime should not terminate the investigation. All elements of the crime must be proved beyond a reasonable doubt. Some crimes have unique elements or possible defenses. The investigation should continue until all evidence, positive or negative, is gathered to prove the crime, to identify the perpetrator, and to disprove, when possible, defenses such as justification, an excuse, lack of specific intent, lack of malice, diminished capacity, intoxication, ignorance, error, insanity, and the like.

Basic leads suggest lines of inquiry likely to provide an investigator with two types of information (Figure 5–2). **Active information** leads to the establishment of a group of suspects. The strength of the information accumulated against each member depends on the nature of the evidence, but it may indicate prime suspects. **Passive information** is associative evidence that can be of use only if a group of suspects has been developed. Passive information often confirms suspicions that a person is a prime suspect by associating him or her with the crime scene or the victim. These basic types of information lead, by two routes, to evidence sufficient to reveal the person or persons who are guilty of the crime under investigation.[1]

Victim's Background

Police investigators have been criticized for cross-examining a victim and for probing into his or her background and relationship to the crime. To the uninitiated, prying information from the unfortunate victim of a crime instead of promptly taking up the hue and cry for the perpetrator seems unjustifiable. However, a chase without a clearly defined objective is just aimless activity. Promising leads can be developed from a review of the victim's background, which can give the pursuit defined goals.

Many classic avenues must be probed with regard to the victim. Eight of these classic queries are as follows:

1. Does or did the victim know the perpetrator? If so, what is or was their relationship?
2. Does the victim suspect any particular person? Why?
3. Does the victim have a history of crime? A history of reporting crimes?
4. Did the victim have a weapon?
5. Does the victim have an aggressive personality?
6. Has the victim been the subject of any field contact reports?
7. What is the license number and description of the victim's car?
8. Was the victim mistaken for someone else?

Such inquiry should not boomerang into an investigation of the victim rather than an investigation of crime. However, any significant fact about the victim should be unearthed at this stage of an investigation because it may contribute a vital basic lead, and it may aid in future evaluation of the case by the prosecuting attorney.

Benefit

The question of who might **benefit** from a crime provides an excellent focus of inquiry. The factor of benefit can often provide investigative leads. In homicide cases, the motive of jealousy or elimination is a standard avenue of inquiry. Whenever a wife or a husband dies and the death is unexplained, the survivor is suspect. Necessary action is taken to discover the classic love triangle. If a third party is involved, the triangle is considered a promising lead. In arson cases, the benefit may be complex: a rational motivation for financial gain in fraudulent fires of insured premises or an irrational motivation in psychopathic fire setting.

These motives are particularized in that the perpetrator's identity can be deduced from exposure of his or her relationship to the victim or the crime. Generally, in homicides, the relationships between the victim and persons who might benefit from the victim's death are most productive in providing significant leads. The more universal motives of profit and sexual release common to burglaries, robberies, rapes, and other sex crimes do not usually offer investigators specific leads about the identity of the person who will benefit from the crime.[2]

Opportunity

Searching for and identifying persons with the opportunity to commit a crime is a valid basic lead. An admitted or a suspected presence at the crime scene at or around the time of its occurrence may be no more than an immediate investigative aid, but it is a lead.

When offenders know they are suspected of being at the crime scene and are thus vulnerable to this **opportunity** line of inquiry, they often fabricate an **alibi**—a claim of being elsewhere. Investigation into an alibi will often disclose any fabrication, which will justify other inquiries directed at the suspect. However, an effective alibi does not summarily exclude a suspect from further screening.

Knowledge

In theft cases, the victim is questioned about the identity of persons who might know about the presence and location of articles of value and know their way around the premises. This questioning is done to establish who may have had the **knowledge** necessary for committing the crime. In armed robberies, the victim is questioned about the identity of persons who knew the victim's routine or the business firm victimized. This tracing of knowledge provides a natural group of suspects, including the following three:

1. Persons who have access to the premises at which the crime occurred or who are familiar with the premises
2. Persons who knew of the value and the place of storage of property or the routine of the victim or the business victimized, such as
   a. Any present employee or spouse
   b. Any former employee or spouse
   c. Service and maintenance personnel (individuals employed in the area or the building, or those making frequent service deliveries)
   d. Neighbors
   e. Criminals with contacts among the persons listed in a–d
3. Persons noticed recently in the area or on the premises who were
   a. Acting strangely (sex offender cases, fires, homicides)
   b. Applying for work, soliciting sales, conducting surveys, and so forth

Possession of the knowledge needed to commit a crime also suggests possession of the skill and capacity to have done it. What kind of criminal could accomplish the crime under investigation? Did it require a special (an identifying) skill such as using a torch to open a safe or knowledge of the fast cutting action of demolition-type burning bars? Did the crime require special knowledge acquired in a particular trade or occupation? Use of a hydraulic jimmy suggests a person who has worked in body-and-fender repair shops, where this device is used to pry apart bent fenders and employees know about its fast and powerful push-and-heave action. Did the crime require a person who was not afraid to kill, such as the cat burglar who enters occupied homes—even occupied bedrooms?

The multiple murders of the Clutter family in Kansas would have been solved months earlier if investigators had pursued the basic lead of former employees. Floyd Wells, a prisoner in Kansas State Prison, had worked on the Clutter ranch and had mentioned the extent of the ranch to a cell mate. The murders took place shortly after the cell mate's release. Weeks after the crime, Wells identified himself as a former employee of the victims and supplied the authorities with this basic lead; it identified one of the two killers. A check of this man's associates led to rapid identification of his crime partner.[3]

Field Contact Reports

Field contacts (or interviews) are an aggressive police patrol tactic. **Field contact reports** record the "stop-and-frisk" interviews conducted by police with persons stopped in their cars or on foot because of their suspicious appearance or actions. These reports place in police records the names and descriptions of the persons coming to police attention, and the time, date, and place they were seen and interviewed. These reports are confidential in that they are not disclosed to the public but are filed in police records systems for investigators' use. The data on who was "about," and where and when, are valuable aids to investigators seeking basic leads. Field contacts represent a broad surveillance involving observations of an entire patrol sector by an alert assigned officer. Often an investigator confronted with a burglary without apparent clues to the offender's identity will find a field contact report describing a known thief who was stopped in the early morning only a few blocks from the crime scene. An apparently innocent suspect in a sex offense case who pleads that he hardly ever leaves his home at night may be found, through field contacts, to be a nocturnal roamer in city parks.

Some police units have an automated filing system for field contact cards of individuals younger than 17 or 18 years old to reveal group identification. Because most juvenile crimes are committed by groups, this cross-reference offers information about an offender's associates. When a juvenile's field contact cards are requested, these group associations should be probed for basic leads along the lines of race, sex, age, and associates in crime from previous arrests.

Vehicles

Nothing provides a better clue to a criminal's identity than vehicle identification. Time is important when a stolen vehicle is involved because professional bank robbers and other criminals who plan their crimes with care abandon the getaway car before an alarm can be broadcast.

Even a fragmentary description of a vehicle is often helpful. In a series of bank robberies in northern California, the robber walked away from his crimes. The first basic lead offering any promise followed the third robbery, in which a witness noticed a man who was acting suspiciously walking from a bank to the parking lot. All the witness could offer was a fragment of a license number: EPC. Federal Bureau of Investigation (FBI) agents sought help from the California Department of Motor Vehicles, with no results. Then, the EPC fragment was checked against reports of cars stopped at barricades set up after each robbery. The agents found one promising lead. A car with registration letters CPC had been stopped and had passed through a roadblock. Again, motor vehicle records were scanned. The vehicle was registered to a used car dealer. Motor vehicle files provided an in-the-course-of-business exemplar of the dealer's signature on a registration application. Agents compared it with another basic lead, previously useless for lack of a suspect—the handwriting on a fictitious money order dropped by the robber at one of the crime scenes. The handwriting was similar. Other evidence corroborated these leads, and the suspect was arrested and convicted.

Enterprising detectives scan stolen vehicle reports for similarities to descriptions of cars used in crime. The anxious criminal who uses his or her car may become worried that witnesses have seen the vehicle and abandon it. Then, after an appropriate interval, he or she will report it stolen in the hope that doing so will throw off suspicion. Usually, the fragments of description are not sufficient to locate a vehicle, but they are sufficient for alert detectives when a criminal directs attention to an automobile by reporting its loss.

Motor vehicle records are statewide records filed by name and license (registration) number. Often, a name that the suspect under investigation has not been known to use will be detected during a search for the owner of a vehicle used in a crime or known to be operated by the suspect. Motor vehicle records may contain a thumbprint, a photograph, or both, and these records will usually have some physical description of a licensed operator. Both owner and operator records usually contain a person's date of birth, previous residences, and dates of residence at such locations. Accident and violation reports, cross-indexed to these basic motor vehicle records, may reveal some of the suspect's activities, such as the dates and locations of accidents and his or her driving record.

The importance to investigators of using motor vehicles as a basic lead is the finality of identification that is possible. Time and again, a suspect's shock on learning that he or she has been identified has led to full cooperation with police and a guilty plea.

Weapons

Clubs and other blunt instruments are seldom engraved with an owner's name, but firearms are marked with the maker's name and a serial number, and their ownership can often be traced through sales and firearm registration records. The lead developed from such tracing may reveal that the weapon was stolen. Such a fact links the crime under investigation with another crime—and that is a basic lead.

Knife ownership can often be identified even though knives do not have serial numbers. Clubs and other striking weapons also often provide promising leads to identity. Poisons and drugs used in crime can sometimes be traced, and the purchase of dynamite is often traced in bomb cases. Likewise, bullets and fired cartridge cases, wound patterns, and the distinctive effects of several poisons provide passive information useful for associating a suspect, when identified, with a crime.

Fingerprints

Fingerprints found at crime scenes have a high potential for identifying perpetrators of crime once the imprints of the victim and other nonsuspects are screened out. Increasing emphasis has been placed on searching for these chance imprints at crime scenes. Latent imprints, normally invisible, are developed by dusting various surfaces at the crime scene with contrasting fingerprint powders or by iodine fuming. The growth in the use of evidence technicians at crime scenes has resulted in more-effective searches for these hidden fingerprints.

Computerized fingerprint searching systems permit rapid scanning of thousands of ten-digit fingerprint records against chance imprints found at crime scenes. Police expertise at other police agencies is developing slower, but equally effective, procedures for rapidly comparing fingerprints found at crime scenes with the fingerprints on file for known offenders. The fingerprint identification procedure comprises three steps:

1. Crime scene fingerprints are determined to be of value or of no value. Imprints of value have an adequate number of identifying characteristics.
2. Crime scene fingerprints are compared with the imprints of persons who are legally at the scene: the victim, witnesses, the police, and other known visitors.
3. Fingerprints on file are searched to identify the suspect who left his or her fingerprints at the crime scene. Three types of searches can be conducted:[4]
   a. *Request Search.*   The investigator assigned to the case names one or more suspects and asks for a search.
   b. *Single-Digit Search.*   To identify a suspect from a single fingerprint, identification technicians search files such as those containing other crime scene fingerprints or containing the ten-digit fingerprints of repeat or career criminals.
   c. *Cold Search.*   Identification technicians search through an entire ten-digit fingerprint file. Unless the police agency is small or has a computerized search capability, the scope of this cold search should be reduced to, first, known criminals operating in the same geographic area or with the same modus operandi, and, second, recent arrestees.

The finality of identification by fingerprints is important. Fingerprints found at crime scenes reveal the opportunity, or presence, factor—an important lead. When fingerprints pinpoint a person with a history of like crimes or link the suspect's prints with latents from another crime, the lead is significant.

Stolen Property

A search for stolen property is a search for identifiable items. Police have been skillfully using this technique for so many years that it is sometimes overlooked as a routine, albeit successful, technique. Novice investigators are unaware of its potential value until they work on cases in which stolen property is recovered. In tracing the possession of the property, they often note the ease with which a burglar's or a thief's identity can be developed.

Tracing the proceeds of a theft is facilitated by the establishment of special investigative squads whose duties are (a) to visit pawnshops, secondhand dealers, junk shops, and other places where stolen property is likely to be offered for sale, and (b) to coordinate the local search for locally stolen property. Such tracing is also supported by many state and municipal laws that require pawnbrokers to report to the police the pawning or purchase of specific secondhand merchandise (guns, watches, televisions, VCRs, computers, and similar article that are commonly stolen). These laws often require places of business handling such merchandise to maintain a log or register of their business that describes each item purchased. This record is open to police inspection at any time. The level of cooperation many such business managers extend to police—often far exceeding the legal demands—has resulted in the recovery of vast amounts of stolen property. In some cities, pawnshop proprietors have personally defrayed the cost of hotlines to, and silent alarms in, nearby police stations for prompt notification of offerings by suspicious persons.

The Sacramento County Sheriff's Department has established a database of information supplied by pawnshop dealers. This information includes the transaction date, item description, and name and address of the person pawning the item. Each month, a compilation of all transactions for that month is printed and sent to investigators. In one instance, investigators noted that a woman had pawned eight wedding rings in a month. Another individual had pawned a number of televisions and VCRs at various pawnshops around the city. This information supplied investigators with important investigative leads, outside the theft and burglary investigations, that might have started a search for stolen property.

A computerized stolen property record system within a police department will do the following:[5]

- Shorten the time required to search the reports for items of stolen property
- Allow searches that can lead to the identification of persons who frequently sell or pawn used property

- Offer opportunities, long after a crime has been committed, for periodic examination of the records of manufacturers' repair services (authorized agents) to locate stolen office equipment

Serial numbers and other positive identification data necessary for property recovery are not always available from the theft victim. The victim (or the investigator) may need to visit the store in which the property was purchased. Most merchants keep a detailed record of sales. When jewelry and furs are stolen, merchants can provide information about scratch marks on jewelry items or hidden identification stamped on the inside lining of fur garments or on their skins. These merchants, along with pawnbrokers, sometimes mark this type of property when it passes through their establishments for repair or cleaning or as collateral for a cash loan. Often, markings are hidden and require information about where to look for them or must be viewed with ultraviolet light. Thus, when skilled thieves believe they have removed all labels and identifying marks from stolen property, these markings remain for the investigator's use.

When an investigator describes the identifying characteristics of stolen property, he or she should not make assumptions. Recovery depends on identification. For instance, when jewelry must be described, the best approach is to state the appearance of the metal and stones instead of assuming a basic classification. When a victim describes a ring as yellow gold, the wanted notice should say "a yellow metal ring," and the diamonds and rubies said to be part of the setting of such rings are best described as "white and red stones" of a particular size and cut. Notices of stolen property sometimes contain lengthy listings of the property; for this reason, these notices are indexed by number to each item of property listed, starting with the first. Investigators also group property into general classifications, such as jewelry, clothing, and furs, within this numbered sequence. When agencies must communicate with each other to locate stolen property, this numbering system aids in identification and shortens the necessary communications between agencies. Know-how based on experience and training can lead an investigator to the prompt recovery of stolen property, which will offer a valuable investigative lead.

Similar to tracing stolen goods is verifying the use of stolen credit cards. Such use leaves a trail that offers many opportunities for basic leads. Large commercial organizations issuing credit cards are generally nonlocal because a central accounting office provides nationwide coverage. However, their billing procedures provide effective assistance in tracing fugitives, which more than justifies the labor of communicating with these organizations. Because gasoline is a prime credit card item, local service station dealers provide good opportunities for inquiries about a suspect and the use of a credit card. Recent receipts, not yet forwarded to the central accounting office, may still be available at gas stations and will reveal the purchaser's name, the credit card number, and the name of the gasoline company handling the purchaser's account. These credit card accounts reveal recent billings and the suspect's activity on the days when purchases were charged to the credit card. Problems resulting from loss, theft, and misuse of credit cards have led to a security consciousness among the accounting personnel of these firms, and their cooperation with police is usually excellent.

Modus Operandi

The choice of a particular crime to commit and the method selected to commit it is the *modus operandi* of a criminal. A criminal's modus operandi is his or her **signature**. Not every criminal has a particular modus operandi, but enough criminals have distinctive methods of operation to justify classifying crimes by like characteristics.

For this reason, investigators compare the manner in which a crime was committed with information in relevant records stored in the modus operandi section of the police record systems. If any of these comparisons is successful, the detective obtains data on possible suspects. The use of modus operandi by police agencies is both current and extensive. Its successful use in robbery, burglary, grand theft, fraud, sex offense, and fraudulent check cases amounts to a mandate to search the modus operandi files for basic leads when such crimes are committed.

A modus operandi file contains information about the methods of operation of known criminals and the methods used in unsolved crimes. This file has three major capabilities:

1. Identifying a perpetrator by naming suspects whose modus operandi in past crimes fits the facts of the crime being investigated
2. Linking an unknown perpetrator with the modus operandi of past crimes committed by unknown perpetrators to structure a suspect's identity from the modus operandi and leads from several connected crimes
3. Storing data on unsolved crimes according to modus operandi to allow comparison of modi operandi with the crime technique of an apprehended criminal

Past offenses in methods of operation must be sufficiently similar to the crime under investigation to be meaningful. Both must have a number of features in common to warrant the inference that if the suspect committed the other acts, he or she must have committed the act being investigated. Similarities (in combination with other basic leads) are also an important tool in the realm of identification because they decrease the likelihood of a claim of a mistake—or that of a real mistake—in suspecting a person of crime.

Computer Databases

At the local level, police and sheriff's department computer databases contain information about who has been victimized and where, the wanted person, his or her criminal history, and stolen property information. At the state or regional level, motor vehicle files can be accessed for driver's license, registered vehicle, and stolen vehicle and vessel information. Other statewide or regional databases may contain wanted person, stolen property, and firearms registry files.

The National Crime Information Center (NCIC) is the computer system dedicated to serving the needs of law enforcement throughout the United States, Mexico, and Canada. Operated by the FBI, the system processed 2 million inquiries in its first year of operation in 1967. Currently, the system handles 2.5 million inquiries a day, most of which are generated by local law enforcement officials. The system was upgraded in the year 2000 and now contains files or databases on wanted persons, stolen property, criminal histories, missing and unidentified persons, convicted sex offender registration, and convicted persons on supervised release. This system is now supported by digital images. Upon request, the system can provide mug shots, fingerprints, signature samples, and as many as ten identifying photographs of wanted, missing, or unidentified persons. Photographs can also be attached to identify stolen vehicles, boats, or other property. The system can match fingerprint records and link related records across associated NCIC files for the same crime or criminal.[6]

The **National Integrated Ballistic Information Network (NIBIN)** is a networked computer database of ballistic images for forensic laboratories to use in solving open firearms cases. It allows comparison of gun evidence (such as projectiles and cartridge cases) that is recovered at crime scenes with gun evidence recovered in other cities and states. The ballistic images are scanned electronically and stored by using a microscope connected to the system. This database—which is maintained by the Bureau of Alcohol, Tobacco, Firearms and Explosives (ATF)—rapidly compares new images with images in the regional and national databases and generates a list of potentially similar entries. A firearms examiner then visually examines the evidence to confirm that the cases are linked.[7]

Offender Registration

In 1994, the U.S. Congress passed the Jacob Wetterling Crimes Against Children and Sexually Violent-Offender Registration Act. The act required states to create sex offender registries within 3 years. Offenders who commit a criminal sexual act against a minor or commit any sexually violent offense must register for a minimum of 10 years from the date of their release from custody or supervision. All fifty states now have sex offender registration laws. In 1996, the act was amended to establish a national sex offender database that the FBI maintains. This national tracking system gives investigators access to sex offender registration data from all participating states.

Registry information typically includes the offender's name, address, birth date, Social Security number, physical description, fingerprints, and photograph. Usually, offenders must register within a certain number of days following their release from custody or placement on supervision. The registration requirement is in effect for at least 10 years; some states require lifetime registration for all or some offenses. Most states make knowingly failing to register or report subsequent changes in information, such as the registrant's name or address, a criminal offense.[8]

California, the first state to pass an offender registration law in 1947, requires not only convicted sex offenders, but also convicted arsonists and drug offenders to register. The drug offender registration terminates 5 years after discharge from custody or expiration of parole or probation. However, sex offender and arson offender registration is a lifetime requirement. This registration is required of California residents even if the crime was committed in another state or federal jurisdiction.

A new tool in the law enforcement arsenal used to combat sexual predators is the nationwide **Amber Alert system**. This system aims to assist officers in capturing kidnappers and sexual predators who have recently abducted children. The system disseminates information to the general public about the suspects and their vehicles by means of highway signs, television spots, and radio broadcasts. The system is named after Amber Hagerman, a 9-year-old Texas girl whose abduction and murder inspired a similar alert system in that state.[9]

XREF#:	**5000324**
Last:	**CARVER**
First:	**DANIEL**
DOB:	**06/06/66**
Sex:	**MALE**
Race:	**WHITE**
Height:	**6'02"**
Weight:	**210**
Hair:	**BLOND**
Eyes:	**GREEN**
Charges:	

Mug shot taken at the time of arrest.

Photographs of Known Criminals

A search through modus operandi records often provides photographs of suspects taken at the time of a previous arrest. These photographs are called **mug shots**, and if the crime under investigation has been witnessed, the investigator can ask an eyewitness to view them. Usually, such viewing is a casting-out process. The witness is not asked to identify a photo but is requested to scan no less than a half-dozen photographs and to cast out those that offer no resemblance to the perpetrator. When one or more photographs appear to resemble the perpetrator, further inquiry is conducted. The investigator concentrates on the whereabouts of the persons selected as "possibles." Perhaps the suspect was in prison, out of town, or living in a distant city at the time of the crime. Every reasonable circumstance that eliminates persons from a group of suspects reduces the group and allows concentration on the remainder. The investigator or associates also cast out any suspect known to be working and living within his or her means and to have a reputation for no longer being involved with crime.

Mug books are often prepared. The FBI provides photos of known bank robbers to agents investigating bank robberies. These photographs were collected before the crime under investigation occurred and thus permit an eyewitness to rapidly view persons who have committed similar crimes.

This practice does not destroy the validity of these witnesses' future testimony so long as the photographs show five or ten suspects of various types and origins. However, when a photograph of only one person is shown to an eyewitness, or when the other photos in the group are of a nature that a single suspect is isolated by some physical or racial characteristic, the witness's future testimony is compromised and his or her potential credibility toward establishing identity may be ruined. When two or more eyewitnesses are available, investigators may use one to view photographs for basic leads to the offender's identity and reserve the remaining witness or witnesses for later identification. Little justification exists for ruining the potential of a major witness by having him or her confirm identification at this initial stage.

Composite Sketches

When photographs are not available, the victim and any witnesses may be asked to collaborate with a police artist in developing a **composite sketch** of the suspect. Artists have the necessary skill to develop a portrait of a suspect from a victim's or a witness's description or the descriptions given by several witnesses. The usual procedure is for the artist to make a tentative sketch and then show it to the victim or witness and ask how closely it resembles the suspect. After some trial and error, this collaboration of the artist and the victim or witness frequently results in a drawing likely to be of value in identifying the suspect.

The **Identikit system** is another visual means for suspect identification by victims and witnesses. The Identikit system consists of several hundred plastic slides containing photoreproductions of one small portion of a human face: hairstyle, forehead, eyes, nose, mouth, chin, ear, eyeglasses, and so on. Police personnel trained in the use of the Identikit system can work with a victim or witness in developing a composite sketch in accordance with the description and trial-and-error viewing.

Computer software is now available that will produce composites created in response to a witness's answers to queries posed by the computer program. When completed, these composites can be checked against a database of known criminal mug shots by using facial-recognition software. In the past, the use of composites always relied on someone's recognizing the person and coming forward with that information. Facial-recognition software, however, measures the spatial relationships among facial features and converts that information into a mathematical map of the face. The computer then picks the most similar set of mathematical features and displays the corresponding faces in an electronic lineup.[10]

Injured Suspects

In homicides, assaults, and arson cases, the criminal is sometimes bloodied or burned. Therefore, an injured person may be a basic lead. In most states, physicians are required to report gunshot and knife wounds when patients seek treatment. In some cases, local hospitals are asked to be alert for persons seeking treatment for various injuries. In one case, the investigator believed that blood and a broken glass window suggested a wound with glass in it. The emergency department of the local hospital was requested to report any such wound, and 48 hours later, a call was received describing "a wound with a great deal of powdered glass." In a rape case, the attacker was surprised in the act and ran off in the dark through a wooded area. Two days later, the police received a call about "a patient . . . who did not seek treatment for his broken ankle for 2 days." An anxious suspect may wash off blood and postpone treatment for a severe injury, but when medical treatment is sought, an excellent chance for a basic lead is created.

Searching for injured persons during development of a group of suspects is similar to an exhaustive search for witnesses. The search may develop information and it may not, but this work of the investigator reveals a determination to follow every reasonable line of inquiry in seeking leads to the perpetrator's identity.

A similar determination to follow every suggested line of inquiry as basic leads are developed not only reassures the people of a community that criminals are being sought systematically, but also favors exoneration of an innocent person originally suspected of the crime. Diligent inquiry in following up basic leads gathers the active and passive information that will identify "who did it," that will sometimes reveal the perpetrator's presence at the crime scene, and that will often contribute to an understanding of why the crime was committed.

Linkage Between Suspect and Crime Partners

When more than one person is responsible for a crime, the assigned investigator must develop the identity of all individuals involved. An arrested suspect may or may not identify his or her crime partners. An identified but unapprehended suspect may be located by identifying and locating one or more crime partners.

While crime partnerships may be based on an individual's underworld skills (ability to neutralize burglar alarms, drive a getaway car, be a "torch" for opening safes and locked boxes), they also depend on mutual trust and compatibility. When crime is a person's business, partnerships are formed only with someone who is known, liked, and trusted.

Six types of relationships that form strong personal links between persons engaged in criminal activity—or **linkages**—are as follows:

1. *Neighborhood Friendships.*   Neighborhood friendships may date from early childhood, such as from membership in a youth gang, or may result from the social interactions between neighboring families and members of ethnic groups.
2. *Juvenile Hall and Prison Contacts.*   Incarceration in a correctional facility brings persons who are convicted of a crime, or who are adjudicated as delinquent and made wards of a children's court, into close contact. Many of these contacts ripen into friendships that can be traced through juvenile institutions to prisons for adult offenders. Inmates band together with others they trust.
3. *Family Relationships.*   Many persons have a strong sense of family trust and loyalty, which may be extended to persons without kinship linkage who have exercised some form of unofficial parental control, guidance, or support.
4. *Coethnic Contacts.*   In ghetto neighborhoods, juvenile halls, and prisons, each ethnic group tends to band together. This situation is emotionally similar to family relationships.
5. *Buyer-Seller Interactions.*   A buyer-seller relationship is a business relationship between the person wanting the crime committed for profit and the criminal actor. Common types of buyer-seller relationships are the business owner and the "torch," the planner of a murder and the "hit man," and the receiver of stolen property and the thief.
6. *Lovers.*   An identifiable and often easily traced friendship is one between husband and wife (legal or common law), a "triangle" relationship in which a lover of either sex is added to the husband-wife duo, or heterosexuals or homosexuals living together or otherwise identified as lovers.

When basic investigative leads do not disclose a crime partner's identity, investigators must probe among the common kinds of relationships for "possibles."

The investigator who probes into a criminal or personal relationship may gain information meaningful to the success of the investigation. Few relationships can survive the temptation of **"better him than me."** Ethnic gangs have informants or potential informants, prison friendships may succumb to self-preservation, families often have hidden internal hostilities, and the instances of lovers-grown-cold are legion.

INFORMANTS

Informants have long been a source of information to investigators seeking basic leads to a crime under investigation. In fact, one class of informants has been termed the **basic-lead informant**. However, informants are not basic leads, but a means through which basic leads can be developed. One criticism of criminal investigation in its early years was that when solving crimes, police investigators relied too heavily on informants and paid little or no attention to processing the crime scene or to following up on available basic leads. Currently, the starting point for investigating any crime is a thorough examination of the crime scene, if known, and a scrutiny of the basic leads discovered during this examination. In the follow-up investigation, the investigator picks up these data and expands and develops them. Investigators no longer depend on informants but do seek the general public's help in locating anyone with information about the crime under investigation.

Revealing other people's secrets is **snitching**. In the world of crime and criminals, snitching is a social felony. When a crime partner reveals his or her associates to police investigators and becomes a prosecution witness at subsequent court proceedings, he or she has committed underworld treachery.

Words long used to describe individuals who "inform" to police are denigrating; they disparage the character or reputation of the informer: *snitch, tipster, stool, stool pigeon, rat, canary.* More recently, police investigators have used *informant* as a generalized—and euphemistic—term. Anyone can be used as an informant. Most informants can testify in a criminal trial as long as they are acceptable witnesses and their testimony meets the rules of admissibility.

Informants generally want to remain anonymous. They particularly want to avoid the public identification inherent in becoming a witness for the prosecution. The ability to conceal an informant's identity or to protect him or her from attack once his or her identity is disclosed is lifesaving because professional criminals are more than willing to maim or kill informants. However, concealment of an informant's cooperation is difficult because criminals use every available means of learning an informant's identity.

Because the investigator relinquishes his or her basic role when seeking the help of criminals or persons associating with criminals, the use of informants is a questionable option in criminal investigation. Even noncriminal informants are often less objective than they claim. Some of their more common motivations for snitching are less than benevolent: hatred, revenge, jealousy, and greed.

Informing is a "dirty business" because informants may lie to implicate innocent persons or to exculpate a favored crime partner. In some forms of

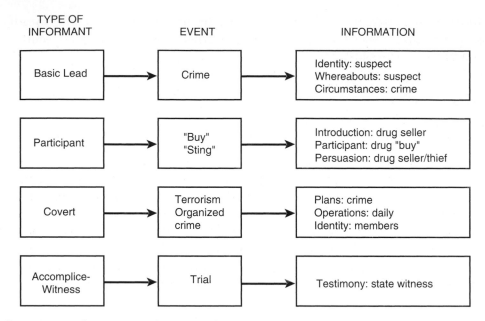

TYPE OF
INFORMANT   EVENT   INFORMATION

| Basic Lead | → | Crime | → | Identity: suspect
Whereabouts: suspect
Circumstances: crime |

| Participant | → | "Buy"
"Sting" | → | Introduction: drug seller
Participant: drug "buy"
Persuasion: drug seller/thief |

| Covert | → | Terrorism
Organized
crime | → | Plans: crime
Operations: daily
Identity: members |

| Accomplice-
Witness | → | Trial | → | Testimony: state witness |

FIGURE 5–3   Informant network in criminal investigation.

snitching, the snitch trades his or her version of what happened during a crime for immunity from prosecution, a reduced charge, or leniency at the time of sentencing.

Informants can be classified in four major categories: basic lead, participant, covert, and accomplice-witness (Figure 5–3). These four types of informants are discussed in more detail next.

Basic-Lead Informants

Informants are a traditional starting point for seeking basic leads. In fact, informants sometimes offer data about an unreported or undiscovered crime or one in its planning stages.

The successful use of basic-lead informants is a complex process. An alert and knowledgeable investigator must know where to seek information, find the contacts who have it, and probe and pry to gather as much meaningful information as possible.

This type of informant is motivated to divulge information to a police investigator for many reasons. He or she may have encountered the information by chance or want to do his or her civic duty by divulging it. Alternatively, criminals may provide information to eliminate a competitor, which is a common practice in the fields of gambling, drugs, and prostitution and is not uncommon among thieves and receivers of stolen property. Jealousy and revenge sometimes motivate such informants. For example, the "woman scorned" has done great harm to the victims of her fury by informing about their criminal activities.

Former girlfriends and wives often serve as unpaid informants. In the world of crime, the women friends of criminals often justifiably fear these individuals. A frightened and knowledgeable ex-girlfriend or ex-wife, in self-defense, has often allied herself with police efforts and delivered vital information about the criminal activities of her ex-boyfriend or ex-husband.

Other informants seek pay for information leading to arrests. Investigators with unsolved jewelry thefts, suspicious fires, and homicide cases are often contacted by such informants, who propose to supply information. Recently released prison inmates may be confronted with the choice of going back into crime or "earning" money, and they know of this resource. They often sell information as a stopgap livelihood until they find employment or return to crime.

In many areas of the United States, "secret witness" programs sponsored by local news media are an innovative way of paying informants for basic leads. Cooperating business firms contribute to an "informant" fund; local police request publicity about the most serious crimes or those without substantial leads. The news medium involved publishes the details of the crime and specifies the amount of the reward (which varies with the nature of the crime). Inherent in these programs is a means by which informants can contact local police investigators without revealing their identity, such as by providing a code word or a number that will substantiate their claim to the reward. Rewards are paid when police have verified the information and found it meaningful and useful in the identification of a suspect, in learning the whereabouts of a known suspect, or in discovering what happened at the time of the crime.

Participant Informants

The role of the **participant informant** in enforcing the law against illegal drug sales is that of go-between: to identify the drug seller and introduce the undercover investigator as a potential buyer, or to "instigate" the transaction in some fashion.[11] Participant informants are workers who participate directly in gathering sufficient evidence to warrant an arrest. One type of participant informant is the special employee. He or she is paid a fee, set in advance, for this work. A special employee may be hired because of his or her knowledge of the local drug scene, friendships among local drug sellers and users, or ability to deceive suspects about his or her role.

Another type of participant informant on the drug scene is the arrestee who has been "turned," or "**flipped**," by the arresting officer. In this procedure, the arrest is for a minor charge of possessing or selling illegal drugs, and the arresting officer persuades the arrestee to cooperate and identify his or her source or supply of drugs—in effect, a more important arrest is made in return for some consideration by the police, prosecutor, or court because of the informant's cooperation. At one time, this procedure was informal, but current procedure usually requires discussion with the prosecutor and approval of the "deal" by this official. Often, a formal plea bargain is entered into between the prosecution and the defendant and his or her legal counsel.

An investigator may use participant informants in solving crimes other than those involving the sale of illegal drugs. A few of these informants have been used as **shills** (decoys) in police "sting" operations aimed at discovering burglars and thieves and recovering stolen property. This role requires the informant to sell property to the police "buyers" to lure real burglars and thieves into doing likewise.

The FBI used a participant informant to uncover political corruption in Chicago. The informant's role was to lure politicians to meetings where FBI agents could videotape payoffs.[12]

The FBI's Abscam investigation pioneered the practice of videotaping public officials accepting bribes. The name *Abscam* derives from the original cover story about the informant's relationship to a group of wealthy Arabs owning "Abdul Enterprises, Ltd." In the Abscam prosecutions, a U.S. senator, six U.S. Congress members, several local public officials in Pennsylvania and New Jersey, and numerous associates were found guilty. These verdicts were reached despite defense claims of unfairness and entrapment in this cash-for-political-favors scam. The videotapes presented to the juries in these trials apparently convinced them that the government's action was not unfair, unscrupulous, or unethical.[13]

Covert Informants

Covert informants are not classified as persons who assist in developing basic leads in a criminal investigation, nor do they serve the "instigator" role of participant informants. They are men and women who report information to a police investigator about a terrorist or another criminal organization from a position of trust and confidence within the group. These agents-in-place are known as **moles** in the area of international espionage, because they are often "buried" for years before being activated.

These persons may or may not be remunerated for their work. They are not used for spot intelligence. The use of such persons is akin to the practice of having spies in the enemy's camp. These agents-in-place are a spin-off from military and international intelligence.[14] They can provide information during a lengthy period as long as their identities are protected. Such individuals must be developed fully, cultivated for a long period, and used only when absolutely necessary. These sources of information are not developed solely to provide information for current investigations, but can be set up to provide information at a future time.

The ever-widening organized crime syndicate and hate extremist groups are sites for agents-in-place. Homicides are frequent among hate groups, and organized crime is constantly expanding its operations. The hoodlums and extremists are an ever-present threat. When information is needed, after-the-fact intelligence operations are useless with either group.

A man or woman may be established within the terrorist or crime group when he or she begins cooperating with an investigator. Alternatively, the investigator may recruit a person whom he or she believes trustworthy and capable and suggest a means by which the new covert informant can infiltrate the target organization.

A Canadian woman, a member of the Front de Liberation du Quebec (FLQ), went to the Montreal police to avoid involvement in an armed robbery planned by members of this terrorist group. She was promptly recruited as a covert informant. She was an excellent source of information for several months because she was never suspected of being an informant by any of her terrorist associates. Her police "contacts" avoided disclosing her identity until the day she appeared in open court as a witness.[15]

Most terrorist groups have established high thresholds to any penetration by informants; new members are always greeted with suspicion and distrust. Therefore, in seeking a productive informant, investigators should make every effort to cultivate and recruit an informant who has been an active member of the group for some time.[16]

The "family" aspect of organized crime groups, regardless of its ethnic nature, is a real handicap to infiltrating an informant as a new member. However, the need for covert informants in these groups has diminished in recent years because of the success of prosecutors in "turning," or "flipping," accomplice-witnesses.

Accomplice-Witnesses

An **accomplice-witness** is a person who is liable to prosecution for the identical offense charged against the defendant or defendants in a pending trial. He or she has been arrested along with one or more crime partners, and the police-prosecutor team offers leniency in return for his or her cooperation. Accomplice-witnesses testify for the prosecution, identifying the defendant or defendants and testifying to acts done by them in furtherance of the crime.

Some prosecutors develop compelling evidence of the guilt of one person in a criminal operation, bring him or her to the prosecutor's office for a briefing on the evidence, and offer the alternatives of (a) arrest, conviction, and prison, or (b) cooperation, a bargained plea to a lesser charge, and a "walk."

A special state prosecutor in New York broke a complex case involving many police officers by confronting two of the police suspects with compelling evidence of guilt. Facing prison for their own crimes, these two officers flipped and agreed to inform on their co-workers in exchange for their own freedom. While "wired for sound," they continued their criminal activities (ripping off drug dealers, primarily) while secretly recording and incriminating their colleagues in crime.[17]

Recruiting a defendant in an organized crime case begins with a reiteration of the theme "every man for himself." Once the witness seeks more information, the standard "package" deal is detailed:

- In return for full cooperation, the witness will be given partial or full immunity.
- After testimony is completed, the witness will be accepted in a witness-protection plan (federal or state), which will furnish the witness with a new identity, funds, and assistance in relocating the witness and his or her family, and will provide security measures sufficient to conceal his or her where-abouts.

When a pending case does not involve organized crime members, the accomplice-witness does not usually need the protection afforded by a witness-protection plan, and the prosecutor offers the potential informant only immunity or partial immunity. In a widespread diamond fraud case involving no less than $5.5 million, the mastermind ordered two of his crime partners killed (his accountant and her assistant). After the contract killer in this case was sentenced to more than 100 years in prison for these two homicides plus the wanton killing of three accidental witnesses to the accountant's murder, the prosecutor was determined to indict the mastermind for murder. All the evidence secured by hard-working police investigators, however, was circumstantial. Rather than allow the mastermind to avoid trial and conviction, the prosecutor offered a co-conspirator in both the fraud and the murders a "deal": He would be named in future indictments in the conspiracy to murder unless he freely told all he knew and agreed to testify in any future trial. If he cooperated, he would be granted immunity from prosecution. He talked, and the mastermind was convicted of murder, primarily on the basis of the accomplice-witness's testimony.[18]

CHAPTER REVIEW

CASE STUDY

The Shugars and Smith Case

At 3:40 p.m. on November 5, officers on patrol were instructed to investigate a call from a Greyhound Cab Company driver saying that the door of a pawnshop at 424 J Street was open and the owner not there. On arrival, the officers discovered the body of the proprietor, who was apparently dead of knife wounds to the chest. There was evidence of a struggle, and blood was found in several areas of the crime scene. A display case, which was a container for handguns, was open; the tags (identification of guns) were there, but six guns were missing (Figure 5–4). No wallet was found on the victim. The victim was pronounced dead by the coroner at 1624 hours (4:24 p.m.). The location of the pawnshop is in an area frequented by laborers and transients; occupancies are low-cost hotels and small stores.

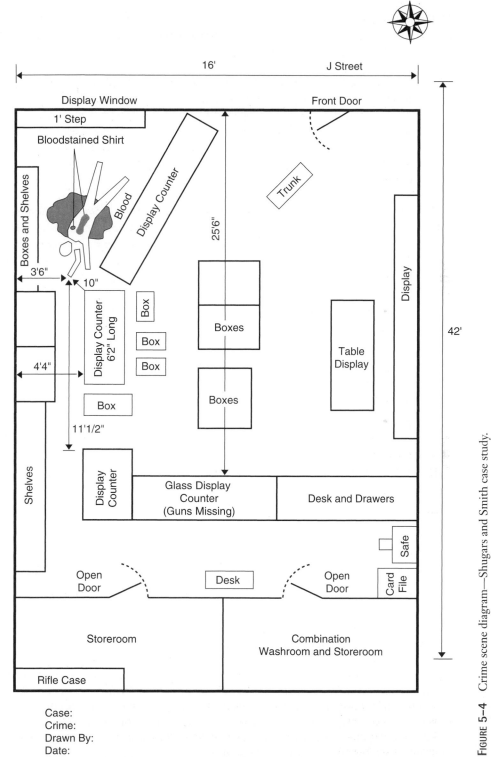

N

16'   J Street

Display Window   Front Door

1' Step

Bloodstained Shirt

Boxes and Shelves

Display Counter

Blood

Trunk

3'6"

10"

25'6"

Display

Display Counter
6'2" Long

Box

Box

Box

Boxes

Table
Display

4'4"

Box

Boxes

11'1/2"

Display
Counter

Glass Display
Counter
(Guns Missing)

Desk and Drawers

Shelves

42'

Safe

Open
Door

Desk

Open
Door

Card
File

Storeroom

Combination
Washroom and Storeroom

Rifle Case

Case:
Crime:
Drawn By:
Date:

FIGURE 5–4   Crime scene diagram—Shugars and Smith case study.

The Investigation

Immediate action was instituted to develop all possible basic leads.

Eyewitnesses

1. Interviewed all employees of hotel and adjoining Greyhound taxi terminal and cab drivers. Checked all neighborhood hotels and shops. Results negative.
2. Questioned bus driver, C. Gardner, who stopped at 4th and J Streets from 2:30 to 3:00 p.m. He noted two people in pawnshop. No definite description. States he saw a green station wagon in front of pawnshop with a woman in front seat and possibly two children in rear (not positive about children).
3. Questioned all cab drivers who worked at that time. Negative.
4. Open book in pawnshop with last entry: Richard Moriarity.
5. Contacted Richard Moriarity at his home. He had redeemed a rifle belonging to his brother at 1500 hours. Negative. Moriarity stated there was a Mexican customer in pawnshop. He gave a complete description of this person and said customer left before he (Moriarity) left the shop. Also interviewed his wife, Celia Moriarity. Negative.
6. Interviewed George Samuel, who told cab driver Petovitch that he saw door of shop open but could see nobody inside. He was worried.
7. Petovitch interviewed, said he went to door, saw the mess, and asked dispatcher to call police. He said he had not seen any suspicious people around at the time.
8. Questioned B. Knursem, cab driver, who picked up a man at 4th and J Street at 4:00 p.m. Man said, "Let's get out of here. Dead man in there." States took man to 8th and E, where he had a soda with him. Six other cab drivers interviewed. Negative.

Victim's Background

1. E. Martin, desk clerk at Olympic Hotel, had received phone call from elderly person (victim's father) earlier but was too busy at the time to call him to phone. (Victim used this phone, no telephone in pawnshop.)
2. Interviewed parents of victim. They said he carried a brown wallet, had no credit cards, and had a car (which was found in nearby parking lot). They said he (father) had worked with son but had no idea of inventory.
3. Outer door of the safe open, but inner door still closed. Money in safe intact, but pocket of victim turned inside out; wallet is missing. Inventory made of money in safe: total was $4,693.70.
4. Questioned cab driver Caleb Leyhe. Saw victim at approximately 3:00 p.m. talking with two men and one woman. Negative.
5. Interviewed Robert Head, cab driver. Negative.
6. Questioned Harry Isuki, jeweler, who was a friend of victim and did work at the pawnshop. He said victim had been beaten up 3 months ago by two men who had given no reason. No report had been made of the assault to police.

Informants

1. James Chambers came to the police station. He said he had information about the murder in the pawnshop. Said he had been standing on the corner of J and 2nd Street on November 5, and a white man asked for "Jerry King." Wanted to know if he was still living on 10th Street. This man said he had heard that King was in trouble because of a "shooting"

in a pawnshop someplace. Chambers stated that King runs with a man named Mason and that both are good with knives. Chambers has not seen them since the murder. King is called the "Cowboy," wears a big white cowboy hat and boots. Chambers also stated that Mason bought a green station wagon, a Ford. Officer sent Chambers back to street for more information.

2. Questioned informant Chambers, who gave a complete description of one Jerry King. He is afraid to tell where he got the information that King was going to borrow a car and "knock over" a pawnshop the night of the homicide. Promises more information. Said he thinks King bought a car at Del Mar Market.

3. Questioned Joe Note at Del Mar Market. Note said that on November 3 he sold a 1990 green station wagon to Eugene Mason. He said Mason had a guy with long hair with him and that Chambers (our informant) lived with Mason.

4. Again questioned Chambers, and he admitted he had lived with Mason and King. King, Chambers stated, had later lived with a Mexican woman on 10th Street. He said some man had told him that Mason and Sanchez had showed up at his house at 1815 6th Street with a 1989 or 1990 green station wagon a couple of nights ago, loaded it up and left, and that there was a third man in the car. He also said that Mason had a reputation with a knife and had knifed someone on 6th Street some time ago. He promised more information.

5. Re: Jerry King. Information from Willie Park (1815 6th St.). Knows of suspect, refers to him as "Big Foot." Big Foot wanted Park in on a deal. Park did not want anything to do with it, so Big Foot talked about getting "Walkie Talkie" to go in on the deal with them. Park stated that Walkie Talkie is a BMA [black male adult] about 50 years old, 5' 8", 175 lb, sort of heavy build; wears a cap made of corduroy material and a grayish-type suit coat and blue pants. Park stated that Walkie Talkie sometimes sleeps in the shack behind 1815 6th St. Park stated that Big Foot, in talking about the job he had lined up, said they were going to use three men on the job. One was to be on the outside, one would be on the roof, and one was to be let down by the fellow up on top through the skylight into the shop. Big Foot talked about a lot of guns, watches, and cameras that were in the place. When they were done, they would take the stuff to a room they had. Big Foot is supposed to see Park tonight (1815 6th St., November 12) and bring over some pants and a bottle of wine. This is supposed to be around 1800 to 1900 hours.

6. Re: Elroy Robin (Walkie Talkie), DOB [date of birth] 7/19/49 (Texas), BMA [black male adult], gray/black [hair color], brown eyes. Elroy Robin was spoken to in the detective division regarding the above offense. Robin stated he did not know anyone by the name of Jerry King and that the nickname Big Foot meant nothing to him. Stated he knew only what he had heard on the street about the killing at the pawnshop. Robin was asked if he had ever been approached by anyone who attempted to get him to go along on a burglary of a pawnshop. He stated he had not, that he had been in prison once and didn't want to go back.

7. Re: George Brendon Williams ("Tex"), WMA, bald/gray, DOB 2/6/56 (Texas). Williams stated he was approached by a subject he knows as Jerry King on Saturday at 0900 hours at 2nd and K Street in front of the Bank Exchange Bar the day the pawnshop man was killed. King asked him to loan him his car. Williams asked King why he wanted his car. King stated he had to go pick up some money. Williams told King that his car was not running. King was with a small man with gray hair at this time. Williams later saw the two walking east on

J Street near the Olympic Hotel about 0930 hours. Williams stated he did not see King again until November 10 around 1200 hours. This was at 6th and S Street near the park. After a short conversation of small talk, King told Williams he had a hot gun he had bought down on 2nd Street. Williams asked what kind of gun, and King replied it was a .22 caliber pistol. Williams stated he advised King that he had heard the cops were looking for him. King stated he knew they were. Williams told King if he knew the cops were looking for him, why didn't he go in and get it straightened out. King stated he was going to do that but he was going to throw the gun in the river first. The same man who was with King when they had met on 2nd Street was with him at this time. He had walked away, going to a nearby gas station. On his return, King stated he was fixing up to leave town. He was going to steal a car and make it. Williams stated that the last time he saw King, he and the other man were walking in the direction of town. Williams described the man with King as short, thin, gray hair, about 45 or 50 years old.

8. Received phone call at police department from J. Drum of 1909 P Street. Drum stated that on the previous night he was drinking at the Village Club and a man said he had killed the pawnbroker. This man was about 37 years old, 5'10". He stated the bartender seemed to know him because he changed a lot of dimes to bills for him, no questions asked.

9. Contacted bartender at Village Bar re: customer changing dimes. He stated the man works for the Purple Heart Thrift Shop, that his name is Bill Donal, and that he was drunk at the bar with Drum and probably did talk about the murder because the victim of the homicide had refused Donal a loan at an earlier date. This story was checked out with Donal. Negative.

10. Donal was in Los Angeles en route on bus (checked out) at time of murder.

Willie Park (informant) called and said King would visit the 6th Street address in the evening (November 12) for sure.

Benefit and Motive

No reports.

Knowledge

No reports.

Field Interview Reports

1. Jerry King is a supposed associate of a Eugene Mason. Field interview cards checked: On July 20, Eugene Mason, PD [police dept. no.] S-7836 was stopped at 2nd and I Streets. DOB given: May 3, 1938, WMA, 5'9", 155 lb. Add[ress] of California Apartments in Broderick. Car being used was an '85 Mercury, 4 dr., lt. blue, ANZ-009. At the time he was with an Agapito Casteneda.

2. FI [field identification] card on Agapito Casteneda shows DOB 11/20/38, 5'7", 138 lb. Add. 100 Lucas Street, Laredo, Texas.

Weapon

1. No weapon found at crime scene.

2. Interviewed Mr. John Daven, a resident of Olympic Hotel, who said he observed a man displaying a knife with an 8-inch blade in the lobby around the time of the homicide. Daven identified Albert Richards, who surrendered the knife to officers and said he was intoxicated that day and lives in neighboring hotel. Identified himself. Negative.

Latents at Crime Scene

1. Six latent prints were lifted and photographed at crime scene.
2. Compared latent prints found at scene. Found they were of victim, of the last customer in shop (Richard Moriarity), and remainder not identified at this time.
3. The latent prints obtained were checked against all persons on the list of police and coroner's personnel present at crime scene, with negative results.

Stolen Property

1. Thorough check of inventory of shop. Six tags for handguns found in showcase, but no guns. Description and serial numbers of guns on tags. This case had been broken into. Missing were one .25-caliber automatic, three .22-caliber revolvers, one Smith & Wesson .38-caliber revolver, and one .32-caliber revolver. It also appeared that some rifles were missing. Further checks with accountant.
2. With assistance of brother-in-law of victim, checked records in pawnshop and made list of all guns on hand, guns taken in pawn and not redeemed, and guns sold. Checked all guns bought by victim for past year and a half. Bookkeeper contacted. He had invoices for all new guns. Impossible to find out what weapons should be in shop—poor records.
3. After further check with accountant: seven guns (handguns) missing.
4. Inspector Serro of the pawnshop detail called and said he had picked up a 17-year-old WMA by the name of Steven Russell while he was attempting to pawn some "junky" jewelry. A search of his car revealed a .38-caliber Smith & Wesson revolver, serial #190452. Inspector Serro stated that he had seen the TT [Teletype alarm, wanted notice] on the pawnbroker stabbing and noticed that some as-yet-unidentified guns had been stolen, and he offered this information for what it was worth.
5. Phone call received from Wayne Cooper. Has in his possession three guns obtained from a Henry Smith as security on a loan. Checked serial numbers—all three missing from pawnshop. Cooper called after he had been told by his sister that Smith was wanted. These guns were taken as evidence.

Modus Operandi Comparison

1. Checked all local pawnshop owners for any unusual occurrences. Negative.
2. Attempted holdup at Southside Junk Yard. Gun displayed but victim could not identify make. There is a good description of the robber who was scared off by a customer.

Photographs of Known Criminals

None available. Identikit likeness prepared from descriptions given by informants. [The Identikit is a trademarked device that uses plastic slides of facial characteristics to reproduce a likeness of a suspect from verbal descriptions and visual supervision. It is a substitution for a police artist portrait sketch.]

Injured Suspects

1. Checked adjacent hotel. Interviewed witness who saw a man with blood on face and hands in washroom of hotel at the time of the homicide. This was traced to a resident who had a fight with another resident. Negative.
2. Went to the Olympic Hotel and took two photographs of the blood droplets in the lobby and in the bathroom in front of the toilet bowl. Obtained a sample of this blood at the same location and booked it as evidence. Receipt #30551.

3. Patrol Division Captains: Re: Homicide at 424 J Street, Pacific Jewelry & Loan Co. It appears that the victim fought with the suspect and perhaps the suspect has injuries. Please be on the alert for subjects being arrested with injuries that may have been caused during a struggle and bring it to the attention of the detective division.

4. Contacted the clerk at the desk in the Travelers Hotel and obtained a list of checkouts this morning. There were six, and R/O [reporting officer] in company with the housekeeper (Clacey Brown) checked each room; three had been made up, and the floor maids indicated that no sign of blood or other evidence was noticed. Three rooms not yet made up were checked, particularly bathrooms and towels, but no sign of blood or anything of evidential value seen. The janitor responsible for cleaning the common washrooms on each floor was also contacted and he reported that there were no bloodstains or anything suspicious noticed in any of them.

The Arrest

On November 12, about 1800 hours, a team of investigators went to 6th Street in separate vehicles, positioning their cars to keep the vicinity of 1815 6th Street under observation. After a short interval, a man wearing a white cowboy hat and having the general appearance of the suspect Jerry King was observed on the sidewalk walking toward the house at 1815. The suspect was stopped and questioned. Also stopped with the suspect was another man who identified himself as Henry Smith and who said they both lived at 912 S Street. Smith had identification. King had none. Both men were searched; King had a .22-caliber revolver, loaded, in his belt, and Smith had a .22-caliber revolver, loaded, in his right pants pocket. Both King and Smith were handcuffed and taken to the police station.

Postarrest investigation revealed Jerry King to be Lyle E. Shugars. His companion was identified as Henry E. R. Smith, the person named as Eugene Mason during the investigation by informants. Both men were warned of their rights to silence and legal counsel (the Miranda warning) but waived these rights and made statements to police.

The Trial

Both Shugars and Smith were represented by legal counsel. However, guilty pleas were entered for both men. The proceeding was brief; both men admitted their guilt in open court. They were sentenced to state prison for life.

Critique

1. The lack of eyewitnesses, despite diligent search, indicated this case was likely to be one in which the police would not have a named suspect.
2. Investigator's reports of their day-to-day activity document a series of parallel inquiries along avenues suggested by basic investigative leads.
3. There was an excellent gathering of information from reliable informants.
4. Investigators followed the doctrine of warning suspects of their constitutional rights to silence and to legal counsel. Grand jury testimony indicates rights of both accused persons were fully protected while they were in custody during questioning. Wording of statements and content indicates voluntariness.
5. Continuing and diligent search for witnesses and evidence indicated impartial attitude of investigators, which allowed the case to focus within its own evidence structure and without any preconceived theory of who did it.

Source: Sacramento, California, Police Department and Public Defender's Office.

DISCUSSION QUESTIONS

1. Compare the objectives of investigations in which the offender is known with those of investigations in which the offender's identity is unknown. Compare these objectives with the basic objectives of any investigation.
2. Discuss in some depth one of the classic queries to be probed in victim-offender relationships.
3. Explain the concept of *benefit* in relation to motive for a crime.
4. Is the basic lead of knowledge more likely to be concerned with motive or opportunity for a crime?
5. Are field interviews justified? Why?
6. Why does the shock of being connected with a crime often lead to a prompt acknowledgment of guilt? What basic lead or leads are likely to have this "finality of identification"?
7. Can the imprint of a single finger found at a crime scene lead to identification of a suspect? Explain.
8. Discuss the role of tracing stolen property in the day-to-day investigation of crime and criminals.
9. Discuss the three major capabilities of a modus operandi file.
10. What is the common theme between the use of photographs for identification and the hue and cry for injured suspects?
11. What is the role of composite drawings in identifying a suspect?

LIBRARY ASSIGNMENT

Search available literature on homicides and list at least five bibliographic references on motivations for murder. If possible, itemize page references of motives for murder related to the concept of benefit. Prepare an abstract or digest (100 to 200 words) of the most meaningful reference.

WORKBOOK PROJECT

Review the case study in this chapter. Describe the items of information that helped identify the perpetrators, and name the basic investigative lead concerned with each.

RELATED WEB SITES

To learn more about the history of fingerprints and the answers to the most frequently asked questions about fingerprint examination, visit this Web site: *www.onn.com.*

Want to know more about computer databases? If so, visit the FBI's NCIC Web page: *www.fas.org/irp/agency/doj/fbi/is/ncic.*

NOTES

1. M. A. P. WILLMER, "Criminal Investigation from the Small Town to the Large Urban Conurbation," *British Journal of Criminology* 8, no. 3 (July 1968): 259–74.

2. JAMES W. OSTERBERG, "The Investigative Process," in *Law Enforcement Science and Technology*, ed. I. S. A. Yefsky, 591 (Chicago: Thompson Book Co., 1967).

3. TRUMAN CAPOTE, *In Cold Blood* (New York: Random House, 1965), 159–64.

4. JOAN PETERSILIA, *Processing Latent Fingerprints—What Are the Payoffs?* (Santa Monica, CA: Rand, 1977), 13–14.

5. JOHN E. ECK, *Solving Crimes: The Investigation of Burglary and Robbery* (Washington, DC: Police Executive Research Forum and the U.S. Department of Justice, National Institute of Justice, 1983), 269–70.

6. STEPHANIE L. HITT, "NCIC 2000," *FBI Law Enforcement Bulletin* 69, no. 7 (2000): 12–15.

7. JENNIFER BUDDEN, "Linking Crime Through Ballistic Evidence," *Law and Order*, November 2002, 51–54; South Dakota Division of Criminal Investigation (DCI), "National Integrated Ballistics Information Network (NIBIN)," DCI, *http://dci.sd .gov/lab/nibin.htm* (accessed November 30, 2004).

8. ALLAN D. SCHOLLE, "Sex Offender Registration: Community Notification Laws," *FBI Law Enforcement Bulletin* 69, no. 7 (2000): 17–19.

9. JULIET EILPERIN, "Congress Approves 'Amber Alert' System," *Washington Post*, April 11, 2003, A2.

10. CHRISTOPHER SWOPE, "The Digital Mugshot," *Governing*, August 1998, 54.

11. JAMES Q. WILSON, *The Investigators—Managing FBI and Narcotics Agents* (New York: Basic Books, 1978), 62.

12. IRA ROSEN, "Wheeler, Dealer, Squealer," *60 Minutes* transcript, March 6, 1988, 5–9.

13. IRVIN B. NATHAN, "ABSCAM: A Fair and Effective Method of Fighting Public Corruption," in *ABSCAM Ethics: Moral Issues and Deception in Law Enforcement*, ed. G. M. Caplan, 1–16 (Cambridge, MA: Ballinger, 1983).

14. THOMAS WHITESIDE, *An Agent in Place: The Wennestrom Affair* (New York: Viking Press, 1966), 150.

15. CAROLE DE VAULT, *The Informer—Confessions of an Ex-Terrorist*, with William Johnson (Toronto: Fleet Books, 1982), 115–44.

16. JAMES M. POLAND, *Understanding Terrorism—Groups, Strategies, and Responses* (Upper Saddle River, NJ: Prentice Hall, 1988), 196.

17. MIKE MCALARY, *Buddy Boys—When Good Cops Turn Bad* (New York: Putnam, 1987), 25–37.

18. RICHARD HAMMER, *The CBS Murders* (New York: Morrow, 1987), 215–20.

6

Major Investigative Techniques

Identifying a suspect with compelling evidence of guilt often goes beyond hours of making inquiries and miles of footwork and driving. The combination of an eyewitness, a suspect, and a police lineup may achieve this goal.

Monitoring a subject's activities by ordinary observation can be supplemented by videotaping, court-ordered wiretaps, and fluorescent chemicals. Such monitoring can reveal contacts and actions of great importance to an ongoing investigation—even when the suspect is aware of (or fears) a police interest. Patience is essential during monitoring because, on occasion, a suspect is not as cautious as he or she should be and, as a result, the investigator can unearth a valuable piece of information.

Investigators assigned to covertly scan the activities of the known criminals of organized crime are often not the arresting officers. However, when homicides occur, the information these investigators can provide their associates will lead to arrests.

Undercover police agents assume a similar role. Seeking information in this manner can be life threatening to an agent. Nevertheless, facts gathered in this way become solid evidence when the agent testifies in court.

SURVEILLANCE

Surveillance is the observation of people and places by investigators to develop investigative leads. Often hidden, not just unobtrusive, it involves seeking for specific activity and significant information rather than merely passive onlooking. Its basic objective is to bring an investigation into sharp focus by supplying detailed information about the activities of a person or place and about the associates of a person or the individuals who visit a place.

Visual Surveillance

Visual surveillance is simply keeping a watch on a particular suspect, vehicle, or place. It may be aided by binoculars or a telescope or replaced by photographic surveillance. The use of binoculars permits observation from a distance of two or three city blocks. A twenty-power telescope is effective at ten to fifteen city blocks. A robotic camera can replace personnel performing fixed surveillance. Infrared viewing devices permit observation in the dark.

A **fixed visual surveillance**—a **stakeout**, or plant—is located within a building, if possible, and observations are made through available windows or doors. Panel trucks and campers have been converted to fixed observation posts with peepholes or curtained windows for viewing. Rooftops are excellent for long-range surveillance; stores and hallways are suitable sites for short-range viewing. Sometimes long-term positions are possible; in some instances, the surveillance must be moved frequently to avoid notice. The static quality of a fixed surveillance requires skilled judgment in selecting a rewarding area of observation. To be effective in scrutinizing a suspect's activities, the observing investigator must not be detected. For this reason, a fixed observation post in a building is preferable because the investigator not only is concealed, but also, through a rental arrangement, has a resident's or tenant's rights.

Some investigators, because of their height, size, race, or national origin, may have difficulty blending into certain environments as residents or tenants. In fact, several well-hidden fixed surveillances in apartments have been compromised by the appearance of the investigator entering the premises. In the de facto segregated ghetto areas of urban centers across the United States, an investigator not conforming to the residents' or tenants' appearance is certain to be suspect.

A **moving visual surveillance**—a **tail (shadow)**—may be on foot, may be in a vehicle, or may use a combination of walking and riding. The suspect being followed is often alert and may take evasive action. Suspects "double door" the trailing investigator by entering a street-level shop and leaving by a rear, side, or basement entrance. They use the modern traffic system, with its "platoons" of traffic and one-way streets, to break contact or to force the investigator too close to a point at which his or her presence can be noted by an alert suspect. Supplementing a moving surveillance optically is difficult, although camera equipment can be used. A moving surveillance is a dynamic technique that does not depend on the appearance of the suspect at a certain place; rather, it keeps the subject in view from place to place.

To avoid detection, a mobile surveillance often uses a two- or three-person surveillance team, with members rotating in the "close contact" position. This leapfrogging technique of following persons under surveillance is useful on foot or in vehicles. Its particular value is that the chance of detection by the suspect is diminished because the same person is not following the suspect continuously. The close contact position is behind the suspect, and an alert and anxious suspect will identify a person who is in this position for an extended period. With the leapfrogging technique, the suspect almost makes an identification when a new member of the surveillance team or a new vehicle moves up into contact and the other team member drops back into a position well to the rear or across the street. All that is required of the personnel who drop back is to keep the contact position investigator in sight. When vehicles are used, such contact can be maintained by radio.

A device that electronically signals the location of automobiles, or other objects to which it is affixed, is known as a **bumper beeper**. Another device used for this purpose is the **global positioning system (GPS) device**. As an example, wireless carriers are required by law to make a cell phone user's location traceable when they make 911 calls. Carriers that track callers by means of the GPS can locate the caller within 160 feet.[1] Sophisticated receivers in the vehicle or vehicles of a mobile surveillance continually trace the otherwise silent signals emanating from the bumper beeper and locate the vehicle (or other object) under surveillance. These devices are particularly helpful during investigations of ongoing, conspiratorial criminal activities involving a high degree of organization (gambling, fraud, drug selling) and in which the person or persons under surveillance are likely to "make" (identify) one or more of the vehicles in a mobile surveillance if they follow the target car too closely.

Monitoring beeper signals from a radio transmitter that was placed in a container of chloroform has been held not to invade any legitimate expectation of privacy and not to constitute search or seizure under the Fourth Amendment. In *United States v. Knotts*, the U.S. Supreme Court noted that the scientific enhancement of the beeper raised no constitutional issues that would not be raised by visual surveillance.[2]

Investigators develop their own methods for blending with the surroundings on mobile surveillances. A device or technique suitable for one individual may draw attention to another. Appearances can be corrected to some extent. A change of clothing may suffice for one individual; another may use clothing to suggest a trade or service. Conduct and behavior can be coordinated with appearance to communicate some cover or excuse for being in a neighborhood. Carrying something is a common practice with some investigators adept at hiding their occupation, and most persons are not suspicious of a person carrying a bag of groceries or some similar load.

Vehicles used in mobile surveillances do not blend with surrounding traffic units if they are too distinctive in design or color. The number of occupants and the seating arrangement may also identify a vehicle to a suspect under surveillance, as can the design and position of headlights at night. Apparent changes in the number of occupants and their in-car positions are a defense against identification, as is driving without lights when safe, or using a vehicle with the ability to change the appearance of headlights.

Fortunately for investigators, most suspects are alert but anxious; they are on the lookout for a surveillance but do not want to discover one. They want to know whether the police are watching them, yet they do not want to know.

A combination of fixed and mobile surveillances (both on foot and by vehicle) has been effective in on-the-scene apprehensions of criminals who have committed a series of crimes. The irrational fire setter who sets several fires a night and who cannot be traced by normal investigative leads can be apprehended by isolating the area of suspicious and known incendiary fires and establishing extensive surveillances. Burglars and serial rapists who enter residences and continue their operations until arrested may also be surprised in their operations by the technique of staking out an area.

The objective of a surveillance is to collect information on the activities of a suspect, the persons in contact with him or her, and the places frequented. Therefore, the assigned investigator and associates must keep a running commentary, or log, of their observations. Notes are made in the field as the surveillance discloses the suspect's associates, the cars used by the suspect and associates, and the ownership or reputation of places frequented. When surveillance is aligned with the use of the investigator as a witness to what he or she observed, the surveillance investigator must personally verify vehicle registrations, identities of unknown persons in contact with the suspect, or data on the premises or locations frequented by the suspect or others. With such a foundation, the witness can show personal knowledge of the surveillance and the investigation that disclosed pertinent and related facts.

Audio Surveillance

Wiretapping and electronic eavesdropping are the primary forms of **audio surveillance**, surveillance by listening. The U.S. Supreme Court has termed this observation technique a "dirty business," and it is viewed with mixed emotions by law-abiding citizens, who apparently see it as the epitome of an unjustified and nondirective invasion of privacy.

Interception of telephone communication is a difficult surveillance to detect. Telephone wires lead from the instrument cable to a house cable, to an area cable, to a main cable, and to the "bays" of a central office. At each point, a junction box containing an array of wires and binding posts facilitates the work of telephone company service personnel in providing service to subscribers. The wires of an individual telephone appear in terminal boxes and are identified by pair and cable numbers located at various points from the telephone instrument to the distant central office. A telephone tap can easily be hooked up at any of these locations.

Testimony is sometimes required on the mechanics of the interception—for example, how the wires used were selected as the wires of the telephone that was meant to be tapped. A common practice is to use a regular portable telephone instrument equipped with wire clips. The investigator hooks up to the selected wires, makes certain no one is using the line, and dials the subscriber's number. If the hookup works, the investigator will hear the distinctive sound of the busy signal, without conversation on the line. In other areas, an associate may have to call the subscriber and hold a "survey" conversation while the listener clips in and verifies the line by recognizing the associate's voice. Tape-recording devices permit direct recording of overheard conversations and offer a verbatim record for review.

In another type of audio surveillance, places or people may be wired for sound. This practice has been termed **bugging**. When properly installed, the electronic equipment necessary for eavesdropping is almost as difficult to detect as wiretap connections and equipment. The pickup microphone may be wired directly to a tape recorder, or it may broadcast the conversation by radio a short distance to a receiver located either on the person of an investigator or in a nearby car or building. Surreptitious or covert entry of private premises to install a microphone (bug) is in conflict with expectations of individual privacy. However, in a 1979 case, *Dalia v. United States*, the U.S. Supreme Court stated the following:[3]

> We find no basis for a constitutional rule proscribing all covert entries. It is well established that law officers constitutionally may break and enter to execute a search warrant where such entry is the only means by which the warrant effectively may be executed. (p. 247)

The facts of *Dalia* are that the U.S. District Court authorized the interception of specified oral communications at a particular location in compliance with Title III of the Omnibus Crime Control and Safe Streets Acts of 1958. Dalia was convicted of receiving stolen goods and conspiring to transport, receive, and possess stolen goods. At a hearing on petitioner Dalia's motion to suppress evidence obtained under the "bugging" order, the defense showed that the order did not explicitly authorize entry of the petitioner's business office. However, the district court ruled that a covert entry to install electronic eavesdropping equipment is not unlawful merely because the court approving the surveillance did not explicitly authorize such an entry. (FBI agents assigned the task of implementing the court order had entered the petitioner's office secretly and installed an electronic bug in the ceiling.)

The court considered two questions in *Dalia*: First, may courts authorize electronic surveillance that requires covert entry into private premises for installation of the necessary equipment? Second, must authorization for such surveillance include a specific statement by the court that it approves of the covert entry? The court held that the Fourth Amendment does not prohibit per se a covert entry performed to install otherwise legal bugging equipment; Congress has given the courts statutory authority to approve covert entries for the purpose of installing electronic surveillance equipment; and the Fourth Amendment does not require that a Title III electronic surveillance order include a specific authorization to covertly enter the premises described in the order.

Audio surveillance is an investigative technique about which appellate courts have rendered many decisions. Fortunately, the U.S. Supreme Court, in *Katz v. United States*, consolidated judicial thinking in this area and established the doctrine that such eavesdropping may properly be conducted under court supervision similar to procedures now available to police securing search warrants and arrest warrants.

Katz was convicted on the basis of telephone evidence obtained through electronic eavesdropping of a public telephone. No court order had been obtained for this audio surveillance. The U.S. Supreme Court reversed Katz's conviction, saying,[4] "Wherever a man may be, he is entitled to know that he will remain free from unreasonable searches and seizures" (p. 359). In this decision, the court slashed away at a confusing collection of previous decisions in this area, involving, among other things, whether a physical penetration or a technical trespass had occurred, by pointing out that the trespass doctrine is no longer controlling "for the Fourth Amendment protects people, not places" (p. 359). The final words of the decision suggest that antecedent court review of the probable cause for eavesdropping and a court order similar to a search warrant would have resulted in the court's sustaining Katz's conviction. (See Appendix A, Case Briefs, for a digest of *Dalia* and *Katz.*)

Consensual electronic surveillance (as opposed to nonconsensual) is also known as **participant monitoring**. Its primary use is to secure a record of a conversation to which the person wired for sound is a participant. Undercover police agents and cooperative informants, such as accomplice-witnesses, can provide police with a record of conversations in which they participated. This record proves exactly what was said and is important when one of the other participants later disputes the substance of the conversation. Since electronic surveillance carried out with the consent of one party to a conversation is not a "search" within the meaning of the Fourth Amendment, this type of surveillance does not require previous judicial authorization. Telephone conversations recorded with the consent of one participant are in this class of consensual electronic surveillances. Since a collateral purpose of consensual electronic surveillance is to expose wrongdoing, particularly in relation to an ongoing investigation, police investigators need to know that the Fourth Amendment does not shield a suspect-defendant from a misplaced belief that a person to whom he or she voluntarily confides wrongdoing will not reveal it.[5]

Investigators contemplating the use of audio surveillance should avoid it unless the means-end factor justifies its use. Because of its overtone of being dirty business, any results obtained by this technique are often mitigated or negated by the means used.

When an electronic eavesdropping technique is used, it may be subject to countermeasures. Technicians skilled in surveillance countermeasures make extravagant claims about "debugging." An electronic device (bug) that is wired to its receiver is difficult to detect, as is a properly connected wiretap, or the installation of a device to record the numbers to which outgoing calls are directed. If an electronic transmitting device is used, however, its radio transmissions can be detected by other commercially available electronic devices.

Countersurveillance activities may also include deliberate conversations intended to be heard and recorded, such as incriminating statements involving innocent persons, exculpatory conversations transferring or excusing guilt or guilty knowledge, and scenarios intended to "blow" the surveillance by confirming the target suspect's belief in police eavesdropping. Fortunately, police investigators carefully screen incriminating or exculpatory conversations for their basic worth and avoid acting on any conversation calling for a police response (search, arrest) unless such information can be confirmed by other independent information.[6]

Contact Surveillance

Contact surveillance techniques are based on the ability of certain fluorescent preparations to stain a person's hands or clothing on contact and thus to offer observable proof of a connection between the stained person and the object under surveillance. Denying the connection and offering a reasonable explanation for extensive and vivid fluorescent blue, orange, or green stains is difficult. Contact surveillance techniques may be used alone or to supplement a visual surveillance. They are extremely useful when visual surveillance is not feasible, as in cases of dishonest employees and of transactions involving the payment of money.

The tracer preparations are usually in the ultraviolet spectrum and become visible only under ultraviolet light. Persons who make contact with the object under surveillance are not aware of the treated surface or of the transfer to their clothing or hands until they are questioned about the contact and examined under ultraviolet light. Tracer paste is available for objects exposed to the weather, such as fire alarm boxes, automobiles, and the drops used in underworld or espionage activity. A marking powder is available for putting tracer powder on money or any object not exposed to weather. Felt pens are available for tracer marking objects such as money or merchandise.

Ultraviolet light is not always required for contact surveillance. A dye powder is available that is also invisible when dry but becomes visible when wet, although it is difficult to wash off. Use of such powder is convenient in cases of petty thefts investigated in schools and business offices because a school or an office supervisor can monitor the surveillance without ultraviolet light equipment.

These tracers are available from police equipment suppliers, and most police agencies have an assortment in stock from which an investigator can select the appropriate dye, powder, paste, crayon, or pen. The selected preparation should be applied liberally to the object likely to be contacted by the suspect or suspects. It should be tested before field use for its invisibility, its ability to blend in normal light, its adhesiveness, the life of each application, and the difficulty of removing the stain by ordinary washing with soap and water.

A variation of this type of contact surveillance is the technique of adding a tracer substance to objects or liquids commonly subject to theft. The U.S. government adds various dyes to gasoline at federal garages to enable the ready identification of government gasoline in privately owned vehicles; state agencies mark containers of foodstuffs for state institutions (when unauthorized possession is suspected); and department stores attach tracer tags to merchandise that alert personnel at store exits unless the tags are removed by a sales-clerk upon purchase.

SEARCH WARRANTS

Issuance of a **search warrant** is guided by the Fourth Amendment to the U.S. Constitution. This amendment states the following:

> The right of the people to be secure in their persons, houses, papers, and effects, against unreasonable searches and seizures, shall not be violated, and no Warrants shall issue, but upon probable cause, supported by Oath or affirmation, and particularly describing the place to be searched, and the persons or things to be seized.

Meeting the standard of probable cause requires a demonstration to the judge or magistrate that a crime has occurred, or is occurring, and that evidence relative to that crime will be found at a particular location. The investigator must swear, under oath, that the information establishing this probable cause is true to the best of his or her knowledge. The application for the search warrant must describe in detail the place to be searched and the items or person to be seized.

In 1968, in Title III of the Omnibus Crime Control and Safe Streets Act, Congress codified the requirements for obtaining court authority to include oral and wire communications. This act was subsequently amended in 1994, when Congress passed the Communications Assistance for Law Enforcement Act (CALEA). Most states have enacted similar legislation on the issuance of search warrants for electronic surveillance. The courts and Congress have long considered any form of electronic surveillance extremely invasive. Because of this view, the prerequisites for obtaining a warrant authorizing electronic surveillance of oral, wire, and electronic communications, as well as silent video, are extremely strict. Investigators must comply with the probable cause and particularity requirements of the Fourth Amendment. In addition, Title III requires (a) that the surveillance be confined to only relevant conversations or activities, (b) that investigators specify the length of time the technique will be used, and (c) that investigators certify that normal investigative techniques have been tried and failed, are reasonably unlikely to succeed, or are too dangerous to attempt. These requirements are designed to ensure that electronic surveillance is not used as a first resort when other, standard, less intrusive investigative techniques would expose the crime.[7]

POLICE INTELLIGENCE: CRIMINAL INVESTIGATION INFORMATION

Intelligence is the information about crime and criminals not normally available to investigators through overt sources that is secretly or clandestinely collected and evaluated. Detection and investigation of crime and pursuit and apprehension of criminals require reliable intelligence; otherwise, the investigator is limited to overt acts and volunteered information and thus is severely handicapped in many cases.

Collection and analysis of information discovered by undercover police agents or confidential informants is usually channeled to a special unit within a police department. There, the data are analyzed and evaluated so that they may be used in current or future investigations. To a certain extent, intelligence is warehoused until it is needed.

The police intelligence process is cyclical: it involves a series of linked activities, beginning with the needs of users (consumers) and ending with intelligence reports disseminated to specific users and reevaluation of the process (Figure 6–1). The six stages of the police intelligence process are as follows:[8]

1. *Needs.*   Clear needs for information develop as police investigate unsolved crimes and attempt to block the commission of planned crimes. Police personnel demonstrating such needs are the users of police intelligence.
2. *Collection.*   The gathering of information on matters of interest, in response to user needs, is investigatory reporting: raw intelligence (information) is reported along with a field evaluation of the information, its source, and how access to the reported information was gained. **Overt collection** of information is from public sources or from nonintelligence police personnel. **Covert collection** of information is from sources such as undercover police agents and confidential informants, or from various types of surveillance of unaware targets.
3. *Evaluation and Collation.*   **Evaluation** of information screens out useless, incorrect, irrelevant, and unreliable information. **Collation** is the orderly arrangement, cross-indexing, and filing of evaluated information so that meaningful relationships can be developed between apparently unconnected bits and pieces of information.
4. *Analysis and Interpretation.*   **Analysis** is the core area of the police intelligence process. This activity converts information into intelligence. Unanalyzed raw information provides few data about a developing pattern of criminal activity or a target suspect. As a result of analysis, a new recognition of the significance, meaning, and interrelationships of incoming information can be developed. **Interpretation** is an inseparable part of analysis—it is the dovetailing of collated information with the problems of users. Interpretation is developing a hypothesis and a tentative statement about the meaning of the information involved.
5. *Dissemination.*   Police intelligence reports are released only to users with a legitimate need for such intelligence. This need-to-know factor must be credibly established and strictly enforced. Unused or misused police intelligence reports sabotage a criminal investigation technique that is

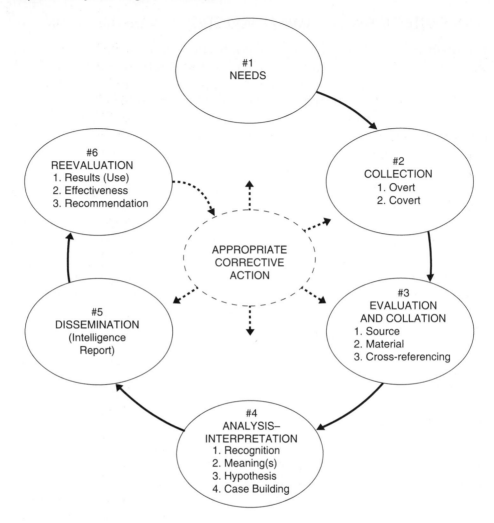

FIGURE 6-1   Six stages of the police intelligence process.

unique and is often the only means of disclosing information about ongoing
and planned crimes to police.

6. *Reevaluation.*   The final element of the police intelligence process is a postmortem review of the effectiveness of police intelligence reports and of subsequent action likely to improve the process and its effectiveness.

Criminal investigation information is police intelligence oriented to the
solution of ongoing investigations. A **criminal investigation information
center (CIIC)** within a police agency can assist investigators in clearing assigned cases by doing the following:[9]

1. Reviewing and collating items of information common to police reports
2. Providing information in response to investigators' requests

3. Organizing information on criminal activities in other jurisdictions for connections to local crime activities
4. Arranging for information sharing between investigators and investigative units

Proactive Investigation

Proactive investigation is an innovative technique that moves into attack mode long before an arrest occurs. Cases begin with a "quiet" investigation and often move into the "hustle" mode. A proactive investigation should be based on information provided by informants, coconspirators, and intelligence-gathering activities, or from data of ongoing crimes.

One tool used in proactive investigation is **link analysis**. Link analysis, which can be performed by computer programs, is ideal for profile work. It assists in visually showing the relationships among a number of people and organizations.

Charting techniques have proven extremely valuable for clarifying or visually illustrating such relationships. The types of charts that can be drawn are limited only by the user's creativity and needs for a chart. Chart types include, but are not limited to, link analysis charts, time lines, telephone toll analysis charts, case correlations, modus operandi (MO) comparisons, and chronologies.

Undercover Police Agents

The use of police personnel as undercover agents is an ethical approach to the problem of securing information about criminal operations from the inside. It is surveillance from a position of advantage. It is dangerous work, but often preferable to using an underworld informant—probably the only other source of such information. Undercover agents make excellent witnesses. Unlike underworld informants, whose credibility can be attacked because of their criminal histories, the police agent is a person of good reputation and character. Jurors recognize the hazards of this work and usually accept police undercover agents as extremely credible witnesses.

Investigators often go underground to search out the operations of criminals. In one case, a covert investigator arranged, through an underworld informant, an introduction to a gambling operator. The agent had a good cover story of being interested in gambling, and he posed as a man who had been arrested and sentenced to prison. A few weeks later, this agent was able to identify thirteen members of a gambling syndicate operating illegally and extensively and to offer legally significant evidence against them at their trial.

In many police units, recruits fresh from the police academy are used for this work. The recruits are not known to local members of the underworld, and they uncover meaningful information of help to the investigator. Statewide narcotics and alcoholic beverage control units also use trainees in undercover work during their first year or two of employment. Likewise, federal agencies transfer suitable personnel to areas in which they are unknown to facilitate the clandestine collection of information.

LINEUPS

The solution of a crime may rest on the identification of a suspect in custody. The lineup has been the traditional identification procedure used to focus a case against a suspect when eyewitnesses are available, but this process has the inherent evil of suggestibility, which has now been legally recognized. The postindictment lineup has been cited as a critical stage of the pretrial period in which the suspect is entitled to legal counsel (*United States v. Wade*).[10]

The major objective of placing a suspect in a lineup with other persons for viewing and possible identification by an eyewitness, or several such witnesses, is to make certain the suspect is the perpetrator of the crime. The witnesses are asked: "Is any of them the man (or woman) who committed the crime?"

The lineup format is similar throughout the United States: Four to six persons are used. They are allowed to select their position, then they are placed in line under a numeral against a wall marked to clearly indicate their height in feet and inches. A record is made of their descriptions and physical characteristics. They should be photographed for the record—in color, if possible. Viewing is under lights, with the witnesses out of view of the persons lined up for identification. Many police units have installed complex dimmer switches to permit simulation of the lighting conditions at the time of the crime. The individuals lined up may be asked to speak for identification; in some cases, they are also asked to put on various items of clothing. The witness or witnesses viewing the lineup may be requested to prepare and sign a statement noting whether they could make an identification.

The potential for prejudice, intentional or not, in the pretrial lineup is grave. U.S. investigators are now aware of this fact and are beginning to understand why, in many foreign countries, the presence of a suspect's friends or legal counsel is required during this type of identification. In England, the suspect must be allowed the presence of a solicitor or a friend. In Germany, a retained counsel must be present. In France, the suspect cannot be confronted with any witness in the absence of counsel.

Eyewitness testimony has been destroyed on cross-examination in certain offenders' trials because of substandard investigative procedures in arranging the identity lineup. Contentions of abuse of the integrity of a lineup can be overcome by the testimony of the eyewitness, the investigator, and police officers present at the time.

Defending a lineup when the eyewitness is asked to view an injured person in a hospital bed is difficult. When a witness is told that the culprit has been apprehended and the hospital bed is guarded by a uniformed police officer, the situation is difficult to justify; however, when police use professional care in the arrangements, a hospital-bed identification may be justified.

One suggestion has been that the presence of legal counsel at lineups would avert prejudice of any kind and ensure a meaningful confrontation at trial. This concept persuaded the U.S. Supreme Court to determine that the lineup is a critical stage of the proceedings against the defendant and that he or she has a right to counsel at such lineups. In 1972, the Court modified its position on lineups by specifying that the provisions of the *Wade* decision applied to only indicted defendants.

Many investigators believe the presence of legal counsel at a lineup impedes legitimate inquiry. However, if the presence of counsel prevents the taint of an improper lineup from affecting the eyewitness testimony at trial, such a presence is actually an aid to the investigator. The attorney cannot interfere with the witnesses; they view the lineup and make or do not make their identification without help or hindrance from such legal counsel. Furthermore, the attorney's presence can bring the identity evidence into court without taint and strengthen the testimony of the prosecution's eyewitness.

Defense counsel are divided on what their duty is in the lineup procedure. Some think their role should be passive. However, most of them see their role as a new and active one. If they do not actively seek a fair lineup, they will be in a poor position to complain about it at the trial or on appeal. A look at the types of actions a defense counsel might take during a lineup will alert investigators to possible problem areas. Basically, a defense counsel proceeds under the following theory: miscarriages of justice are related to the degree of suggestion inherent in the manner in which the prosecution presents the suspect to the witness for pretrial identification.

The defense counsel will request an interview with the accused before the lineup. At such an interview, he or she obtains an overview of the defendant's involvement by asking about the circumstances of the arrest, whether any witnesses have seen the defendant since the arrest but before the lineup, and what statement has been made to the police. Counsel advises the accused of basic rights and answers questions the accused may ask about future proceedings.

After talking to the accused, the defense counsel should interview the investigating officer and request the names and addresses of the witnesses who are to view the lineup. Information about the nature of the offense and the time and place of its commission—as well as whether the witness or witnesses have previously described the suspect (and if such a description has been reported in an official police report), have been shown photographs of the accused, or have viewed the suspect since arrest but before the lineup—should be considered.

The defense counsel will request that others in the lineup be of the same general age, build, and appearance as the accused. Counsel will note the physical procedure of the lineup, should request that a photograph be taken of the lineup viewed by each identification witness, and may suggest that the accused person be allowed to change positions after each witness has viewed the lineup. Counsel will request a separate lineup for any other accused persons. Counsel may object to any voice identification, but if overruled will insist that all persons in the lineup say the same words.

Counsel will insist on being present when each witness views the lineup and says whether he or she does or does not identify any person there. Counsel will also note any comments the officer or investigator makes in front of the witnesses.

This new constructive role of the defense counsel depends on the fairness of the procedure used in the particular police department. The presence of an attorney representing a suspect during a lineup is *not* akin to his or her presence during interrogation of the suspect when the attorney is likely to advise his or her client not to talk at all or not to answer certain questions. An attorney in the bystander role at a lineup should be welcomed and used by police to strengthen their identification procedures and thus strengthen their eyewitness case at trial by foreclosing the charge of unfairness or of suggestion heretofore often raised by the defense counsel.

CHAPTER REVIEW

CASE STUDY

The Brown Case

The Brown case is one in which the perpetrator's identity was not known when the investigation started, and only extensive work by assigned investigators disclosed the suspect's identity and led to prompt apprehension. A known identity case is likely to be underinvestigated, but the work commonly necessary in a serious felony investigation in which the perpetrator is unknown develops the type of evidence structure necessary in any prosecution of an accused person.

Although the killing of this liquor store proprietor might be considered accidental, it was legally classified as murder because it was a homicide committed in the course of committing a felony (robbery).

Synopsis

At approximately 3:20 p.m., March 12, officers on patrol received a call to proceed to the Bank Bottle Shop, a liquor store. The first patrol officer arrived at 3:25 p.m. and walked into the scene of a murder. The scene survey showed the appearance of a struggle and robbery, and a victim apparently dead from massive wounds and extensive bleeding. The officer checked the body for signs of life, looked for other occupants, then called for detectives and the coroner. A neighborhood inquiry by the responding police officers located two witnesses. One witness, an adult, observed

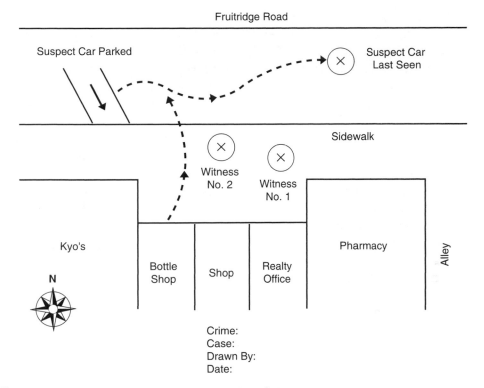

FIGURE 6–2   Brown case crime scene area—position of witnesses.

what was believed to be the killer's automobile in the parking area immediately in front of the liquor store. Another witness, a child, observed what was believed to be the killer and his automobile leave the parking area immediately in front of the liquor store. This witness also saw the automobile scrape the curb in front of the liquor store. Two nights later, evidence was found in a ditch near a golf course along a nearby street. Among the items in the ditch was a hammer, which later proved to be the murder weapon. A witness who observed the automobile from which the items were thrown obtained its license number, and this information led police to the defendant. This witness also identified the defendant as the driver of the car at a later lineup. In a jury trial, the defendant was found guilty and sentenced to death.

The Investigation

The police prepared sketches and diagrams to detail the crime scene pictorially. Photographs of the crime scene and the extension of the scene were taken. Along with the sketches were (a) a written report describing the items depicted on the sketches, and (b) measurements to show the exact location of the evidence illustrated (Figures 6–2 and 6–3).

Physical evidence recovered at the crime scene included a hat, hair samples, paint scrapings from the area of the parking lot curb in front of the store, and glass particles from the floor. Physical evidence recovered at the extension of the crime scene (the ditch) included clothing in a bundle and, separated from the bundle, a wheel weight tool (hammer) and hair samples from the clothing.

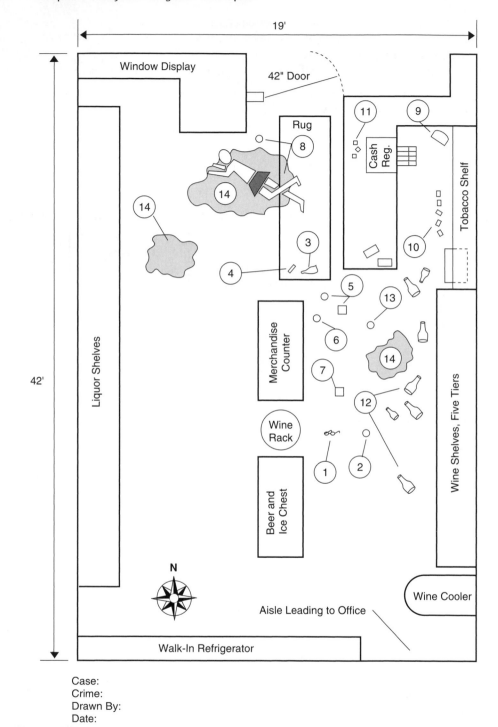

FIGURE 6–3   Brown case crime scene sketch. Numbered locations indicate items of evidence (listed on crime report).

When the suspect was arrested, his shoes and a hair sample were secured. At the suspect's home after the arrest, a sample of the suspect's dog's hair and a sample of paint from the tire of the suspect's automobile were taken for comparison tests.

Interviews of the two witnesses at the scene developed the following evidence at the trial:

Witness No. 1. (Previous questioning elicited testimony that established the age and identity of the witness.) The questioning included a number of leading questions, which are sometimes necessary and permissible when the witness is young. This witness was 11 years old. The prosecutor phrased the questions:

Q: Do you know the shopping center that is located on the corner of Fruitridge Road and 24th Street?
A: Yes.

Q: On March 12th, a Sunday afternoon of this year, were you in the area of that shopping center?
A: Yes.

Q: What was your purpose for going there?
A: Had to get something at the grocery store.

Q: What were you going to get?
A: Some milk.

Q: And that was at which store?
A: Raley's.

Q: Raley's Market located in that shopping center?
A: Yes.

Q: Which way did you come from when you approached Raley's?
A: By Fruitridge Road.

Q: Do you know where the Bank Bottle Shop is?
A: Yes.

Q: Did you walk past that?
A: Yes.

Q: Do you know where Kyo's is?
A: Yes.

Q: Did you walk past that?
A: Yes.

Q: You passed Kyo's before you approached the Bank Bottle Shop?
A: Yes.

Q: Did you look in the Bank Bottle Shop as you passed?
A: Yeah.

Q: Did you see anything?
A: Saw a pair of legs lying down on the floor.

Q: Did you see anything else?
A: Blood.

Q: Where did you go then?
A: I went to the store.

Q: And what did you do?
A: I just got the milk, and I left after I paid for it.

Q: Did you go back past the Bottle Shop again?

A: Yes.

Q: How long did it take you between the time you passed the Bottle Shop on the way to the store and the time that you passed it on your return?

A: About 5 minutes.

Q: Would you tell these ladies and gentlemen what you saw?

A: Well, I saw a man coming out from the store. I didn't see him run out from it, but he was coming from that direction. Then he got in his car and drove away.

Q: What did you notice about the man, if anything?

A: He had blood on him, a lot of blood, and he was carrying something in his hand.

Q: What was he carrying in his hand?

A: A small hammer.

The witness continued to relate that the man appeared as if his leg was injured and that when he started to drive away, his car scraped the curb in front of the liquor store. (When arrested, the defendant had a broken leg.)

Witness No. 2.   This witness was an adult who saw the car used by the robber and killer while it was parked in front of the liquor store, the Bank Bottle Shop. After giving testimony concerning his identity, he was questioned by the prosecutor as follows:

Q: Are you familiar with the shopping center at the southeast corner of Fruitridge Road and 24th Street?

A: I live in that area.

Q: Did you have occasion to be in front of that area, the shopping center, on Sunday, March 12th, in the afternoon?

A: Yes, I walked down the sidewalk past the Bottle Shop.

Q: Are you referring to the Bank Bottle Shop at 2346 Fruitridge?

A: Yes.

Q: Where were you going at that time?

A: I was going to Kyo's right next door.

Q: What time was it?

A: Approximately three or a few minutes after.

Q: Did you see any automobiles in that area?

A: There was one car parked out in front.

Q: Would you describe that automobile, please.

A: It was a light, cream-colored, two-door Thunderbird with chrome down the side, and curved-fenders, and it had "Thunderbird" written across the side on the front fender. (This described the defendant's automobile.)

Medicolegal (Autopsy) Evidence Developed from the Autopsy Report

Countless wounds were found about the scalp, ears, forehead, and eyes (Figure 6–4). These lacerations are generally sharp in character and are made by a relatively sharp instrument. They show a bruising along the edge and vary in size from 3 to 4 inches in length to virtual puncture wounds. There is one virtually continuous laceration across the entire frontal area from right temporal bone to left temporal bone. Both ears have been partially divided, again by a sharp instrument. There are innumerable other smaller marks, approximately six around the left eye, approximately six to eight around and under the right eye. There is extensive bruising in these areas.

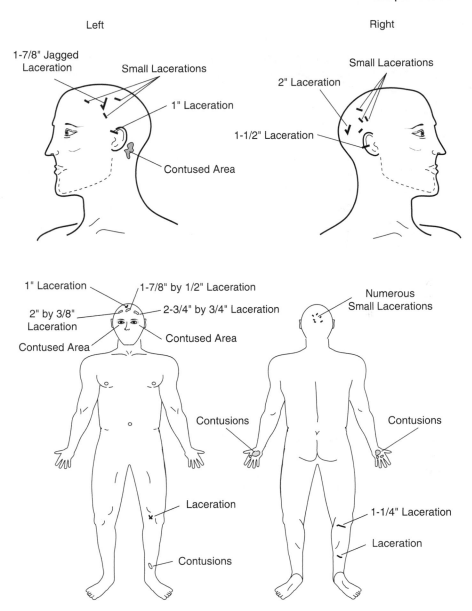

Left

Right

1-7/8" Jagged
Laceration

Small Lacerations

Small Lacerations

1" Laceration

2" Laceration

1-1/2" Laceration

Contused Area

1" Laceration

1-7/8" by 1/2" Laceration

Numerous
Small Lacerations

2" by 3/8"
Laceration

2-3/4" by 3/4" Laceration

Contused Area

Contused Area

Contusions

Contusions

Laceration

1-1/4" Laceration

Contusions

Laceration

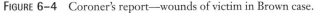

FIGURE 6-4   Coroner's report—wounds of victim in Brown case.

These wounds are basically small and appear to be virtual gross puncture wounds. Through one of the lacerations over the left frontal area, there is a palpable fracture.

> ***Extremities.***   There are several small bruise lacerations about the left upper arm, left fore-arm, and left hand. There are similar lacerations over the right hand. There are two or three superficial abrasions and lacerations over the left lower extremity and a laceration over the right heel. All of these wounds—head, arms, and lower extremities—appear to be made by basically the same type of instrument.

FIGURE 6–5   Murder weapon in Brown case.

Head.   There are three areas of fracture involving the skull. The first is in the left frontal area, the second is in the right posterior temporal area, and the third is in the right occipital area. All of these are relatively undisplaced fractures, the intracranial depression being approximately 5 to 10 millimeters in each case. The most severe of these is the right temporal bone fracture, and even in this area there is little or no underlying hematoma. No trace of glass fragments found in head area.

I had occasion to reexamine the subject for the purpose of comparing the wounds inflicted with a weapon supplied by the coroner's office. This weapon was a hammer with a green composition handle and a peculiar type of head. There was a flat surface at the front, a side extension resembling a screwdriver, and in the rear a two-pronged structure, one prong being relatively straight and the other being curved, somewhat on the order of a bottle opener. The sutures over the left frontal area were removed and the area of peculiar dual penetration of the skull was exposed and, upon examination, was found to fit perfectly with the end of the hammer described above as two pronged. In addition, multiple lacerations over the hands and face demonstrated virtually perfect conformity to the small screwdriver-like side arm on this hammer. It was my impression, after examining the wounds again, and the hammer supplied by the coroner's office, that this instrument or one very similar inflicted said wounds. The skull fracture in the left frontal area appeared to have been made by the pronged end of the hammer; the two other skull fractures appear to have been made by the flat end of the hammer. The hammer was then returned to the custody of the coroner's officer (Figure 6–5).

Cause of Death.   Cerebral concussion due to multiple skull fractures with multiple lacerations of the head.

Laboratory technicians in criminalistics tested the physical evidence and reported their five findings as follows:

1. The hair samples from the hat recovered at the scene were similar in appearance and physical characteristics to the hair samples taken from the suspect.
2. The hair samples found on clothing recovered at the scene extension (ditch) were traceable and similar to the hair samples of the suspect's dog.
3. Glass fragments from the crime scene and glass fragments in the soles of the suspect's shoes could not be differentiated one from the other.
4. Paint scrapings from the curb in front of the crime scene store appeared similar in color and type to the paint transfer found on the tire of the suspect's car.
5. Blood on the hammer and clothing found at the scene extension (ditch) was human and the same type as that of the deceased.

> **Critique**
>
> The prosecution's success was ensured by the following six factors:
>
> 1. Careful documentation and recovery of physical evidence at the crime scene
> 2. Location of and interviews of the two witnesses at the scene
> 3. Careful documentation and recovery of physical evidence at the scene extension (ditch)
> 4. The initiative of the witness at the scene extension (ditch) in recording the automobile license number and his ability to identify the driver
> 5. Postarrest documentation and recovery of physical evidence from the suspect and his home and car
> 6. Successful comparison of physical evidence connecting the suspect to the crime scene
>
> *Source:* Sacramento, California, Police Department and Public Defender's Office.

DISCUSSION QUESTIONS

1. Explain the public's approval of visual surveillance and its rejection of electronic eavesdropping.
2. Why is collected police intelligence vital to the success of investigation into the operation of organized crime?
3. What restrictions are placed on the surreptitious entry of homes or places of business by police to install hidden microphones (bugs)?
4. Under what circumstances would a court be likely to authorize police to enter a home or an office surreptitiously to install hidden microphones?
5. How does consensual electronic surveillance differ from nonconsensual electronic surveillance?
6. What is the common scope of countermeasures used by "targets" of police electronic surveillance?
7. Justify the sequential arrangement of the six stages of the police intelligence process.
8. Are undercover police agents useful? Is their work ethical?
9. Regarding the case study, how would the presence of a surveillance camera have affected the outcome of this investigation?
10. What cases can you think of that have gained nationwide attention because of the presence of a video camera?
11. What effect will surveillance equipment have on the future of criminal investigation?

LIBRARY ASSIGNMENT

Prepare a selected bibliography on wiretapping; list at least ten references. Abstract or digest no less than three of the references that appear to have unusual or timely significance in this area of audio surveillance.

WORKBOOK PROJECT

List five methods of becoming the "invisible investigator" during a visual surveillance.

RELATED WEB SITES

Interested in a surveillance camera concealed in a pair of eyeglasses or in a necktie? Check out the latest in video security at: *www.supercircuits.com*.

A full line of surveillance equipment can be seen at: *www.spybase.com*.

Think your home or office is being bugged? Information on counterintelligence, bug sweeps, and surveillance countermeasures can be found at: *www.tscm.com*.

NOTES

1. JEFFREY SELINGO, "Protecting the Cellphone User's Right to Hide," *New York Times*, February 5, 2004, e5.
2. *United States v. Knotts*, 460 U.S. 276 (1983).
3. *Dalia v. United States*, 441 U.S. 238 (1979).
4. *Katz v. United States*, 389 U.S. 347 (1967).
5. RICHARD G. SCHOTT, "Warrantless Interception of Communications: When, Where, and Why It Can Be Done," *FBI Law Enforcement Bulletin*, 72, no. 1 (2003): 25–31.
6. NATIONAL COMMISSION FOR THE REVIEW OF FEDERAL AND STATE LAWS RELATING TO WIRE-TAPPING AND ELECTRONIC SURVEILLANCE (NWC), *Electronic Surveillance* (Washington, DC: Government Printing Office, 1976), 151–52.
7. THOMAS D. COLBRIDGE, "Electronic Surveillance: A Matter of Necessity," *FBI Law Enforcement Bulletin*, 69, no. 2 (2000): 25–31.
8. E. DREXEL GODFREY, JR., AND DON R. HARRIS, *Basic Elements of Intelligence: A Manual of Theory, Structure and Procedure for Use by Law Enforcement Agencies Against Organized Crime* (Washington, DC: U.S. Department of Justice, Law Enforcement Assistance Administration, 1971), 11–35.
9. DON R. HARRIS, *Criminal Investigation Information Center: A Manual Describing the Organization and Analysis of Criminal Information* (Washington, DC: U.S. Department of Justice, 1979), 1–8.
10. *United States v. Wade*, 388 U.S. 218 (1967).

7

Interviewing and the Detection of Deception

An **interview** is a person-to-person conversation engaged in to obtain information about a crime or its circumstances. Interviews should be conducted in private. The actual interview begins only after the investigator has made the interviewee comfortable and established rapport. While establishing rapport, the investigator must assess the potential witness's competency and credibility.

The type of interview conducted at the crime scene is a four-step process designed to elicit complete and accurate information from the person being interviewed. These types of interviews are unstructured and are used to determine exactly what happened at the crime scene. Follow-up interviews are more structured and designed to address specific areas of concern.

While conducting an interview, the investigator must be a good listener. Listening is an interactive process that involves interpreting both visual and oral input. During the interview, the investigator should be mindful of the possibility that the person being questioned will be deceptive. Clues to deception can be obtained from the interviewee's body language, demeanor, and comfort level with the interviewing process. A polygraph examination can be scheduled when the issue of whether the person is being deceptive must be resolved.

Persons who cannot recall specific details of an event can often have their recollections refreshed. Investigative hypnosis, when used by a trained practitioner, can be useful for memory recall. Another technique used to refresh a witness's recollections is the cognitive interview process. The final step in the interview process is to transcribe the witness's oral statement to written form.

INTERVIEW ESSENTIALS

Privacy

Ideally, interviews should be conducted at the police station, but doing so is not always possible or practical. About 80 percent of all interviews are informal and occur outside an office setting.[1] These interviews, conducted at the crime scene or at a person's home or workplace, still need to be conducted in private. Privacy can be obtained by conducting the interview inside a patrol vehicle, in another room of a house, or anyplace where other witnesses or outsiders cannot overhear and possibly be drawn into the discussion.

Privacy is important because it insulates the witness from others' input. An unacceptable situation would be if a witness was giving a vehicle or suspect description and another person joined the conversation to try to aid the witness's recollection. Knowing that discrepancies in testimony and differences of perception commonly occur among witnesses, the investigator must obtain the independent recall of each witness. Conducting interviews in private also guards against the possibility of **reverse transference**. This process occurs when a witness overhears other witnesses discussing their observations and then unknowingly takes on some if not all of their information as his or hers.[2]

Interviewers should also not forget that a witness is much more likely to reveal any secrets in private than in the presence of additional persons.[3] Another important reason interviews are conducted in private is that privacy enhances the bonding process between the witness and the interviewer. This bonding process, known as **rapport building**, is essential if an investigator is to obtain the maximum amount of information.

Rapport Building

Rapport is a harmonious relationship with another person. The investigator begins the process of rapport building by making the interviewee comfortable. The investigator should introduce him- or herself, explain the reason or purpose for the interview, and be aware of the witness's stress resulting from being a victim or a witness to a crime. This person may need to be reassured about his or her personal safety and to have anxiety and personal comfort issues addressed. The goal of rapport building is to make the interviewee feel comfortable with the interview process and the investigator. To accomplish this, the interviewer should always treat the person being interviewed with respect and be sympathetic and empathetic when necessary. A person who is comfortable with the investigator and the interview process is more likely to become an active participant and to supply more information than someone who is uncomfortable and wants to terminate the experience as soon as possible.

Prior to beginning the interview, the investigator should take a few minutes to discuss subjects unrelated to the crime. A well-rounded interviewer can always find a subject the witness is willing to talk about. Most people like to talk about themselves, so a discussion about where they were born is always appropriate, as is a discussion about the weather or current events. Although this step may seem like a waste of time, it is important. This conversational process makes the person feel comfortable talking with the investigator and more likely to answer questions. The investigator should use this step as a means of observing the witness when he or she is not under stress and answering questions truthfully. This demeanor is that person's norm for truthful responses, and any deviations from this norm may indicate deception.

Competency and Credibility Issues

Another benefit of the rapport-building process is that the investigator can make some assessments about the person being interviewed. The investigator should be aware of competency issues as they relate to the person's age, intelligence, mental state, and intoxication. No age limit is placed on witnesses who can testify in court. However, a very young person must know the difference between right and wrong and that telling a lie is wrong. For an elderly person, the issue is soundness of mind. This issue can be addressed with a few questions to determine whether the person is rooted in reality and his or her answers to questions are responsive.

As with the age issue, a witness to a crime is not subject to minimum intelligence requirements. However, the potential witness should be able to focus and not be easily confused. A person's mental state will affect his or her ability to testify in court. A person who hears voices or is delusional will not make a good witness, and such a state should become apparent to the interviewer after a few questions.

The question of intoxication is a matter of degree. A person who is intoxicated will not be a competent witness, but the person who has had only a few drinks might be. The standard is whether the person's speech is clear or slurred and whether his or her answers are responsive to the questions being asked.

Credibility issues involve considerations that would make the witness's testimony unbelievable. The witness's relationship to either the victim or the suspect would affect his or her credibility because testimony driven by love or hate is rightly suspect and often unbelievable. Biases and prejudices are another factor that would affect credibility. If a witness uses racial slurs or other hateful epithets during the interview, this information should be noted in the official police report. Bringing a witness's biases to the prosecuting attorney's attention will be appreciated because these officials rarely like surprises at trial time. Other credibility issues that should be brought to the attention of the prosecutor and the defense could be the following:

- Any physical impairments that might affect the individual's ability to observe an event, such as needing eyeglasses or hearing aids, and whether corrective items were in use at the time.
- Conditions, such as weather or lighting, existing at the time of the crime that could have affected a person's ability to perceive an event.
- The witness's reputation for being truthful. A person with a long criminal history is not as believable as other members of society are.

Interview Structure

Interviewing witnesses contacted at the crime scene is a four-step process. The first step starts with the basic open-ended questions of What happened? and What did you see or hear? Once a question is asked, the witness should be allowed to answer without interruption. Notes are not taken and audio or visual recording is not conducted at this point. Taking notes only slows the witness and interrupts his or her concentration. Notes and recordings are also intimidating to most witnesses, and when they are aware of such recording, they will choose their words carefully, which is exactly what the investigator does not want.

Once the witness tells his or her story and the interviewer has a good grasp of the information the witness gave, the interviewer should proceed to the second step. This step involves having the witness repeat the story; however, this time the interviewer will take notes or record the conversation. Because the witness has already given the interviewer the information, notes taking or recording will not be as intimidating to him or her. In this step, the interviewer should also ask questions addressing any competency or credibility issues that might arise: Do you wear eyeglasses and were you wearing them at the time? Were you under the influence of alcohol or drugs at the time? What is your relationship to the victim or suspect? If appropriate, the interviewer should ask any or all of these questions.

In third step of the interview process, the interviewer reviews his or her notes with the witness. This step ensures that the interviewer has accurately recorded or paraphrased what the witness said. Because this step involves action on the part of the interviewer, the pressure is off the witness. This step allows the witness to think about his or her testimony and to fill in any areas that might have been missed.

The final step in the process involves thanking the witness for his or her cooperation and asking whether he or she wants to add anything. The witness should be given a business card as a means of contacting the investigator if he or she forgot something important during the interview and remembers it later.

Follow-up interviews are not conducted at the crime scene. These interviews are more structured because they occur after the event and the investigator has a good idea of what happened and the type of questions that the witness needs to be asked.

Listening

Being a good listener is not easy. Most people speak at a rate of about 125 words a minute, which is extremely slow compared with how fast a person can think.[4] As a result, a poor listener's thoughts drift away into daydreams or outside thoughts and fail to return for crucial spoken words. To aid concentration, a listener should use the extra thinking time to stay ahead of the talker, formulate ideas about where the talker is headed, and connect this information to what has already been said.

Words alone convey only a part of any message. Sixty-five percent of our conversation with another person is nonverbal. Therefore, the interviewer must think beyond mere words, gathering meaning from tone of voice, eye contact, facial expression, hand gestures, and body language. Interviewers must remember that what is important is not *what* is said, but *how* it is said.

Being a good listener requires active involvement. The interviewer's body movements, eye contact, hand gestures, head nodding, facial expressions, and tone of voice must convey to the witness an interest in what is being said and an interest in the witness as a person. Leaning toward the witness conveys the nonverbal signal that the interviewer is interested, even enthused, about the information being given. In contrast, the interviewer's tone of voice, facial expression, and body movements can convey emotions of disgust, boredom, disbelief, and contempt, which can make a witness defensive or evasive.

DETECTION OF DECEPTION

Repeated studies have shown that traditional methods of detecting deception during interviews succeed only 50 percent of the time, even for experienced interviewers.[5] Despite this fact, investigators still need the ability to test the veracity of individuals they interview.

Physical Signs of Deception

An alternative paradigm for detecting deception, based on four critical domains—comfort or discomfort, emphasis, synchrony, and perception management—can increase the odds in the interviewer's favor.

Comfort.   A person's comfort or discomfort level is one of the most important clues interviewers should focus on when trying to establish veracity. People who tell the truth more often appear comfortable because they have no stress, nor do they have guilty knowledge to make them feel uncomfortable. People who are being deceptive, however, first display discomfort physiologically. Their heart rate quickens, hairs stand up, and perspiration and breathing increase, all of which are autonomic responses. Nonverbally, they tend to move their bodies by rearranging themselves, jiggling their feet, fidgeting, or drumming their fingers. Deceptive people tend to distance themselves from those with whom they feel uncomfortable. They will lean away from the interviewer or create artificial barriers either with their shoulders and arms or with inanimate objects in front of them. Other clear signs of discomfort include rubbing the forehead near the temple region, squeezing the face, rubbing the neck, or stroking the back of the head with the hand. Research has also shown that when people are nervous or troubled, their blink rate increases, a phenomenon often seen with liars under stress.

Emphasis.   When people speak, they naturally incorporate various parts of their body, such as eyebrows, head, hands, arms, torso, legs, and feet, to emphasize a point. For the most part, liars do not emphasize with nonverbal behavior. They will think of what to say and how to deceive, but rarely do they think about the presentation of the lie.

Synchrony.   In an interview setting, the tone of each party should mirror the other's with time. A certain amount of harmony occurs in speech patterns, sitting styles, touching frequency, and general expressions. An interview that is "out of sync" or lacks harmony indicates that the interviewee is uncomfortable and possibly being deceptive. A lack of **synchrony** often occurs when a person says "I did not do it" while nodding his or her head as if to say "Yes, I did it." Or, when asked "Would you lie about this?" his or her head again bobs up and down. Synchrony should occur between what is being said and the events of the moment. The information and facts should remain pertinent to the issue at hand, the circumstances, and the questions. When the answers are asynchronous with the event and the questions, the investigator may assume that something is possibly wrong or that the person is stalling for time to fabricate a story.

Perception management.   Liars will try to influence their intended targets of deception with verbal and nonverbal behavior designed to demonstrate the implausibility of their involvement in committing a crime. They may use **perception management** statements such as "I could never hurt someone," "Lying is below me," and "I have never lied," all of which should alert the interviewer to the possibility of deception. Statements such as "To be perfectly frank," "To be honest," "To be perfectly truthful," and "I was always taught to tell the truth" are intended solely to influence the interviewer's perception. Nonverbal behaviors such as yawning, indicating boredom, and stretching out on a couch, as if to demonstrate comfort, are examples of perception management.[6]

Polygraph Testing

One technique useful in investigation is the instrumental detection of deception. With a cooperating subject, it is a valid investigative tool.

Modern polygraphs have three components, or channels—that is, three separate capabilities—for recording anatomic responses to the questioning situation. These components and their actions are as follows:

1. The **pneumograph** records respiration (breathing rate and depth)
2. The **galvanograph** records the electrodermal response (skin electrical resistance changes)
3. The **cardiograph** records changes in pulse rate and blood pressure

Generally, the cardiograph is considered the most reliable indicator of deception. The **galvanic skin response (GSR)**, which is measured by the resistance of the skin to the passage of a small electric current, is the least dependable.

Instrumental detection of deception is based on human anatomy. The sympathetic division of the **autonomic nervous system**, when stimulated by reactions such as anger and fear, mobilizes the body and its resources for emergencies. The effects are similar to those produced by adrenaline. Sugar is released from the liver for use by the muscles, the heart rate increases, and blood coagulability is heightened.

Because the autonomic nervous system reacts automatically to threat with this fight-or-flight reaction, a subject cannot hide his or her involuntary responses to a situation. If something poses a threat to the subject, fear will occur, and when a person is fearful, an involuntary, animalistic preparation within the body for fight or flight—a prehistoric form of survival insurance—occurs.

A guilty subject fears relevant questions during an examination. He or she is in a stress situation: fear of telling the truth, which would expose him or her as the guilty person, and fear of lying, which may be revealed by the "box" and expose him or her as a liar and, therefore, a suspect in the case.

If these tests for deception are to succeed, cooperation between the investigator and the examiner is necessary. The investigator must guard against contaminating the subject of a lie detection test by not taking any action before the testing session that will make creating or administering an effective test difficult or impossible for the examiner. The investigator should not discuss the lie detector or the possibility of such a test with a suspect until a decision has been made to request a test. The reason is not so much that silence is a safeguard against the subject's use of tranquilizers, since a drugged response level will be apparent when the subject is initially tested on the instrument. Rather, silence is a safeguard against any future allegations that the subject had been threatened with the use of this scientific device. When talking with possible subjects about the use of tests, investigators should also avoid any mention of key facts of the crime and its circumstances. Examiners use these facts for questions at the peak of tension. For example, in larceny cases, the exact amount of money taken (or perhaps the denominations of the larger bills in cash thefts) and, in assault and homicide cases, the type of weapon used and a detail about the weapon are facts useful for questions at the peak of tension.

The procedure in lie detection sessions may vary slightly with the examiner, but it is similar to that for interviews and interrogations in that these sessions have an introductory period, the actual testing phase, and a closing. During the introductory period, the examiner explains the operation of the instrument and its ability to detect body responses. The use of questions calling for a simple "yes" or "no" response is also explained, and the subject is instructed to remain silent if he or she does not understand the question and to reserve explanations for the period after the questioning. The subject is put at ease and allowed to ask questions, to which the examiner replies in an easily understood conversational style. The transition to the testing session for suspects in criminal cases is usually accompanied by an assurance that questions will be asked only in relation to the event under investigation. The questions may even be shown to the subject before the test. Some operators believe this is a more effective procedure. It reassures the subject that the testing period will not be a "fishing expedition" into a lifetime, and it validates responses as emanating from the current situation and not from any past feelings of guilt or fear about other crimes.

The testing begins after the subject is comfortably seated and the various tubes and wires have been attached securely and without discomfort. The first questions are irrelevant questions that are used to establish a normal response level for the individual being questioned. After these questions have established a response level, the examiner may demonstrate the capability of the machine by asking the subject to select a card from a deck of cards. The examiner directs the subject to answer "no" to questions about the value of the card. Then, by examining the graph, the examiner determines the identity of the card and tells it to the subject. The examiner is cued to its identity by the subject's reaction shown on the graph when the subject lied by giving the required "no" response.

The core area of the testing session follows this display of the device, and the relevant questions are interspersed with irrelevant questions. The so-called peak-of-tension questions relate to the circumstances of the crime; the remaining relevant questions may relate to events shortly before or after the crime.

No suspect can be forced to take a lie detector test. The privilege against self-incrimination, guaranteed to individuals by the Fifth Amendment to the Constitution, protects against such coercion. However, an element of psychological coercion is involved in merely requesting a suspect to take a lie detector test, and this element is likely to negate any claim of voluntariness. That is, this testing has "damned if you do and damned if you don't" overtones.

The process of detecting lies by using instruments and a skilled examiner has not gained sufficient general acceptance in its field to warrant court acceptance of the process as scientifically valid. In 1923, in *Frye v. United States*, this doctrine of general acceptance was established:[7]

> While courts will go a long way in admitting expert testimony deduced from a well-organized principle or discovery, the thing from which the deduction is made must be sufficiently established to have gained general acceptance in the particular field to which it belongs. (p. 1014)

One major criticism of the lie detector is that the examiner's role and the mechanics of testing jeopardize the scientific aspects of the instrument. The relationship of the examiner to the instrument in the detection of deception has been compared with that of a pilot to an airplane. The emphasis on operating skill brings the entire process into question as a way to detect truth or lies.

RECOLLECTION REFRESHMENT

Frequently, a witness forgets some critical details of a crime. The "I don't remember" response can be overcome by refreshing the witness's recollection through investigative hypnosis or the cognitive interview process.

Investigative Hypnosis

Hypnosis is a state resembling normal sleep. A person may be placed under hypnosis by the suggestions and operations of a **hypnotist**—a person who has studied the science or art of inducing hypnosis. Hypnosis in one form or another has been practiced for centuries, but its use in criminal investigation is a relatively recent phenomenon.

The use of hypnotically aided recall to enhance the memories of persons who have witnessed a crime but are unable to recall critical facts about the event is based on the belief that human memory is like a videotape machine. It faithfully records, as if on film, every perception the witness experienced; permanently stores such recorded perceptions in the brain at a subconscious level; and accurately "replays" them in their original form when the witness is placed under hypnosis and asked to remember them.

This "videotape recorder" theory of law enforcement hypnotists, however, is not supported by a survey of professional literature in this area. Highlights of these writings are the following:

1. Hypnosis is, by nature, a process of suggestion, and one of its primary effects is that the person hypnotized becomes extremely receptive to suggestions that he or she perceives as emanating from the hypnotist.
2. The person under hypnosis experiences a compelling desire to please the hypnotist by reacting positively to suggestions and hence to produce the particular responses that he or she believes are expected.
3. During the hypnotic session, neither the subject nor the hypnotist can distinguish between true memories and pseudomemories.
4. Neither the detail, the coherence, nor the plausibility of the resulting recall is any guarantee of its veracity.

The California legislature, in response to the California Supreme Court's banning the testimony of witnesses who have been hypnotized to aid in recollection, enacted legislation that allows such a witness to testify under extremely limited circumstances. For instance, the substance of the prehypnotic memory of the witness must be preserved in written, audiotape, or videotape form prior to the hypnosis session; the session must be extensively recorded; and the hypnosis must be performed only by a licensed medical doctor or psychologist experienced in the use of hypnosis and independent of and not in the presence of law enforcement officers, the prosecution, or the defense. Finally, the testimony of a witness who has undergone a memory-jogging hypnosis session is limited to "those matters which the witness recalled and related prior to the hypnosis."[8]

Therefore, the criminal investigator who uses investigative hypnosis is taking a risk. In some cases, the importance of discovering the identity of the person or persons responsible for a crime is so overriding that an investigator is justified in suggesting a hypnosis session for a witness whose recall of events appears to be blocked. Kidnappings in which the victim is still under the control of the kidnappers, terrorist acts, and series crimes such as rape and murder are examples of instances in which hypnosis may be justified. However, in effect, the investigator sacrifices any future value of the witness in court to gain information about the identity of the criminal and associates, if any.

Cognitive Interview

Cognitive interviewing is an investigative technique used to enhance a witness's ability to recall events. This technique has proved to be as effective as hypnosis but does not jeopardize the witness's credibility in court. The witness's ability to recall events is improved by taking one or more of the following steps: reinstating the context of the event, recalling the event in a different sequence, and looking at the event from a different perspective.

Reinstating the context of an event involves having the witness recall all his or her experiences before, during, and after the event. Instead of asking what happened, the interviewer asks that the witness relive the part of the day surrounding the crime: how the witness got to the scene, what route was taken, what the weather was like, what was being done during and after the event. This process enhances a person's retrieval of stored information. The witness can see the details of the crime in the proper sequence and context.

Changing the sequence involves having the witness recall the event in reverse order or out of order. Normally, a witness is asked to recall events in chronological order, a logical sequence of events from beginning to end. By recalling the event out of order, the witness must view each segment of the event independently. This process keeps the witness more focused and may reveal details that might otherwise be missed.

Changing perspective requires the witness to recall the event from the perspective of another person, such as the victim or another witness, or from that of an object, such as a camera mounted on the wall. This technique gives the witness the opportunity to recall more of his or her experiences and lessens the trauma of the event.[9]

WRITTEN STATEMENT OF A WITNESS

Statements are an excellent means of documenting the story the witness tells the investigator. They are usually little more than ruled forms on which a summary is recorded of what the witness has seen and heard and of how he or she happened to be in a position to make this observation. Investigators are expected to exercise judgment about the number of statements taken if witnesses are plentiful.

When a statement is taken, it should have a dual accuracy. It should reflect both what the witness has said and what the witness is prepared to testify to, under oath, about his or her observations. If any contradiction between the two exists, defense counsel may seize it as an opportunity to destroy the witness's credibility.

The purpose of taking a statement from a witness is generally threefold:

1. To provide a written record that will allow a prosecutor to evaluate the case and plan its presentation at trial
2. To enable the prosecutor to monitor the witness's testimony in court
3. To "hold" a witness; that is, to discourage surprise testimony by providing a possible base for impeaching the witness

If statements are taken, or if the interview develops as a situation in which a statement should be taken in accordance with standard local operating procedures, a note about taking the statement, or the failure to do so when a statement is warranted, should be made part of the investigator's field notes and report.

CHAPTER REVIEW

CASE STUDY

Robbery Interview

Victim Terri Shaw, age 34, was contacted on July 3, at her place of employment, The Mini Mart, 3751 Shore Road, at 2215 hours (10:15 p.m.). Following is a summary of her statement:

I have been working for The Mini Mart for about 2 years now; it will be 2 years in August. I work the swing shift, from four to midnight. Today I arrived at work at about 3:45 p.m. to relieve Tom, who works the day shift. It was a pretty busy shift, with the holiday tomorrow and all. I had to keep running to the back to stock the beer cases as well as wait on customers. I am the only one working tonight, as the other clerk called in sick.

At around 9:30 p.m., it began to slow down and I had three customers at the counter and one in the back of the store near the beer case. I waited on the customers at the counter, and then when they left, the remaining customer approached the counter. He was carrying a six pack of beer and placed it on the counter and asked for two packs of cigarettes. When I reached up to get the cigarettes, I noticed that he was reaching for something under his shirt. I thought he was getting his wallet, but when I looked back, I saw that he had a small gun in his right hand.

He told me, "Keep your mouth shut and you won't get hurt. Give me the money and place it in a bag." I did as I was told and opened the register and placed the money in a small bag. There was a lot of money in the register because it was busy and I didn't get a chance to make a drop. He had me lift the tray, and I placed that money in the bag also. He then had me put the cigarettes in the bag, and he told me to get on the floor and to count to 1,000 before I got up and called the cops. He told me that he would come back to check on me to make sure I was still counting. I got on the floor and counted slowly to 1,000, and because I was afraid that he might come back, I counted to 1,500 before I got up and called the police. When I got up, I noticed that the bag and the beer he had placed on the counter were gone.

The guy was a white male, about 20 to 25 years old, 5' 10" to 6' 0" tall, thin build, about 150 pounds, clean shaven, with brown eyes and hair. He was wearing blue jeans and a white T-shirt. I didn't see any writing on the shirt. The gun was dark blue and appeared to have a short barrel; I think it was a semiauto. I would be able to identify him if I saw him again; that desperate look on his face was unforgettable.

End of statement.

DISCUSSION QUESTIONS

1. In reference to the case study, would you have included any other information or asked additional questions? Does this witness need to be reinterviewed?

2. Is interviewing persons at their place of employment a good practice? In the case study, were any other options available? If so, what were they?

3. Think back to the professional contacts you have had with your doctor, dentist, or lawyer. How did the professional build rapport and make you feel comfortable in his or her presence?

4. In addition to the issues addressed in this chapter, what other issues affect a person's credibility as a witness?

5. A crime occurs in a bar, and all the potential witnesses have been drinking. Discuss how you would handle this situation and determine which, if any, of the witnesses is competent to testify in a court of law.

6. Explain the difficulties of being a good listener.

7. Discuss why you think you are a good listener.

LIBRARY ASSIGNMENT

Search the available literature on the detection of deception and prepare a brief abstract on five methods experts use to determine a witness's veracity.

WORKBOOK PROJECT

Research the legal status of investigative hypnosis in your jurisdiction and discuss your findings.

RELATED WEB SITES

Interested in becoming a polygrapher? For more information on this career choice, contact the American Polygraph Association at *www.polygraph.org*.

For answers to frequently asked questions about the polygraph, consult the following site: *www.polygraphplace.com*.

For information about the shortcomings of the polygraph, see *www.antipolygraph.org*.

NOTES

1. PAUL SZCZESNY, "Suspect Interviews: Asking for the Necessary Information," *Law and Order*, June 2002, 126.
2. LARRY DANAHER, "The Investigative Paradigm," *Law and Order*, June 2003, 133–34.
3. FRED INBAU et al., *Criminal Interrogation and Confessions*, 4th ed. (Gaithersburg, MD: Aspen, 2001), 51.
4. EDGAR MINER, "The Importance of Listening in the Interview and Interrogation Process," *FBI Law Enforcement Bulletin* 53, no. 6 (1984): 12–16.
5. PAUL EKMAN, *Telling Lies: Clues to Deceit in the Marketplace, Politics, and Marriage* (New York: Norton, 1985), 287.
6. JOE NAVARRO, "A Four-Domain Model for Detecting Deception," *FBI Law Enforcement Bulletin* 72, no. 6 (2003): 19–24.
7. *Frye v. United States*, 293 F. 1013 (D.C. Cir. 1923).
8. *California Evidence Code*, sec. 795 (1984).
9. MARGO BENNETT and JOHN E. HESS, "Cognitive Interviewing," *FBI Law Enforcement Bulletin* 60, no. 3 (1991): 8–12.

8

INTERROGATION OF SUSPECTS

An **interrogation** is the adversarial questioning of a suspect with the goal of soliciting an admission or a confession of guilt. Because of their adversarial nature, confessions have been challenged in the courts over the years. These legal challenges have ultimately led to the *Miranda v. Arizona* decision, which established procedural safeguards for in-custody questioning of a suspect. An interrogation can be conducted only in an in-custody environment when the suspect voluntarily waives these safeguards.

Unlike an interview, an interrogation is highly structured. Prior to the interrogation, the investigator must thoroughly investigate the crime and its circumstances. As a result of this investigation and during the rapport-building process with the suspect, the investigator must assess the person who is to be interrogated. This assessment will determine the approach for the investigator to take during the interrogation. During interrogation, suspects may admit guilt, give a full confession, or invoke their Miranda rights and terminate the interrogation.

INTERROGATION LAW

In the case of *Brown v. Mississippi*, the defendant was suspected of murder and was picked up by sheriff's deputies and taken to the sheriff's office. Once there, Brown was stripped to the waist and forced to bend over a desk. The deputies then repeatedly whipped him with their belts until he confessed. This confession was then used to convict him of the charge of murder, and he was sentenced to death. On appeal, the U.S. Supreme Court determined that confessions were an essential part of the investigative process; however, the confession must be made voluntarily. Accordingly, the confession was invalidated and the case was returned to the state courts.[1]

Other cases dealing with police procedure include *Ward v. Texas*, which was decided in 1942. In this case, the defendant was a suspect in a murder case. He was picked up for questioning and taken out of the county. He was transported from county to county, taken more than 100 miles away from his home, during a 3-day period and was not allowed to contact family or friends. He finally confessed and was found guilty of murder. On appeal, the Court found that holding a person incommunicado was inherently coercive.[2] Likewise, in the case of *Fikes v. Alabama* (1957), the defendant was held in solitary confinement for 10 days until he confessed,[3] and in the case of *Ashcraft v. Tennessee* (1944), the defendant was questioned for 36 straight hours until he confessed.[4] In both cases, the Supreme Court found these practices to be coercive and the confession to be involuntary.

The Court also examined the characteristics of the accused. In the 1948 case of *Haley v. Ohio*, the Court determined that questioning a 15-year-old from midnight to 5:00 a.m. until he confessed was coercive.[5] In the case of *Davis v. North Carolina* (1966), Elmer Davis was suspected of committing several burglaries and a homicide. He was questioned once or twice a day for 16 straight days until he confessed. Throughout the questioning, Davis was not told the true reason for the questioning: that he was a homicide suspect. Because of his low level of intelligence, having completed only the third or fourth grade of school, such questioning was determined to be coercive.[6]

The Court also examined the suspect's physical condition. In the case of *Mincey v. Arizona* (1978), the defendant was involved in a shoot-out with police. One officer was killed and the defendant was seriously wounded in the exchange of gunfire. The defendant was taken to the hospital and admitted to the intensive care unit. A short while later, a detective began to question the defendant, even though a tube had been inserted in his throat to help him breathe. To answer, the defendant responded by writing his answers on pieces of paper. During questioning, the defendant lost consciousness several times, and questioning was delayed for medical treatment. After 4 hours, the defendant finally confessed and was convicted of murder. On appeal, the Court found that the defendant's will was weakened by pain and shock; therefore, his confession was not voluntary.[7]

In the case of *Townsend v. Sain* (1963), the defendant was a suspect in a robbery and murder. He was a heroin addict and during questioning began exhibiting symptoms of withdrawal from the drug. The detectives summoned a doctor, who administered medication to alleviate the discomfort of the withdrawal symptoms. Unknown to the detectives, the medication had the effect of a truth serum and the defendant confessed. On appeal, the Court determined that the confession was not the product of the defendant's free will and therefore not voluntary.[8]

In 1964, the Court heard the case of *Escobedo v. Illinois*. The defendant's brother-in-law was fatally shot, and the following morning the defendant was taken into custody and questioned. He did not make a statement and was released that afternoon on a writ of habeas corpus obtained by his lawyer. A few days later, his crime partner confessed and stated that Escobedo had fired the fatal shots. Escobedo was again picked up for questioning and transported to the police station. En route to the station, he requested to speak to his attorney and the request was denied. Shortly after Escobedo reached the police station, his attorney arrived and asked to speak with his client, and this request was denied. After about 4 hours of questioning, Escobedo confessed to the crime and was convicted of murder. On appeal, the Court held the following:[9]

> [When] the investigation is no longer a general inquiry into an unsolved crime but has begun to focus on a particular suspect, the suspect has been taken into police custody, the police carry out a process of interrogations that lends itself to eliciting incriminating statements, the suspect has requested and been denied an opportunity to consult with his lawyer, and the police have not effectively warned him of his absolute constitutional right to remain silent, the accused has been denied "the Assistance of Counsel" in violation of the Sixth Amendment to the Constitution. (p. 491)

Two years later, the Court expanded the procedural safeguards established in the *Escobedo* decision. In the case of *Miranda v. Arizona*, the Court held that when a person is taken into police custody, in which his or her freedom of movement is lost,[10] and he or she is being interrogated with questions designed to elicit an incriminating response,[11] the police must advise the suspect of the following four points of law:[12]

1. You have the right to remain silent.
2. Anything you say can and will be used against you in a court of law.
3. You have the right to talk to an attorney and have an attorney present before and during questioning.
4. If you cannot afford an attorney, one will be appointed free of charge to represent you before and during questioning, if you desire.

The Court established that, procedurally, if a person indicates in any manner that he or she does not want to talk to the police, the interrogation must stop. If the suspect indicates that he or she wants an attorney, the interrogation must stop until the person has had the opportunity to consult an attorney. The suspect may waive these procedural safeguards; however, when he or she does, the prosecution has a "heavy burden" to prove that the waiver was freely and knowingly given.

THE WAIVER

Police are routinely seen in the movies or on television advising a suspect of his or her so-called Miranda rights while they are handcuffing the suspect. Although this approach may be acceptable procedure, it is not required by the *Miranda* decision, and few people would agree to be questioned at such a time. The so-called Miranda warning needs to be given only when the two-pronged test of custody and interrogation is met (Figure 8–1). A suspect may be interrogated and not be in custody—be questioned over the telephone, for example—or be in custody

154

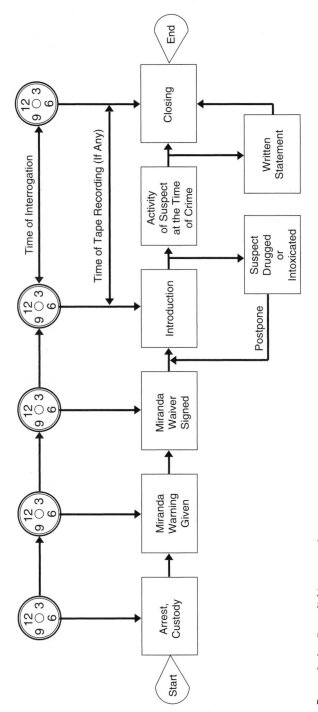

FIGURE 8–1 Custodial interrogation.

and be asked questions not designed to elicit an incriminating response. In these situations, the Miranda warning is not required.

As in an interview situation, the investigator must build rapport before beginning an interrogation. Although small talk with a suspect may not be appropriate, obtaining background information is. Questions about a person's place of birth, for example, and other related questions need to be asked. These questions offer opportunities for further informal questions. Such questioning, which does not meet the definition of *interrogation* per *Innis*,[13] allows the investigator to build rapport with the suspect.

After rapport is built, the suspect should be advised of his or her Miranda rights. As mentioned previously, the Court determined that the prosecution has a "heavy burden" to prove that this waiver was freely and knowingly given. This burden can be met by using the Miranda advisement form most U.S. police agencies use (Figure 8–2). However, this form is not required by the decision, and other means, such as audio- and videotaping, can be used to meet this legal burden.

INTERROGATION ESSENTIALS

Privacy

As with interviews, interrogations should be conducted in private. A suspect is more apt to reveal secrets, such as his or her involvement in a crime, in the privacy of a room occupied by only him- or herself and the investigator. The room should be free from outside noises and should be off limits to anyone not directly involved in the interrogation. The interrogation room should not contain any ornaments, pictures, or other objects that would in any way distract the attention of the person being interrogated. Even small, loose objects, such as paper clips or pencils, should be out of the suspect's reach so that he or she cannot pick them up and fumble with them during the interrogation. These tension-relieving activities can detract from the effectiveness of the interrogation, especially during the critical phase when a person may be ready to confess.[14]

Prior Investigation

Prior to conducting an interrogation, the investigator needs to know as much about the crime in question as possible. What do the victim and witnesses have to say about the suspect's involvement in the crime? What evidence implicates the suspect, and how does this evidence apply to the suspect? The investigator's goal is to know as much about the crime as the suspect does. In many cases, especially homicides, the suspect may be the only person alive who knows what happened during the commission of the crime.

A thorough investigation is important because if the investigator is not prepared and is only on a fishing expedition, the suspect will know it. Such a

Miranda Warning

Report #_____

1.   You have the right to remain silent.

2.   Anything you say can and will be used against you in a court of law.

   a.   Do you understand that you have the right to remain silent?

      ☐ YES_____   ☐ NO_____

   b.   Understanding that right, do you wish to talk to me now?

      ☐ YES_____   ☐ NO_____

3.   You have the right to talk to an attorney and have an attorney present before and during questioning.

4.   If you cannot afford an attorney, one will be appointed free of charge to represent you before and during questioning, if you desire.

   c.   Do you understand you have the right to talk to an attorney?

      ☐ YES_____   ☐ NO_____

   d.   Understanding that right, do you wish to talk to me now?

      ☐ YES_____   ☐ NO_____

SIGNED_____

OFFICER:_____   BADGE: _____

OFFICER:_____   BADGE: _____

TIME: _____   DATE: _____

The suspect should initial the appropriate answer to each question (yes, no) and sign the waiver. The officer should then sign and date the form.

FIGURE 8–2   Miranda warning—action indicating a suspect about to be questioned by police while in their custody has thoughtfully waived his or her Miranda rights. (See Appendix A, Case Briefs, for a digest of the *Miranda* case.) From Sacramento, California, Sneriff's Department.

lack of preparation allows the suspect to lose respect for the investigator's abilities and gives him or her license to lie. To prevent this, the investigator needs to know the answers to the questions before they are asked.

Approach

During the investigative phase and while building rapport, the investigator needs to assess the person to be interrogated. The investigator needs to consider the suspect's personal characteristics, the type of offense, the probable motivation for the commission of the crime, and the suspect's initial response to questioning. On the basis of this assessment, the investigator can determine if the person to be interrogated is either an emotional or a nonemotional offender.

An **emotional offender** is a person experiencing a considerable amount of feelings of remorse and mental anguish as a result of committing the offense. This individual has a strong sense of moral guilt, or, in other words, a troubled conscience. Typically, these offenders have committed personal crimes, such as homicides, rapes, or physical assaults, or are first-time offenders. For these offenders, a sympathetic approach that uses expressions of understanding and compassion is appropriate.

A **nonemotional offender** refers to a person who does not ordinarily experience a troubled conscience as a result of committing a crime. This offender may be the product of an antisocial personality disorder, may be unemotional as a conditioned response from repeated prior success in escaping punishment through lying, or may perceive committing crimes as a business. In the last case, the suspect approaches arrest, prosecution, and possible conviction as an occupational hazard and experiences no regret or remorse as a result of exploiting victims. The most effective tactic to use on this offender is the **factual analysis approach**. This approach appeals to the suspect's common sense and reasoning rather than to his or her emotions. This approach is designed to persuade the suspects that their guilt is established and consequently the intelligent choice to make is to tell the truth.[15]

WHY PEOPLE CONFESS

Most people would think that when suspects are taken to the police station to be questioned about their involvement in a particular crime, their immediate reaction would be a refusal to answer any questions. Most people would also think that once a suspect senses the direction in which the interrogation is heading, the conversation would come to an end. However, for various psychological reasons, suspects continue to speak with investigators. In most cases, suspects commit crimes because they believe that doing so offers the best solution to their needs at the moment. If the investigator can convince suspects that the key issue is not the crime but what motivated them to commit the crime, they will begin to rationalize or explain their motivating factors.

Investigators must conduct interrogations with the belief that suspects, when presented with the proper avenue, will use it to confess their crimes. Research indicates that most guilty persons who confess are, from the outset, looking for the proper opening during the interrogation to communicate their guilt to the interrogators. However, before a suspect will confess, he or she must feel comfortable in the surroundings and must have confidence in the interrogator, who should attempt to gain this confidence by listening intently and allowing the person to verbalize his or her account of the crime.[16]

THE SUSPECT'S DILEMMA: THE CRIME PARTNER

When a suspect has committed the crime with a partner, he or she has a problem: an accomplice. The suspect must decide whether to sacrifice a crime partner for some mitigation of involvement in the crime and must make the decision before the crime partner does. This dilemma is often referred to as simply *"better him than me."*

Advising a person being interrogated that a crime partner has talked is a practice that may taint an interrogation if done to persuade a suspect to waive his or her right to remain silent. If done honestly, it can, at times, be an effective technique. The offensive-defensive situation of an interrogation session is replete with covert communication. The threatening aspect of the experience may be perceived with little outward awareness, but subliminally the person being interrogated has a strong anxiety response. The interrogator need not comment; the worry and concern about whether a crime partner has talked is a natural form of anxiety. Many offenders assume that their partner has talked or is about to talk and that the only smart thing to do is to talk first, or better, to spill everything.

Interrogators should be alert to situations in which the person about to be interrogated is a professional criminal with an amateur crime partner. The pro may be the "torch" of an arson ring, may be the hired killer of a heavily insured partner in commerce or industry, or may be the burglar and thief with a businessperson receiver who buys all the thief can steal. Regardless, these pros apparently look at this relationship in crime as future insurance, rather than a dilemma, in the event of arrest.

DOCUMENTATION OF THE CONFESSION

Three methods are used to document a suspect's confession: video recording, audio recording, and writing. Each method has its strengths and weaknesses.

The strength of video recording is that it captures exactly what happened during the interrogation. Video recordings can help meet the burden of proof required to demonstrate that a waiver of Miranda rights was freely and knowingly given and that no coercion was used to obtain the confession. Because the video records not only what was said, but how it was said, the triers of fact can view firsthand any deception on the part of the suspect.

Video recording done surreptitiously allows the interrogation process to be viewed by others without the suspect's knowing that it is being recorded. State or local law may bar surreptitious taping. However, the federal constitution should not be a bar since a suspect would be hard pressed to prove that he or she had a "reasonable expectation of privacy" while under police interrogation in a station-house interview room. Indeed, the Miranda warning states explicitly that anything suspects say can and will be used against their interests.[17]

Covertly recording an interrogation allows other detectives to watch the interrogation and be a resource to the interrogator regarding areas of concern, deceptive movements, and officer safety issues. Such covert recording allows for the removal of one-way mirrors in interrogation rooms. These mirrors are well known by everyone who watches popular crime stories on television. Such mirrors work against the concept of privacy and do not aid the rapport-building process because the suspect is aware that other persons are on the other side of the mirror monitoring everything going on in the interrogation room. Another benefit of covert recording is that a suspect can be left alone in the room and his or her activities can be monitored while the person is alone. In such situations, a suspect often begins to talk to him- or herself and make incriminating statements. This tactic is even more effective when crime partners are left alone in the interrogation room and are allowed to talk to each other.

One weakness of video recording is that it can be edited or altered. To guard against this allegation, the investigator must ensure that the interrogation room has a clock on the wall, and that this clock is included in the recording. Any edits would be apparent to the viewer because the time would change if the tape were edited. Interrogation sessions often last for hours, and another weakness of using this technology is that the prosecuting attorney, the defense attorney, and the jury do not want to have to view the entire contents of the videotape of an interrogation. Another problem is that suspects, especially emotional offenders, may begin to sob or cry during the interrogation and become difficult to hear when they are making a confession. These problems can be overcome by reducing the confession to writing.

The strength of audio recording is that this technology is available for field use: for interrogations that occur outside an interview room. This technology can be used to capture the voluntary nature of the waiver as well as the confession. To guard against the allegation that these tapes can be easily edited, the investigator needs to state the date and time when the interrogation begins and ends. The lack of any time differences ensures that the tape has not been edited. However, during the taping, the investigator must not turn the recorder off and on. Taping an interrogation ensures that the investigator correctly records what the suspect has to say.

On the negative side, tape recorders are often intimidating to some people if not used surreptitiously. Once again, the overt use of a tape recorder will work against the concepts of privacy and rapport building. The issues of using a tape recorder surreptitiously are the same as those for video recording.

The third method of documenting an interrogation is with a written confession supplied by the suspect. This means of documenting a confession captures the words spoken by the suspect but does not capture the unspoken body language revealed by the suspect. A written form documenting the waiver of Miranda rights and the written statement supplied by the suspect are an effective means of documenting the voluntary nature of a waiver and confession. In the final analysis, the confession documented by video recording or audio recording must be memorialized in writing. Reducing the confession to writing allows the confession to be condensed to a concise statement of what happened, which can be included in the police report.

CHAPTER REVIEW

CASE STUDY

Interrogation of a Robbery Suspect

Detectives question a suspect in an armed robbery of a credit union and obtain the following statement:

Statement of Suspect

DeRose: I am Detective Bob DeRose, and this is Lt. Jacob Saylor. The time is now 1532 hours; the date is August 24th. We would like to interview you regarding the offense today. Before doing so, I will advise you of your rights, which I will read to you from this form: "I acknowledge that I have been advised, by officers Lt. J. Saylor and Detective R. DeRose, that I have the right to remain silent and that anything I say can and will be used against me in a court of law. I have the right to a lawyer and to have him present with me during questioning, and a lawyer will be appointed to represent me before any questioning if I cannot afford to hire one and desire to have a lawyer. Each of these rights has been explained to me, and I understand them. Having these rights in mind, I nevertheless waive them and consent to talk to the officers." Do you understand that?

Straus: I understand them, and I waive them.

Saylor: You understand and you want to waive and talk to us?

Straus: Yes.

DeRose: How far did you go in school?

Straus: Just about finished the second year of college.

DeRose: Concerning the robbery that occurred at the Credit Union, could you first describe what happened from the time you got up this morning?

Straus: Concerning the robbery?

Straus: I got up; I thought, well, should I go to work? Today's the 24th and the railroad gets paid on the 24th, and people will be cashing their paychecks at the office, at the Credit Union office. So having made up my mind to touch and go, I called in to work and told them I had a doctor's appointment and wouldn't be there until approximately 10:00 or 10:30. And I proceeded to arrange a pair of blue coveralls, a ski mask, gloves and the piece—the pistol, the thirty-eight.

DeRose: Where did you get the coveralls and the other stuff?

STRAUS: I bought them on the 9th of this month at The Emporium, I believe. I bought the ski hat at a sporting goods store next to Allen's Shoes on Temple Boulevard. The thirty-eight is registered to my brother-in-law and I took it without his knowledge, hoping to return it today.

DEROSE: Then what happened?

STRAUS: Then I got into the car and went down to the Credit Union. It is sort of hazy from there. I circled the block a couple of times. I parked the car in a loading zone and went to see if they were open, and the door was unlocked, from which I figured they were open at the time. So I had the coveralls on and the hat on my head. . . . I didn't have it over my face, and I had my fist in my pocket. And I heard loud noises in there . . . people talking, so I figured there was someone in there. I chickened out and I went back to the car and started to leave, and I said if I don't do it now, I won't do it. So I went back and parked in the parking place I showed you. Then I got out of the car. I walked over to the Credit Union. I went in the door and I heard the same loud male voices. There was two females. There was a couple female clerks in there. So I chickened out again, and I walked halfway back to the car. I say well, if I don't do it, I'll never do it again. And so I went back and got inside the building. I locked the door, the front double doors, behind me, went in and opened the inner door. And there was a man standing at the counter. He didn't turn around, and I put the gun . . . pointed the gun at the man and I said, "This is a holdup." I believe—I don't know exactly what I said.

DEROSE: Do you remember what the man looked like?

STRAUS: No. I only saw the back of his head. And I told him, "Keep quiet and everything will be all right." I said to the girl behind the counter, "Give me the money." And I had a paper bag in my hand, and I put the bag on the counter. And the man said, "Do as he says." And I was holding the gun on him.

DEROSE: Before you committed this robbery, did you anticipate what could happen?

STRAUS: No.

DEROSE: Did you ever think about getting caught?

STRAUS: No. I didn't worry about getting caught because I figured if I got caught—I got caught.

DEROSE: Well, all of the foregoing statements you have made have been given voluntarily and we haven't promised you anything?

STRAUS: No. Not yet.

DEROSE: And everything has been given of your own free volition, this statement?

STRAUS: Yeah.

DISCUSSION QUESTIONS

1. What has been the impact of the U.S. Supreme Court's *Miranda* decision on criminal investigation? What are its future implications?
2. Is the offensive-defensive situation common to all interrogations?
3. Explain the similarities and differences between interviewing witnesses and interrogating suspects.

4. What is the likelihood that a case would cease being a general inquiry into the circumstances of a crime when a person is taken into custody and questioned by police as a suspect?
5. Describe the Miranda warning. What are its related procedural safeguards?
6. What is meant by the *adversarial nature* of interrogations?
7. Explain the sympathetic approach used during an interrogation and discuss the type of person with whom this approach works best.
8. In the case study, when advising the suspect of his "rights," the detectives do not quote the exact wording of the *Miranda* decision. Could this be a problem for the prosecution?
9. At the start of the interrogation, why did the detective ask the suspect about his schooling?
10. How would the fact that this subject is an admitted heroin addict affect the interrogation process?
11. What is the importance of asking the suspect about promises?

LIBRARY ASSIGNMENT

Review the available literature on constitutional laws regarding police interrogation and confessions. Prepare a list of U.S. Supreme Court cases, with appropriate citations, that traces the body of case law known as the *confession cases*.

WORKBOOK PROJECT

Prepare an outline of the introductory segment of an interrogation that could serve as a guideline for your opening in an interrogation session with any suspect or accused person.

RELATED WEB SITES

To research U.S. Supreme Court cases, consult the following site:
    www. findlaw.com.

To learn more about the Supreme Court of the United States, visit its Web site at
    www.supremecourtus.gov.

NOTES

1. *Brown v. Mississippi*, 297 U.S. 278 (1936).
2. *Ward v. Texas*, 316 U.S. 547 (1942).
3. *Fikes v. Alabama*, 352 U.S. 191 (1957).
4. *Ashcraft v. Tennessee*, 322 U.S. 143 (1944).

 5. *Haley v. Ohio*, 332 U.S. 596 (1948).

 6. *Davis v. North Carolina*, 384 U.S. 737 (1966).

 7. *Mincey v. Arizona*, 437 U.S. 385 (1978).

 8. *Townsend v. Sain*, 372 U.S. 293 (1963).

 9. *Escobedo v. Illinois*, 378 U.S. 478 (1964).

10. *Beckwith v. United States*, 245 U.S. 341 (1976).

11. *Rhode Island v. Innis*, 446 U.S. 291 (1980).

12. *Miranda v. Arizona*, 384 U.S. 436 (1966).

13. *Innis*, 446 U.S. 291.

14. FRED INBAU et al., *Criminal Interrogation and Confessions*, 4th ed. (Gaithersburg, MD: Aspen, 2001), 51–58.

15. Ibid., 209–11.

16. DAVID D. TOUSIGNANT, "Why Suspects Confess," *FBI Law Enforcement Bulletin* 60, no. 3 (1991): 14–18.

17. U.S. DEPARTMENT OF JUSTICE, NATIONAL INSTITUTE OF JUSTICE, OFFICE OF JUSTICE PROGRAMS, *Videotaping Interrogations and Confessions* (Washington, DC: Government Printing Office, 1993), 4.

9

THE ARREST OF
THE ACCUSED PERSON

The accused person may be known and easily located. Alternatively, the suspect's name may not be known, he or she may have no known address, or he or she may be in hiding or in flight. Early in the investigation, an alarm, containing only fragmentary identification, is broadcast, or transmitted, by radio for local units in the field to be on the lookout for a suspect or a vehicle. The purpose of this alarm is to aid in the apprehension of the perpetrator in flight. After the initial hue-and-cry alarm fails, the investigator must collect and publish, in printed form, more detailed information about the crime and the perpetrator (a wanted notice). This information is the means by which other officers, distant in time and space from the crime, locate and identify a person in flight from justice.

Tracing fugitives depends a great deal on the expertise with which sources of information are exploited for adequate and meaningful information about the wanted person. Although the crime and its circumstances provide the basic information, data about the suspect as a person are also available in the records of criminal justice agencies, credit reports, telephone records, employment histories, and public records. Basic research often rewards the diligent investigator with meaningful information.

An arrest brings the investigation into close focus. The prisoner can be searched and booked, and during the process of recording facts, fingerprinted for positive identification. Evidence that can be collected at this time is collected, recorded, and preserved. The prisoner may be eager to talk to the police and may deny or admit to being the criminal. At this time, an arrested person must be warned of his or her constitutional rights to silence and legal counsel, and the investigator must ascertain whether the accused person will waive such rights and participate in an interrogation session by cooperating.

THE BROADCAST ALARM

The initial hue and cry in pursuit of the perpetrator of a crime emphasizes the distinctive identifying characteristics of the person, vehicle, or property wanted. The **broadcast alarm**, or order to be on the lookout for a suspect, a vehicle, or stolen property, is usually transmitted first by radio to the local unit and then, if appropriate, by Teletype, fax, or computer to adjacent jurisdictions to alert them to the recent crime. The first police officer at the crime scene or the investigator receiving the report of a crime is responsible for obtaining the best possible physical description of the criminal and his or her car, if any. A broadcast detailing a want is most effective when it is sent promptly.

Despite the urgency for getting the alarm on the air to alert other officers, accuracy must be emphasized. Law enforcement agents no longer ask leading questions when obtaining descriptions, and they emphasize in their reports that the description is a composite inasmuch as it is usually secured from both the victim and witnesses. Officers do not change the composite description once it is entered in their field notes or other records, nor is the composite description changed when the wanted person is arrested or when a wanted vehicle is recovered and found to differ from the description.

Identifying characteristics that distinguish a person or a vehicle from other persons or vehicles are the basis for success in the apprehension of suspects. Partial descriptions, if distinctive, such as a damaged fender on a vehicle coupled with a fragment of the registration number, have resulted in apprehensions. In cases involving juveniles, a painted identification or another marking on the car may be distinctive. Several weak, general descriptions of persons individually insufficient for identification often total to significant identifying characteristics when they are broadcast about the occupants of a vehicle.

The content of a broadcast alarm at this time in the investigation is oriented toward characteristics that are observable and that will guide searching police. Although a brief description of the crime (including the proceeds of a theft) is included, the major content is usually limited to describing persons, vehicles, and weapons.

The brief description of the crime basically includes the offense the offender is suspected of committing and the date, time, and location of its occurrence. Stolen property is not described, but a few details on the amount of currency taken or the kind of item stolen are included. If a weapon was used, its type and description are included in the broadcast to alert police that the fleeing suspect is likely to be dangerous.

When more than one perpetrator is described, a listing by number (Suspect No. 1, Suspect No. 2) is recommended. The following characteristics, in the order listed, are standard for these alarms: race, sex, adult or juvenile, age, height, weight, build, hair color, eye color, and distinguishing characteristics. A suspect's height and weight are usually reported in blocks or ranges: upward from 5 feet in 3-inch intervals and from 100 pounds in 20-pound intervals.

Clothing is an observable characteristic that affords excellent opportunities for recognizing a wanted person. In the "How Dressed" section of the alarm, each suspect's clothing is described, and the color, cloth, and design of the outer garments are noted. The absence of garments normally worn by other individuals in the area is also noted. The following items, in the order listed, are standard elements in broadcast alarms across the United States: bareheaded; hat (color and design: black, gray, porkpie, skimpy brim); cap (color); overcoat (color, cloth, design); jacket (color, cloth, Windbreaker, fingertip); suit (color, cloth, design); shirt (color, dress, or sport); dress; slacks; or shorts (color, cloth, design).

Vehicle descriptions in these alarms are generally limited to the following: year, make, model, color, state license plate number, any damage or suspected damage, and number and sex of occupants. The usual categories of sedan, station wagon, van, convertible, and sports car have been supplemented by pickup, "crew" pickup, jeep, and pickup with camper.

The direction of flight, if known, is also included in the alarm. Roadblocks may be set up, and buses and other public transportation vehicles may be searched. A surveillance of the area may be conducted for criminals who seek temporary refuge by hiding in yards, in basements, in hallways, and on roofs along the escape route.

The initial alarms are usually concluded with a statement of the authority for the alarm. At the local level, the name of the investigator and his or her assignment are listed; at other levels, the name of the issuing police department is cited.

All broadcast alarms are distributed locally, but their coverage is expanded as the interval from the time of the crime indicates the possible enlargement of areas of flight. An **all points bulletin (APB)** is justified when adequate descriptive information is available. The geographic coverage of an APB depends on the locale and may extend to neighboring states.

As facts become available to investigators during the search, adding information to what was originally broadcast becomes urgent. This added information may simply be a notice that the vehicle, when located, should be protected but not processed until the evidence technicians can visit the scene and search the vehicle for fingerprints and other evidence. Additional facts about the identity of a vehicle, such as the full license plate number and the name and description of the registered owner, may be secured from the Department of Motor Vehicles. Additional knowledge about the suspect may be no more than a fragment of information about appearance, or it may be a full name and description of the perpetrator when a prompt and specific identification has been made. The objective of broadcasting facts as soon as they are available is to provide searching police with enough identification to pick out a fleeing person or vehicle with some certainty that the person or vehicle being stopped is the subject of the alarm.

RECORDS AS SOURCES OF INFORMATION

Agencies that may provide an investigator with information useful in locating a fugitive range from criminal justice agencies that might have processed the suspect at some previous time to the vast data banks of agencies providing credit or telephone service. Investigators develop a knowledge of where to look for useful information. It may be found among records systems common to all localities, but it may also be in the records native to a specific locality. For instance, in Reno, Nevada, county clerk records contain information on every divorce granted in this mecca of unhappy spouses, and these records are dated and cross-referenced with the names of wives, children, parents, and witnesses. Likewise, public records in the Miami-to-Hollywood section of Florida have been a source of information about holidaying husbands and their girlfriends when they were arrested on a minor charge. A local record system can be found in every section of the United States. Such records contain unique information and are generally known only to investigators who have stumbled upon them or have been advised of their existence by friends or associates.

Investigators should develop their own ready-reference file on sources of information. When working on an investigation, the assigned investigator usually has a general idea about what he or she is looking for. A ready-reference file will aid in locating such information, indicate the form in which it may be found, and describe how to gain access to it.

A suggested form for this kind of file includes type of information, source, and name of and other identification data on a contact (e.g., telephone number).* Among the categories of sources of information are the following four: [1]

1. *City and County.*   Vital statistics; tax, welfare, court, school, juror, and voting records; the prosecutor and the public defender; and so forth
2. *State.*   Tax and corporate records; court, alcoholic beverage, and consumer affairs data; motor vehicle license and registration files; and so forth
3. *Federal.*   FBI and other federal law enforcement agencies (Secret Service, U.S. Treasury, U.S. Postal Service, courts, U.S. Attorney, Immigration and Naturalization Services, Securities and Exchange Commission, Social Security, military, etc.)
4. *Private.*   Moving companies, the telephone company (public directory, and directories on file at company office), other public utilities, credit reporting agencies, banks and finance companies, the Better Business Bureau, chambers of commerce, business (trade) directories, industry and trade associations, professional associations, and so forth

---

*These contacts are invaluable when a speedy response to queries is necessary, despite the reciprocity inherent in these calls. Some networks include graduates of the Federal Bureau of Investigation (FBI) Academy, former members of the FBI and the New York Police Department, and alumni of college and university criminal justice degree programs.

WANTED NOTICES

A **wanted notice** is a printed version of a broadcast alarm that follows a short time later. It provides probable cause for a stop-and-arrest. Thus, it should provide full information about the fugitive and about areas in which he or she is likely to be found. Copies of the notice are sent to police in neighboring areas and mailed to police in areas that the fugitive is likely to visit. These cities are usually large and in adjacent states and resort centers. The basic content of a wanted notice is a photograph or sketch of the fugitive, fingerprints, and an extensive personal description (Figure 9–1).

The standard mug shot taken at the time of a previous arrest is made part of the wanted notice. When this photo is not available, any close-up photograph from public records or from the suspect's associates may be substituted. Full-length shots of the suspect alone or with a group of associates can be used to supplement the standard front and profile photographs. Ideally, color photography and printing should be used in a wanted notice because they offer a lifelike image of the wanted person.

The fingerprint classification of a fugitive in the wanted notice is a major point of identification. Often, these notices contain a facsimile of a suspect's fingerprints, and a comparison can be made by the local agency making the arrest. In recent years, fingerprinting persons not charged with a crime has increased, and these records are available to police agencies preparing wanted notices. Classification and comparison of fingerprints prevents apprehension of the wrong person. Any other type of identification always includes the possibility of error. For this reason, investigators should search diligently for a fingerprint record for the wanted notice.

Observable and distinctive characteristics are used to describe a person. Identifying physical characteristics are necessary to locate the fugitive and to offer some positive identification for an arrest. The standard base of details for describing wanted persons is race, sex, age, height, weight, color of eyes, and hair color. Racial appearance or national origin is an identifying characteristic. Many police units use a standard listing and suggest that the most descriptive designation applicable to the fugitive be used. The usual list is as follows: White, African American, Mexican, Indian, Chinese, Japanese, and Other.

Observable physical characteristics found useful by police in tracing fugitives have been codified in a "relevant matter" listing of key items in a personal description. The following twelve items of identity are believed to be important:

1. *Face*—shape
2. *Hair*—color, type, and cut
3. *Eyes*—color, type, and defects
4. *Nose*—shape and size
5. *Mouth*—shape, size, and unusual characteristics
6. *Chin*—shape, size, and if dimpled

ARMED ROBBERY SUSPECT

Date: **2/23/2005**

Case # **00-0070**

Height: **5 Feet 9 inches**

Weight: **160**

Age: **20**

Sex: **M**

Race: **White**

OTHER INFORMATION BELOW

On Monday, 2-14-05, approximately 11 P.M., a university professor was robbed on the pathway between Green and Gray Halls at Valley University. The suspects assaulted the victim with a stun gun and departed with his wallet. The suspects are described as followed:

1. White male, early 20s, 5'9" to 5'10", 160 to 180 lb., sparse, straggly beard. He was wearing a dark blue sweatshirt with some type of writing on it. (A composite of the suspect is shown above.)

2. White male, early 20s, no further description.

3. Hispanic female, early 20s, 5'0" to 5'2", 100 to 105 lb., described as "petite".

The University Police at Valley University are asking the public's help in identifying the suspects.

University Police Department, Valley University
(555) 555-5555

TRAK (136:1.6.48) This flyer produced on a TRAK system. For more information about TRAK see www.trak.org

FIGURE 9–1   Typical wanted notice.

7. *Ears*—type, size, and defects
8. *Eyebrows and beard*—appearance
9. *Scars and marks*—location and type
10. *Amputations and physical deformities*
11. *Speech*—accent or defect
12. *Peculiarities*—a limp or a distinctive way of walking

When these relevant characteristics are used, a person may be described as round faced with long, red, wavy hair; blue, bulging, crossed eyes with hooded lids; a broken nose; a wide mouth with full lips; a receding chin; flaring ears; bushy eyebrows meeting in the center; long sideburns, a mustache, and a light beard; a forehead scar about 1 inch long over the right eye; and needle marks on the left arm. The person may also be described as walking with a pronounced limp.

A fugitive's occupation, associates, friends, relatives, habits, and hobbies are often significant factors in a police search for a suspect. A person's occupation or profession is often a form of habituation. Known criminal associates are likely to offer promising leads, and data on relatives and friends may suggest promising areas of inquiry. Habits and hobbies are related to places frequented or areas in which the fugitive is likely to be found. Amusement and resort areas may offer promise in one instance; theatrical and cabaret districts may be indicated in the habits of another person. This field is wide open to innovative practices by both the investigator preparing the wanted notice and police seeking the fugitive.

A final segment of the description of a fugitive concerns whether he or she may resist arrest. All investigators seeking the apprehension of a fugitive have a duty to specify in every wanted notice whether the fugitive is armed, whether a weapon has been used in the crime, and whether the fugitive has used weapons on previous occasions to avoid capture or to escape from custody. The cliché "armed and dangerous" may appear to be routine, but the unnecessary injury and death of arresting officers is not routine and can be avoided by adequate notice. Officers staffing roadblocks and stopping suspicious cars on the highway late at night are usually prepared for any aggressive action by the occupants of a vehicle. However, on many other occasions, officers in pursuit of a fugitive are not always as alert to possible aggression unless they are warned in advance.

Armed with the knowledge that a person is wanted, all police seek fugitives. Apprehending fugitives is part of the general police role. Traffic officers making so-called routine stops have apprehended fugitives. Police on patrol, when responding to a call for help or handling a minor crime investigation, encounter fugitives and take them into custody. Investigators allow some time out of their daily routine for inquiries about wanted persons.

Investigators, however, must exercise care in questioning a person about a fugitive. They may encounter a person who knows the suspect's whereabouts but who is more friendly with the fugitive than with the police. The person may warn the suspect of the inquiries, which may result in the fugitive's flight and a lost opportunity for his or her capture.

Traditionally, a wanted notice has always been aimed solely at locating and apprehending the fugitive. It now has an additional purpose: to discover, to collect, and to preserve evidence at the time of the arrest. The four purposes of a modern wanted notice for a fugitive from criminal justice are as follows:

1. To provide sufficient identifying characteristics (constituting reasonable grounds for belief) to allow other law enforcement agents to provisionally identify the fugitive upon initial contact and to make positive identification when the suspect is taken into custody
2. To alert other law enforcement officers to the fugitive's nature and character, his or her criminal history, and whether he or she is armed and dangerous
3. To suggest activities and areas in which a search or surveillance may locate the fugitive
4. To delineate the crime in sufficient detail to alert arresting officers to potential legally significant evidence available at the time of arrest

THE ARREST

In the past, investigators believed that legally significant evidence could be developed after an arrest had been made. Although at the time of the arrest, meaningful evidence can still be collected, investigators now assemble evidence beyond the strong suspicion or probable-cause level basic to any lawful arrest *before* they attempt to arrest the major suspect in a case.

The time of arrest provides an excellent opportunity to find further evidence that will connect the prisoner with the crime, the crime scene, the victim, or other crimes and other criminals. It is also an excellent point in the investigation to guard against faulty identification of an arrestee.

All arresting officers should be alert to the nature and type of evidence that might normally be encountered at the time of arrest. While collecting evidence at this time, the finding officer must exercise the same care he or she would use if the evidence had been discovered in a crime scene search. The officer finding evidence should make an appropriate entry in his or her field notes and in the arrest records, mark the evidence for identification, and protect its integrity.

The search incidental to an arrest may not only recover the proceeds of a theft, but also produce transfer evidence that will link the suspect to the crime, the scene, or the victim. The search should be confined to the person of the arrested individual and to the vicinity of the arrest.[2] A complete body search is conducted at the time of booking. When a serious crime has been committed, the suspect's clothes are often seized for processing by a vacuum cleaner in an attempt to collect dust and debris for analysis, and the clothes are searched for blood and other stains that may connect the defendant with the crime scene or the victim.

The search of a person should not verge on conduct that shocks the conscience, as in the case of *Rochin v. California*, in which an offender's stomach was pumped to recover two heroin capsules.[3] Instead, the search should fulfill only the arresting officer's obligation to remove any material that might aid the arrested person in escaping and to prevent the destruction of evidence or the failure to collect evidence.

The doctrine of **immediate control** indicates the area in which a search is justified. If the arrest is made on the street when the suspect is walking, his or her person and the immediate public area may be searched. If the arrest takes place in a parked or moving vehicle, the vehicle may be searched. If the arresting officer witnessed the suspect jettisoning an article just before the arrest, the officer should search for the article. If the arrest is made inside a premises, the search is usually restricted to the area over which the arrested person has control. (See Appendix A, Case Briefs, *Chimel v. California*.)

The police department issuing the wanted notice is notified of an arrest, cancels the notice by issuing a Teletype announcement of the arrest, and makes the necessary arrangements to pick up the prisoner. If the locale of the arrest is outside the state in which the crime was committed, extradition proceedings, unless formally waived by the fugitive, are required.

When a perpetrator is arrested locally, the search incidental to the arrest may involve the prisoner's home if it is the place of arrest. Burglars and thieves in possession of recently stolen property often conceal it in their homes. Experienced detectives know that "hitting" the residence of a suspect in burglary and theft cases holds a great deal of promise. Current protocol is to seek a search warrant to look for evidence in any building during the postarrest period unless the search is incidental to the arrest. The investigator, citing the fact that an arrest has been made, should be able to establish probable cause for a search of a specific location for particular items of evidence. The investigator can arrange for a surveillance of the premises to be searched, which will secure it from disturbance while the warrant is being obtained. The search warrant prevents tainting of evidence. Conducting a search pursuant to a warrant and fully reporting the results to the court is simple.

An investigator may ask the arrested person to consent to a search of an office or a residence. If another person has dual or joint control of such premises, consent should also be requested of that individual. Landlords and managers of multiple housing or office structures can consent to a search of only the so-called public portions of such buildings and cannot consent to the search of a room, an apartment, or an office under the sole control of a tenant. Since the *Miranda* decision, the compelling atmosphere of police custody has been delineated as inherently in conflict with the intelligent waiver of any constitutional right. Therefore, the waiver should be formal, should state that consenting to the waiver is a voluntary act, and should be signed by the prisoner and by a witness. Ideally, the police should discuss with the prisoner the nature of the evidence and where on the premises it will be found. A postarrest consent to search is not illogical conduct if the arrestee is cooperating with police, and it should be requested.

Pedigree

At the time of arrest, the booking process either begins the prisoner's criminal history file or adds to it. The police apprehension process concentrates on identifying a logical suspect as the perpetrator and, after sufficient information is ascertained about the suspect's appearance for a pursuit, locating and arresting him or her. In these pursuits, the searching police are advised of the suspect's name and whereabouts when they are available. Sometimes, however, pursuits for wanted persons are based on little more than an eyewitness description and a sketch. Therefore, when an arrest is made, the arrestee must be positively identified.

The arrest record should reflect as much information about an arrestee as possible. Such basic information should include the following ten elements:

1. Name (including alias, a.k.a., and nickname)
2. Sex, race, age
3. Residence, employment
4. Social condition, next of kin
5. Physical description
    a. Height and weight
    b. Hair color and style
    c. Eye color and any defects
    d. Ears, nose, lips, chin, teeth
    e. Complexion and general build
    f. Facial hair or lack thereof
    g. Tattoo marks, amputations or physical deformities, visible scars, moles, birthmarks, needle tracks
6. Speech—accent or defect
7. Peculiarities—a limp or a distinctive way of walking
8. Habits (known to . . . , frequents . . . , hobby is . . .)
9. Type of crime, area of geographic operations
10. Associates (neighborhood, crime partners, other)

Fingerprints and photographs should be taken of every person arrested unless local laws forbid doing so with minors. Sufficient copies of fingerprints should be made for circulation to other records systems, and both front and profile photographs should be taken. The basic records systems for a fingerprint search are the files of the arresting agency, the state criminal justice files, and the huge records system of the FBI. The search reveals whether the prisoner's fingerprints are on file. The fingerprints taken at the time of this arrest are matched against the base files of these agencies, a report of the search is made to the police agency forwarding the prisoner's fingerprints, and the fact of this arrest is filed in all these records.

The report of the records search may be a simple "No record." However, it must bear a date and a person's name, and it is evidence that a records search in that agency, based on a set of the arrestee's fingerprints, was made and failed to disclose any record. In contrast, the report may be several pages long and list arrests and imprisonments in various sections of the United States. (This report is the **rap sheet** of a person with a criminal record. Prior arrests and other contacts with police and criminal justice agencies were once referred to as *raps*, a name synonymous with *criminal record* or *criminal history*. The term *bum rap*, signifying a false charge of crime, is common in criminals' lingo.)

While the agencies are searching their fingerprint files, they are also reviewing the current criminal justice status of the arrested person. When warranted, the arresting agency is notified if the arrestee is wanted by police in other jurisdictions as a suspect in a crime, as a fugitive from justice, or as an escapee from a correctional institution or a mental health facility; is under a probation or parole officer's supervision; or is out on bail pending trial for a previous arrest and charge of crime.

The criminal histories of persons are serially numbered in local agency records, the state records system, and FBI records. In effect, the arrestee is given a lifetime identification (ID) number. In some areas, a letter prefix reveals the grade of the crime: serious—usually a felony but sometimes a "high" misdemeanor; or minor—usually a misdemeanor but sometimes not including minor offenses such as traffic violations. In New York City, the prefix *B* is for serious crimes, and *E* for lesser crimes. In the state records systems, the number usually has a simple prefix of letters representing the name of the agency. In California, it is *CII*, for the California Bureau of Identification and Investigation. At the federal level, it is *FBI*.

If an arrestee has never been arrested within the jurisdiction of the local police agency in which he or she is being booked, a local number will be assigned. If previously arrested locally, the arrestee is booked under the previously assigned ID number.

The collection of data about the prisoner at the time of the arrest does not relate primarily to the offense but rather to the offender's pedigree. **Pedigree** is an odd word; yet the questions asked and the information sought at the time of booking an arrestee provide just that—complete information about a person. When an arrested person is in contact with law enforcement agencies as an arrestee for the first time, the facts of the pedigree may be minimal. As a criminal prosecution moves from arrest to trial to sentencing, a great deal of information is collected and filed under the arrestee's ID number. It is then more than a personal description; it is a person delineated against the background of the crime charged and sometimes a record of behavior when in prison and on parole. When another arrest occurs, similar data are collected and integrated with the base file. This compilation is probably the reason the term *pedigree* has persisted as a reference to a person's criminal history. For an investigator, the compilation of a first offender's data sheet is a routine that should be performed with full recognition that such data may be used as a future investigative aid by other investigators.

CASE PREPARATION

Case preparation is organization. It is the orderly array of information collected during an investigation—all the reports, documents, and exhibits in a case. It is also the preparation of a synopsis of the individual material in the case, an abstract written without personal conclusions, opinions, or "facts." A so-called final report is undesirable. The collected reports and other data are the final report—the package forwarded to the prosecutor with no intrusion by the investigator. The synopsis is no more than a summary of the package contents. In the evaluation of a case in this pretrial period, investigators must discriminate between evidential material and personal conclusions and opinions, between potential evidence and "facts." In a criminal action, fact leads to truth, and courts admit relevant evidence at trial to determine fact.

Case preparation is the roundup time of an investigation. The investigator collates the work of the entire investigation, confers with associates, prepares the case folder and its synopsis, forwards the case to the prosecutor for preparation of the formal accusatory pleading and the legal development of the case before trial, and marks the case closed by arrest.

The Defendant's Identity

Before a solid case can be made, the investigator must establish that the defendant is the person accused of the crime. Such identification leads to an array of witnesses and evidence. Identification usually results from some combination of testimony and other evidence. This evidence structure is sometimes supported by a pretrial statement made by the accused person and is oriented toward proving the identity of the individual as the person responsible for the crime alleged in the **accusatory pleading**—the indictment or information.

Evidence likely to have legal significance in establishing the identity of the person or persons responsible for a crime can be summed up as six possibilities:

1. A witness (or witnesses) who saw the offender commit the crime or some part of it
2. A witness (or witnesses) who saw the offender at the crime scene at or near the time of the crime
3. A witness (or witnesses) who observed the offender in the neighborhood of the crime at or near the time of occurrence
4. Physical evidence discovered in the crime scene search that indicates the offender was at the crime scene or in contact with the victim

5. Physical evidence found on the offender or among his or her effects at the time of arrest, or secured by other lawful means, that indicates the offender had been at the crime scene or in contact with the victim
6. Connect-ups:
   a. The offender's possessing the vehicle that witnesses will testify was used in the crime
   b. The offender's having the proceeds of the crime (in theft and burglary cases)
   c. The offender's having an unexplained injury (in assaults and homicides)
   d. The offender's possession of the weapon used in the crime
   e. The offender's having been interviewed by an officer at or near the crime scene at or around the time of the crime (the officer reported it in the regular course of business and is available to testify)

This list appears to be a formidable array of witnesses and evidence, but it must be evaluated against the background of the problem areas in proving the identity of a person accused of crime. These problem areas are as follows:

- Variances in the original descriptions and the actual description of the accused person
- Other errors in evidence or variances in witnesses' statements
- A well-supported **alibi**—claim of being elsewhere at the time of the crime
- A widespread distrust of eyewitness identification because of the many publicized mistakes in such identifications

The Defendant and the Corpus Delicti

The accusatory pleading must show that at a specified time and date, in a specific place, the person named committed an act or an omission in violation of a particular law, specified by both name and section number and in force at the time of the act or omission. Therefore, the first major area of case evaluation is the affirmative evidence of a real-life *corpus delicti*—the classic "body of the crime" plus the identity of the person charged with it:

- The time and date of the crime, and the territorial jurisdiction in which it happened (the **venue**)
- The name by which the accused person has been identified
- The essential elements of the crime charged
- Specification of the criminal agency used to accomplish the crime and of the victim's name.

This process of affirming the corpus delicti is a combining of "what happened" and "who did it" with the knowledge that the happening as reported violates a specific law and that the offender is legally responsible for answering for this violation.

Negative Evidence

The second major area of case preparation concerns negative evidence and is oriented to countering defenses to the crime charged. The three standard defenses are as follows:

1. The defendant did not commit the crime. The defense allegation is that the accused person is the victim of mistaken identification, faulty police work, or pure coincidence and was somewhere else at the time.
2. The defendant did commit the crime, but
    a. It was excusable (usually a claim of self-defense or provocation).
    b. It was an accident.
    c. It was the result of legal insanity.
    d. Mental factors diminished the defendant's responsibility for the act.
3. No crime was committed.
    a. The sufficiency of the corpus delicti is attacked.
    b. The sufficiency of the evidence is attacked.
    c. One or more of the essential elements of the crime charged (intent, proximate cause, etc.) is attacked.

If any essential element of the crime charged is not proved beyond a reasonable doubt, the defendant is entitled to an acquittal.

Lawful Procedures

The third major area of case preparation concerns procedural foundations used to secure evidence. Affirmative proof is required to dispel any allegations of unlawful activity by police that may be presented to a court. The investigator must point out the procedural lawfulness. In most cases, such evidence will show one or more of the following:

- Nothing suggestive or otherwise improper in the procedure for locating and interviewing witnesses
- The reasonableness of the search and the integrity of collecting and preserving evidence
- A reasonable surveillance that meets the requirements of due process
- The voluntariness of a confession or an admission, together with the other due process requirements

Arrangement of Evidence

Evidence must be tabulated in some orderly array. A suggested outline includes the name and a summary of the background of each witness, a synopsis of the story told, and a reference to the names of one or more witnesses who can give corroborating or supporting testimony. The array is usually as follows, in order of importance: the defendant's identity, relationship to the corpus delicti of the crime, essential elements of the crime charged, and negative evidence likely to block common defenses.

Another means of tabulating testimonial evidence is to prepare a timetable of the crime. The timetable is a chronological exposition of the movements of all persons involved in the crime and a brief description of the evidence that pinpoints the time and the relationships. It can be broken into any convenient subdivisions.

Tabulation of evidence in some relevant arrangement helps an investigator avoid disorder in an investigation, facilitates review by others, and permits an overview of the case not possible in any other fashion. This "taking in of the case at a glance" was a principal objective of Hans Gross's "table" of a crime, which allowed the investigator to determine whether work on the case was complete or where additional work was necessary.[4]

The "Package," or Case Folder

Police reports and other documents are usually placed in chronological order. The offense or crime report is on top, and the various supplementary or progress reports follow in sequence. Photographic exhibits in the form of color or black-and-white prints or transparencies are included in the folder. Physical evidence, if any, may be delivered to the prosecutor or held until requested. The content of the various reports should be sufficient to indicate the physical evidence and its nature.

A brief synopsis should accompany each case folder. In preparing a synopsis, an investigator must keep in mind that it is an abstract or a digest of the material in the case folder, nothing more and nothing less. It must be brief. It should deal only with the pertinent facts in the complete case folder being forwarded to the prosecutor. Every point covered in the synopsis must be supported by a police report or another document in the case folder being forwarded, and the elements of the synopsis should be organized in the same order as the police reports and documents in the case folder. A quick reading of the synopsis and scanning of the case folder should inform the prosecutor of the crime committed; the time, date, and place of its happening; and the evidence collected.

THE DECISION TO CHARGE

In the prosecutor's office, the case is reviewed and assigned to a staff member for further investigation and preparation for trial, if warranted. This review of the case by a public official trained in law is a learned review of the investigator's work. Conferences with the investigator and witnesses are usually scheduled by this legal expert, and the physical evidence and reports of its analysis are examined. If the case is a homicide, the staff of the coroner or medical examiner and their reports may be involved in these sessions. The assigned prosecutor makes his or her decision and moves through the necessary stages for trial or recommends that no action be taken at the time and details reasons for not taking action. The decision to charge is not a function or responsibility of the investigator.[5]

Cases are not moved for trial or rejected as possible trial material solely on the basis of the investigator's, work and the legal significance of the collected evidence. Tactical factors and the needs of law enforcement may indicate that a trial is not advisable. Prosecutors may waive prosecution in exchange for information or testimony against a more hardened criminal; the conservation of resources may suggest a negotiated plea of guilty to a lesser charge. Or, for example, when first offenders and persons who are emotionally disturbed are processed, application of the sanctions of the criminal justice system may not appear justified by the circumstances of the case.[6]

The prosecutor's staff may review the case preparation before the arrest. An investigator habituated to the traditional separation of the roles of investigator and prosecutor may be reluctant to ask the prosecutor to step into an ongoing investigation. However, when the measure of proof is less than the amount necessary to move the case to the prosecutor, the natural tendency is to seek help. The prosecutor may accept a difficult investigation as just that—incomplete and insufficient. In such instances, and in a case with promise, the prosecutor has an ideal investigative device in the local grand jury, with its powers of subpoena and the right to administer oaths and take sworn testimony. This route may be taken for promising cases previously marked by police with the notation "No further results possible."

CLOSURE OF AN INVESTIGATION

An investigation is successful when the crime under investigation is solved promptly and the case closed. Measurable results occur when the case is closed by the perpetrator's arrest. Cases cleared by arrest are a statistical measure of the efficiency of the criminal investigation function of any police unit. However, case clearance may also be a statistical measure of efficiency when an investigation is terminated without an arrest. A review of reasons given by police executives for closing investigations in this manner shows the following authorized case clearances in lieu of an arrest:[7]

- The investigation discloses that the case is unfounded; no crime occurred or was attempted. (However, the return of stolen property, restitution, or refusal by the victim to prosecute does not justify this classification.)
- The offender dies.
- The case is found to be a murder-suicide; one person kills another person and then commits suicide.
- The perpetrator confesses on his or her deathbed.
- The arrest and charge of an identified offender is blocked by an uncooperative victim.
- A confession is made by an offender already in custody for another crime.

- The person identified as the perpetrator is located in another jurisdiction and an unsuccessful attempt is made to gain custody, or the prosecutor does not believe the expense of an attempt to gain custody is justified.
- The person identified as the perpetrator is prosecuted, upon the decision of the assigned prosecutor, for a less serious charge than that cited at the time of arrest.

If the investigator's case preparation reveals that the perpetrator's identity has been definitely established, the perpetrator has been located, and sufficient information and evidence exist to support an arrest and a charge of crime, no valid reason exists *not* to close the case by arrest if it is not covered by any of the foregoing exceptional clearances. Identification of the perpetrator solves the case and justifies such action.

An investigator should recommend, on a supplementary report, the termination of a case when no further results can be secured. In addition, a follow-up officer should have the authority to file cases in an inactive, or "hold," file when no further results can be obtained despite due diligence.

Therefore, the criminal investigation function can be terminated in the following three instances:

1. Results have been obtained in full; the case is cleared by arrest or exceptional clearance.
2. Results have been obtained in part, and no further results can be obtained.
3. No results can be obtained.

Recognition that a bona fide conclusion to a case can be achieved without an arrest is important to the new frontiers of investigation. Such action strips the deadwood from an investigator's workload, leads to new definitions of responsibility and accountability in the criminal investigation function, and strengthens the concept that arrests are not the primary objective of criminal investigation.

In pursuing the truth—the main objective of an investigation—investigators must view all aspects of a case, particularly information pointing to the innocence of the accused person. Presenting a prima facie case and hoping and trusting it will withstand the contradiction of a defense attack is no longer sufficient. The case must be prepared so that legally significant evidence presented in court will withstand attack by the defense and establish guilt beyond a reasonable doubt.

An investigation is a search for truth in which all possible information in a post-factum inquiry is searched for, collected, and analyzed. The investigative process involves examining all the data, both for and against the person accused of crime. Therefore, viewing a case throughout an investigation from the viewpoint of the defense is always appropriate, and particularly appropriate during preparation of the case for presentation to the prosecutor. Along with using scrupulous accuracy in reporting information, viewing the defense side of a case is the ultimate technique for conducting investigations that exonerate the innocent and discover and identify the guilty.

CHAPTER REVIEW

Double Murder—Ms. Wylie and Ms. Hoffert

The Wylie–Hoffert case involved a double murder and a lengthy investigation in which George Whitmore, Jr., was arrested and charged with the crime. For clarity, the case is presented in a chronological format, beginning with the day of the crime.

Wednesday, August 28

The Day of the Crime

Janice Wylie, 21, and Emily Hoffert, 23, were found bound and stabbed to death in Apartment 3-C at 57 East 88th Street, New York City. Their bodies were found by Max Wylie, father of Miss Wylie, and by Patricia Tolles, a roommate who shared the murder scene apartment with the two victims.

Miss Tolles, who had last seen the victims when she left for work at 9:30 that morning, returned from work at 6:40 p.m. and found the apartment in disarray. Shocked and upset, she did not go through the apartment, although she did glance into the bathroom. She called Max Wylie from the telephone in the foyer of the apartment, and he came directly over from his home a few blocks away. They examined the apartment and found the bodies of the two victims in a bedroom—between a wall and a bed. Miss Wylie was nude; Miss Hoffert was fully clothed. Two knives were found near the bodies, and there was another knife on the basin in the bathroom, which was opposite the crime scene bedroom. The wrists and ankles of both victims were tied, and their bodies were bound together at the wrists and waists. Cloth strips, torn or cut from a bedsheet and a bedspread, were used for this restraint (Figure 9–2). There was no blood in any room other than the bedroom in which the victims were found. The drawers of dressers and cabinets were open, and their contents were dumped on the floor, on beds, and on dresser tops. Miss Tolles said that nothing was missing, and that neither the victims nor she herself possessed any valuable jewelry or large sums of cash. Preliminary police investigation revealed no sign of forced entry, and no witness who had seen or heard anything suspicious was found. Chief Medical Examiner, Dr. Michael Halpern, said the bodies of the victims had been mutilated viciously, but there was no apparent evidence of sexual assault.

Thursday, August 29

1 Day After the Crime

A search of the apartment by police identification technicians revealed numerous fingerprints. All such traces were collected and then processed by the police. The two knives found in the crime scene bedroom had broken blades, but the broken-off portions of the blades were recovered from the floor nearby. The knife found in the bathroom was intact and identified as a standard pointed steak knife. The origin of the knives was apparently the kitchen of the apartment.

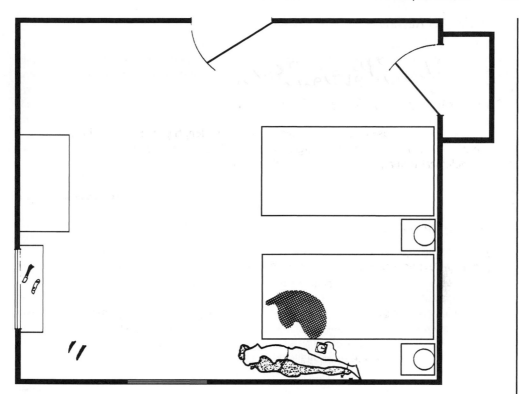

FIGURE 9–2   Janice Wylie and Emily Hoffert were found dead, tied in one of the bedrooms of their two-bedroom apartment.
From Weston, Paul B., CRIMINAL JUSTICE AND LAW ENFORCEMENT: CASES, © 1972, p. 103. Reprinted by permission of Prentice Hall.

Continued questioning of neighbors and building employees failed to locate anyone who had seen or heard anything suspicious or directly related to the crime apartment. One neighbor reported meeting a stranger in the elevator, whom he described as of medium build and "baby faced."

Chief Medical Examiner Halpern said, in a preliminary autopsy report, that the cause of death for both victims was multiple stab wounds in the neck, chest, and abdomen, and that Miss Hoffert had head wounds in which glass was found, which indicated blows by a weapon such as a soft drink bottle. An electric night table clock was found near the bodies. Its plug was out of the wall and on the floor a few feet from a wall outlet, and a good portion of its electric cord was partially under the torso of victim Wylie. The time on the stopped clock was 10:35 a.m.

Max Wylie stated that his daughter Janice had received a threatening phone call on or about August 18, and that she was terrified by it. The caller left a name, Joe Hunter, and a telephone number, Wylie added, but when his daughter called the number, a woman who identified herself as the subscriber for that telephone number said she knew of no man named Hunter or any similar name.

Friday, August 30

2 Days After the Crime

Newsweek, where Miss Wylie had worked, offered a $10,000 reward for information leading to the arrest and conviction of the murderer or murderers. Continuing investigation revealed that Miss Hoffert had left the apartment shortly after her roommate, Patricia Tolles, left for work at 9:30 a.m. The victim then drove north to Riverdale to return a borrowed car and pick up her own automobile. She was placed in the Riverdale area up until 11 a.m., through contacts with friends and the garage proprietor. The time span of the crime could now be set between 9:30 a.m. and 6:40 p.m. for victim Wylie and 11:30 a.m. to 6:40 p.m. for victim Hoffert. Police established a public information telephone number and asked for public cooperation in their search for both witnesses and the person or persons responsible for the killings.

Friday, September 6

9 Days After the Crime

No substantial clues were revealed by the continuing investigation, despite a far-reaching search for witnesses, and numerous inquiries among relatives, friends, and associates of the victims. No motive for the crime was discovered either. Burglary was not believed to be the actual motive, although an attempt was apparently made to create the illusion of a burglary. However, no cash was stolen, and several pieces of jewelry and a watch were left untouched. Over 100 detectives were assigned to the case by this time. The canvass for witnesses had been concluded without success. All known sex offenders and all known daytime burglars had been questioned by the police, and their activities on August 28 had been investigated—all to no avail.

Friday, September 13

16 Days After the Crime

The report of the fingerprint search and processing revealed that no fingerprints were present on the suspect murder weapons (three knives) and that a total of nine partial sets of fingerprints were found in the apartment. Seven of these sets corresponded with those of the victims, relatives, friends, or occupants of the apartment. The two remaining sets of partial fingerprints did not have sufficient characteristics for overt identification by any search of criminal justice files, but they were marked for possible use as suspects were developed through other information and evidence in the case.

September 27

33 Days After the Crime

In the continuing investigation of the Wylie–Hoffert murders, detectives had interviewed over 500 persons, but to date no identity of the murderer or murderers had been revealed, nor had any witness been found who observed anyone leaving the apartment or any suspicious person in the building during the time span of the crime. Investigators had been seeking someone who observed a blood-spattered person, or one carrying a bundle or bag. The police believed that the killer's clothing was splashed with blood during the crime, and he then would have had blood-stained clothing when he fled from the scene—unless he had changed clothes at the crime scene. In that case, he would have carried out his bloody garments in a bag or bundle.

Thursday, October 31

64 Days After the Crime

Continuing investigation exhausted all leads contained in telephone and memorandum books of the victims and in all other memoranda, such as cards and letters with names, telephone numbers, or other identification that were found in the apartment. Police had also investigated all names and other leads supplied by friends and relatives of the victims, including the "Joe Hunter" lead supplied by Max Wylie. They also followed leads gathered through the over 1,000 telephone calls received by the special public information number. To date, no description or other identification of the murderer or murderers, or of any suspicious person seen leaving the death scene apartment or its vicinity on the day of the crime, had been secured. The detail of detectives, now reduced to twenty-four, had reoriented the continuing investigation to investigate (a) all previous crimes in which knives were used, (b) all persons moving out of the neighborhood, and (c) persons who left state mental health institutions or prisons just before the crime or who had been admitted or committed since the crime.

Thursday, February 27

183 Days After the Crime

Detectives assigned to the continuing investigation had now interviewed, questioned, and investigated over 1,000 suspects. Most suspects had been fully exonerated. About 10 of these individuals required some verification of their activities on the day of the crime. To date, no one of these persons was classed as a major suspect, and no substantial clue to the identity of the murderer or murderers had been discovered.

Saturday, April 24

240 Days After the Crime

George Whitmore, Jr., age 19, was arrested for the Wylie–Hoffert killings. At about 6:00 a.m., Friday, April 23, a Brooklyn police officer who was searching an area in which an assault, a robbery, and an attempted rape had been committed a few hours earlier spotted a suspect and took him to the police station. The victim of the robbery and attempted rape, Mrs. Ella Borrero, was brought to the police station and identified the suspect, George Whitmore. He confessed to the crime. He was booked for the robbery and attempted rape of Mrs. Borrero. A search revealed no weapon and no drugs, but two photographs were found in his wallet. The suspect said they were "girlfriends." Further questioning led to Whitmore's confessing to the murder of Mrs. Minnie Edmonds, age 46. Mrs. Edmonds's body had been found in a backyard at 444 Blake Avenue, Brooklyn, on April 14—10 days earlier. Death had resulted from multiple stab and slash wounds from a knife or similar weapon.

Detective Edward Bulger, who was present at the questioning of Whitmore in the Edmonds case, had been assigned to the investigation of the Wylie–Hoffert murders in its early stages. He thought the two photographs found in Whitmore's wallet resembled the blonde, blue-eyed Wylie girl and her roommate-victim. Further questioning resulted in Whitmore's admitting to the murders of Misses Wylie and Hoffert. Whitmore's formal statement of guilt in the double murder was taken under the direction of Peter Koste, an assistant district attorney in the Manhattan district attorney's office.

Whitmore seemed to know details of the double homicide that had never been made public. In his statement, Whitmore gave the brand name of the broken soft drink bottle that had been found, and he stated that he broke the blades of two of the knives used in the attack by using his heel and the floor, as in breaking a stick of wood. Last, he admitted that he took the photograph of Miss Wylie from the dresser of the crime scene bedroom.

Whitmore was arraigned before Judge James J. Comerford in a Brooklyn court. An attorney, Jerome Leftow, was appointed to represent Whitmore when he stated that he was without legal counsel. After a brief out-of-court conference between Whitmore and his new attorney, both returned to court and Mr. Leftow told Judge Comerford that his client had made certain statements to the police but that they were made under duress and stress and that his client had now recanted and repudiated all the confessions he had made. Whitmore was remanded to jail without bail by Judge Comerford for a hearing on the next Thursday.

Tuesday, April 27

243 Days After the Crime

Jerome Leftow now claimed that his client, George Whitmore, Jr., had asked police to give him a lie detector test when he was arrested. Additional data released by police connecting Whitmore to the Wylie–Hoffert murders was the substance of an unofficial statement published in the *New York Journal-American*. This press story stated that Whitmore knew the location of a razor blade found on the floor of the crime scene bedroom, knew where its wrapper had been found in the bathroom, was able to describe a Noxzema jar left on the bloody floor, and told of blood spots that were found on the bedroom window shade.

Wednesday, May 6

253 Days After the Crime

Whitmore was indicted by a Manhattan grand jury in the knife slaying of Janice Wylie and Emily Hoffert. The jury presented a two-count murder indictment to Justice Charles Marks, who ordered Whitmore taken into custody and arraigned for pleading. Whitmore pleaded "not guilty" to the murder charge.

Friday, October 17

317 Days After the Crime

Psychiatrists at Bellevue Hospital found George Whitmore, Jr., sane and able to stand trial for the Wylie–Hoffert murders. The finding concluded the longest study of any one patient in the long history of Bellevue's Psychiatric Center. Whitmore had been committed to Bellevue the previous May by Justice Charles Marks, following Whitmore's arraignment and not guilty plea in the Wylie–Hoffert case.

Saturday, January 2

393 Days After the Crime

Manhattan's district attorney, Frank S. Hogan, refused comment on the 8-month delay in the trial of Whitmore for the Wylie–Hoffert killings. Police reporters pointed to two factors that might account for the delay: (a) the identity of the young blonde girl in the photograph found on Whitmore was in dispute, and (b) whether the photograph was really taken from the death scene apartment in 88th Street was also in dispute.

Note. A few weeks after detectives arrested a new suspect in this case, D. A. Frank Hogan quietly asked the Manhattan court to release Whitmore in "the interest of justice." Whitmore was released to the Brooklyn district attorney for trial in homicide cases in that jurisdiction.

Source: Weston, Paul B., CRIMINAL JUSTICE AND LAW ENFORCEMENT: CASES, © 1972, pp. 101–111. Reprinted by permission of Prentice Hall.

DISCUSSION QUESTIONS

1. What is the rationale for organizing a final review of an investigation around a theme of witnesses and exhibits of evidence?
2. What is the emerging concept inherent in an exhaustive search for witnesses? An intensive and scientific crime scene search for evidence? The objective and scientific laboratory services for processing physical evidence? Setting limits on suggestibility during interviews with witnesses and lineups for identification?
3. On the basis of available legally significant evidence likely to be admissible in court upon trial, is further action by the prosecutor against George Whitmore, Jr., for the Wylie–Hoffert killings justified?
4. Does the prosecutor's role in making the decision to prosecute an accused involve a preliminary evaluation of evidence on the issue of guilt or innocence?
5. What evidence collected by police, other than Whitmore's confession to the double murder, supports the police theory about this crime and the conclusion about Whitmore's guilt?
6. Present an argument in support of the validity and reliability of reviewing a case from the defense frame of reference—that is, from the point of view of the case for the accused person.

LIBRARY ASSIGNMENT

Prepare a list of at least five cases (court decisions) about the rights of defendants in custody awaiting trial.

WORKBOOK PROJECT

Summarize any one of the case studies in preceding chapters.

RELATED WEB SITES

Want to know if federal law enforcement is looking for someone you might know? Check out the U.S. Department of Justice most wanted. This Web site includes persons wanted by the FBI, the Drug Enforcement

Administration (DEA), the Bureau of Alcohol, Tobacco, Firearms and Explosives (ATF), and the U.S. Marshals Service: *www.usdoj.gov/09fugitives*.

The U.S. Marshals Service has a variety of law enforcement responsibilities, one of which is fugitive investigations. To learn more about the Marshals Service as a career choice, see the Web site at *www.usmarshals.gov*.

NOTES

1. HERBERT EDELHERTZ et al., "Appendix B: Sample Guide to Sources of Information," in *The Investigation of White-Collar Crime: A Manual for Law Enforcement Agencies* (Washington, DC: U.S. Department of Justice, Law Enforcement Assistance Administration, 1977), 267–75. For in-depth coverage of the sources of information, see Harry J. Murphy, *Where's What: Sources of Information for Federal Investigators* (Washington, DC: Brookings Institution, 1975).

2. *Agnello v. United States*, 296 U.S. 20 (1925).

3. *Rochin v. California*, 342 U.S. 165 (1952).

4. HANS G. A. GROSS, *Criminal Investigation: A Practical Handbook for Magistrates, Police officers, and Lawyers*, trans. John Adam and J. Collyer Adam (Madras, India: Higginbotham, 1906), 34–35.

5. WAYNE R. LAFAVE, *Arrest: The Decision to Take a Suspect into Custody* (Boston: Little, Brown, 1965), S-6, 320–24.

6. INSTITUTE OF DEFENSE ANALYSES, *Task Force Report: The Courts*, a report to the President's Commission on Law Enforcement and Administration of Justice (Washington, DC: Government Printing Office, 1967), 5–7.

7. INTERNATIONAL ASSOCIATION OF CHIEFS OF POLICE, *Case No. S: Criminal Investigation* (Washington, DC: International Association of Chiefs of Police, 1966), 18.

PART II INVESTIGATION OF MAJOR CRIMES

10

Physical Assaults

Physical assaults include attacks on the person that produce death or serious bodily injury. These assaults include attacks by others, self-inflicted injury, and physical abuse of children. Stalking may also result in physical assaults on victims.

HOMICIDE

Criminal homicides, from murder to manslaughter, and common and aggravated assault are major crimes against the person. First, the crime scene and, second, the circumstances of the attack are the focus of these investigations.

Criminal homicide is usually divided by statute into murder in the first degree, murder in the second degree, and manslaughter. **Murder in the first degree** is well defined by statute, but **second-degree murder** is frequently defined as any murder that is not first-degree murder, and **manslaughter** may be defined as any criminal homicide that cannot be legally classified as murder.

The corpus delicti of all criminal homicide comprises three elements:

1. An evidentiary showing of the death of a human being
2. An evidentiary showing of a criminal agency
3. An evidentiary showing that the criminal agency was the proximate cause of the death

The death must be of a human being and must occur within a certain period after the act causing the injury. The time may vary in different jurisdictions from 1 to 3 years. The **criminal agency** is the means of death: another person's unlawful act or omission that caused the death.

"Suspicious Death" Investigation

Police investigators conduct a **suspicious death** investigation in all cases in which the circumstances of the death indicate violence or **foul play**—that is, some criminal agency; when death occurs in a place other than the deceased's residence; or when the deceased was not under a physician's care at the time of death. From the preliminary investigation of a suspicious death, the facts may result in either a decision to close the case because death resulted from natural or accidental causes or was a suicide, or a decision to continue the investigation because the facts disclosed indicate a criminal—an unjustified or unexcused—homicide.

The suspicious death concept is more comprehensive than "foul play is suspected" (the circumstances of a death strongly suggest murder). It is a classification of certain unexplained deaths so that they will be investigated until either the circumstances indicate that death was due to natural, accidental, or self-inflicted causes, or the criminal agency is determined and the **criminal agent** (person) identified.

The autopsy is a major method of detecting murder. This postmortem examination of the victim in a suspicious death case is performed by a competent physician, usually a surgeon specializing in this field. Autopsy surgeons are the professionals who determine the cause of death. If the autopsy surgeon reports that the nature of death is natural, accidental, or suicidal, the death is not classified as a criminal homicide. However, when the autopsy surgeon's report states that a death resulted from a criminal agency, a criminal homicide has been detected.

Although police investigators can make no contribution to an autopsy surgeon's professional conclusions about the cause of death, they can assist these surgeons by supplying information related to the means used to cause death. Current prevailing practices in the detection of criminal homicide have led autopsy surgeons throughout the United States to expect a report from a police investigator, before an autopsy, that informs the autopsy surgeon of all the known facts in the case. These facts include details about the crime scene, possible weapons, and other matters that relate to the death. The autopsy surgeon does not participate in linking the perpetrator to the criminal agency that caused death. This role is the investigator's.

Thus, the detection of criminal homicide is based on finding the answers to four classic questions:

1. What was the cause of death?
2. What were the means (agency) that caused death?
3. Was the homicide excusable or justifiable?
4. Who was responsible for causing death (the agent)?

In summary, the autopsy surgeon has the major responsibility of determining the cause of death. He or she and the police investigators work together to find the agency of death and whether the agency is criminal, excusable, or justifiable. The police accept sole responsibility for identifying the person responsible for the killing.

The Autopsy as an Extension of the Crime Scene

In homicide cases, the autopsy performed on the victim is an extension of the crime scene and offers an additional opportunity to search for clues and evidence useful in the investigation. The pathologist's examination goes beyond the determination of the cause and time of death. This examination is also conducted to search for evidence such as foreign hairs and fibers, or the presence of defense wounds, for example. The investigator searching the scene and the evidence technician lack the professional background of the medical examiner, the pathologist, and the toxicologist. Therefore, any examination of the victim in a homicide case by the investigator searching the scene must be superficial.

Many coroners and medical examiners consider an examination of the victim's clothing to be a segment of the postmortem inquiry and require the same laboratory personnel processing the deceased's vital organs to carefully examine the clothing. However, in suspicious death cases, the police investigator's duty is to ensure that an examination is conducted in a police laboratory.

Medicolegal Laboratory Services

Most local laws governing investigative jurisdiction in cases of suspicious death require the coroner or medical examiner to be notified promptly and the victim's body not to be moved without this official's permission. The basic medicolegal service is to determine whether a death was caused by criminal agency and to identify the deceased person and the cause of death.

The report on the postmortem examination contains the autopsy surgeon's findings. The five parts of this report are as follows:[1]

1. The preamble (date, place, and identity of the deceased and of witnesses to the identification)
2. External appearance (the site, character, and dimensions of any wounds or marks related to the cause of death)
3. Internal examination (a description of the brain, spinal column, organs, and contents of the body)
4. A reasoned opinion of the cause of death based on the facts found
5. Signature of examiner (title and qualifications)

The autopsy technique comprises external examination and dissection. During this work, the pathologist may dictate his or her findings to a stenographer, an assistant, or a recorder. When transcribed, these notes, along with any sketches, diagrams, or photographs, are the raw notes on the examination.

The autopsy surgeon investigates all the body cavities and makes incisions on the side of the neck to expose the neck organs for examination. A knife, a saw, and a chisel are used to open the head; the brain is removed and examined. The spinal cord and extremities are also examined. If any of the substances appear to be abnormal, the substances are examined microscopically. The pathologist must be systematic and thorough. As mentioned previously, recognition of the cause of death is his or her professional responsibility.

External postmortem appearances are informative when a criminal agency is involved in the death. The areas of the body showing lividity indicate the position after death. Wounds and their appearance are particularly significant because they often assist in reconstructing the circumstances of a crime, the nature of the murder weapon, and the manner of its use. Significant data include an accurate description of where the wounds are situated, their shape, their size, and their direction. Generally, pathologists classify and report the nature of wounds as follows:

- *Incised Wounds.*   Spindle shaped in stabbing, linear in cutting
- *Lacerated Wounds.*   Irregularly edged, some tearing
- *Contusions.*   Bruises, discolorations, hematoma
- *Abrasions.*   Scratches, trivial wounds
- *Gunshot Wounds.*   Shotgun: "rat hole" to dispersion; rifles and pistols: contact, entrance, exit
- *Antemortem or Postmortem.*   Wound occurred before or after death
- *Age of Wound.*   Signs of healing of the wound
- *Opinion about Wound.*   Accidental, suicidal, or homicidal; "hesitation" wounds in suicides, and "defense" wounds in homicides

A practitioner skilled in medicolegal procedures can reconstruct the shape of the striking area of the weapon used and the degree of force in relation to the weight and striking surface of the weapon. This information can permit possible matching of a murder weapon when it is found, and if the offender has not been identified, possibly an estimate of the perpetrator's sex and size.

Body temperature, lividity, and rigor mortis indicate an approximate time of death in on-the-scene examination, but the general appearance of the body and its stomach contents afford the pathologist a means of fixing the time of death within reasonable limits. The clinical history of the case, its revelations about persons who were the last to see the victim alive, and the victim's activities assist the pathologist in determining the time of death.

Classically, the autopsy report should provide information on the following seven topics:[2]

1. Cause of death
    a. Natural causes
    b. Accident
    c. Suicide
    d. Homicide
    e. Undetermined origin

2. If a weapon or a substance caused death, the nature of the fatal wounds or injuries
3. Time of death in relationship to time of wound
4. Whether the scene where the body was discovered was the death scene; whether marks and signs indicate that the victim was mobile or that the body was moved
5. Evidence of chronic illness or other disease
6. Evidence of blood, hair, or skin other than the victim's
7. Evidence of sexual knowledge or deviancy

In suspected poisoning cases, the pathologist must correlate his or her clinical postmortem findings with the deceased's history, if available, and suggest to the toxicologist the most promising area of investigation. The history in a medicolegal autopsy includes all available information about the circumstances of a case—manner of death, preceding manifestations of illness and pain, and investigation at the death scene if foul play is suspected. After the toxicologist's report is received, the pathologist evaluates the significance of the toxicologist's findings with regard to the body conditions at autopsy and against the background of the clinical history of the deceased. The pathologist then bases an opinion on the cause of death on these three types of facts.

Identification after death is determined by characteristics that distinguish the deceased from all other individuals. In the usual police investigation, attempts are made to disclose the deceased's name so that responsible persons (relatives or friends) can be located to view the body and identify it. The deceased person is frequently fingerprinted, and the inked impression may be forwarded through the criminal justice information system for identification or verification.

Teeth provide leads to identification, and dentists can elicit valuable clues to identity. A wealth of dental information is now in the hands of the dental profession and can be useful in the identification of deceased persons.[3]

Sex, age, marks and scars, and other physical features such as old bone fractures or physical deformities are identification factors.[4] Death masks are sometimes made, photographed, and included in police bulletins when identification is a problem. These flyers are circulated in the same manner as wanted notices.

The unrecognizable remains of a human body present problems. Fire, water, explosion, mutilation, and exposure to the elements and to animals often make identification difficult or impossible. Nevertheless, pathologists can establish some clues to identity. By correlating all available data, they may arrive at a determination of race, sex, age, and approximate height and weight.

Suicide, Accident, or Criminal Homicide?

Persons who kill themselves adopt methods similar to techniques used in criminal homicides. Many suicide victims do not leave classic notes explaining their reasons for self-destruction and do not foreshadow their intent to commit suicide in any observable fashion. Even when the circumstances of a suspicious death reek of murder, a comprehensive investigation may indicate that the death was suicidal.

Circumstances of a suspicious death often invite an investigator's conclusion of self-destruction. However, many murderers attempt to hide their crime by cloaking it in the dressing of clues and traces that will indicate suicide. The greatest problem exists when the circumstances of the death show that someone has a motive, or could have a motive, for murder. An investigation into a victim's background may strongly indicate that an apparent suicide is out of character with the victim's lifestyle—a fact that must be weighed heavily before a suspicious death case is closed as a suicide.

The techniques of criminal homicide are similar to accidental causes of death. Death can result from being pushed out of a high window or from accidentally falling out of the window. It can result from being shot by another person or as the result of an accident while cleaning a firearm. Death can be caused when another person plunges a knife into a vital area, or an accidental fall on a bottle can drive shards of glass into the same vital area and cause similar fatal injuries. A fatal dose of poison can be administered by another individual or can be taken by mistake. A skull can be crushed with a blunt instrument, or the same injuries may result from falling down a flight of stairs.[5]

Identification of Victim

In most homicides, identifying the victim is not a problem. He or she is known and can be identified by relatives and friends. Identifying a victim becomes a problem, however, when death occurs in a public place, a hotel, or a place not the domicile of the victim. Identification especially becomes a problem when the victim is a member of the large transient population in the United States. Although the transient population comprises primarily homeless men, the drug scene has contributed a great number of runaway girls and boys to the ranks of those who move about from place to place in the United States.

Victim identification is also a major problem when the killer attempts to avoid detection by doing away with the remains of his or her victim through burning, sinking the victim in a substantial body of water, cutting the victim up, or destroying the victim's remains by chemical means. Sometimes the killer does not seek complete destruction of the body but may attempt to destroy only portions of the remains to prevent or delay identification. Scientific means can be used to identify the partial remains of victims in suspicious deaths. Among the possibilities are the following four:

1. *Fingerprints.*   If the victim was fingerprinted in his or her lifetime, the prints are a positive means of identification.

This victim was strangled, shot, and then set on fire.

2. *Dental Work.*   The dental work of a victim may be matched with the dental work of a person who has been missing from home or otherwise unaccounted for.
3. *Bones.*   Bones serve as a broad index of identification when other means are not available because of the condition of the victim's remains. Bones may indicate sex, height, and age, and sometimes time of death, cause of death, and other features of identification.
4. *Surgical Procedures.*   Surgery performed on the victim during his or her lifetime may also aid in identification.

Estimates of a homicide victim's size, age, sex, and race are possible from studying the victim's remains, but identification of the unknown victim depends on finding a sufficient number of unique physical characteristics for comparison with records made during the victim's lifetime. Insofar as skeletal remains are concerned (no fingerprints), dental records and body X-rays are the most likely means of identification: Dentists can be queried and identification made from dental records. Bone injuries severe enough to suggest hospitalization during the victim's life can lead to existing X-rays in hospital records and also result in a positive identification.[6]

Time of Death

Criminal homicide investigations have a built-in time clock keyed to the time of death. Methods for establishing this vital time, or period of time, range from the testimony of one or more witnesses (the persons who saw the killing, who last saw the victim alive, or who discovered and reported the crime) to the autopsy surgeon's testimony about the condition of the victim's body when it was found or examined.

In homicide cases, the time of death connects the events that happen before the crime with the actual killing. The important questions related to this time-clock sequence are as follows:[7]

- What activity was the victim engaged in at the time of the fatal assault?
- What activity did the victim engage in immediately before death (24 to 48 hours, and longer if warranted)?

The only certain time element in the beginning phases of a homicide investigation is the time the crime was discovered. As a result, the witness or witnesses who can testify to this aspect of the case are questioned carefully about the circumstances that first aroused their interest or suspicions and the time of that event; how they found the victim and whether he or she was found dead; the time of the discovery of the victim; and the circumstances and time of reporting this discovery to police.

As a homicide investigation continues, witnesses are located who talked to the deceased victim prior to the fatal assault, either in person or over a telephone. Such witnesses can provide information about the content of the conversation and its time. Sometimes, the activities in which the victim was engaged prior to or at death can be timed within reasonable limits. This process is known as establishing the **window of death**.

When no witnesses to a homicide exist, the forensic scientist and the pathologist may establish the time of death within the window of death. Estimating the time of death is important in determining opportunity to commit the crime. These estimates are based on the postmortem, or after-death, changes that occur in the body and on the activity of insects that may attack the body.

After death, the body begins to cool. This process is known as **algor mortis**. The body temperature will decrease until it reaches the ambient air temperature, which usually occurs within 18 to 20 hours. Algor mortis is considered one of the more reliable indicators of time of death. However, as a result of a number of variables, including body temperature at the time of death, amount and type of clothing, surface temperature, humidity, and air movement across the body, these estimates are not exact.

Biochemical changes in the body after death produce stiffening of the muscles, known as **rigor mortis**, which usually appears within 2 to 6 hours after death. The process begins in the jaw and neck and proceeds to the trunk and extremities and is complete within 6 to 12 hours. This rigidity remains for 2 to 3 days and disappears in the same order in which it appeared.

As a result of gravity, when the blood stops circulating, it begins to settle to the lowest portion of the body. This process, known as postmortem **lividity**, is noticeable within approximately 1 hour after death and is fully developed within 3 to 4 hours. Lividity appears as blue or reddish marks on the skin. By 12 hours after death, fresh livid stains are no longer produced by a change in body position. Lividity discoloration indicates two types of information: the time of death and a change of position or movement of the body after death.

Decomposition, or **putrefaction**, begins at the time of death as a result of two processes: autolysis and bacterial action. **Autolysis** is a chemical breakdown of the body that results in the softening and liquefaction of body tissue. Bacteria convert body tissue into liquids and gases. Within 24 hours, a discoloration of the skin is noticeable. This greenish-red or blue-green color change is pronounced within 36 hours. **Bacterial action** produces gases that cause the body to swell and produce an unpleasant odor. The environment affects the rate of decomposition—colder temperatures impede the process, whereas warmer temperatures increase it.

Various kinds of insects feed on dead bodies. These insects lay their eggs, which develop into larvae, or maggots. They can reduce a body to skeletal remains in less than 2 months under favorable conditions. The life cycle of these insects is constant, and the forensic entomologist can determine how long a body has been exposed to the action of these insects.[8]

Exhumation

A court order must be secured for **exhumation**—removal of a deceased person's body from its burial place—so that a medicolegal examination can be conducted to disclose the presence of previously unknown or improperly identified injuries or reveal the presence of poison or another noxious substance that would indicate a criminal agency caused death.

Examination after burial is rarely as satisfactory as an autopsy before burial. However, full autopsy procedures should be carried out, the body should be fully X-rayed before and after the autopsy, and both color and black-and-white photographs of the body should be taken before and after the autopsy.

Checklist for the Investigation of Criminal Homicide

A checklist for a criminal homicide investigation should be divided into stages to allow for the orderly progression of the investigation from its beginning to its focusing and then to the arrest of the perpetrator and crime partners, if any (Figure 10–1):

Stage 1: Crime Scene

1. Be alert at the approach to and the entrance of the crime area for the perpetrator and others leaving the crime scene. All persons at or leaving the crime scene should be stopped and identified before they leave. Such persons may be interviewed at the scene or later.

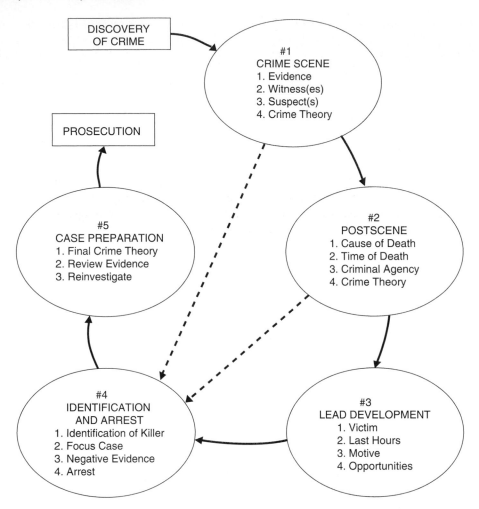

FIGURE 10–1   Investigation of criminal homicide.

2. Take a "good hard look" when entering the crime scene.
   a. **The Victim.**   Give first aid or summon medical help, if necessary. Note if the victim is apparently dead or has been pronounced dead by a physician. Take a dying declaration, if possible.
   b. **The scene.**   Check entrances, exits, and the extent of the scene. Protect weapons and other evidence. Prevent the entrance of unauthorized persons. Call for technicians (if available) to take photographs and process the scene for fingerprints and other physical evidence.
3. Protect the integrity of the scene by warning all individuals present not to smoke, use any plumbing (sinks, tubs, showers, toilet bowls) or towels, touch any objects or surfaces, or walk in or otherwise contaminate blood traces.
4. Identify witnesses, interview them, obtain statements of their knowledge of the crime, and begin the search for additional witnesses.

5. If an apparent suspect is at the scene (case is focusing), warn the person of his or her rights; note the person's appearance, clothing, and physical and mental condition; and record any spontaneous utterances. Everyone present at the scene is a possible suspect until the case has focused. Begin a search for suspicious persons and vehicles that were at the scene before or at the time of the crime.

6. Record the scene.
   a. Photograph the scene.
   b. Measure and sketch the scene.
   c. Take notes.
   d. Collect evidence and record where it was found and who found it; mark the evidence, transport it, and secure it with the property officer.

7. Seal the scene. Do not open the scene without the previous agreement of associates, technicians, and the prosecutor.

8. Identify the victim.

9. Develop a tentative crime theory.

Stage 2: Postscene

1. Determine the time of death; "bracket" the time period by using the following sources:
   a. Witnesses who saw the victim alive or talked to the victim by telephone before his or her death
   b. Witnesses who discovered the victim (the crime)
   c. Medicolegal testimony setting a maximum and minimum limit for the time of death (autopsy surgeon's report)
   d. Other evidence

2. Determine the place of the fatal assault (when different from the place of discovery of the crime).

3. Determine the cause of death by using the following information:
   a. Apparent cause at the scene
   b. Medicolegal autopsy report

4. Determine the means of death, including the following:
   a. Criminal agency
   b. Specific weapon
   c. Weapon recovered

5. Develop a tentative crime theory.

Stage 3: Lead Development

1. Determine the victim's background and activities.

2. Investigate the victim's last hours, including where he or she was and with whom:
   a. Contacts: Family, friends, and co-workers
   b. Activity at the time of death and before death

3. Determine the vehicle or vehicles used.

4. Interview injured suspects.

5. Interview informants.

6. Locate the weapon.
7. Investigate tie-ups with other crimes.
8. Determine the perpetrator's knowledge of the victim's activity and access to the premises.
9. Establish motive: the "pattern" of the criminal homicide.
10. Determine opportunity for these individuals:
    a. Persons known to have been at the scene
    b. Persons who were possibly at the scene
11. Develop a tentative crime theory, including identification of one or more "prime" suspects.

Stage 4: Identification and Arrest

1. Develop evidence that will identify the killer. Review the evidence for the corpus delicti, identification, and consistency with the crime theory.
2. Focus the case.
3. Exonerate innocent suspects.
4. Arrest the killer and his or her crime partners, if any.
5. Gather negative evidence as needed, including the following:
    a. Alibi
    b. Self-defense
    c. Intent
        i. Suspect's mental state
        ii. Suspect's sobriety
        iii. Suspect's crime record
    d. Crime or treatment (medical, psychiatric) records of witnesses and victim

Stage 5: Case Preparation

1. Reconstruct the crime.
2. Summarize the physical evidence.
3. Summarize the witnesses' testimony.
4. Review the motive (reason) and intent.
5. Confer with associates and the prosecutor.
6. Reinvestigate as warranted or directed by the prosecutor.
7. Prepare a brief synopsis to forward with case records to the prosecutor.

Patterns of Criminal Homicide

The basic pattern of a criminal homicide is ordinarily disclosed in the initial investigation of a suspicious death. Even though a killer may attempt to falsify the facts of a dispute or cast the suspicion of guilt on another person, a routine investigation should disclose the facts.

Among the basic patterns of criminal homicide are the following eight:

1. ***The Anger Killing.*** The **anger killing** pattern is an extension of the crime of assault. A dispute occurs, and anger develops. The victim is attacked, with or without weapons, and is fatally injured.

2. *The Triangle Killing.*   The possibility of an errant husband, a lover, or a mistress should rarely be ignored. If a wife is dead and another woman is involved in a triangle situation, grounds exist for suspecting the husband, who may have wanted to rid himself of an unwanted wife. The reverse situation is frequently encountered; the wife is eager to rid herself of an unwanted husband because of a developing romance. When the person who may have the motive in this triangle was also the last one to see the victim alive, the investigation starts to gather momentum in its development as a **triangle killing.**

3. *The Revenge or Jealousy Killing.*   In a **revenge or jealousy killing**, the initial investigation of who the victim was and the history of the involvement between the victim and suspects will usually disclose the motive of revenge or jealousy—and thus a suspect.

4. *Murder for Profit.*   Elimination of another person because the murderer would gain some benefit has long been a standard motive for murder. Who would profit? This avenue of investigation is extremely effective for developing suspects. When the circumstances of a suspicious death show that persons who would profit from the death are among those who last saw the victim alive, support exists for developing a theory of criminal homicide along these lines. **Murder for profit** is closely aligned with the triangle-killing situation; the victim is eliminated to gain some benefit.

5. *The Random Killing.*   Every killer has a motive, if *motive* is defined as a reason for the slaying. Even the random killer, who has no previous connection or tie to the victim, has a motive. The random killing is often termed *unmotivated* because the reason for the killing is clouded and unknown until the suspect is discovered. The killing of a complete stranger, or **random killing**, is perhaps the most difficult to solve. This pattern of murder may be disclosed by first excluding the usual or common patterns of criminal homicide.

6. *Murder-Suicide.*   The **murder-suicide** pattern of criminal homicide is one in which the killer self-destructs shortly after the fatal assault on the victim. These killings often involve a "compact" in which a husband and wife, boyfriend or girlfriend, or parent and child agree that both should die and one takes the responsibility for killing the other and then committing suicide.

7. *Sex and Sadism Murder.*   The **sex and sadism murder** is marked by unusual violence. It may follow child molestation, rape, acts of perversion, or sadistic acts. It often has bizarre overtones. In one New York case, the two female victims were stabbed repeatedly, one was undressed, and they were tied together face to face. The killer rubbed Noxzema face cream on and around the rectums of his victims. In a Nevada case, the victim's vagina and breasts were slashed deeply with a sharp instrument.

8. *Felony Murder.*   In **felony murder** cases, the victim's death does not result from an angered attack; from a triangle, revenge, jealousy, or profit motivation; or from random chance, a murder-suicide compact, or sex and sadism. Rather, death results from injuries inflicted by someone in the act of committing a felony. The criminal intent of the original crime carries over to the killing.

The investigator must not close his or her mind or the investigation too quickly. A homicide investigation may initially appear to fit one of the criminal homicide patterns, then evidence develops in the continuing investigation that reveals sufficient data to change its classification to another pattern or combination of patterns. For instance, a criminal homicide case in St. Paul, Minnesota, first appeared to be a burglary gone wrong. Mrs. Carol Thompson was found semiconscious and bloody in her home. She was rushed to a hospital, where she died as a result of bleeding from multiple skull fractures. The deadly weapon was a blunt instrument, and when fragments of pistol grips were found in a pool of blood in the Thompson living room, investigators assumed a pistol-whipping had occurred. Evidence of a burglary was apparent at the crime scene: a bureau and desk drawers had been ransacked. However, continued inquiries revealed that the victim's husband had been intimate with another woman, and a new potential pattern developed: elimination of an unwanted wife. A few days later, when local insurance executives responded to police inquiries with the news that the housewife victim was insured for more than $1 million and the husband was sole beneficiary, the murder-for-profit pattern was added as a possible motive for the crime.[9]

Motive for Murder—Relationships

In a trial for murder, proof of motive is always relevant but never necessary. In a criminal homicide investigation, a motive is necessary and useful. It may surface while the investigator is following the basic leads of benefit and opportunity or reviewing the victim's relationships. Current and former spouses and lovers of the victim promptly become suspects because friends and relatives, not strangers, are often the killers. Such relationships are as follows:

- Spouse (or ex-)
- Common-law spouse (or ex-)
- Boyfriend or girlfriend (or ex-)
- Live-in boyfriend or girlfriend (or ex-)
- Sister or brother
- Mother or father
- Daughter or son
- Other relative (including in-laws)
- Friend of family; relative of friend (specify)
- Neighbor
- Business associate (partner, co-worker, other)
- Acquaintance
- Seen before (such as "known from the neighborhood")

The frequency of contact in a relationship is classified as follows: live together, see daily, see weekly, see monthly, or hardly see at all.

Multicide

Multicide is the killing of a number of victims by one or more persons working in concert. Mass murder, spree murder, and serial murder are the various types of multicide. **Mass murder** is the homicide of four or more victims during a single event at one location.[10] The mass murderer appears to give little thought or concern to his or her inevitable capture or death. Some mass murderers are killed by the police during the attack; others kill themselves once they complete the massacre. In some cases, these killers surrender to the police and offer no resistance. Most appear to commit their crimes in public places. When families are murdered, the killer usually leaves ample evidence to lead to his or her arrest.[11]

Spree murder is the killing of three or more persons within a relatively short time frame. Most of these cases last from only a few weeks to as long as a year. The victims may be men, women or children and are often randomly selected.[12] The so-called D.C. Sniper, who killed 13 persons and wounded 6 others in five states and the District of Columbia during 3 weeks in the fall of 2002, is an example of a spree killer.

Serial killers, by contrast, may make special efforts to elude detection. They may continue to kill for weeks, months, and often years before they are caught, if at all. The definition of a **serial murder** is two or more separate murders when an individual, acting alone or with another, commits multiple homicides during a period of time, with time breaks between each murder.[13] Four types of serial murderers have been identified according to their motivation for the killing:[14]

1. The **"visionary" serial killer** is compelled to kill by voices he or she hears or visions he or she sees. These breaks from reality demand that he or she kill certain kinds of people. This kind of offender is truly out of touch with reality—a psychotic. This killer's competency to stand trial for his or her actions is a consideration for the court to decide.
2. The **"mission" serial killer** feels a need on a conscious level to eradicate a certain group of people. This offender is not psychotic. He or she is in touch with reality but acts on a self-imposed duty to rid the world of a certain class of people: prostitutes, or religious or racial group members, for instance.
3. The **"hedonistic" serial killer** has made a connection between personal violence and sexual gratification. The **lust or thrill killer** is a subtype of this category. These offenders murder because they derive pleasure from the act; for them, killing is an eroticized experience. These killings are process focused, take some time to complete, and include torture, mutilation, and other fear-instilling activities.

      Another type of serial killer in this category is the **comfort-oriented serial murderer**, who kills for personal gain. Professional assassins and people who kill for personal gain fall under this category.

4. The **"power and control" serial killer** experiences sexual gratification from complete domination of the victim. This type of killer derives gratification from the belief that he or she has the power to make another human being do exactly what he or she wants. This murderer is psychologically rooted in reality; a true sociopath, he or she lives by personal rules and guidelines.

The crime scene or lack of a crime scene will determine whether the killing was the work of an organized or a disorganized offender. **Organized offenders** are usually of above-average intelligence. They are methodical and cunning. Their crimes are well thought out and carefully planned. They are likely to own a car that is in good condition. The crimes are usually committed out of their area of residence or place of work. These killers are mobile and travel many more miles than the average person. Fantasy and ritual are important, and organized offenders select victims, usually strangers. Most of their victims share some traits. These killers are considered socially adept. They use their verbal skills to manipulate and gain control over their victims until the victims are within the killer's "comfort zone." Organized offenders are likely to follow news reports of the event and will often take "souvenirs" from their victims as reminders, which are sometimes used to relive the event or continue with the fantasy.

Disorganized offenders, in contrast, are inadequate individuals who are experiencing intense sadistic sexual fantasies and may suddenly "act out" these fantasies on a victim of opportunity. The crime scene will be disorganized, and the killer's actions and behavior could be viewed as psychotic. These offenders are usually of below-average intelligence. They are generally loners, are not usually married, and live either alone or with a relative in proximity to the crime scene. They experience difficulty in negotiating interpersonal relationships and are described as socially inadequate. They act impulsively under stress and usually select a victim from their geographic area. In most instances, these offenders do not own a vehicle but have access to one. They use a "blitz" style of attack, which catches the victim off guard. This spontaneous action, in which the offender suddenly "acts out" his or her fantasy, does not allow for a conscious plan or for even a thought of being detected. This spontaneity is why the crime scene will be disorganized and clustered. A **clustered crime scene** involves a situation in which most of the activities occur at one location: the confrontation, the attack, the assault, and sexual activity.[15]

Although knowing the kind and type of serial killer involved will not tell the investigator who is committing these crimes, this information will aid the investigator in determining where to look and the type of person who may be involved. The real benefit of this information is its value at the time of interrogation. Knowing these killers' motivation will aid in the formation of the proper questions to ask when the serial killer is caught.

The mobility of the organized offender presents a problem for the investigator because this killer may intentionally cross jurisdictional lines of authority to avoid detection. For instance, Ted Bundy, an infamous serial killer, killed twenty-nine victims in five states and avoided capture for several years primarily for this reason. The Violent Criminal Apprehension Program (VICAP), administered by the Federal Bureau of Investigation (FBI), is the clearinghouse for information about serial killers. Investigators send in data on local murders, and when cases are linked, the reporting investigators in the local agencies are given each other's names so that they can coordinate their work.[16]

STALKING

About half the states in the United States now have penal code provisions to combat stalking. For instance, in Kentucky, **stalking** is defined as an intentional course of conduct that

- Is directed at a specific person or persons
- Seriously alarms, annoys, intimidates, or harasses the victim
- Serves no legitimate purpose

Stalking ranges from making telephone calls and sending letters to confronting an individual personally to attempting murder, committing murder, or committing rape. The following typology of stalkers may be helpful to investigators who are suddenly confronted with a stalker's activity:[17]

Celebrity Stalker.   Knows the victim (e.g., actor, sports star) on an impersonal level

Lust Stalker.   Engages in predatory sex* that escalates to murder

Hit Stalker.   Is a professional killer

Love-Scorned Stalker.   Intends violence against a known victim who has rejected the stalker in some way

Domestic Stalker.   Is an ex-lover or ex-spouse who uses "get even" violence

Political Stalker.   Selects a victim who is a stranger but who has a known political or religious view

ASSAULTS

An **assault** is an unlawful attempt, coupled with the current ability, to commit an injury to the person of another. In other words, it is an attempt to commit a **battery**: an unlawful beating or other wrongful physical harm inflicted on a human being without his or her consent.

In an assault, the victim is usually alive and willing to cooperate with investigators. In many cases, the assailant is known to the victim, and the investigation becomes one in which establishing the perpetrator's identity is

---

*Predatory sex offenses are those in which the victim is a stranger to the assailant.

not a problem. However, when the assailant is not known to the victim, the investigation of assault is closer to a homicide investigation than it is to any other type of investigation.

Assault without a weapon and in which serious injury is not inflicted on the victim is a relatively minor crime. Assault with a deadly weapon or in which serious injury is inflicted with or without a weapon is **aggravated assault**—a serious crime. Aggravated assaults are often murder attempts that have failed as a result of the intervention of witnesses, prompt medical treatment, or pure luck. For this reason, the characteristics of assailants in both crimes are likely to be similar.

The term **violent injury** is synonymous with *force* in assault cases. It includes any application of physical force, even if such force entails no pain or bodily harm and leaves no marks.

The assault scene must be protected and its integrity preserved. The victim must be given first aid and prompt medical attention, if required. Furniture may have to be moved to care for the victim. The investigating officer at the scene should make note of any changes in the crime scene, and if the victim is moved from the position he or she was in at the time of the officer's arrival, the victim's original position should be noted.

The crime scene is processed for evidence that will assist investigators in reconstructing the crime and identifying the participants as the attacker and the victim; witnesses at the scene are interviewed for the same purpose. The work of investigators at this time is concentrated on securing the details of the attack and of the dispute that led to the attack.

When the victim is seriously injured and requires medical care, the investigating officer should accompany the assault victim to the hospital. The situation is flexible, but the objective is to gain as much information as possible from the victim about the circumstances leading to the attack, the nature of the attack, and the attacker's identity. The information provided by a victim in periods of consciousness after being seriously injured may be compelling evidence in a future trial. If a victim is in extremis and is aware of impending death, the officer may secure a dying declaration indicating the victim's mental condition and the circumstances of the attack.

If the circumstances warrant, the officer accompanying an assault victim to the hospital should collect, mark, and retain the victim's clothing as evidence. Future processing by criminalists may indicate the direction of force from bullet holes and the damage caused by knives or other sharp instruments, bloodstains and their origin, and similar evidence.

Promptly identifying and recovering the weapon or weapons involved in the assault and relating them to a participant in the assault event is particularly important. The police search of the crime scene should disclose the presence of all weapons at the scene when the police arrive. Interviews of eyewitnesses should be aimed at disclosing any weapons used in the attack but not found at the crime scene.

Before an assault, the offender and the victim have usually had some interaction. Generally, this interaction was an **altercation**—a verbal dispute. The origin of the dispute may have been domestic difficulties or a pushing-and-shoving situation to prove masculinity among drinking partners. Although intoxication (drugs or alcohol) may not be a factor, the high incidence of assaults during late evening and early morning hours suggests that many disputes arise during, or because of, some leisure-time pursuit. Investigators must seek out the details of the dispute in assault cases to cast some light on the reason for the attack and the roles of both the victim and the assailant.

Sometimes in the preliminary investigation of an assault case the investigating police charge both participants with assault or disorderly conduct. A "fielder's choice" of responding police has often been to charge the apparent victim (the person most seriously injured) with disturbing the peace until the police can ascertain whether the victim was responsible for the attack on him- or herself.

Data in assault investigations are usually organized within the following four major segments:

1. *The Scene.*   Reconstruction of the assault event
2. *Dispute Origin.*   Place, time, participants, witnesses
3. *Weapon or Weapons.*   Existence or nonexistence, identified with user (attacker, victim), recovered at scene, recovered elsewhere
4. *Negative Evidence.*   Whether lawful resistance, victim armed, victim previously in fear of attacker (state of mind)

CHILD ABUSE

Child abuse is the intentional and deliberate assault on a child in which serious bodily injury is inflicted by a parent, a foster parent, a babysitter, a day-care worker, or a person in a nonparental relationship. **Serious bodily injury** is a standard that excludes police intervention in cases involving only minor assaults that could be described as corporal punishment incidental to disciplining a child.[18] In most areas of the United States, however, cases of child abuse brought to the attention of police—or discovered by them—are more properly classed as **battered child syndrome**.

Signs of physical abuse, in the absence of a reasonable explanation for the injury, include the following:[19]

- Damage to the skin (burns, bruises, abrasions, lacerations, or swelling)
- Brain damage (convulsions, coma, retardation)
- Bone damage (pain on movement, deformity)
- Internal injuries (shock, abdominal pain, signs of internal bleeding)

Burn injuries comprise about 10 percent of all child abuse cases. Immersion burns result from the child's falling or being placed into a tub or another container of hot liquid. In a **deliberate immersion burn**, the depth of the burn is uniform. The wound borders are distinct, sharply defined "waterlines" with little tapering of depth at the edges. Little evidence exists that the child thrashed about during the immersion, which indicates the child was held in place. **Contact burns** are caused by flames or hot, solid objects. Cigarette and iron burns are the most frequent types of these injuries. Cigarette burns on a child's back or buttocks are unlikely to have been caused by walking into a lighted cigarette and are more suspect than facial burns. Accidental burns are usually more shallow, irregular, and less well defined than deliberate burns. Multiple cigarette burns are distinctively characteristic of child abuse. Purposely inflicted "branding" injuries usually mirror the objects that caused the burn, such as cigarette lighters and curling irons, and are much deeper than the superficial and random burns caused by accidentally touching these objects.[20]

Shaken baby syndrome, another type of child abuse, occurs primarily in children 18 months old or younger because the neck of a child this age lacks muscle control and the child's head is heavier than the rest of the body. These injuries are caused by a violent, sustained shaking action in which the infant's head is violently whipped forward and backward so that it hits the chest and shoulders. The baby begins to show symptoms such as seizures or unconsciousness within minutes of infliction of the injury. The result may be respiratory arrest or death.

A classic medical symptom associated with shaken baby syndrome is **retinal hemorrhage**, which is bleeding in the back of the eyeballs. Simple household falls and tossing a baby into the air in play are not good explanations for retinal hemorrhage. Not enough force is involved in minor falls and play activities to cause retinal hemorrhage or the kinds of severe, life-threatening injuries seen in infants who have been shaken.

Munchausen syndrome is a psychological disorder in which the patient fabricates the symptoms of a disease or an injury in order to undergo medical tests, hospitalization, or even medical or surgical treatment. In cases of **Munchausen syndrome by proxy**, parents or caretakers suffering from this disorder attempt to bring medical attention to themselves by injuring or inducing illness in their children. Common occurrences in these cases are as follows: The child experiences "seizures" or "respiratory arrest" only when the caretaker is present—never in the presence of a neutral third party. While in the hospital, the caretaker will turn off life-support equipment, which causes the child to stop breathing, and then turn the equipment back on and summon help. The caretaker induces illness by introducing a mild irritant or poison into the child's body.

Sudden infant death syndrome (SIDS) is not a positive finding; rather, it is a diagnosis made when no other medical explanation exists for the abrupt death of an apparently healthy infant. SIDS rarely occurs in infants older than 7 months and almost never is an appropriate finding for a child older than 12 months. Before SIDS can be ruled the cause of death, the investigator must ensure that every other possible medical explanation has been explored and that no evidence exists of any other natural or accidental cause for the child's death. An investigator's suspicions should be aroused when multiple alleged SIDS deaths have occurred under the custody of the same parent or caretaker.[21]

When child abuse is suspected, the assigned investigator should take the child to a local hospital for examination by a physician. This examination and the physician's report will indicate the nature of the injuries and some age dating, but the reporting physician may be reluctant to diagnose the case as child abuse.

Six factors likely to influence physicians to link discovered injuries in a child with child abuse are as follows:

1. Delays in seeking medical care
2. Injuries not reported by the parent or guardian
3. Bruises or broken bones in an infant
4. Age dating of bruises indicating that they were sustained at different times (Figure 10–2)
5. Characteristic "wraparound" bruises caused by whipping with a belt, a rope, or an electrical cord
6. Discrepancies in the parent's or guardian's story about how the injuries occurred: inconsistencies between the described circumstances and the nature of the injuries

When the report of child abuse originates in a hospital, the examining physician may have been alerted by one or more of the preceding factors or simply because the parent or guardian bringing the child to the hospital were "hospital shoppers": bringing the child to a hospital outside their community when a local hospital was readily available to them.

Determining the Age of a Bruise by Its Color

Color of Bruise	Age of Bruise
Red (swollen, tender)	0–2 days
Blue, purple	2–5 days
Green	5–7 days
Yellow	7–10 days
Brown	10–14 days
No further evidence of bruising	2–4 weeks

FIGURE 10–2 Age dating of bruises. From U.S. Department of Justice, Office of Justice Programs, Office of Juvenile Justice and Delinquency Prevention, *Recognizing When a Child's Injury or Illness Is Caused by Abuse* (Washington, DC: U.S. Department of Justice, Office of Justice Programs, Office of Juvenile Justice and Delinquency Prevention, 2002), 5.

At this time, the investigator must decide whether to take the child victim into protective custody. The action taken should be in the child's best interest. If a person in the home environment of a child is a suspect in the abuse, adequate cause exists to remove the child from this environment. (It also warrants action with regard to other children in the same household, if they have been abused or may be the subject of abuse.)

During the initial contact with a child victim, while present in the hospital, or following the physician's examination, the investigator must gather what facts he or she can from the child. Doing so may be difficult when the child is very young (2 to 4 years old) or the child has been instructed by the person responsible for the injury not to talk to anyone about how it happened—or instructed to repeat a false story. Once a child realizes the investigator is truly interested in discovering the truth, the details of the assault are usually forthcoming.

The when, where, and what-happened factors in these cases may cover a broad period, several locations, and different assaults. Once these factors have been correlated, the investigator can determine whether a crime was committed, what the crime was, and who was responsible for it.

CHAPTER REVIEW

CASE STUDY

Autopsy Surgeon

The doctor (witness) was qualified at the beginning of his testimony. The direct examination on how long the victim lived after being stabbed is just ending.

Direct Examination Prosecutor

Q: Doctor, can you tell us what then would, in your opinion, be the maximum time that it could have been?

A: Well, he could not have lived an hour, I am sure, but all outside limits—I mean it could possibly be, but in my opinion it would be less than that.

Q: Less than an hour?

A: Oh, yes.

Cross Examination Defense Attorney

Q: How long did the autopsy take?

A: About an hour and a half.

Q: Was that consistent work or were there lapse times in the hour and a half?

A: It was consistent work going over the body, yes, sir.

Q: What did your autopsy consist of, Doctor?

A: External examination of the body.

Q: As to the external examination of the body, would you tell us what that consisted of?

A: Examining the wounds, examining the depth of the wounds, examining the positions of the wounds.

Q: You examined those by probes?

A: Yes, sir.

Q: And the width of the wounds you examined, you examined those with some measuring device?

A: We have a ruler type of thing.

Q: How long did that part of your examination last, your external examination?

A: Approximately 30 minutes.

Q: How many actual—how many wounds actually penetrated into and through the lung wall into what you call where the air would be in the lung?

A: There were nine of them.

Q: All nine penetrated actually—

A: Yes, sir.

Q: Were those large wounds, sir?

A: They were approximately three-eighths of an inch—approximately three-eighths of an inch in width. None greater. They were still of the stab wound type.

Q: There were some less?

A: Yes, sir, there were. The more distant ones, there were two that were approximately a quarter of an inch. But there were nine little wounds going right down in this medial border of the lung, and each of them would have been enough to let some air into the chest cavity.

Q: Would that depend upon the position in which the person was in? Would that at all be a factor?

A: I don't think position would have so much—

Q: Well, would the position tend to either close or open the wounds?

A: You mean when he was standing up or lying down?

Q: Not only lying down—or curled up, or any other position.

A: I don't think position would have so much to do as possibly activity from breathing, and activity—muscular activity.

Q: But as you move, and your chest cavity moves, don't your internal organs also tend to move or contract?

A: Well, see, your lungs—when you breathe, your lungs contract and expand, the diaphragm comes up and your chest muscles contract, and there is a pumping action, like a bellows on the lung. Now, a lung that is punctured, and a lung cavity where the—instead of being a vacuum, has atmospheric air in it, and where there is a loss of blood, a rush of blood into it, that lung just contracts right down.

Q: Let's get back now to your external examination in the detail that we started with before we got off on this track—which took half an hour. Your external examination, you probed, you say, to determine the depth of the wounds, right?

A: Yes, sir.

Q: Also, Doctor, what other examinations did you make with your external examination?

A: Looking for other wounds, looking for fractures, looking for signs of trauma, and the general configuration of the body, and looking into the mouth and checking the eyes, and I was looking for any extraneous marks or anything that would give me any more of a clue as to the cause of this man's death.

Q: Did you find any except the puncture wounds and the two marks on the neck?
A: No, sir, I did not.

Q: There were no other signs of trauma?
A: No, sir.

Q: By "trauma" you mean a blow of some kind?
A: Yes, blows, bruises, any other types of mark that would, you know, have a bearing on the death of this individual.

Q: I presume you examined very closely for those kind of things?
A: Yes.

Q: You gave an opinion as to the time between the injury and death. What factors are involved to determine that particular thing?
A: The factors involved, of course, are the wounds, the number of wounds.

Q: How do you mean the wounds? That is rather a general thing.
A: Let me put it under classification of wounds, then your subheading of that would have the number of wounds, number 2 under that you would have the size of the wounds, number 3 you would have the location of the wounds, and number 4 you would have to figure the rate of bleeding. Then there are variable factors under that, there would come blood pressure, coagulability of the blood. That is about all, I believe, under those factors.

Q: All right, any other factors?
A: I believe that would cover just about everything, I mean when you figure time of death.

Q: Are there any others? You say just about all of them, and are there any other factors that would be important?
A: Not that I think of extemporaneously here.

Q: On what facts do you base your opinion?
A: On the above.

Q: Well, that is pretty general. Would you detail that for us, please?
A: All right, and in doing that, of course, I would have to describe the wounds again.

Q: What I want is your detailed basis for your opinion.
A: The detailed basis of the opinion would be a description of the wounds as described above. First of all, I believe I described an incised wound, 4 inches long in the neck going through the skin and superficial fascia of the neck.

Q: Did that have something to do with the time of death, that particular wound?
A: Yes, it would have something to do with bleeding.

Q: All right, go ahead.
A: I would then take into consideration the wounds on the rest of the body, namely, the extremities, which as I said before, were supplementary and contributing factors of death but not actual causes of death. Then I would take into consideration the stab wounds of the chest. And I would take into consideration the multiplicity of those wounds, their location, nine in number. Relatively an educated guess from what I have seen before, and what I know about medicine, yes.

Q: But it still would be a guess, wouldn't it?
A: Yes, sir.

DISCUSSION QUESTIONS

1. Define a *criminal homicide*.
2. What is the role of the medical examiner (autopsy surgeon) in evaluating suspicious deaths?
3. List and describe the common patterns in criminal homicides. What patterns in criminal homicides are often related?
4. What are the possible routes (techniques) for identifying victims in suspicious deaths?
5. Why is the determination of the time of death important in the investigation of criminal homicides?
6. What procedures should be followed to protect the integrity of an autopsy in exhumation cases?
7. List five major segments of the on-the-scene phase of a criminal homicide investigation.
8. What are the similarities and differences between the investigation of criminal homicides and the investigation of criminal assaults?
9. How can a pattern of "serial murders" be established? Why are they difficult to close out with an arrest?
10. What circumstances are likely to indicate physical child abuse?
11. What is the goal of cross-examination in the case study?
12. The time of death is vital to this case—why?

LIBRARY ASSIGNMENT

Research the killer-victim relationship in criminal homicides.

WORKBOOK PROJECT

Chart or diagram an outline of the investigation to be used when an investigator is confronted with a serial murder investigation.

RELATED WEB SITES

To learn about homicide trends in the United States, visit the FBI's Uniform Crime Reports Web site at *www.fbi.gov/ucr/ucr.htm*.

For information about homicide in the workplace, see *www.cdc.gov/mmwr/preview/mmwrhtml/00024907.htm*.

Researching serial murderers? If so, you might want to take a look at Court TV's crime library at *www.crimelibrary.com*.

NOTES

1. THOMAS A. GONZALES et al., *Legal Medicine: Pathology and Toxicology* (New York: Appleton Century Crofts, 1954).

2. WILLIAM F. KESSLER AND PAUL B. WESTON, *The Detection of Murder* (New York: Arco, 1961), 44–47.

3. LOWELL J. LEVINE, "Forensic Odontology Today: A New Forensic Science," *FBI Law Enforcement Bulletin* 41, no. 8 (1972): 6–9, 26–28.

4. T. D. STEWART, "What the Bones Tell Today," *FBI Law Enforcement Bulletin* 41, no. 2 (1972): 16–20, 30–31.

5. WILLIAM F. KESSLER AND PAUL B. WESTON, *The Detection of Murder*, 1–9.

6. LARRY MILLER et al., *Human Evidence in Criminal Justice* (Cincinnati, OH: Anderson, 1983), 115–46.

7. EDWARD A. DIECKMANN, SR., *Practical Homicide Investigation* (Springfield, IL: Charles C Thomas, 1901), 23–25.

8. BARRY A. J. FISHER, *Techniques of Crime Scene Investigation* (New York: CRC Press, 2000), 445–50.

9. DONALD JOHN GIESE, *The Carol Thompson Murder Case* (New York: Scope Reports, 1969), 5–20, 38–50.

10. VERNON J. GEBERTH, *Practical Homicide Investigation: Tactics, Procedures, and Forensic Techniques* (New York: CRC Press, 1996), 849.

11. ERIC W. HICKEY, *Serial Murderers and Their Victims* (Pacific Grove, CA: Brooks/Cole, 1991), 5.

12. RONALD M. HOLMES AND STEPHEN T. HOLMES, *Mass Murder in the United States* (Upper Saddle River, NJ: Prentice Hall, 2001), 3.

13. VERNON J. GEBERTH, *Practical Homicide Investigation*, 348.

14. RONALD M. HOLMES AND STEPHEN T. HOLMES, *Profiling Violent Crimes*, 2nd ed. (Thousand Oaks, CA: Sage, 1996), 63–67.

15. VERNON J. GEBERTH, *Practical Homicide Investigation*, 419–21.

16. JAMES B. HOWLEIT, KENNETH A. HANFLAND, AND ROBERT K. RESSLER, "The Violent Criminal Apprehension Program—VICAP: A Progress Report," *FBI Law Enforcement Bulletin* 55, no. 12 (1986): 14–22.

17. R. M. HOLMES, "Stalking in America: Types and Methods of Criminal Stalkers," *Contemporary Criminal Justice* 8, no. 4 (December 1993): 318–26.

18. JOSEPH GOLDSTEIN, ANNA FREUD, AND ALBERT J. SOLNIT, *Before the Best Interests of the Child* (New York: Free Press—Macmillan, 1979), 72–77.

19. CALIFORNIA DEPARTMENT OF JUSTICE, *Child Abuse Prevention Handbook* (Sacramento: California Department of Justice, 1982), 7–9.

20. U.S. DEPARTMENT OF JUSTICE, OFFICE OF JUSTICE PROGRAMS, OFFICE OF JUVENILE JUSTICE AND DELINQUENCY PREVENTION, *Burn Injuries in Child Abuse* (Washington, DC: U.S. Department of Justice, Office of Justice Programs, Office of Juvenile Justice and Delinquency Prevention, 2001), 1–8.

21. U.S. DEPARTMENT OF JUSTICE, OFFICE OF JUSTICE PROGRAMS, OFFICE OF JUVENILE JUSTICE AND DELINQUENCY PREVENTION, *Battered Child Syndrome: Investigating Physical Abuse and Homicide* (Washington, DC: U.S. Department of Justice, Office of Justice Programs, Office of Juvenile Justice and Delinquency Prevention, 2002), 1–11.

11

SEXUAL ASSAULTS

RAPE

Forcible rape is an act of violence. It is not a crime of sexual desire but an act of brutal violence, as in murder with intent and **malice**. Rape should be investigated in the same manner as criminal homicides and just as thoroughly.

In common law, **rape** was defined as "having carnal knowledge (sexual intercourse) of a woman by force and without her consent." Consent induced by fear of violence is not consent, and it is against the woman's will if her male attacker uses an array of physical force to overcome her mind so that she dare not resist. Of necessity, since force or fear is an essential element of the crime of rape, evidence should be developed that the victim resisted, that her resistance was overcome by force, or that she was prevented from resisting by threats to her safety.[1]

The means used to overcome the female victim's will is of major importance in rape investigations:

- Force or threat of the use of force
- Administration of drugs (including alcoholic beverages)
- Incapacity to consent (victim's physical or mental condition or age)

In the terminology of state legislatures, **aggravated rape** is said to occur when the rapist is armed with a dangerous weapon, kidnaps the victim, inflicts bodily injury (assault), or is in a position of trust with regard to the victim: official authority (custody or control) or a familial relationship.

Date rape, or "acquaintance rape," is male sexual aggression in which the female half of a twosome is forced to have sexual intercourse. Sexual coercion by dates or acquaintances is rape. This type of rape is not the "blitz" type of rape in which no previous interaction occurred between offender and victim and the offender immediately threatens or uses force to overcome his victim. In date, or acquaintance, rape, the offender and the victim have had a previous relationship, but the victim has been forced to have sex without her consent.

The prevalence of forced sex among dates and acquaintances may be increasing, but, more likely, victims are now more aware of their basic rights.

After years of being underreported, this so-called simple rape is now being reported for what it is: forcible rape.[2]

Although most sexual assault victims are women, a man can also be victimized sexually. However, depending on the jurisdiction, the crimes involved when a man is a victim are usually sodomy, forcible oral copulation, or both, rather than the crime of rape. The investigative protocol is the same, regardless of the victim's sex.

Initial Action

The initial task of police upon receipt of a report of a forcible sexual assault is to aid the victim (Figure 11–1). The injured victim may require immediate transportation to a local hospital providing emergency services; apparent "shock"—known as **rape trauma syndrome**—should also warrant medical attention. Men and women taking these reports must do their best to avoid contributing to the victim's mental distress. The professional reporting officer must realize that the person reporting a forcible sexual assault has just been through an emotionally shattering experience and act accordingly.

Depending on the victim's condition, the next step is the initial interview, in which the victim is asked about the circumstances of the crime and the suspect's identity. If the victim requires medical attention or is in a state of shock, questioning should be extremely brief and limited to the facts of the crime and a description of the suspect for a radio broadcast alarm. If the victim can be questioned, this interview should probe all the circumstances of the crime and the suspect's identity.

At the conclusion of this interview, the victim should be told about the necessity of a physical examination. The victim should be informed that this exam is voluntary, but that the exam is vital to the collection and preservation of evidence that will reveal and corroborate the acts done and contribute to identification of the suspect.[3]

A medical examination of the victim of a forcible sexual assault may be conducted as part of the victim's medical treatment when he or she is hospitalized or by special arrangement with the victim. The examining physician's report becomes part of the record of the case. It is usually concerned with the victim's bodily injuries, evidence of force in relation to the perpetrator's sex act, evidence of the completion of the sex act to the penetration required by statute, and evidence likely to identify the suspect.

The victim of a forcible sexual assault may not know exactly where the crime occurred, or may have been in the suspect's car, and the vehicle is not usually available until the suspect is arrested. If a crime scene has been located, however, it must be promptly secured until properly searched.

Correlated with the victim's detailing of what happened, who did it, and where it happened is the search for witnesses. Their identity and where they

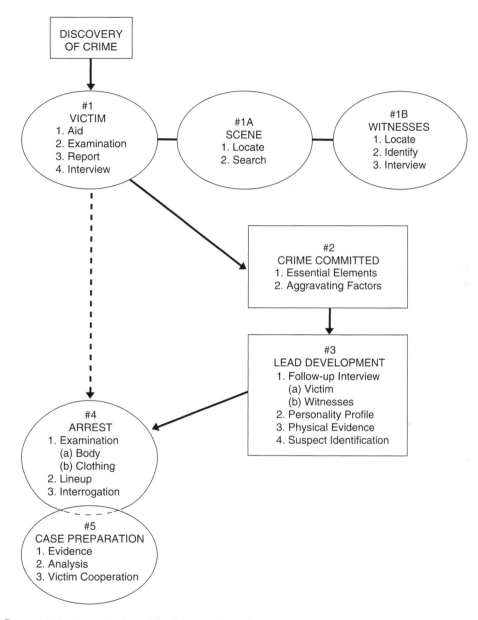

FIGURE 11-1   Investigation of forcible sexual assault.

can be located is important at this time in the investigation. What they observed can be secured later.

When the reporting officer believes the circumstances of the attack spell out the elements of a forcible sexual assault (lack of consent, use of force or fear, resistance by the victim, and penetration), the case should be so classified and emphasis placed on identifying and apprehending the suspect. When the victim identifies the suspect by name or as having been seen before the assault, the emphasis should be on locating this suspect. The same is true when the victim provides information about the color, design, or license plate number of a vehicle used by the suspect.

Unless the suspect is promptly identified by information supplied by the victim or witnesses, or is arrested in the "hot pursuit" phase of the police apprehension process, discovering the suspect's identity is likely to be the major problem in such investigations. Identification of a sexual assault suspect is a problem because, as a general rule, informants are not helpful, modus operandi files do not supply any leads unless the suspect is a repeat offender (serial rape cases), photographs of suspects are not usually available, and field interrogation reports are usually nonproductive. Leads to the identity of an unknown suspect may be developed from the same six areas as in criminal homicide investigations:

1. Victim's background
2. Persons in contact with the victim or places the victim visited in the hours immediately preceding the assault
3. Weapons found at the scene
4. Persons with "knowledge" or "opportunity"—access to the victim and crime scene, or actually at or near the scene at the time of the assault
5. Injured suspects (when the victim believes he or she scratched or otherwise injured the suspect)
6. Connect-ups with previous forcible sexual assaults

Follow-Up Interview of Victim

If a suspect is arrested before the follow-up interview of the victim, the focus of this interview is identification that will be legally significant in court at the trial. Inquiries should concern how the victim identifies the attacker. A lineup in which the suspect is placed among others to be viewed by the victim is warranted. All the standard legal safeguards protecting this identification from suggestibility or other invalidating factors must be in operation.

When the victim cannot identify the suspect in a lineup but police believe they have arrested the correct person, concentration is on other evidence of identity that will be compelling and overcome this failure to positively identify the suspect in a lineup. Even when the victim does identify the suspect in a lineup, other evidence of identity is important in case the defense counsel attacks the lineup identification at trial.

If the suspect has not been identified, the focus of the interview is on what the victim can remember about the circumstances of the assault that will contribute to the suspect's identification. What did the suspect look like? How was the suspect dressed? Was a vehicle included in the circumstances of this assault? These and related questions should develop the physical characteristics of the suspect and how he or she was dressed at the time, and perhaps some vehicle identification. Investigators must probe the victim's recall of events to uncover any particular physical characteristics or distinctive or unique article of clothing. Even the most fragmentary description can be helpful.

Arrangements with a police artist or an Identikit specialist may be indicated. The victim should approve the final artwork as a reasonable illustration of the suspect.

Computer searches are now available in most state motor vehicle bureaus, and "possibles" may be obtained, which will indicate vehicles matched to a fragment of a license plate number or a partial description, or both.

Extensive searches for the unidentified perpetrator of multiple sexual assaults (serial rapist) by police in several urban jurisdictions have indicated the need for information on a suspect's behavior. Therefore, the victim should be questioned about the suspect's "approach": how he exerted control over the situation, the sex acts attempted or communed, and whether the suspect made any effort to conceal his or her identity.

Was the approach friendly ("sweet talker") or brutal and surprising? What was the victim doing during this initial contact? What had the victim been doing just before this contact? Where had the victim been? Who had the victim seen there? Who might have witnessed this initial approach? These questions and others will provide behavioral dimensions to the first contact of the suspect with the victim.

Sexual assault suspects control their victims by some combination of the following:

- Verbal activity, particularly threats
- Display of a weapon
- Physical force

Threats and orders are the usual verbal activity, but some suspects are animated conversationalists. The essence of what was said and its pace are important aspects of the suspect's behavior. The details of weapon display are also part of the suspect's behavior. What weapon was displayed? How does the victim describe it? What did the suspect do with it?

The use of physical force and its extent is one of the most important factors in defining the suspect's behavior during the crime. A precise description of the force used should disclose whether it was minimal, excessive, or brutal. Another important factor is the suspect's reaction to any resistance by the victim.

A problem area of these follow-up interviews of the victim may occur when the investigator seeks details of the sex acts attempted or committed by the suspect. Perhaps the best technique is to inform the victim that these queries are necessary to determine the suspect's behavioral pattern and, possibly, to connect the suspect with other assaults.

This in-depth interview of the victim may be postponed because of the victim's injuries or mental condition, lack of a suitably private place, or a departmental ruling that such interviews be conducted by specially trained personnel.[4]

Follow-Up Interviews of Witnesses

The police officer accepting the report of a forcible sexual assault has the duty of securing the names and addresses of possible witnesses and, if time permits, of briefly interviewing them about what they might have observed. Then, when the crime scene is located and the time of occurrence firmly fixed, investigators may interview or reinterview these witnesses.

Follow-up interviews of the person to whom the victim reported the sexual assault, or from whom he or she initially sought help following the attack, are mandatory. These persons are primary witnesses to the victim's appearance and condition at the time. Of almost equal importance are witnesses who observed the victim and possibly the suspect just before the attack occurred.

Usually, sexual assault suspects find some area in which they will not be observed to commit their assault on their victims. Therefore, investigators are unlikely to find witnesses to the crime. Nevertheless, experienced investigators make every effort to find the chance onlooker who was a witness. Failing in this discovery, investigators depend on the individuals who observed the "before" and "after" phases of this crime.

The focus of the follow-up interviews of witnesses is to find evidence supportive or corroborative of the victim's report of a sexual assault.[5]

Personality Profile of the Serial Rapist

The victim's description of a rapist's behavior, upon analysis by competent personnel, reflects the rapist's personality. From data secured in the follow-up interview of the victim, a criminal personality profile may be prepared. These profiles require the services of persons trained in the behavioral sciences who can review the manner in which the rapist behaved and can portray the rapist as a person.[6] On the basis of victims' descriptions of rapists' behavior and the results of personal interviews with convicted rapists, three major types of rapists emerge:

1. *The Anger Rapist.*   The **anger rapist** commits the crime of rape as a means of expressing and discharging feelings of pent-up anger and rage. The assault is characterized by physical brutality. The rapist uses far more force than necessary to overpower the victim and achieve sexual penetration. This offender "attacks" his victim, grabbing her, striking her, knocking her to the ground, beating her, tearing her clothes, and raping her. He may use a blitz style of attack or he may use a confidence-style approach to gain access to the victim and then launch a sudden, overpowering attack. The anger rapist typically finds little or no sexual gratification in the rape. The act is more of a weapon—a means by which he can defile, degrade, and humiliate

his victim. These attacks are usually short and infrequent because it takes time for his frustrations and aggravation to reach a volatile point again. In summary, his intent is to hurt and degrade his victim, his weapon is sex, and his motive is revenge.

2. *The Power Rapist.* The **power rapist** uses sex as a means of compensating for underlying feelings of inadequacy and of expressing issues of mastery, strength, authority, and control over another person. His goal is sexual conquest, and he uses only the amount of force necessary to accomplish his objective. His aim is to capture and control his victim. He is often armed with a weapon as a means of intimidation. His victim may be subjected to repeated assaults during an extended period. This offender finds little sexual satisfaction in the rape because it never lives up to his fantasies. The amount of force and aggression used in the assault may increase with time as the offender becomes more desperate to achieve that indefinable experience that continues to elude him. His offenses become repetitive and compulsive, and he may commit a series of rapes during a relatively short period. Frequently, the power rapist denies that the sexual encounter was forcible. He needs to believe the victim wanted and enjoyed it. Following the assault, he may insist on buying the victim a drink or dinner and express a desire to see her again.

3. *The Sadistic Rapist.* The **sadistic rapist** finds the intentional maltreatment of his victim intensely gratifying and takes pleasure in her torment, anguish, distress, helplessness, and suffering. The assault usually involves bondage and torture and frequently has a bizarre or ritualistic quality to it. In extreme cases—those involving sexual homicide—he may commit grotesque acts such as sexually mutilating the victim's body or engaging in necrophilia. Usually, his victims are strangers who share a characteristic such as age, appearance, or occupation. They are symbols of something he wants to punish or destroy. The assault is deliberate, calculated, and preplanned. The offender takes precautions against discovery by wearing a disguise or blindfolding his victim. The victim is stalked, abducted, abused, and sometimes murdered. The sadistic rapist's intent is to abuse and torture his victim. He has made the connection between the infliction of pain and sexual gratification.

Examination of the incidence of these primary patterns of rape reveals that power rapes are most common. More than half (55 percent) of all cases involve a power rape, approximately 40 percent are anger rapes, and about 5 percent are sadistic rapes.[7] In essence, the crime of rape is primarily about anger and power and not about sexual desire. Although this information may not be considered a basic investigative lead in the identification and apprehension of the rapist, it is useful for interrogation of the suspect when he is eventually caught.

Arrest of the Suspect

Time is of the essence in arresting suspects in forcible sexual assault cases. If the arrest is made within a reasonable period from the time of the crime, medical personnel at a local hospital should conduct a full body examination of the suspect. Most hospitals with emergency treatment facilities have kits containing medical equipment and supplies used in these examinations. The report of the medical personnel conducting the examination becomes part of the total investigative report.

Since this report is nontestimonial evidence, no legal problems should be encountered. Delays incidental to securing a court order could result in the destruction of evidence. If the arrestee consents to this examination, appropriate forms should be prepared for the suspect's signature.

Scratches, bites, bruises, and other wounds are searched for and reported; scars, moles, and tattoos are detailed; and physical evidence associated with the crime should be secured. In addition, samples of the suspect's blood, urine, and hair (head and pubic) are taken.[8]

If the investigator has reason to believe that clothing worn by the suspect at the time of arrest was worn at the time of the crime, it should be seized and sent to the forensic science laboratory for examination. If the clothing was clearly not worn at the time of the crime, a prompt search should be instituted for such clothing. A search warrant may be required. All suspect clothing should be promptly forwarded to the forensic science laboratory for examination. Reports of these examinations also become part of the investigative record.

The time of arrest is the time for investigators to search for associative evidence that will corroborate the victim's testimony by placing the arrestee at the crime scene or in contact with the victim.

Case Preparation

Investigators assigned to a forcible sexual assault investigation must develop and hold the victim as a cooperative witness for the prosecution. The reinterviewing of the victim common in these cases, the time gap between arrest and trial, and the procedural safeguards protecting all accused persons will turn off most men and women who have been victims of a serious, violent crime and want the criminal punished.

Lack of victim cooperation may seriously complicate case preparation and make developing evidence proving the necessary elements of a forcible sexual assault difficult or impossible. This aspect of sexual assault investigations, along with the humanitarian aspects of treating a victim decently and exhibiting a sincere concern for his or her well-being during the postassault period, should motivate an investigator to do his or her best to close the case with an arrest and move it to trial without loss of time.

To overcome the common defenses of a forcible sexual assault charge, the investigator must prepare a case in which the victim is cast as the most truthful witness in the trial. Confirming and compelling evidence must be available at the trial to depict the victim in this truthful witness role.

Problems of Proof

When a defendant denies any involvement in a sexual assault, the most common defense is mistaken identity plus an alibi for the time of the crime (a claim of being elsewhere at or about the time of the crime).

Identification of a defendant as the suspect is a major problem of proof. Some suspects pull a pillowcase over the victim's head or cover his or her face with an article of clothing, others wear gloves to avoid leaving conclusive physical evidence, and a few have been known to command their victim, "Don't look at me!" In recent years, ski or stocking masks have become popular headgear for blitz-type sexual assaults. This problem can be overcome by a combination of the victim's identification of the defendant, the testimony about the initial meeting between victim and defendant (the suspect's "approach"), and "transfer" physical evidence linking the defendant to the victim or the scene of the assault.

When a suspect admits to sexual intercourse with the victim, the usual defense is consent. This defense is effective when the prosecution cannot show that the victim's resistance was overcome by an immediate threat or an overwhelming use of force, or that the victim did resist and did attempt to flee from the defendant. In cases involving date, or acquaintance, rape, the element of consent is likely to be a major problem. However, the fact of a prior relationship in these cases no longer implies such consent.

Problem-solving assistance is available from the Federal Bureau of Investigation's (FBI's) Investigative Support Unit (ISU). It offers profiles, assessments, and other support and may be able to link the details of the case under investigation with multiple sexual assaults elsewhere. Evidence from these "foreign" cases may provide a starting point for an investigator's case development.[9]

Sperm and blood are the common forms of evidence in sexual assault cases. In fact, this evidence has become such a given that many investigators have developed a "mental block" with regard to other physical evidence that may be effective in proving guilt or innocence or possibly penetration in these cases.

As the use of condoms increases, suspects will also probably use them more frequently. Investigators aware of the potential for traces from condoms to associate a suspect with one or more sexual assaults will find that many problems in investigating these sexual assaults will diminish and possibly disappear. The reason is the emerging forensic science procedure for extracting condom lubricant traces from evidence items in sexual assault cases. If condom lubricant traces are to have significant evidentiary value, new collection procedures at crime scenes and in subsequent transport to a crime lab must be developed. This professional "how-to" is likely to include instructions for the doctor conducting the medical examination, the investigator collecting crime scene evidence, and the detective interviewing the victim and the suspect.[10]

CHILD SEXUAL ABUSE

When children are the victims of criminal activity, they must be treated as persons to be helped (similar to victims of forcible sexual assault). The shock of being a crime victim, particularly when it involves sex acts, is heightened by police inquiry into the circumstances of the crime. Investigators must promptly recognize that the child victim may require medical attention for possible injuries and the emotional shock of such a crime.

Investigators are the community's agent in redressing the harm done to the child victims of crime. The investigator's role in cases involving child abuse, sexual exploitation, or abduction is that common to all investigations: reconstruct the event or events; determine whether a crime has been committed and, if so, what crime; identify the person or persons responsible; and take appropriate action. The investigator's role is not medical practitioner, social worker, counselor, or psychologist. However, the investigator is responsible for referrals to professionals in any of these disciplines whenever the investigation discloses that the child victim requires such help.

Incest

A person commits the crime of **incest** when he or she has sexual intercourse with a person known to be his or her parent or child, brother or sister, uncle or aunt, or nephew or niece. Most state laws use a broad definition of incest: any sexual contact between family members who are not permitted such behavior by social norms.

So-called **psychological incest** is sexual activity between a child and a stepparent, foster parent, or live-in boyfriend of the child's mother. It also includes such nonrelated family members as stepbrothers and stepuncles.[11]

This degrading form of child sexual abuse should be investigated along the same lines as physical child abuse: gathering facts about when, where, and what happened; identifying the adult involved; and determining the adult's family relationship to the victim.

Four important validations of the fact that incest has been committed are as follows:[12]

1. The acts committed were continuing and progressive.
2. The child's story of sexual abuse provides explicit detail in his or her own words.
3. Secrecy was encouraged, and the victim was pressured to keep silent (gifts, threats, family disgrace).
4. The victim retracts the accusation because of familial pressure.

Child victims should be transported to a hospital for an examination like that conducted in cases of forcible sexual assault. A similar examination of the suspect at the time of arrest may be warranted. Both examinations are oriented to discovering and collecting evidence supportive of the victim's story of the sexual abuse.

Pedophilia

A **pedophile** is someone who "loves" children. **Pedophilia** is a sexual interest in children that ranges from fondling to mutilation and murder. Two types of pedophiles are recognized: situational and preferential.

Of the two, the **situational child molester** has fewer victims. This type of molester does not have a true sexual interest in children but will experiment with them when the opportunity presents itself. This offender may also molest other vulnerable persons, such as persons who are elderly or physically or mentally impaired. These molestations are often the result of dealing with stress and poor self-esteem issues.[13]

The **preferential child molester** prefers children to adults as providers of sexual satisfaction. This person's interest in children is persistent and compulsive. Many pedophiles can be classified as preferential child molesters, and these offenders are the most likely to be extremely dangerous to children.

Diligent inquiry will disclose a network of other incidents, victims, and pedophiles. This **mushroom factor** links activity likely to identify a previously unknown child molester. Evidence available upon the arrest of a suspect (address book, identity of friends and associates) will often disclose the full details of a network of pedophiles and their victims. Common to this organization of pedophiles and child victims are registered sex offenders.[14]

Victims are good sources of information about these networks, particularly boys or girls who have participated in this activity voluntarily either because of their friendship with the molester or because they were paid for their services. Teenaged runaways of both sexes have admitted to this type of prostitution as a survival technique in a hostile environment.

Many molesters operate in their home or business neighborhoods, sometimes using one victim to recruit others in the age group of the molester's sexual preference. Other molesters gain access to victims by seeking leadership positions in a church or a community child-centered program. Given any organization for youths or occupation providing contact with children, some adult identified with it has been arrested for child sexual abuse. The mushroom factor in these cases takes little more than simple queries to develop: Who are the victim's friends in the neighborhood? What children's group is involved?

Pedophiles (a.k.a. **chicken hawks**) now use computers and available online services to locate potential child victims. They pose as another youth and begin their conversations with teenage subjects (e.g., drugs, girls, school, parents). As the friendship develops, they suggest a meeting. Child exploitation through computer bulletin boards and online information services is a rapidly growing problem.[15]

Investigators can learn more about this crime when they make their first arrest, questioning the offenders about their activities. When their acts do not imply guilt, but merely a displayed interest in the area, these offenders are likely to talk—and teach.

The need for police investigators to detect and discover child sexual molestation is great. Detection may originate from a casual inquiry of a runaway child encountered in other police activity about how he or she survived "on the street," from the investigation of an unrelated crime, or from the willingness of a knowledgeable defendant in a case awaiting trial to reveal significant information about child molestation in exchange for help with his or her plea negotiations.

A medical examination of the victim in these cases is more than warranted, as is a similar examination of the suspect upon arrest. This examination should be aligned with the reported sexual abuse and be focused on discovering urogenital or anal injuries, pain, irritation, and evidence of a venereal disease or any illness related to child molestation.

Clothing worn by the victim at the time of the attack and clothing belonging to the suspect that is seized by police as evidence at the time of arrest or in the postarrest period should be sent to the forensic science (crime) laboratory as physical evidence. Such clothing may contain trace evidence linking the suspect to the victim or place of occurrence of the attack, or it may contain evidence of the sexual contact or contacts.

When, where, what happened, and who did it are the classic queries likely to develop the circumstances of these crimes (Figure 11–2). If the collected evidence indicates child sexual molestation, the investigator should act promptly to identify and arrest the adult responsible. The investigator should work hard to link the suspect with other victims and other cases of child sexual abuse from evidence developed by the investigator at the time of arrest or in the postarrest period.

The Child as Victim-Witness

Children may testify in court in a variety of cases, but they are most likely to be classified as "key witnesses" in child-abuse trials. In these cases, the child is not only the victim, but also the only eyewitness. Moreover, in these criminal proceedings, police and court personnel are especially alert about protecting the defendant's constitutional rights. The rights of the child victim-witness will not be disregarded, but the child's competence as a witness will be examined in depth and the testimony given in court will be sharply scrutinized.

Investigators usually operate on the assumption that the child is telling the truth. This behavior is desirable for any "first-line" agent—parent, teacher, neighbor, physician, or police officer. However, the assigned investigator must work beyond this assumption and critically appraise the child's story during

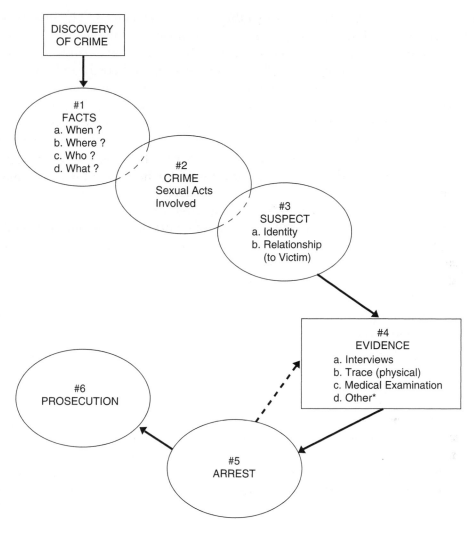

*Includes Network Development–Sex Abuse.

FIGURE 11–2   Investigation of child sexual abuse.

interviews and in postinterview periods when evidence supporting the child's story is sought. Linked to this appraisal is an ongoing demand that the investigator "carrying" the case offer an opinion about the child victim's competency as a future key witness. In forming an opinion about the child's competency, investigators should be mindful that the child must be observant, articulate, know truth as opposed to lies, and understand that a witness must testify truthfully.

Supporting evidence of a child's story of physical or sexual abuse should include evidence that totals to the "probable-cause" level, along with basic leads likely to upgrade the case when they are fully developed. The investigator needs this level of evidence for his or her decisions during the investigation; the child victim needs such support for his or her testimony in court.

California's McMartin Preschool case was long and costly and a revelation to criminal investigators about deficiencies in their inquiries. Police investigators attempted to jump-start their investigation by sending a letter to nearly 400 parents of children enrolled in this school. The letter encouraged parents to question their children about any sexual abuse by their teachers. However, many parents promptly mentioned it to one or more of the suspect teachers, which alerted these teachers to the threat of an ongoing investigation. The case went on for several years to an unsatisfactory conclusion: no one convicted, no truth of the accusations proved in court.[16]

Investigators need to learn the how-to of securing information from children. A nonsuggestive interview is likely to be more productive and have a basic integrity. The basic structure of this interview should contain several "don'ts": don't suggest—or even appear to suggest—anything to the child or his or her parents; don't reveal the allegations of other children involved in the same investigation; don't use dolls of any kind until subsequent interviews, and then only with good reason; and avoid news releases until the crime and its facts are clear and focused.

Missing Children

Any unemancipated young person under the legal adult age who, without a parent's or guardian's permission, remains away from his or her home for 24 hours or more is generally termed a **runaway** by local police.

Police in large cities often field a "Diaper Squad" to patrol local bus stations and "gut" areas containing occupancies such as adult theaters and bookstores, the "stroll" section in which local prostitutes operate, and the "meat rack" frequented by boys and young men catering to older men.

When runaways spend the funds they carried with them when they left home, they have difficulty replenishing their money through legitimate employment. "Hustling" is an aggressive reaction and is generally focused on sex for sale. Less aggressive runaways are picked up by pimps or sexual deviates and sometimes forced into prostitution.

Unfortunately, despite the work of police officers to locate missing children and return them to their parents or guardians, the number of runaway children in the United States provides pedophiles with recurring opportunities to find child victims. The many runaways create a major obstacle to searching for and finding a missing child. In addition, local police must depend on police from other jurisdictions in this search-and-identify task. So-called Runaway Programs operated by various youth organizations are emerging as a new resource for runaways, getting them off the street and encouraging them to contact their parents or guardian. These programs may also become a resource for investigators seeking missing children, particularly when evidence indicates the child has fled to a particular city.

When some aspect of a child's disappearance indicates abduction, local police will generally make an effective and timely response. The 1982 Missing Children's Act placed federal resources at the service of local police. The National Crime Information Center's Missing Person File of the FBI can be used to search for missing children believed to have been abducted.

The first step in the investigation of child abduction is to ensure that the child has not been abducted by a parent or grandparent. Once the investigator ascertains that the child is not a pawn in a family dispute, every reasonable means should be used to broadcast the facts of the case and a description of the missing child. Since many of these victims are murdered, this description should contain the child's dental chart, medical information, and fingerprints if available. (In emerging police programs, police fingerprint local children and provide the parents with the prints in case the child becomes a victim of an abductor.)

The investigation into an abduction generally follows the outline of any criminal homicide investigation. Since the victim is not available for interviewing, the investigator must concentrate on securing data about the victim's movements just before his or her disappearance. As facts are gathered, data are added to the published alarm. Collaterally, investigators probe among registered sex offenders, suspected pedophiles disclosed as part of a network in child sexual abuse investigations, and suspect persons or vehicles seen in the neighborhood of the child's disappearance.

Investigators must move promptly along two general lines: find the child, and identify and locate the suspect. One experienced detective described this type of investigation as "frantic," which is a graphic description of the fast-breaking and aggressive investigation likely to produce results in these cases.

CHAPTER REVIEW

CASE STUDY

East Area Rapist

The first rapes occurred in the eastern part of the county; thus the rapist was named the "East Area Rapist." In all, fifty-five rapes were reported to the police in five counties. However, many more rapes may have been committed but not reported. These rapes started in northern California and eventually ended 10 years later in Southern California. Police now believe this rapist made the transition to serial killer and may be responsible for as many as ten murders. Despite investigating and eliminating 5,000 possible suspects and spending more than

$2.5 million on the investigation, investigators have no clear picture of the armed man in a ski mask who terrorized his victims.

The rapist cased his victims with eerie diligence, which led some people to believe he had military or law enforcement training. Sometimes he would first slip into their homes, swiping a photograph or other small items that barely raised suspicion. He would gather details, like the floor plan, how the garage door operated, how an outside light timer worked, or the occupants' names and schedules. At one home, he removed bullets from a gun tucked under a mattress, then put it back. Then, he would come back during the night, armed with a gun or knife, carrying shoelaces to tie up his victims. He started with women living alone but soon moved to couples.

For as long as 3 hours, he would terrorize the victims. He kept the men from moving by putting dishes on them, threatening to kill if he heard anything break. He would then attack the women, disappear quietly in the house—eating pumpkin pie at one place—then come back again. The victims never knew for sure when he was gone. In later rapes, he grew more violent, more forceful in his threats. He was bold. He would telephone victims after the attack and would seem to know which lines were tapped. At town-hall meetings set up by the authorities, as many as 700 people would jam inside. At one, a couple raised doubts about the rapist's methods, questioning his existence. They were the next victims and investigators are sure he was in the audience, watching.

In Southern California, he also invaded quiet neighborhoods. He would sometimes prowl beforehand, then slip in through unlocked windows or doors. He would bring his own cord to tie up victims. He would sexually assault the women before bludgeoning them to death. Because of the similarities in these attacks, investigators, using long-shelved DNA evidence, have connected these crimes. Investigators are optimistic that this new evidence will lead to identification of a suspect.

Source: Adapted from M. S. Enkoji, "New Hope in the Hunt for Rapist," *Sacramento Bee,* May 24, 2001.

DISCUSSION QUESTIONS

1. What is the major responsibility of the first police officers on the scene of a forcible sexual assault?
2. What are the "aggravating" factors in these cases?
3. Is medical examination of the victim of a forcible sexual assault necessary? When should it be conducted? What should its scope be?
4. Outline the major factors to be covered by investigators during the follow-up interview of a victim.
5. What is the focus of the follow-up interview of a witness in sexual assault cases?
6. Does the previous relationship between a victim and the suspect in date rapes create a problem for the police-prosecutor team?
7. Describe "network" development in child sexual abuse cases.
8. Can police detect child sexual abuse? How?
9. How do child molesters use computers to find potential victims?
10. Which type of rapist is discussed in the case study?

LIBRARY ASSIGNMENT

Review available material on police-victim relations in sexual assault cases and outline substandard police practices.

WORKBOOK PROJECT

Develop a list of all the items of evidence likely to contribute to the identification of a rapist. Divide this list into two segments: evidence tending to identify the rapist before arrest, and evidence tending to identify the arrested rapist as the person guilty of the rape or rapes under investigation.

RELATED WEB SITES

Interested in knowing the sexual assault statistics in the United States? If so, visit the Men Against Sexual Assault Web site at *www.sa.rochester.edu/masa*.

For information about what a sexual assasult is and preventive measures, consult this Web site: *www.sao.co.st-clair.il.us/sexalt.asp*.

NOTES

1. PAUL B. WESTON and KENNETH M. WELLS, *Criminal Law* (Santa Monica, CA: Goodyear, 1978), 253–62.
2. SUSAN ESTRICH, *Real Rape* (Cambridge, MA: Harvard University Press, 1987), 7–26.
3. JOSEPH A. ZECCARDI and DIANA DICKERMAN, "Medical Exam in the Live Sexual Assault Victim," in *Practical Aspects of Rape Investigation—A Multidisciplinary Approach*, ed. Robert R. Hazelwood and Ann Wolbert Burgess, 315–25 (New York: Elsevier Science, 1987).
4. LISA BRODYAGA et al., *Rape and Its Victims: A Report for Citizens, Health Facilities, and Criminal Justice Agencies* (Washington, DC: U.S. Department of Justice, Law Enforcement Assistance Administration, 1975), 37–42.
5. JERRY D. MOODY and VICKI ELLEN HAYES, "Responsible Reporting: The Initial Step," in *Rape and Sexual Assault: Management and Intervention*, ed. Carmen Germaine Warner, 27–45 (Rockville, MD: Aspen Systems, 1980).
6. ROBERT R. HAZELWOOD, "The Behavior-Oriented Interview of Rape Victims: The Key to Profiling," *FBI Law Enforcement Bulletin* 52, no. 9 (1983): 8–15.
7. A. NICHOLAS GROTH, *Men Who Rape: The Psychology of the Offender* (New York: Plenum Press, 1979), 12–59.
8. RICHARD BRAEN, "Examination of the Accused: The Heterosexual and Homosexual Rapists," in *Rape and Sexual Assault: Management and Intervention*, ed. Carmen Germaine Warner, 85–91 (Rockville, MD: Aspen Systems, 1980).
9. C. R. VAN ZANDT and S. E. ETHER, "Real Silence of the Lambs," *Police Chief* 61, no. 4 (1994): 45–52.
10. R. D. BLACKLEDGE, "Collection and Identification Guidelines for Traces from Latex Condoms in Sexual Abuse Cases," *Crime Laboratory Digest* 21, no. 4 (October 1994): 57–61.

11. ROBERT J. BARRY, "Incest: The Last Taboo," *FBI Law Enforcement Bulletin* 53, no. 1 (1984): 2–9.

12. MARVIN R. JANSSEN, "Incest: Exploitive Child Abuse," *The Police Chief* 51, no. 2 (1984): 46–47.

13. SETH GOLDSTEIN, "Investigating Child Sexual Exploitation: Law Enforcement's Role," *FBI Law Enforcement Bulletin* 53, no. 1 (1984): 22–30.

14. VINCENT DEFRANCIS, *Protecting the Child Victim of Sex Crimes Committed by Adults* (Denver, CO: American Humane Association, 1969), 1–2.

15. T. M. DEES, "Cyberchip Chickenhawks: A Mix of Kids, Computers, and Pedophiles," *Law Enforcement Technology* 21, no. 10 (1994): 52–55.

16. NANCY WALKER PERRY and LAWRENCE S. WRIGHTSMAN, *The Child Witness: Legal Issues and Dilemmas* (Newbury Park, CA: Sage, 1991), 2–10.

12

ROBBERY

COMPONENTS OF ROBBERY

To substantiate charging a suspect with robbery, the investigator must uncover legally significant evidence that a crime was committed, that this crime was robbery, and that the defendant committed it. In such investigations, the basic evidence must prove each of the three essential elements of the crime of **robbery**:

1. Taking of personal property from the person or the presence of a possessor
2. Against the possessor's will
3. By force or fear

Taking "from the person" means from the victim's body or his or her clothing, and "from the presence of a possessor" means within the victim's sight or hearing. The nature of robbery is that an offender not only takes personal property with the intent to steal, but also carries it away. Taking a possession away from the victim and into the robber's control is sufficient. Control by the robber rather than the distance moved is the issue. "Against the possessor's will" is implied in the force or fear element of robbery. This force or fear must be adequate to frighten the victim and make the victim part with his or her property against his or her will.

Robbery is generally divided into two degrees to express the legislative intent that armed robberies are more serious than unarmed robberies:[1]

First Degree. Robbery while armed with a dangerous or deadly weapon likely to cause death or serious wounding

Second Degree. Robbery accomplished by physical force or its threat but without a weapon, including purse snatching

Robbery is a felony-level crime likely to result in a convicted robber's receiving a lengthy sentence and may be aggravated (which leads to a longer sentence) when the robber has an armed crime partner at the scene and either of them inflicts serious bodily injury on the victim or a witness.

Related crimes, such as kidnapping, must be substantiated similarly. However, larceny and assault merge with the robbery. In contrast, kidnapping may not merge with the robbery. In 1969, the top court in California repudiated the doctrine that any movement of the robbery victim amounted to kidnapping. In *People v. Timmons*, the court held that the true test was whether the movement of the victim substantially increased the risk of harm beyond that inherent in robberies.[2] If it did, kidnapping would be added to the charges against the robber or robbers; if not, the "movement" would be considered part of the robbery activity.

During the robbery investigation, the investigator need not decide whether these crimes join with the robbery or are separate crimes. The investigator's role is simply to collect all available evidence and develop the existence of related crimes from the array of collected evidence.

Another area of concern is the difference between robbery and extortion. One essential of robbery is consent resulting from force or fear. In extortion, the victim consents more willingly; consent may be induced by persuasive threats related to future harm or disgrace rather than here-and-now harm. A close call for investigators is a **scam** described in 1890 by Chief of Detectives James Byrnes of the New York Police Department as the **badger game**. This scam is an extortion scheme in which a woman places a selected victim in a comprising position (nude, in bed, in a hotel room) and then victimizes him by demanding money. Next, her male accomplice breaks in and pretends to be an outraged husband threatening violence, scandal, or the like. The victim's harassment is the key to the success of this scheme.

Identification in an armed robbery case often relates to the tactics or style of the robbery. Robbery has been categorized as having three styles: the ambush, the selective raid, and the planned operation. The **ambush robbery** is the least planned and is based on the element of surprise. The **selective-raid robbery** involves a minimum of planning but involves some "casing" of the robbery scene. The **planned-operation robbery** is carefully structured: The robbery group examines all aspects of the situation and plans for all foreseeable contingencies. In fact, the group may stage "dry runs" in this style of robbery.

Crime partners in a robbery group form a loose partnership that provides the skills for the various tasks necessary to carry out different types of robberies. They participate in planning the robbery, including the basic decision about whether a certain target can be successfully robbed. Crime partners are usually associates from **spontaneous "play groups"** in the underworld: persons who live in or frequent the same neighborhood, who purchase drugs from the same source, or who have served sentences in juvenile or adult institutions together.

New York's notorious "Robert's Lounge Gang" comprised customers frequenting a small bar near the cargo area of John F. Kennedy Airport. This gang was of varying size—depending on the availability of targets—but in total its membership was drawn from the spontaneous play group that assembled daily

A video surveillance camera picture of a robbery in progress. From Sacramento, California, Sheriff's Department.

in this popular drinking place. Seven members of the gang carried out a robbery at the Lufthansa Air Cargo terminal at Kennedy Airport. Their loot totaled $8 million in cash, jewels, and gold. Investigators were frustrated in their probing, until one suspect led them to Robert's Lounge and his gang associates.[3]

Investigators assigned a single robbery or series of robberies should search for linkups, or connect-ups, that will indicate a group's operations. In many instances, a gang of two to six robbers will not allow more than two robbers to "surface" on the scene of a robbery. A Chicago robber, whose robbery group specialized in ambushing lone pedestrians late at night in streets and alleys, explained this switching of the group's membership in various robberies: "Now we never did nothing with the four of us together, always two. I'd be with George when we'd get one guy, and next I'd be with Percy."[4] Linking or connecting several robberies may develop the identification of four or five members of a gang, and such data may lead the investigator to some clues about the style of a particular robbery gang.

The fact that a robbery mob may be involved in a robbery or series of robberies can be developed by the investigator through a study of the style of the robbery: if it was a selective raid or a planned operation, whether a getaway driver aided the robbery, and whether backup people were present at the scene.

Inquiries may reveal data identifying one or two persons, who are not similar in description to the armed robber or robbers who committed the crime, loitering around the premises and inquiring about employment or making other inquiries that would permit them access to the premises and would allow them to scan the crime scene before the robbery ("casing" the robbery).

The presence of a getaway driver may be established from witnesses who can offer data about how the robber or robbers who committed the robbery fled the crime scene. A **getaway driver** is a driver specialist who remains in the escape vehicle until the robbers have completed the robbery, then picks them up and flees the scene.

A **backup person** is a member of the gang who remains in the background unnoticed and, in case of trouble, supports the gang members who are committing the robbery. The presence of backup people may be more difficult to discover because the backup person often does not flee from the scene in the same car as that used by the armed robber or robbers. Since he or she has not been identified with the crime, he or she may stay at the scene for some time, then walk away to meet with his or her crime partners at some prearranged location. The role of backup person in modern robbery gangs is to protect his or her crime partners from the unexpected. He or she is "buried" in the store (when customers are not the victims) or outside the robbery scene, where he or she can view the crime scene and its approaches. His or her job is to fight off police who might chance on the scene or respond to a silent alarm.

Robberies have some signature aspects. These so-called trademarks are part of the modus operandi of a crime and distinguish it as work of a specific robber or a group of robbers who have committed previous crimes in which the same identifying circumstances occur. The investigating officers pick out from the modus operandi the most likely identifying "signature" characteristic and develop their investigation to lead to the identity of the robber group. For instance, the "paper bag robber" was a robber who carried a brown paper bag to the scene of the robbery and told the victims to put their money and valuables in the bag. The "lovers'-lane robber" frequented lovers' lanes and his victims were always a boy and a girl. The "Mutt and Jeff" team of robbers were always described as a tall man and a short man.

Traditionally, weapons indicate violence. However, violence is used in robberies only as a tool for carrying out the robbery. A new measure of violence in robberies indicating some hostility on the robber's part has emerged only recently. Such hostility can serve as a "signature" characteristic to identify suspects

Although most robberies are committed by men, women also commit this crime. From Sacramento, California, Sheriff's Department.

because it is unusual among robbers. Most robbers view the use of violence to overcome resistance as only a "self-defense" measure. Nevertheless, the number of wanton pistol-whippings or shootings of victims has been increasing. Such violence is the use of force beyond that necessary to control the robbery victim or victims. As one convicted robber said, "The last thing you want is trouble. If you gotta shoot somebody you gotta run, and you don't get any money. The thing is to get in and get what you are after and get out with the least trouble possible."[5]

The use of addicting and dangerous drugs by a robber is indicated when the modus operandi reveals that restricted drugs are part of the proceeds of a robbery. Even when restricted drugs are not part of the proceeds of a robbery, an investigator can identify the robberies of a drug addict by the time span between robberies and the proceeds of each crime. This assumption is based on other modus operandi information identifying a "series" of robberies as the work of one or more robbers, the amount of money stolen, and the date of the next robbery by the robber or robbers under investigation. The time gap between the robberies is extended when a good "score" allows the robbers to buy sufficient drugs for a specific habituation level ($100-a-day habit; $200-dollar-a-day habit). A characteristic of the addict-robber is that robberies are not committed when the addict is on a drug "high," but rather when he or she needs money for drugs.

In the investigation of robberies, investigators must realize the potential for conflict between data contained in police reports and the testimony of witnesses in court. Accuracy in recording witnesses' statements is of primary importance. Investigators should neither encourage a witness to guess nor record a guess as a fact. They should not suggest facts to a witness who is unsure. They must let the witness describe the person, car, weapon, clothes, disguise, marks, hair, speech, and the like in his or her own terms and record the witness's terms, not use interpretive terms. Normal mistakes in descriptions will be made, but the investigator should not compound these mistakes by adding to or interpreting the witness's descriptions.

THE TARGET IN ROBBERIES

The determination of a criminally oriented person to rob a specific and predetermined person or place, when and how to do it, and whether he or she cruises to find a place to rob are mental processes of considerable interest to an investigator. The selection of a target in robberies offers clues as to who did it. In planned robberies, the acts done in planning before the crime can suggest suspects or indicate persons in the suspect group who are unlikely suspects. In the unplanned robberies of the cruising criminal, an investigator can develop some theory as to who did it solely on the basis of the target selection.

In planned robberies, the offender considers not only the victim of the robbery, but also such operational facts as the number of accomplices necessary, the weapons to select, the number of persons likely to be present during the robbery, and the escape route. In unplanned robberies, the offender acts on impulse, generally selects a weapon according to its availability, and haphazardly cruises an area in search of a victim.[6] Nevertheless, the "cruiser" does avoid victims likely to be armed or places that might be wired for a silent alarm that will alert police to a robbery in progress.

When using the target aspects of a crime to further an investigation, the investigator must first attempt to determine if the robbery was planned or unplanned. Beginning with information about the victim and whether he or she was alone at the time, and information about the place of the crime, the investigator tries to evaluate the need for precrime planning. The cruising robber seeks victims who will present little or no operational problem (resistance or alarm operation). Lone victims are symptomatic of unplanned robberies, although the place of the robbery may offer more of a substantial clue to target selection and to the planning of the crime.

Residence (**home invasion**) robberies were always considered planned crimes until the advent of **cruising robberies** in above-average-income residential areas and secluded hotel rooms. Bank robberies were also considered planned until the emergence of the **single-teller bank robbery**, in which a person armed with a note and some threat of force victimizes only one teller. Off-street businesses are still the victims reserved for planned robberies. Residence and bank robberies can be placed in the same class when the residence victim has a local reputation for having large sums of cash at home or when the bank robbery extends to more than one teller. Airport cargo areas are also the targets of planned robberies; in such robberies, dishonest air cargo employees supply the robbers with information about the best time to strike for maximum profit.

Markets, liquor stores, and other retail establishments are a no-man's land between planned and unplanned robberies. A cruising robber will enter such premises and appraise their vulnerability within a few minutes of shopping or browsing and then make a decision.[7] Conversely, the attendant circumstances may indicate planning: a fast entry and an apparent knowledge of the routine, the personnel, or both, or timing that coincides with an unusual amount of cash on hand.

ATMs are now popular as a robbery target with younger and potentially violent robbers. Robbery of service stations, taverns, ATMs, drive-in facilities, on-street victims, and victims in vehicles is usually the work of cruising robbers. Such cruising of an area by a robber seeking victims appears to be a nocturnal activity. The lone service station attendant and the little-patronized drive-in or motel offer targets of opportunity, as does the isolated tavern or cafe. Pedestrians and victims in vehicles who are accosted when stopped at a traffic signal, when picking up a hitchhiker, when accepting a taxi passenger, when operating a bus, or when responding to a telephone order to deliver food are victims by chance.

IDENTIFICATION EVIDENCE

In robberies in which the victim is not killed, robbers are identified by their facial characteristics, natural marks or tattoos, hairline and hair color, race, clothing, speech characteristics, and unusual habits or nervous spasms. In robberies in which the victim is killed or is unable to see the robber's face, identification can be made from the robbers' general physical build, fingerprints, footprints, and type of disguise; recovery of the loot; the means of escape (automobile license plate, model, or year, if an automobile is used); and the weapon type. A sufficiently compelling combination of such factors will succeed in convincing a court or jury of the robber's identity. Facial characteristics, fingerprints, or an auto license plate may be sufficiently persuasive without additional factors.

Grounds for attacking the credibility of the identification evidence are as follows:

- Suggestive use of photographs
- Failure to safeguard the accused's rights when a suspect or an arrestee is placed in a police lineup (see Appendix A, Case Briefs, for *United States v. Wade*)
- Conflict between the physical description given by witnesses and the actual appearance of the defendant in court
- Conflict between the weapon described by witnesses, or "constructively described" by the nature of injuries inflicted on the victim, and the weapon presented in court as the robbery weapon
- Conflict between the vehicle, if any, involved in the robbery as described by witnesses and the actual vehicle used in the robbery

Fixed TV surveillance cameras have assumed an increasingly important role in the identification of robbers. This photographic surveillance frequently obtains identifiable photographs of persons engaged in a robbery. Such photographs are used in identification of suspects, in their apprehension, and as identification evidence at trial. Banks pioneered the use of overt, fixed-surveillance cameras, but the rise in robberies of stores and other businesses has extended the use of these cameras to both overt and covert installations.[8]

CHECKLIST FOR THE INVESTIGATION OF ROBBERY

A prompt response by police to the scene of a robbery, a fast-breaking search for the robber or robbers, and a continuing investigation aimed at identifying the person or persons responsible compose the basic routine for successful robbery investigations (Figure 12–1). Following is a checklist for the investigation of robbery:

1. Assume the suspect is present, and arrest him or her if possible.
2. If the suspect has left the scene, ascertain how, his or her description, and whether a vehicle was used.
3. Describe the suspect to the dispatcher, along with the following:
   a. Nature of offense
   b. Weapon involved
   c. Direction of flight
   d. Description of vehicle
   e. Loss, if any
4. Search for the suspect.
   a. Escape route
   b. Refuges (theater, tavern)
   c. Hide-ins (stairways, cellars, yards, trash bins)
   d. Prowler calls
   e. Stolen cars

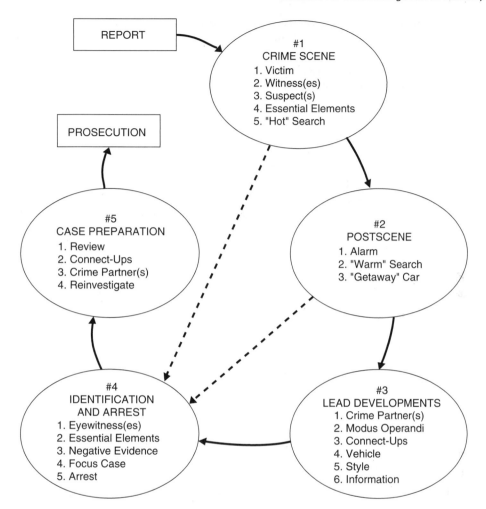

FIGURE 12-1 Investigation of robbery.

5. Search the scene for evidence.
   a. Protect the scene.
   b. Call in a technician.
   c. Extend the scene to the "discard" area.
6. Search the scene for witnesses.
   a. Include latecomers and onlookers.
   b. Canvass the view area and the neighborhood.
7. Advise the superior officer of the following:
   a. Details of offense
   b. Identification of victim and witnesses
   c. Personnel at the scene and assignments
   d. Progress of preliminary investigation
8. Prepare a report on the preliminary investigation.
9. Compile a physical description of the suspects and vehicle, if any.

10. Identify any crime partners or crime group.
11. Ascertain the modus operandi.
    a. Target
    b. Bindings (tape, wire)
    c. Weapon or weapons
    d. Plus rape
    e. Plus kidnapping
    f. Narcotics taken
    g. Signature ("stripper," "rifle mob")
12. Locate and interview informants.
13. Identify robbery groups.
    a. Number in group
    b. Connect-ups
    c. Spontaneous play groups
        i. Prison
        ii. Neighborhood
        iii. Same drug dealer
        iv. Same teen center
    d. Presence of getaway driver
    e. Presence of backup person or people
14. Identify the style of the robbery.
    a. Ambush
    b. Selective raid
    c. Planned operation; "inside" information
15. Use other basic leads for identification.
16. Identify offenders and arrest them.
17. Prepare the case.

REPEAT-OFFENDER CASES

Career criminals are offenders who have had previous arrests, have one or two cases pending in the local courts, and are on the street on some form of conditional release at the time of their latest arrest. Whereas other violent serious crimes may be committed in a series of two or more, the "series" assailant or rapist is not usually a career criminal.

Career criminals comprise a high percentage of armed robbers. Robbery is the violent crime favored by repeat offenders. As a result, many prosecutors have established special units to concentrate on the prosecution of recidivists, particularly armed robbers. From a crime-control standpoint, placing priority on such repeat-offender cases is now considered an appropriate strategy for prosecutors. In the past, prosecutors expended their effort on the basis of the strength of the evidence in a case, the probability of conviction, or the leverage of plea bargaining. Prosecutors are currently realizing that repeat-offender cases are inherently more convictable. Witnesses are generally more cooperative in repeat-offender cases, and the factors leading to the frequent arrests of these robbers also contribute to the weight of evidence indicating guilt.[9]

Investigators must make every effort to build a strong case against a repeat offender to maximize the probability of his or her conviction. However, they must also do so as rapidly as possible to get the repeat offender off the street and into an effective corrections program.

CARJACKING

Carjacking—the theft or attempted theft of a motor vehicle by force or threat of force from the person or the immediate presence of the victim—is armed robbery, a felony-level crime. Even when the carjacker does not display a weapon, the force and fear required for robberies is present (a forced entry of the driver's side door, followed by a rude command to leave the car). When the circumstances and conditions of the robbery lead to a reasonable belief in the victim's mind that he or she may suffer injury unless he or she complies with the robber's demand, the "fear" required in robbery is present. The fact that fewer than half the carjackings from 1987 to 1992 were completed without weapons is evidence that drivers confronted by a carjacker should be frightened. The most common carjacking is committed by an assailant in his or her 20s with a pistol or revolver and a crime partner. Conversely, auto thieves commit crimes of stealth without violence and out of the owner's presence. When they no longer need the car, they abandon it. Investigators in police agencies must stop treating carjackings as they would auto theft (by closing the case when the car is recovered) and consider them crimes of violence, crimes primarily against the person, not against property.

Outline of the Carjacking Investigation

The carjacking investigation is structured around a multiscene routine focused on using the recovery of the car not as a goal but as an aid in identification of the offender. When the offense runs true to form, the carjacking has taken place, the first officers and associates have secured a physical description of the carjacker from the victim along with data on his or her car, and the investigation is turned over to an assigned detective or detectives. An outline of the elements that should be investigated is as follows:

1. *The Crime Scene.* Investigation of a carjacking crime scene is the same as for a robbery crime scene, plus an expanded canvass for witnesses to the offender's, and possibly the crime partner's, precrime activity; the vehicle used; and the offenders' conduct while selecting a victim.
2. *The In-Progress Crime Scene.* An in-progress crime scene includes places such as the gas station where the fleeing offenders purchased gasoline and the area in which the offenders were involved in a traffic accident. Likewise, if the car was equipped with a cell phone, calls made on the phone should be investigated.
3. *The Dump Scene.* Prior notice should be given to patrol units to secure the car where it is "dumped" and to not touch it. The finder should be asked

to notify the assigned detective or command. Arrangements should be made to tow the car to the crime lab, where fingerprint examination of the interior and exterior of the car should be requested. Any damage to the car and any other possible physical evidence should be noted.

4. ***The Prearrest Scene.***   A modus operandi search for "similars" in the past year should be conducted, and incoming crime reports on carjackings, ATM heists, and fast-food restaurant robberies should be scanned hourly. Composite sketches and photo spreads should be arranged. Inquiries should be made in line with relevant basic leads. (The investigator's hunch should be used as a guide to the suspect's home neighborhood and why the crime scene location was selected—for example, the suspect might have been a former employee of fast-food restaurants in the crime scene area.)

5. ***The "Receiver" Scene.***   The receiver scene is where the car parts are sold. The investigator should trace the car parts to buyers and thus seek the offender's identity.

6. ***The "Fraud" Scene.***   If the victim had a handbag in the car at the time of the crime, the carjacker may use the victim's credit cards, pass them to family or friends, or sell them on the street. Each transaction should be traced to determine the offender's identity.

7. ***Postarrest.***   The investigator should try to develop the crime partner, if he or she was arrested with the carjacker; receivers of car parts; and credit card abusers as witnesses against the carjacker at trial.

This outline focuses not only on identifying the carjacker, but also on making "deals" with other involved individuals to ensure a successful prosecution.

PROBLEMS OF PROOF

The first major problem of proof in robbery cases concerns the defendant: identifying him or her as the robber. The second major problem is how to show conclusively that the crime committed is a robbery in which the victim was separated from his or her valuables through force or against the victim's will.

The victim is expected to testify as a major identification witness. After all, the confrontation in robberies is between robber and victim. If a victim's testimony is weak and inconclusive, supporting witnesses need to be positive in their identification of the robber. Often, the defendant not only denies the act done, but claims mistaken identity and offers an alibi in support of this claim. If the alibi has strength and the identification evidence is weak, many jurors will have reasonable doubt.

The victim of a robbery is also mandated by the elements of the crime of robbery to testify that he or she handed over to the robber money and other valuables because of fear. Threats alone are not legally significant unless the victim testifies that he or she believed the robber had the intent to carry them out as well as the apparent ability to do so promptly.

CHAPTER REVIEW

CASE STUDY

This is a Holdup!

A case summary written by assigned detectives details the circumstances of an armed robbery.

Case Summary

0900 Hours.   A WMA (white male adult), armed with a revolver and wearing a ski mask, coveralls, and gloves, entered the State Credit Union office and confronted two clerks and a male customer. The armed suspect demanded money after placing his weapon to the head of the male customer. Demand was met by Anne O'Brien, employee of the credit union. She placed approximately $8,600 in paper monies in a paper bag given to her by the suspect. The suspect then ordered one of the clerks to lie on the floor and then fled through the front door of the credit union, where he had made his initial entry.

0930 Hours.   Detectives Robert DeRose and Lt. Jacob Saylor arrived at the scene. Investigation was made and it was determined that witness O'Brien believed she recognized the robber as being a former borrower whose name she could not recall; but she recognized him by his build, eyes, and voice. She advised that she believed that the suspect had recently applied for a loan at the credit union. The investigation was completed at the scene, and the officers returned to the Detective Division after advising Mrs. O'Brien to come to the Detective Division as soon as possible.

1100 Hours.   Mrs. O'Brien called Detective DeRose and advised that she now recalled the robber's name as being Herbert C. Straus. She stated she obtained this information from a credit application she had on file. She also supplied other pertinent information regarding the suspect.

1120 Hours.   Detective DeRose arrived at DMV (Department of Motor Vehicles) and picked up a Soundex photo of the suspect: Straus. Prior to his arrival, DeRose had contacted DMV and requested the check and photo be made.

1210 Hours.   Mrs. O'Brien arrived in the Detective Division and viewed five driver license photos of like appearance, one of which was that of the suspect Straus. Without hesitation, Mrs. O'Brien picked the photo of Straus and advised that she was positive that this was the person who had robbed her this date.

1245 Hours.   Detective R. Phelps, Detective R. DeRose, Sgt. D. Migliorini, and Lt. Saylor arrived at 402 12th Street after a determination had been made that the suspect lived at that address. Lt. Saylor rang the doorbell and a male voice from within inquired, "Who's there?" Lt. Saylor replied, "Police." The door was opened by suspect Straus and he was immediately taken into custody. He was handcuffed and seated on the couch in the front room. After being apprised of his constitutional rights, the suspect was advised of the circumstances that brought the officers to his residence. A consent to search his home was also obtained at this time.

      The suspect became very cooperative. He admitted that he was the robber. Detective DeRose found a coffee can in the southeast bedroom that contained what appeared to be a considerable amount of money. Suspect then told officers that the gun he used in the robbery was under the cushion in a chair in the front room, and pointed out the chair. Gun, a .38-caliber Smith & Wesson 2-inch "Chiefs Special" was discovered.

1330 Hours.   Identification unit arrived and arrestee's residence was processed.

1510 Hours.   Arrestee was brought to Detective Division. There he again was apprised of his constitutional rights, and he gave a free, voluntary, and complete statement. In his statement, the suspect made admissions that he and he alone was responsible for this offense.

1600 Hours.   The suspect was booked as Herbert C. Straus into the County Jail (Arrest #1068) as the person responsible for this robbery. Monies and gun booked as evidence.

1730 Hours.   Arrest #1068 clears this report. Recovered was approximately $8,600.

DISCUSSION QUESTIONS

1. What are the styles of robbery?
2. Relate the styles of robbery to robbery targets.
3. What are the essential elements of robbery that distinguish this crime from theft?
4. Describe the role of a backup person in a robbery.
5. What facts likely to be disclosed in a robbery investigation can serve as identification of a robber?
6. Why are ATMs a popular target in robberies?
7. Which of the basic leads should be used to develop evidence of identification in robbery investigations?
8. Discuss the groups from which robbers generally recruit crime partners.
9. What are the signature aspects of the modus operandi of robbers?
10. Why is determining whether a robbery suspect may be addicted to restricted drugs useful?
11. What is the role of fixed-surveillance cameras in the robbery investigation?
12. What are the similarities and differences between a series rapist and a repeat offender (robber)?
13. Is giving priority to the investigation and prosecution of career criminals (repeat offenders) a violation of a suspected robber's constitutional rights?
14. Discuss the physical evidence involved in the case study.
15. What kind of evidence was most useful in solving the case in the case study?
16. Discuss the cooperative nature of the suspect after he was arrested. What brought about this level of cooperation?

LIBRARY ASSIGNMENT

Locate and list at least five autobiographical writings by former robbers.

WORKBOOK PROJECT

During a 30-day period, survey one or more of the local newspapers for news stories about armed robberies and felony-murder robberies.

RELATED WEB SITES

For charts and tables about robbery trends in the United States, consult this Web site: *www.ojp.usdoj.gov/bjs/glance/rob.htm.*

To view robbery surveillance photos and robbery prevention tips, check out the Colorado Association of Robbery Investigators Web site: *www.co-asn-rob.org.*

NOTES

1. KENNETH M. WELLS and PAUL B. WESTON, *Criminal Law* (Santa Monica, CA: Goodyear, 1978), 200–211.
2. *People v. Timmins*, 482 F.2d 648 (1971).
3. ERNEST VOLKMAN and JOHN CUMMINGS, *The Heist—How a Gang Stole $8,000,000 at Kennedy Airport and Lived to Regret It* (New York: Franklin Watts, 1986), 1–27.
4. HENRY WILLIAMSON, *Hustler* (New York: Doubleday, 1965), 117.
5. JOHN BARTLOW MARTIN, *My Life in Crime—The Autobiography of a Professional Criminal* (New York: Harper & Brothers, 1952), 68.
6. GERALD D. WOLCOTT, "A Typology of Armed Robbers" (master's thesis, Sacramento State College, 1968), 30.
7. WILLIAMSON, *Hustler*, 188–206.
8. U.S. DEPARTMENT OF JUSTICE, LAW ENFORCEMENT ASSISTANCE ADMINISTRATION, *Selection and Application Guide to Fixed Surveillance Cameras* (Washington, DC: U.S. Department of Justice, Law Enforcement Assistance Administration, 1974), 1–5; *United States v. McNair*, 439 F. Supp. 103 (1977).
9. U.S. DEPARTMENT OF JUSTICE, LAW ENFORCEMENT ASSISTANCE ADMINISTRATION, *Curbing the Repeat Offender: A Strategy for Prosecutors* (Washington, DC: U.S. Department of Justice, Law Enforcement Assistance Administration, 1977), 16–17.

13

Arson, Bombings, and Hate Crimes

Fires set by arsonists and explosives placed to damage property and kill or inflict injury on people are crimes against both the person and property. Because extreme secrecy usually surrounds the fire setting or the placing of explosives, these crimes create problems for investigators.

ARSON

The great eighteenth-century British jurist Sir William Blackstone, in his *Commentaries on the Laws of England*, defined **arson** as the "malicious and wilful burning of the house or outhouse of another man."[1] In common law, arson was considered an offense against the home (habitation). It was defined as the malicious and wilful burning of a dwelling (house or outhouse) of another and extended to structures within the curtilage* of the dwelling.

U.S. arson law has taken many twists, depending on the individual state law examined. Arson may include the burning of buildings other than houses or outhouses, personal property, and crops. The law may distinguish between burning in the day and at night, or between vacant and occupied buildings. The degree of arson may depend on the value of the item burned. Such laws generally make the burning of personal insured property, with the intent to defraud, a crime within the general name of arson. Common, however, to all arson or arson-type crime is the element of burning and the malicious intent of the person setting the fire.

The corpus delicti in arson cases requires the burning to be the result of a criminal agency and an *actual* burning—a consuming-type fire (although the fire need not in fact consume because charring is usually sufficient).[2] Thus, the three facts that must be proved in any prosecution for arson are as follows:

1. That fire occurred—a burning, a charring
2. That the burning was not accidental; that its origin was the result of a criminal agency

---

*The space, usually enclosed, around a dwelling house.

3. That the person who appears as a defendant in court in an arson case is identified as the person who set the fire, or caused it to be set, or otherwise acted in furtherance of a criminal plan for the fire setting

The term **aggravated arson** reflects public and legislative concern about arson as a crime against people as well as a crime against property. It is best described as any arson in which explosives are used and people are present or placed in danger at the site.

Aggravation occurs when explosives are used to injure or harm people or property or, if at the time of fire or explosion, a person other than the arsonist is within or on the structure damaged. Inherent in the "present or placed in danger" element of aggravated arson is the fact that actual physical harm can result from the fire or explosion. Some states use aggravation as essential to first-degree arson; others cite it as adding to the seriousness of arson and, if proved at trial, as calling for additional years to be added to the sentence linked to basic arson.[3]

Motive is an important element in the continuing phase of an arson investigation. However, motive need not be proved in an arson prosecution in order to convict the defendant so long as the defendant can be identified as the fire setter and his or her intent to set the fire is established.

The Suspicious Fire Concept

When investigating a burning (Figure 13–1), the investigator must first seek evidence to prove whether the fire was natural or accidental. When little or no evidence can be secured to identify the fire as accidental, the second step is to seek evidence to eliminate all possible causes except incendiarism. The investigator must evaluate the possibility of persons smoking in bed, spontaneous combustion, a pilot light igniting fumes from flammable liquids, electrical storms, or faulty building construction or maintenance (electrical wiring, motors, space heaters, furnaces, and flues). Also, the investigator must review the possibility that small children, elderly persons, intoxicated individuals, or persons with mental illness may be involved in a noncriminal incendiary fire through carelessness or misfortune.

The third step is to seek evidence that will prove the fire was incendiary. Investigators seek evidence such as separate and distinct fires in different areas of the premises; the residue of inflammables; the odor of petroleum and like fire starters; holes in plaster walls; windows and doors shaded and locked to prevent discovery and retard entry of firefighters; removal of personal effects before a fire; the absence of the owner or occupant, especially at a time when he or she is normally present; excessive insurance; and the presence of ignition devices, or **fire sets**.

Once the suspicious nature of the fire has been revealed, the investigator attempts to classify the burning as a rationally or irrationally motivated fire. *Rational* motivation is based on either hate, profit, or the desire to conceal a

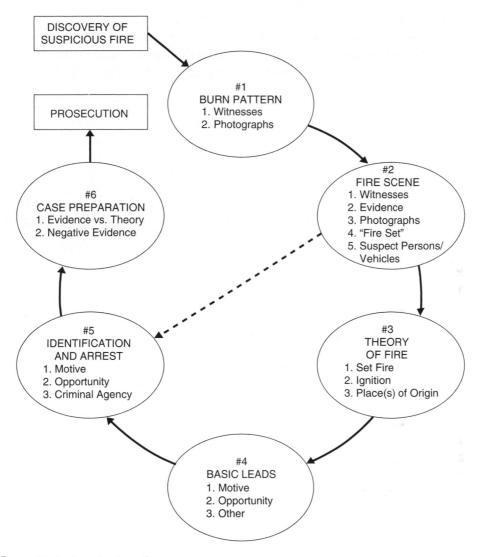

FIGURE 13–1   Investigation of arson.

crime. In rationally motivated fires, the suspects are the people who would want the fire. *Irrationally* motivated arsonists are pathological fire setters, or **pyromaniacs**. Fires set by such individuals offer no focal point for leads.[4]

Hate fires are set because of some dispute. The investigator's work is to question the victim about his or her suspicions and any recent arguments. Landlords may need questioning to help recall a dispute over an unfulfilled tenant request. Querying employers about recently discharged employees or customers with complaints may help them recall a few names. Persons who set hate fires have emotional problems. An unimportant event to an average person may be overemphasized by these individuals and trigger a spite or revenge fire. Religious, racial, and political disputes may be involved. Although the identity factor of the incendiary is not as apparent in such disputes, suspects may be discovered in the opposing group involved in the dispute if the investigator probes and pries.

Profit fire setters are not difficult to expose once hate has been eliminated as motivation. The first step is a general inquiry about the company insuring the building and its contents. Second, a more specific inquiry into the insurance and the policyholder's record is conducted. Collaterally, a general inquiry about the financial status of the insured and his or her business is appropriate and often rewards the investigator with the information that the insured "needed" a fire.

Representatives of the national crime syndicate have been linked to arson more frequently in recent years. They buy into a legitimate business and turn it into an illicit operation. The general procedure in these cases is for the new owners to manipulate the firm's operations to gain full control from the previous owners; to "milk" the business of its readily available assets in merchandise, services, and credit; and then to set a fire for the insurance money.[5]

Alternatively, a fire may have originated as an attempt to conceal a major crime. Evaluation of this motive is not difficult. What crime could be involved? Was there a human victim of the fire? Murder? Was there any hint of missing property? Burglary? Were the record books destroyed, found partially burned, or tented (spread half open with the bound edge up and the leaves spread out for burning)? Tax fraud? Embezzlement? Sometimes the seriousness of the basic crime does not appear to warrant arson, but desperate people take desperate measures.

Pyromania is the obsessional impulse to set fires or a preference for arson as an instrument of damage. Pyromaniacs, the so-called **firebugs** who terrorize entire neighborhoods by their fire-setting activities, repeat their crimes unless they are apprehended and placed in a correctional setting oriented to their needs. These individuals may claim rational motivation, but they set fires for no practical reason and receive no material profit from their incendiarism.[6] "Motive" in these cases is some sensual satisfaction resembling an "irresistible" impulse—the act of setting a fire solves the fire setter's problems more efficiently and often more pleasurably than any other means available.[7]

The pathological fire setter does not usually have any relationship with the victim or the place of burning. A "pyro" fire is similar to a "psycho" murder case in this respect. The fire scene search may reveal a clue to personal identity. The suspect may attract attention by his or her overt and suspicious conduct in the crowd watching the fire. These irrationally motivated incendiaries often act out the role of hero at the fire scene. In seeking a solution to these fires, the investigator may develop a list of suspects by reviewing suspicious juvenile vandals, sex psychopaths, known pyromaniacs, and other individuals with a history of unusual behavior or bizarre acts. When the fires occur in a series within reasonable geographic limits, the technique of working out the pattern of the fire setter and organizing a surveillance for his or her apprehension is sometimes successful.

Burn Patterns: Structural Fires

Structural fires form a burn pattern that can be determined chiefly by evaluating the physical layout of the building involved, the available combustible material, and ventilation. Simply stated, the fire burns upward from its original ignition in an inverted conical shape, with the apex of the cone at the place of origin—where the fire was ignited. Physical characteristics of a building may retard a fire or change its direction. Ventilation will cause a fire to spread away from this conical fire pattern: open doors, open windows, chimneylike physical characteristics (stairways or elevators), and holes in floor, wall, ceiling, or roof (either caused by the fire or some other means) contribute to the spread of a fire and its rate of burning (Figure 13–2). Another variation on the classic fire pattern is caused when the fire encounters highly combustible materials, which will burn more vigorously and will radically modify the direction of a fire.[8]

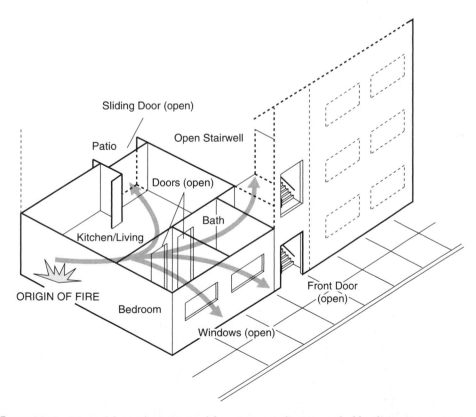

FIGURE 13–2   Normal fire path in structural fires. Arrows indicate spread of fire from origin in kitchen.

Combustibility in structural fires is usually defined in terms of ignitability, rate of heat release, and total heat release. It is a function of the physical characteristics of the furnishings and building materials at the fire scene, their spatial relationships, and the structural features of the place of occurrence.[9] A little-known aspect of structural fires is room **flashover**—a rapid development of the fire that occurs when the volume of active fire becomes a significant portion of the room volume. At flashover, all the previously uninvolved combustibles in a room suddenly ignite. At this time, the rate of the heat release is high and flaming occurs across the ceiling of the room.[10]

A basic key to developing the burn pattern of a structural fire is to determine the approximate time between ignition and flashover in the room in which the fire originates.[11] A fire may be initially classified as suspicious when its burn pattern suggests more than one place of origin, when there is an inexplicable or unexplained deviation from a fire pattern common to the structural characteristics and ventilation of the place burned, or when a rapid buildup of a room fire is not in harmony with the known combustibility of the room and its contents.

Burn Patterns: Nonstructural Fires

In outdoor fires in which a structure is not involved, the fire predominantly spreads horizontally rather than in the typical conical pattern of structural fires. Factors that influence patterns of outdoor fires are wind and the terrain. On level ground—in the absence of wind—a fire will spread from the point of origin in all directions. In the absence of a strong wind, the partial vacuum created by the fire that permits air to flow into the base of the fire tends to retard the spread of the fire. Wind spreads the fire in a fan shape, with the apex of the fan facing the source of the wind. On terrain with an uphill slope, the fire will burn uphill from the point of origin. The combination of the two factors— wind and terrain—may produce a fire that burns uphill and is canted to the left or right because of the direction and velocity of the wind at the time of the fire. A strong wind can sometimes overcome the influence of terrain and cause a fire to burn laterally across a sloping hillside. In some cases, fires have even been spread downhill by a very strong wind.[12]

A wind condition in Southern California known as the **Santa Ana winds** contributes to the ignitability of forest-fire fuels. These winds, with their strong airflow associated with low humidity, quickly dry out the forest fuels. When a fire is started, the increased ignitability of these fuels accounts for a rapid spread in all directions and for the occurrence of many spot fires ahead of the main fire as a result of the wind-driven embers. Under Santa Ana conditions, fire can spread quickly and violently in any direction. A surge or slackening in the airflow or a sudden change in wind direction, rapid heat release, and the Southern California mountainous terrain characterized by numerous canyons that act as chutes or chimneys all contribute to sudden changes in the pattern of the fire.[13]

Ignition and Place of Origin of Fire

One major difference between an accidental fire and an incendiary fire is that accidental fires frequently burn out because of lack of proper ventilation or availability of combustible material. In contrast, the set fire is planned. The fire setter places his or her fire so that it will burn vigorously after being ignited. He or she may use a fire accelerant or may depend on ventilation and the combustible material normally at the fire scene.

Sparks, matches, mechanical lighters, friction, radiant heat, hot objects, and chemical reactions can cause fire. The primary source of ignition can be manual, as in striking a match; mechanical, as in a spark device used by welders; electrical, as in faulty wiring or defective appliances; or chemical, as in spontaneous combustion.

When matches or other simple devices are used to set a fire, little evidence of the means of ignition remain. However, many arsonists construct various mechanical delay devices to afford themselves a few hours in which they can establish an alibi for the time when the fire was started. Candles also provide a delay factor for the arsonist. The time lag depends on the diameter and height of the candle above the **plant**, which is the fire-boosting material used to spread the fire. Alarm clocks are common mechanical devices used to start fires. Both clocks and candles leave traces at the fire scene. When the debris and rubble at the fire scene are searched, some evidence of their use is often located. Electrical fire starters often make a fire appear to be accidental because faulty wiring and careless handling of electrical appliances often cause fires. Spontaneous combustion is often claimed as a cause of fire, but "oily rags" usually require ideal conditions to generate enough heat for self-ignition. In some industrial fires, however, spontaneous combustion might result from the chemical reaction of various oils with air.[14]

Where a fire was ignited is the place of origin. Fire setters often set fires in more than one place to get a rapid buildup of the fire. **Trailers** are often used to spread fires from a point of ignition. Because of this function, they can be considered a secondary incendiary device, carrying the fire from the original place of ignition to other parts of the room or building. The trailer may be nothing more than a rope or a ropelike string of toilet paper, newspaper, or rags soaked in fire accelerant. Sometimes a fire accelerant is simply poured across the floor in a pattern similar to the spokes of a wheel, with each "trail" radiating outward from the original source of ignition.[15]

The major indication of a set fire is when the source of ignition is such that the fire spreads rapidly. Such rapid spreading indicates the use of a trailer and a fire accelerant or that several places are the points of origin.

The investigator should study the lower regions of a fire for the place or places of origin. However, the place of origin may be higher than some of the burned portions of a building. In this case, the fire accelerant used as a source of fuel for the fire or to spread the flames from the original place of ignition might have dripped downward through holes or crevices in the floor before the fire secured enough heat to change the fire accelerant from its liquid state.

The Fire Scene

The best-case scenario in arson investigation is when the investigator arrives at the fire scene while the fire is still in progress. All the firefighters are still on the scene, and occupants of the premises (or the owner of the land on which the fire started), onlookers, and other witnesses are also available at this time. Under these circumstances, the investigator can conduct on-the-scene interviews of persons knowledgeable about the fire and its circumstances. These interviews should point toward securing the following data:

- Who reported the fire
- The color and volume of flames and smoke
- Whether anyone reported the odor of gasoline or another fire accelerant
- Where and when the fire started
- The movements of occupants and others involved in the fire
- Anything unusual at the fire scene

After the fire is over and the investigator can enter the fire scene—which is when most investigators arrive at the fire scene—the onset of the fire and its

The color of the smoke in a suspicious fire is an important investigative lead.

circumstances can be reconstructed. Unfortunately, fire investigators are usually faced with various disturbances or changes in the original fire scene caused by the firefighters' need to "overhaul" after extinguishing a fire. **Overhauling** is the examination and search by firefighters for hidden flames or sparks that might rekindle the fire. To accomplish overhauling, firefighters often throw the contents of a room outside the building and frequently rip cabinets and paneling from walls to expose the space between the studs.

Tracing the root of a fire by examining the manner and direction of burning from the point of origin is the primary means of reconstructing the fire scene.[16] Basically, reconstruction of a fire scene requires the investigator to secure data on how the fire started, how it burned, and whether it was accelerated.

Once an investigator has reconstructed a fire, he or she can develop a theory about it. This theory may be backed up by various items of evidence such as empty containers of flammable fluid found at the scene, traces of fire accelerants, or the remains of a fire-setting device in the rubble of the fire. However, the theory is primarily concerned with the pattern of the fire: how it was ignited, the point of origin, and the source and direction of its burning.

Searching a fire scene is similar to searching any crime scene, except a lengthy period of "freezing" the scene is necessary to protect physical evidence until the searchers can find it among the rubble and debris of a fire. Although the

Arson crime scene.

fire scene search is aimed at discovering the means of ignition and the point or points of origin of a fire, the searchers also look for anything unusual or foreign to the fire scene, evidence that will connect a suspect to the scene by revealing "presence" at the scene (the opportunity to set a fire), clues to the motive of a fire setter, or evidence of the fire setter's intent to set a fire (incendiarism).

Items of evidence suspected of containing volatile substances commonly used to accelerate fires must be found and sealed quickly to prevent loss by evaporation. Such items must be transported to the crime laboratory in airtight containers.

Liquid fire accelerants (e.g., kerosene, gasoline) can and do survive fires. The areas most likely to contain residues of these accelerants are the low points at the fire scene: floors, carpets, or soil. When a suspect is arrested shortly after the fire at or near the scene, the suspect's outer clothing and shoes may contain residual traces if the fire setter used a liquid fire accelerant. The human nose can detect the distinctive odor of a liquid fire accelerant at the scene or on a suspect, but it is best supplemented by flammable vapor detectors. These "sniffers" operate on several principles. The most common type operates on the catalytic combustion principle. However, the recovery and individualization of fire accelerant residues require the services of forensic scientists in a crime laboratory and the use of solvent-extraction devices.[17]

One popular method for separating flammable and combustible liquid residues from fire debris is the **passive headspace concentration method**. In this method, an adsorbent material such as activated charcoal is used to extract the residue from the static headspace above the sample, then the adsorbent is eluted with a solvent. Results of studies have demonstrated that multiple separations can be performed without jeopardizing the recovery and identification of volatile residues.[18] The headspace concentration method is best used when a high level of sensitivity is required because of a low concentration of ignitable liquid residues in the sample. Several variations on this method have also been developed and are effective for separating residues from fire debris.

Solvent-extraction devices backstop the work of fire scene searches by recovering flammable fluids from fire rubble (wood, cloth, and paper). The searchers find and recover the material suspected of containing residues of a fire accelerant and transport it to the crime laboratory for processing by criminalists. Later, the report of these laboratory technicians may contribute to the development of the case, and their expert evidence in court at the offender's trial offers testimony in support of the prosecution's case.

Fire Scene Photographs

Fires and fire scenes are ideal subjects for photo "essays" that communicate otherwise undetectable facts about a fire, its origin, and its pattern of burning. In-progress photos are seldom taken by assigned investigators, but they are taken by the news media, fire personnel, and amateur photographers and can be secured by investigators. Such in-progress photographs, particularly when in color, identify the location of a fire, reveal its spread and intensity, and detail the mixture of smoke and flames. In addition, such photographs sometimes reveal the presence of a suspect at the fire scene, identify one or more vehicles parked at or entering or exiting the scene, and reveal signs of forced entry, attempts to bar firefighters from the structure, or methods used to prevent prompt discovery of the fire.

Investigators and assisting personnel assigned to process the scene of a suspicious fire should take both color and black-and-white photographs of the fire scene and of items of evidence found at the scene. Inasmuch as the corpus delicti of arson is the burning (charring) of a portion of a structure, this burning should be photographed from its place of origin to wherever the fire caused damage to the structure or its contents. Both overall views and close-ups should be taken. Overall pictures reveal the patterns of a fire and offer some clues to its ignition and origin, but close-up photography in the area or areas of the origin of the fire is particularly important for revealing any ignition device and the use of a fire set with trailers and fire accelerants. Although the device itself may have been consumed in the fire, mute evidence of its use to set the fire may be developed from such photographs.

Photographs taken during the postfire processing of the scene of a suspicious fire may exonerate innocent suspects or serve as the only corroboration of an investigator's testimony as to things found (or not found) at the fire scene and their application to the prosecution's theory of the fire, the criminal agency, and the identity of the defendant on trial as the fire setter.

The Continuing Arson Investigation

The preliminary investigation of a suspicious fire is complete when the fire scene examination is recorded, the theory of an incendiary fire has been developed, and the fire can be proved by available evidence to not be accidental.

The investigator assigned to the continuing investigation uses the following lines of inquiry about motive and opportunity (presence at the crime scene): Who would want or benefit from the fire? Who would have the opportunity to set the fire? The specific lines of inquiry suggested by the basic investigative leads are not exhausted until the dual inquiry about motive and opportunity is fully developed. The specific areas of inquiry in the continuing investigation of an arson case depend on the individual characteristics of each case, but ten major areas of inquiry should be explored in an arson investigation:

1. Burn pattern (whether in harmony with structure and contents)
2. Fire scene
   a. Examination for source of ignition
   b. Determination of place or places of origin
   c. Physical evidence

3. Witnesses
   a. Person discovering fire
   b. Fire personnel
   c. Eyewitnesses
   d. Occupants (and owner of premises or place)
   e. Others (onlookers, neighbors, and relatives of person discovering fire)
4. Suspicious persons
   a. At fire scene
   b. At fire scene but left before arrival of investigators (e.g., children playing, strangers in area, transients or homeless persons, former occupants, discharged employees)
5. Suspicious vehicles
   a. At fire scene
   b. Usually parked at fire scene but no longer present
   c. At fire scene but departed before arrival of investigators
6. Theory of fire
   a. Rationally motivated
      i. Hate
      ii. Profit
      iii. Concealment of a crime
   b. Pathological fire setter
      i. Lack of rational motive
      ii. Fire in series
      iii. Neighborhood involved
      iv. Known "pyros"
   c. Criminal agency
      i. Not caused by accident
      ii. Means of ignition
      iii. Place of origin(s)
      iv. Proof fire was set
         (a) Physical evidence
         (b) Witnesses
         (c) Other (e.g., motive, opportunity)
7. Identification of fire setter
   a. Scene
   b. Witnesses
   c. Suspicious person or vehicle
   d. Inquiries—basic leads
8. Review of evidence disclosed by the following:
   a. Burn pattern
   b. Examination of fire scene
   c. Witnesses
   d. Suspicious persons and vehicles
   e. Basic leads
9. Compatibility of evidence—identifying fire setter
   a. Burn pattern
   b. Evidence at fire scene

c. Testimony of witnesses
d. Results of investigation
10. Case preparation; compatibility of identification of fire setter with theory of fire
   a. Criminal agency
   b. Motive (rational, irrational)
   c. Review of negative evidence (to block common defense of accident, alibi, mistaken identification, or lack of motive)

BOMBINGS

Many fires result from explosions. Criminal investigation techniques used in arson investigation can be applied to bombings even though a fire may not result from the explosion. The six stages in the investigation of bombings are as follows (Figure 13–3):

1. ***Determination of Cause.*** An accidental origin, such as a gas explosion or an explosion resulting from the misuse of chemicals, must be eliminated as the cause of the explosion.
2. ***Scene Investigation Pattern.*** The pattern of the explosion must be determined—high or low explosive; approximate amount used (damage).
3. ***Scene Processing.*** The bombing scene is processed by police (responding officers and bomb squad personnel, if available) to locate and interview witnesses and victims, to find and preserve physical evidence, and to identify any suspicious persons or vehicles.
4. ***Case Building.*** The investigator develops a theory of the bombing: target, opportunity, motive, and technical know-how.
5. ***Identification and Arrest.*** Inquiries are initiated to exploit any basic leads, police intelligence, and other clues and traces (scene investigation and processing, case building) likely to result in the identification and arrest of the person or persons responsible for the bombing.
6. ***Case Preparation.*** The case is prepared immediately after the arrest of the bomber and any associates.

Because an explosion destroys traces of the explosives used, explosive "tagging" offers future promise that the scene investigation of a bombing will hold identifiable traces of the explosives used. An explosives tagging program developed at the federal level involves the addition of coded microparticles, or **taggants**, to explosives during their manufacture. The taggants survive detonation, can be recovered at the bombing scene, and can be decoded by crime laboratory examination to show where and when the explosives were made.

The use of police intelligence reports may be the most important factor contributing to the success of a bombing investigation. These reports can provide information that will link suspects to prior bombings and provide data on associates and the possible whereabouts of suspects and associates. In addition,

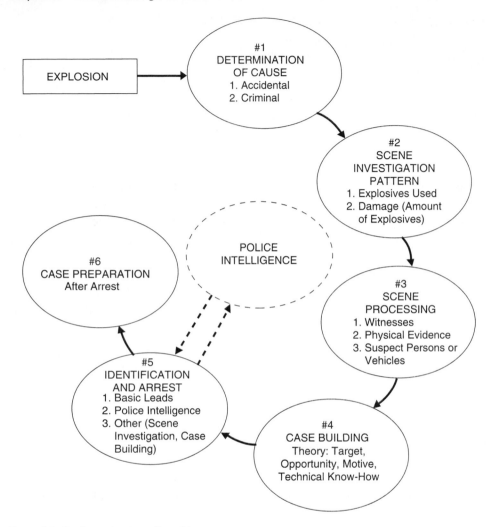

FIGURE 13–3   Investigation of bombings.

a police intelligence unit may initiate preventive intelligence operations to disclose the identity of persons involved in planning future bombings (see Chapter 6).

People who use explosives as the ultimate weapon against persons or property may be linked to the following groups:

- Politically motivated groups (extremists, radicals; see Chapter 16)
- Organized crime (bombings involving known criminals, informants for police, and witnesses or potential witnesses against members of crime syndicates)
- Persons who are mentally ill (including bombers motivated by hate, anger, and revenge)

PROBLEMS OF PROOF IN ARSON AND BOMBING CASES

Two common defenses create problems of proof in prosecuting arson cases: a claim that the fire resulted from an accident, a misfortune, or a natural cause; and if the fire did result from a criminal agency, the defendant was not that agent. To prove that a criminal agency was responsible for the fire, the police-prosecutor team must foreclose all possibilities that the fire resulted from any other cause (accident, misfortune, natural cause) by a strong showing of evidence linking the fire to a single cause: someone set it.

Identifying the defendant as the fire setter is a problem generally attacked along the dual lines of motive and opportunity. The prosecution must, at the least, produce evidence showing that the defendant wanted the fire or would benefit from it, and, that by his or her presence at the fire scene, not only had the opportunity to set the fire but did so, or that the defendant contracted with a crime partner to set the fire.

While cases involving explosive devices may be linked to fires, their investigation is hampered by the fact that the explosion usually destroys most of the physical evidence at the bombing scene. When these cases are prosecuted, the motive and opportunity factors are important. In political bombings, anyone proven to be a member of a terrorist group is assumed to have a motive for the bombings of that group.

HATE CRIMES

Hate crimes are committed by individuals or organizations of people who engage in antisocial and illegal behavior and who pose a danger to agents of the criminal justice system and to the general public. Add to this definition the fact that the hate-violence is commonly directed at African Americans, Asians, Hispanics, Jews, and even the U.S. government (e.g., the Oklahoma City bombing).

Hate groups are organizations such as the Ku Klux Klan (KKK), the Aryan Nation, and the skinheads. In some locales, various militias demonstrate against the government for a specific reason.[19]

Alan Berg, a controversial talk-show host, was shot dead not far from his home on the outskirts of Denver, Colorado. His killers were members of a neo-Nazi group aligned with the Aryan Nation. He was Jewish and openly challenged neo-Nazi and other hate groups. Berg's killing was murder, but also a hate crime. He was killed because he was "different" in his murderers' eyes.

A hate crime is not usually so closely identified with a **community threat group**. It is usually a single offender acting out his or her particular hate. Arson and bombing are common, and often fires and bombings occur in a series a few days apart. Although the motivation is irrational, suspects can be found and evidence can be developed for a trial.

A **cult** can range from a group that preaches revolution or resistance to taxation or similar governmental activity to a group that preaches from the Bible and performs good works among the sick and the poor. A cult may have other problems linked, for example, to the children of the group or the group's lifestyle. Some cults have been targeted for allegations of **mind control**, which is the use of undue influence and unethical means to recruit and retain members.

Despite the negative public perception of groups labeled *cults*, police investigators must remember that the United States has a longtime commitment to religious tolerance and freedom. Investigators should not probe and pry into any such group unless a crime has been reported or discovered and unless strong probable cause warrants police action.[20]

CHAPTER REVIEW

CASE STUDY

Motive for Arson

In this case, a jury convicted the defendant of the crime of arson.

In April 1995, defendant secured fire insurance in the sum of $141,000 on a home located in Corona (comprising rooms numbered on a diagram in evidence at trial as 1 to 10, inclusive). Title to the property was formerly in the name of defendant's son, who, with defendant, was one of the cobeneficiaries of the policy. The house was leased to a Mr. Keys, who resided in it from April 1995 to November 1998. During that period defendant listed the property for sale at $160,500.

On January 5, 1998, defendant came to Corona from her home in Santa Clara where she lived with her husband. She stayed in the Corona house on the nights of January 5th and 6th. On January 7, defendant's insurance agent received a telephone call from defendant informing him that she wanted $10,500 additional insurance. The agent notified the head office to increase the insurance accordingly, effective January 7, 1998. Defendant spent the night of January 9th with a friend in Corona.

A neighbor, living next door to defendant's property, testified that he saw defendant carry an amber-colored gallon bottle into the house on January 7th and saw her again at the house on the morning of January 10th; that he saw lights in the back part of the house about 6 p.m. that night; that he retired about 9 p.m.; and that at 2:30 a.m. of January 11th he was awakened by flames coming from the gabled ends of the defendant's house. The fire department was called. The firefighters forced open the back door and saw no flames in rooms 8, 9, 3, and 4. One firefighter saw evidence of separate fires in rooms 5, 6, and 10. In room 1, other firefighters found an open-faced gas heater on which the valve was open and gas was coming into the house. After the fire was subdued, the fire chief discovered that one of the back doors had been left open.

On January 11th, a deputy state fire marshal and others investigating the fire discovered that the heaviest fire occurred in room 10—a closet—which was separated from room 1 by a door. The fire in that area had burned down through the floor and up through the ceiling, which had resulted in considerable fire damage to the house and roof. Directly across from room 10, in room 1, an area about 36 inches wide had been burned on the wall. Apparently, the fire at that point started from the floor and burned up because the baseboard was entirely gone.

Prosecution

The district attorney focused on the incendiary origin of a fire, which is generally established by circumstantial evidence such as the finding of separate and distinct fires on the premises. Evidence of four separate, simultaneous, and unrelated fires was found in the house in question; holes were found in the plaster behind two of the fires; boxes of combustibles were in the front of the holes; papers were stuffed between the laths in one of the holes; and debris smelling of petroleum products was near another hole in the plaster. The facts amply justify an inference that the fire was of incendiary origin and that it was neither accidental nor from natural causes and that the jury could reasonably infer that the fire was willfully and maliciously set for the purpose of burning the house.

In the opinion of duly qualified experts who testified at the trial, there was no communication or connection between the fire causing the charred condition in room 5 and the burned areas in rooms 10 and 1, nor between the burned area in room 6 and the burned area in rooms 10 and 1, nor between the fires causing the burns in rooms 5 and 6.

Defense

Counsel for the defendant contended that the evidence of the corpus delicti was insufficient because it had not shown that the defendant was present when the fire was set or that the defendant was the means by which the fire occurred. No evidence connects the defendant to the crime.

The identity of the defendant as the person who committed the crime may be proved by circumstantial evidence connecting her to the crime. However, circumstantial evidence must consist of proof of the defendant's motive and conduct that connects her with the crime, and statements that show a consciousness of guilt.

Comment

The jury was justified in believing the defendant had offered the house for sale and that it had not been sold. This fact and evidence of several points of origin, coupled with the fact that she had secured an increase in the insurance on January 7th, 3 days before the fire, justifies the inference that she had a motive for burning the building and collecting the insurance money.

DISCUSSION QUESTIONS

1. Define a *suspicious fire*.
2. How does the burn pattern in structural fires differ from that in non-structural (field and forest) fires?
3. What is a *fire set*? A fire *trailer*? A fire *accelerant*?
4. What basic factors should be considered in investigating fires set because of hate (revenge or jealousy), for profit, or to conceal a crime?
5. What are the basic characteristics of fires set by pyromaniacs?
6. What are the similarities and differences between arson and bombings?
7. Define *combustibility*.

8. In the investigation of a suspicious fire, what information does an investigator seek during on-the-scene interviews of witnesses?

9. How is the ignition and spread of a fire reconstructed at the crime scene? What is the primary objective of this reconstruction?

10. What special care must be taken with evidence suspected of containing residues of a fire accelerant?

11. Outline the major phases of the continuing investigation in arson cases.

12. What are the six stages of a bombing investigation?

13. What are the essential elements of stage 3 in the investigation of a bombing (scene)? Stage 4 (case building)?

14. What individuals or groups may be involved in a bombing?

15. What is explosives *tagging*?

16. Has the corpus delicti been established in the case study?

17. How was the fire in the case study started?

LIBRARY ASSIGNMENT

Update the references in this chapter concerned with burning patterns and the ignition of fires by incendiaries.

WORKBOOK PROJECT

During a 30-day period, survey one or more of the local newspapers for news stories of arson cases and bombings.

RELATED WEB SITES

For information about arson investigation, recent events, and related sites, visit *www.firehouse.com*.

Facts and statistics on arson in America can be found at this Web site: *www.emergency.com/arsonrpt.htm*.

Statistics on hate crime in the United States can be found at this Web site: *www.fbi.gov/ucr/ucr.htm#hate*.

NOTES

1. WILLIAM BLACKSTONE, *Commentaries on the Laws of England* (Oxford, England: Clarendon Press, 1765–1769), bk. 4, chap. 16.
2. KENNETH M. WELLS and PAUL B. WESTON, *Criminal Law* (Santa Monica, CA: Goodyear, 1978), 221–28.
3. *Kehoe v. Commonwealth*, 149 Ky. 400 (1912).

4. BRENDAN P. BATTLE and PAUL B. WESTON, *Arson: Detection and Investigation* (New York: Arco, 1978), 30–42.

5. "Fire Marshalls on Duty—The Intelligence Unit in Fire Investigation," *Fire Journal* 64 (September 1970): 92–93.

6. NOLAN D. C. LEWIS and HELEN YARNELL, *Pathological Firesetting—Pyromania* (New York: Nervous and Mental Disease Monographs, 1951), 86–134.

7. W. HURLEY and T. M. MONAHAN, "Arson: The Criminal and the Crime," *British Journal of Criminology* 9 (1969): 4–21.

8. PAUL KIRK, *Fire Investigation* (New York: Wiley, 1969), 71–81.

9. EDWIN E. SMITH, "An Experimental Determination of Combustibility," *Fire Technology* 7, no. 2 (May 1971): 109–19.

10. T. E. WATERMAN, "Room Flashover—Criteria and Synthesis," *Fire Technology* 4, no. 1 (February 1968): 25–31.

11. T. E. WATERMAN and W. J. CHRISTIAN, "Characteristics of Full-Scale Fires in Various Occupancies," *Fire Technology* 7, no. 3 (August 1971): 205–17; "Fire Behavior of Interior Finish Materials," *Fire Technology* 6, no. 3 (August 1970): 165–78.

12. KIRK, *Fire Investigation*, 82–88.

13. C. M. COUNTRYMAN et al., "Fire Weather and Fire Behavior in the 1966 Loop Fire," *Fire Technology* 4, no. 2 (May 1968): 126–41.

14. BRUCE V. ETTING and MARK F. ADAMS, "Spontaneous Combustion of Linseed Oil and Sawdust," *Fire Technology* 7, no. 3 (August 1971): 225–36.

15. BATTLE and WESTON, *Arson*, 17–29.

16. RICHARD D. FITCH and EDWARD A. PORTER, *Accidental or Incendiary* (Springfield, IL: Charles C Thomas, 1968), 3–26; John J. O'Connor, *Practical Fire and Arson Investigation* (New York: Elsevier, 1987), 81–105.

17. JOHN F. BOUDREAU et al., *Arson and Arson Investigation: A Survey and Assessment* (Washington, DC: U.S. Department of Justice, Law Enforcement Assistance Administration, 1977), 77–89.

18. L. V. WATERS and L. A. PALMER, "Multiple Analysis of Fire Debris Samples Using Passive Headspace Concentration," *Journal of Forensic Sciences* 38, no. 1 (1993): 165–83.

19. JACK LEVIN and JACK MCDEVITT, *HATE Crimes—The Rising Tide of Bigotry and Bloodshed* (New York: Plenum Press, 1993), 1–5.

20. JAMES D. TABOR and EUGENE V. GALLAGHER, *Why Waco? Cults and the Battle for Religious Freedom in America* (Los Angeles: University of California Press, 1995), 147–48.

14

PROPERTY CRIMES

Property crimes are committed for the perpetrator's personal gain. These crimes include burglary, theft, and fraud. While **burglary**, by definition, is entering a structure to commit a *felony or theft* therein, the object of the crime of burglary is almost predominantly breaking and entering a structure to commit a *theft*.

BURGLARY

In the past, conviction for common-law burglary required proof of six essential elements:[1]

1. A breaking
2. An entry
3. In the nighttime
4. Of a dwelling house
5. Belonging to another
6. An intent to commit a felony

Currently, in most jurisdictions, conviction for burglary requires only three basic or essential elements:[2]

1. Entry
2. Of a building (or another structure, place, or thing described by the particular penal code section)
3. With the intent to steal or commit another felony

Burglary is usually separated into first-, second-, and possibly third-degree burglary. Some of the essential elements of common-law burglary are still used to divide the modern crime of burglary into degrees. Depending on the state in which the crime is committed, the division into degrees may be based on whether the crime occurs in a dwelling house; whether such a dwelling is inhabited by a person present at the time; whether the dwelling is entered at nighttime; or whether the act is committed by a person who is armed with a deadly weapon or who, while in the commission of a burglary, arms him- or herself with such a deadly weapon. In recent years, the use of explosives has increased the degree of burglary.[3]

The allied misdemeanor offense of possession of burglar tools assists police in apprehending burglars and in preventing burglaries. Any individual who has on his or her person, or in his or her possession, a picklock or another instrument with the intent of feloniously breaking into or entering any building is guilty of a misdemeanor in California. So is any person who knowingly makes or alters any picklock or other instrument so that it can be used to open the lock of any building without the specific consent of the person having control of the building.[4]

Burglary is a crime of opportunity, a crime of *easy* opportunity. Although many burglars limit their activities to a certain area and thus reduce the scope of their burglaries, every area has many easy opportunities.

Investigators should try to develop some insight into how a burglar selects a site for his or her crime. Why the choice of one area? Why the selection of one house over a neighboring house? The probability of profit and safety are perhaps at the core of this site-selection process, along with having a large "awareness" space in which to evaluate (by search) the opportunity for a successful burglary.[5] If insight into this process can be developed, a roving stakeout of an area may be successful for apprehending the burglar.

Burglary is usually a *passive* crime in that the burglar normally tries to avoid contact with victims. The chances of getting caught in an unoccupied structure are fewer than those of being apprehended in an occupied structure. Persons who are not present at the scene of a burglary can never be eyewitnesses to the burglar's identity in court. Likewise, when no alarm is raised to alert police of a crime in progress, no "hot" search can ensue. In other, more public crimes, when a criminal has fled the scene shortly before the arrival of police, the victim may give the police a physical description of the criminal, of a vehicle, and of the direction of flight, which thus gives the police the opportunity for at least a "warm" search. Even this type of search is not possible when the victim does not know that his or her premises have been burglarized until some time after the burglar has fled the scene. This situation restricts police apprehension to the "cold" portion of the crime-solving process, commonly termed the **investigative phase**. In other words, burglars are usually not apprehended at the scene of their crime or in flight, but instead must be apprehended as a result of an investigative process (Figure 14–1).

The objective of burglars may be something other than theft. It may be assault, usually rape. Sometimes theft and assault are joint goals. Both larceny and rape or any other crime involved is investigated along with the basic burglary. The investigator must be alert to obtain evidence of each essential element of the additional crimes, as well as the essential elements of the burglary.

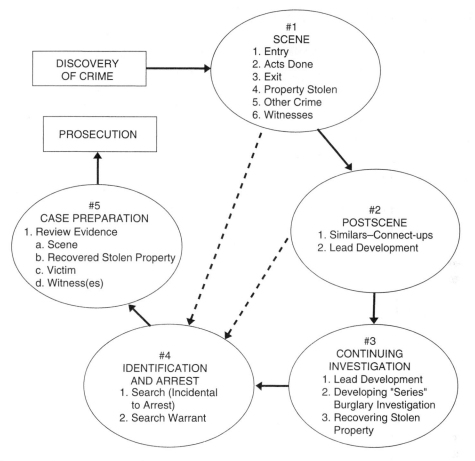

FIGURE 14-1 Investigation of burglary.

Types of Burglars

For years, police schools have taught that two general types of burglars exist: the amateur and the professional. **Professional burglars** are described as persons who work at burglary as a "trade," making their living by burglary and larceny alone and having no other means of income. Other burglars are loosely grouped beneath this plateau of "professionalism." **Amateur burglars** include those who commit crimes primarily to secure money for drugs.

Because burglary is probably the most common serious crime in the United States, constructing a typology of burglars that encompasses skill levels is necessary. This typology categorizes a burglar's skills on two levels:

1. The ability to gain entry to a premises
2. The burglar's business sense with regard to the selection of loot and the method of disposing of the proceeds of the crime (i.e., selling the stolen property)

The skill required to gain entry to a premises may be limited to forcing a door or window open, but it can extend to using lock-picking tools—which keeps pace with the art of the locksmith in providing security against thieves—or to the skill of opening locked containers such as safes. The business sense of a burglar depends on his or her ability to distinguish between valuable and worthless items at the time of the burglary, the burglar's contacts with receivers of stolen property, and whether he or she is in "panic" need (common with drug addicts) to sell the stolen property.

In this typology of burglars, a burglar is described as one of the following three types:

1. Unskilled
2. Semiskilled
3. Professional

The fact that such a typology of burglars exists does not mean investigators should discount the five classic modus operandi items used to describe various types of burglars. These items have served as a working typology for many years:[6]

1. Type of premises entered
2. Means of entry
3. Type of loot (stolen property)
4. Time of operation
5. Presence of crime partners

However, these basic items of modus operandi information should be reviewed from the standpoint of discovering the skills demonstrated in gaining entry to the premises and the business sense demonstrated to some extent by the nature of the property taken at the time of the burglary, its quantity, and its value.

The means of entry differ in various burglaries and are related to the burglar's skill. Nine various means of entry are used:

1. *The Open Door or Window Entry.*   The burglar roams residence areas, apartments, and hotels looking for open doors or windows.
2. *The "Jimmy" Entry.*   The burglar forces a door or window with a tool such as a tire iron, screwdriver, or small crowbar or box opener.
3. *The Celluloid Entry.*   The burglar forces open the spring lock of a door with a small piece of celluloid.
4. *The Stepover or Human Fly Entry.*   The burglar is an aerialist. The **"stepover" burglar** steps from a fire escape, a balcony, or another building to a nearby window. The **"human fly" burglar** can progress upward or downward on the sides of a building to a selected point of entry.
5. *Roof Entry.*   The burglar breaks into a premises through a skylight or an air-conditioning duct on the roof or by cutting a hole in the roof of a building.
6. *The Hide-In Entry.*   The burglar hides in a commercial premises until all employees have left, then breaks out with the stolen property.

7. ***The Cut-in Entry.***   The burglar uses tools of various kinds to cut through the floor, ceiling, or wall of a store or an office to another store or office.
8. ***Hit-and-Run Entry (Smash and Grab).***   The burglar breaks a window of a ground-floor store and takes property from a window or nearby portions of the premises, then flees before police can be alerted to the crime.
9. ***Key Entry.***   The burglar uses a key. The key may have been given to him or her by an informant, it may have been stolen, or the burglar may have obtained a duplicate or master key by various means.

Most unskilled or semiskilled burglars are prowlers who enter a residence and search rapidly for cash or for property that is easily transported and quickly converted into cash. Whether they succeed in finding such cash or property, they leave quickly, taking with them the "portable wealth" of the householder—usually stereo systems, VCRs, computers, and other items that are easily disposed of to individuals seeking bargains or to persons who deal in and sell drugs and are willing to exchange the drugs for the stolen merchandise.

Semiskilled and professional burglars also deal in articles of value, but articles that are not as easily converted into cash and that generally require the services of a **fence**—a professional receiver of stolen property. The loot of such thievery ranges through jewelry, furs, clothing, liquor, tobacco, meat, and textiles.

Burglary as a Behavioral Concept

Burglarizing is the behavior of committing a burglary and, most likely, another and another and another. Burglaries are usually crimes in a series.

Like all behavior, burglary involves needs and the opportunity to satisfy these needs. It also involves a common decision about whether to take advantage of opportunities. The five-step behavior cycle in burglary is as follows:

1. Needs
2. Opportunities
3. Means (skills)
4. Satisfactions
5. Choice

To understand the elements in this burglary cycle is to understand the behavior of burglars. Among burglars whose goals are theft (profit), the economic needs are met through successful burglaries, the successful taking away of stolen property, and its profitable disposition. The opportunity to commit a burglary is perceived; the burglary and its profit will meet the burglar's needs; the burglar has the necessary "technology" to enter a premises successfully to take away the proceeds of a crime and to sell it. The individual with these needs who makes a choice of burglary over other possible activities to meet unmet needs receives not only satisfaction from the work, but also reinforcement of this behavior, both of which increase the probability of the recurrence of this behavior—more burglaries and theft.[7]

Many years ago, burglars stole primarily for economic reasons. Today, the same economic reasons may be complicated by a drug addiction. Although the need for funds to buy drugs is an economic need, a more urgent compulsion is related to the need for the drugs and their effect on the drug user.

Rape-burglars exhibit needs to satisfy various psychological and physical desires. These burglars are abnormal in selecting forcible rape as an outlet, but they follow the burglar's typical cycle of behavior—and each successful crime is reinforcement for continuing this pattern of behavior.

Safe Burglars

Burglars often demonstrate skill at opening locked desks, file cabinets, safes, and other containers. Such entry to locked containers may be accomplished with basic tools such as a jimmy or screwdriver or tools picked up on the premises. Most safe burglars, however, bring to the crime scene whatever special tools they need: torch, sectional crowbar, and so on.

Force used to attack safes generally follows one of eight patterns:

1. *Punching.* In the **punching** manner of entry, a sledgehammer and a drift punch are used to knock the combination dial from the safe and drive the spindle back into the safe, which makes the release mechanism of the lock accessible and allows the safe to be opened.
2. *Pulling.* In **pulling** entry, a device similar to a gear or wheel puller is used to pull the dial or spindle completely out of the safe door, which allows the safe to be opened (similar to punching).
3. *Peeling.* The **peeling** means of entry involves prying off the outer surface of the safe door so that the locking mechanism of the safe is exposed and can be pried open, which allows entry to the safe.
4. *Ripping.* **Ripping** is battering the top, bottom, or sides of a safe with a chisel or another metal cutter such as a ripping bar (burglar's tool) or the hydraulic ramming device used in a body-and-fender shop.
5. *Drilling.* In **drilling**, one or more holes are drilled in the door of the safe to expose the lock mechanism, which allows the safe breaker to align the lock tumblers manually and open the door of the safe.
6. *Burning.* In the **burning** technique, the safe is attacked with an oxygen-acetylene torch, and a section of the safe is burned out to allow entry. When bank vaults are involved, a variation of this burning technique is the use of a thermal burning bar, which makes the original oxygen-acetylene torch much more efficient so that burning through 6-inch tempered steel is possible in 15 to 20 seconds.
7. *Blasting.* **Blasting** is the use of explosives to open safes.
8. *Carrying away.* **Carrying away** is when the burglar removes a safe to a more convenient location to open it.

Intruders often open a safe without force, by means of its combination. A burglar may find the safe open, but when no physical force is used to open a safe, investigators assume it was opened by using the combination. In such cases, the burglar may have found the combination written on the side of a drawer, in a nearby desk, in an account book, or in another convenient place, or he or she may have been given it by a dishonest employee.

Burglary Scene Investigation

The purpose of burglary scene investigation is to ascertain what clues or traces at the scene may identify the burglar and his or her crime partner or partners. Burglary scene investigation has three major phases:

1. Determining the means of gaining entry
2. Learning what the burglar did while in the premises
3. Ascertaining how the burglar exited the premises

The place of entry and tool marks are the classic identifying characteristics found at the scene of a burglary. The burglar's ability to break into any locked containers at the scene is a demonstration of a skill in the use of tools. Various identifying tool marks may be discovered.

Acts done while at the crime scene may be no more than necessary to accomplish a theft. In contrast, the acts of a rapist-burglar spell out the essential elements of a second major crime. In addition, some acts may aid in identifying the burglars. The stolen property is another useful factor in identifying the burglar.

The burglar's means of exit rounds out what investigators can glean from a burglary scene. The burglar may have simply exited from a rear door after a roof entry. However, while determining this fact, investigators may find significant clues or traces in and around the place of exit.

None of the evidence likely to be found at a burglary scene will identify a burglar by name or as a person. Instead, factors related to the burglar's modus operandi may contribute to developing a list of one or more suspects; therefore, this on-the-scene evidence should be preserved for future use. Then, when suspects are uncovered, the investigator can relate the clues and traces to the suspects.

If the investigator has good reason to believe that a suspect still possesses stolen property from one or more recent burglaries, and the investigator can secure reliable information describing this stolen property and where it is located, such data can be tied in with the victim's reports of what was stolen and developed into an application for a search warrant. Execution of the search warrant and recovery of the stolen property in premises controlled by the suspect will support other evidence identifying him or her as the burglar.

Postscene Investigation

Postscene investigation involves developing leads from connect-ups and from comparison of the modus operandi with the modi operandi of other crimes, either solved or unsolved. Such leads may identify one or more suspects as the offenders in a series of crimes, one of which is the burglary under investigation. Identification often involves using informants or recovering the stolen property and tracing it to the burglar.

Connect-ups and informants are classic avenues of investigation to identify suspects in burglary investigations. However, they offer little or no admissible prosecutorial evidence that a particular suspect committed the particular burglary under investigation. Instead, identifying the seller of stolen property by questioning the receiver of stolen property is more promising evidence. When a person is known to possess stolen property, a search warrant can be secured. The resultant seizure of stolen property is lawful, and such evidence can be used in court against the receiver or against the person who sold the stolen goods to him or her—if testimony or other evidence connects the seller to the stolen property.

Known Burglars

When an investigator has developed a suspect who is known to police to be a burglar, but the investigator cannot develop evidence likely to serve as probable cause for an arrest, he or she must continue connecting up subsequent burglaries until sufficient evidence is accumulated to supply probable cause for the suspect's arrest. Innovative surveillance procedures have been used in many police departments to clear burglary cases when a known burglar is identified as the suspect in a series of burglaries. An around-the-clock surveillance of the known burglar (and usually one or more crime partners) is established and continued until the burglar enters a building under circumstances that indicate the intent to commit a crime, at which point he or she is arrested. This type of arrest is opportune and timely.

THEFT

In common law, **larceny** was defined as a trespassory taking and carrying away of personal property belonging to another individual with the intent to permanently deprive the owner of such property. Currently, larceny (theft) is defined in most states as the unlawful taking or stealing of property or articles without the use of force or violence. It includes shoplifting, pocket picking, purse snatching without strong-arm tactics, thefts of and from vehicles, and property or cash taken from a home.

Three terms used in criminal justice statistics describe the scope of common larceny:[8]

1. *Household Larceny.*   **Household larceny** is the theft or attempted theft of property or cash from a residence or the immediate vicinity of the residence. The thief must have a legal right to be in the house—as a guest or maid, for example.
2. *Personal Crimes of Theft (Personal Larceny).*   **Personal larceny** is the theft or attempted theft of property or cash by stealth, in either of the following two instances:
   a. With contact but without force or threat of force
   b. Without direct contact between the victim and the offender
3. *Personal Larceny with Contact.*   **Personal larceny with contact** is the theft or attempted theft of property or cash directly from the victim by stealth, but with no force or threat of force.

Thieves steal money, vehicles, and other property from rightful owners. They sell it to individuals (bargain seekers) or criminal receivers of stolen goods (fences). The profit motive in thefts is too general to offer any promising leads. The solution of these crimes begins with a prompt alarm for the stolen property and an examination of the crime scene to determine the circumstances of the crime and to search for and collect physical evidence. Victims are interviewed to develop suspects, and witnesses to some preparatory or postcrime activity are sought and their help is solicited. Extensive modus operandi comparisons are made. Information about the work of known thieves suspected of operating locally is correlated with the facts known about the crime being investigated. Thieves can be traced when the proceeds of the crime are sold and recovered by police. Persons who buy stolen property frequently reveal the thief's identity. However, thefts are difficult to solve because of the lack of eyewitnesses. They are generally unknown-ID investigations characterized by the absence of a named suspect (Figure 14–2).

Before the recovery of the stolen property, investigators attempt to identify the perpetrator by seeking a characteristic signature in the modus operandi of the crime or a basic lead from field interview reports and tips from underworld sources of information. Physical evidence found and collected at various scenes of thefts compounds in importance. Such scientific evidence is unlikely to identify a suspect or suspects by name, but it can be used as an identifier when the foregoing techniques bring together a group of persons all equally suspect.

Most investigations of thefts involve past thefts. The police patrol force sometimes detects a thief at work or responds to a theft-in-progress call. Often when investigating prowler calls, the responding officers discover a thief. However, usually the victims of these crimes do not discover the theft until after the crime has been attempted or is completed. One unfortunate aspect of thefts is that police must bracket the occurrence between the time of discovery and the time at which the stolen property was last seen or otherwise noticed.

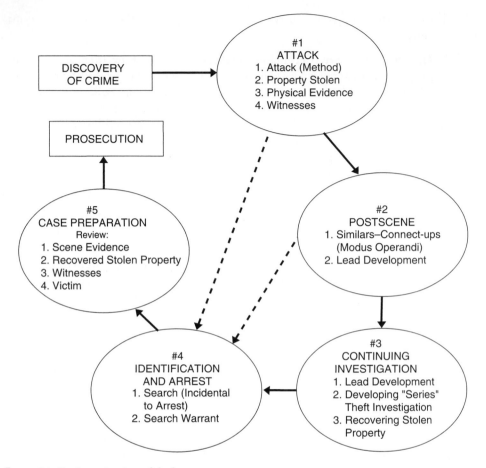

FIGURE 14–2   Investigation of thefts.

Time is likely to favor a criminal. It may blur the focus of an investigation and can aid escape and safe disposal of stolen property. The time element in the past crimes does not encourage the assigned investigator and probably serves as a passive means of discouragement. Crimes of violence have an inherent motivation for any investigator. In cases of theft, the investigator must seek motivation within his or her personal occupational goals for effective work.

The Attack

Money and valuable property are usually safeguarded. To steal either or both requires planning, direction, and operating skills. The entire event is the thief's attack. To be considered are the premises attacked, the method of the attack, and the means used to dispose of the proceeds of the crime. In fact, the proceeds of a crime are the objective of the attack, and they are an important highlight in viewing the attack as an event.

The property stolen is a major clue. The broadcast and Teletype alarms that announce to all cooperating law enforcement agencies the fact of the crime and data identifying the property taken begin the tracing that often leads to recovery of the property and a backtracking to the thief. The stolen property is listed by quantity, kind, material, physical description, serial numbers, and value. Many investigators at crime scenes have discovered that victims cannot describe the stolen property. Therefore, investigators must often question the victim about the stolen property item by item—what each item is used for, what it is made of, whether it is a man's or a woman's item, what marks are on it, and its value (cost and estimated current value).

The characteristics of the stolen property have long been used as part of modus operandi searches, but they are gaining new significance as indicators of the routine decision making of a particular thief. The property stolen is being recognized as the part of the attack event that can help identify a suspect. It is a part of the criteria used to evaluate a target. Some thieves steal money only, which is not grossly incriminating even minutes after a theft. Other thieves consider a proposed theft and reject it because of the difficulty of disposing of the property that will be the proceeds of the crime. Some thieves, having an established disposal route with customers such as housewives, employees of gas stations and drive-ins along a highway, and small merchants in nearby towns and villages, reject all proposals unless the property is suitable for their customers. Other thieves use wholesalers of the underworld—fences—and specialize in property that can be legitimized by removing all identifying marks. A few professional thieves have the necessary friendships among members of the organized crime syndicate to dispose of jewelry, furs, bonds, color television sets, and other merchandise with retail values in excess of $20,000 to $30,000.

Modus Operandi Searches

Modus operandi searches are rewarding in theft investigations because thieves are known as single-pattern offenders. Modus operandi searching will identify a group of suspects as persons actively engaged in committing property crimes and will produce a number of suspects for the crime being investigated. Computerized record searches allow scanning of a huge number of past crimes for modus operandi identification.

A great deal of personal satisfaction is gained by solving a theft in the early stages of a continuing investigation, before the proceeds of the crime have been recovered and the process of tracing back has been initiated. This possibility is not being exploited to its fullest extent; the lack of a named suspect often relegates a theft investigation to a category of "no results possible" until some feedback is obtained about the stolen property being recovered.

The key to an early break in property crime investigation is expanding the modus operandi search to include the decision-making processes the criminal exhibits in his or her operations. By developing an understanding of how thieves make decisions and the nature of the thought processes that underlie this decision making, an aware investigator can learn a great deal about these criminals. Interpreting selected modus operandi data of a theft under investigation provides clues about a thief's decision routines for dealing with each component of the overall task. Then, the investigator's role is to develop an "identifier" from the thought streams of individual thieves. A person's decision making has a pattern because each person learns how to deal with a particular aspect of any task in an individual way. The investigator's use of this decision pattern may disclose the who, the when, the where, or the how, which may make identifying, trapping, or finding the thief possibly before or at his or her next crime.

The Universe of Suspects

Each member of a criminal investigation division should be able to recognize information that is important to all the division members and to advise coworkers of possible suspects in current or future crimes. Unlike solving violent crimes involving named suspects, solving thefts requires criminal investigators to engage in a battle for information, and every investigator needs the help of his or her associates. Although mainly general information about individuals suspected of earning the major portion of their incomes from criminal operations, information obtained from associates and elsewhere can sometimes isolate a number of persons suspected of committing a specific crime.

Field interview reports in the police records systems may hold meaningful data about persons and vehicles stopped and questioned by police officers on patrol. However, a great deal of data about people living and working in a patrol sector is stored in the minds of the officers regularly working the sector. Often, this useful information is never entered into the police records system. At one time, local police communicated this type of information to federal agents, and uniformed police supplied local detectives with similar data about persons considered suspects because of their activity. Recently, the upward supply of information from local levels has been noticeable in its absence. An investigator must work to correct this situation, daily allocating time for developing liaisons with local sources of information among other police officers, for finding out the names and descriptions of persons known to be well supplied with money but without a known source of income, for noting the automobile make and license plate number of a newly arrived hoodlum or a recently released felony parolee, for learning the consensus about a merchant suspected of buying and selling stolen property, and for hearing about a host of seemingly unimportant items shared among police officers in friendship and appreciation of mutual occupational objectives.

Work must also be devoted to remedying current practices about credit and reward for information received. Entries should be made in the service records of the helping officers when such leads assist in breaking a case. More important, such colleagues may be assisted in a normal ambition to step up into investigative work. Willingness to help an investigator is a good recommendation about a person's basic worth for this type of duty.

Investigators must also regularly allocate time for frequenting known thieves' haunts. Taxi drivers, waitresses, cocktail hostesses, bartenders, and tavern owners in such areas are potential sources of information about persons who are new to the area and apparently well supplied with money. Persons in these occupations are less reluctant to talk about thieves than they are about people who rob and commit assault. Underworld informants interviewed clandestinely can provide supplementary information for a better understanding of data already collected, they can assist in interpreting information, and they can offer leads that may be developed through inquiries in these criminals' known hangouts. Such inquiries are necessarily discreet so as not to compromise any ongoing investigation. The investigator's relations with such sources of information must be guarded, substantially different from the friendships necessary to develop information from local police officers.

Learning to appreciate the significance of an apparently minor item of information is a developed skill. However, it is a learned skill that will enhance the value of other information collected during an investigation. It will also increase the universe of suspects and the probability that the group of suspects will contain the person responsible for the crime under investigation. Because of the lack of eyewitnesses in crimes against property, the ability to solve a crime is likely to rest on investigators' entering the necessary information into the police system without loss or distortion and using it to the best advantage.[9]

Criminal Receivers of Stolen Property

Theft investigators would be seriously handicapped if the proceeds of all thefts were cash or its equivalent. Most thefts are of various goods and merchandise. Unfortunately, the market for stolen property is stable and continuing.

The real success in stealing is not completing the crime, but disposing of the stolen property at a profit—without leaving the trace that so often identifies the perpetrators of these crimes. Criminals who commit property crimes are repeat offenders. Perhaps they are fatalistic about this Achilles' heel of property crime and consider it a permanent occupational hazard, but many of them blithely pawn their loot or sell it to someone likely to identify them to the police.

Initially, the receiver of stolen property insulates the thief from identification and arrest. As soon as the property transfer is made, the thief can no longer be caught with the stolen property in his or her possession. However, when police detect and apprehend a receiver with stolen property, the potential for tracing it to the thief is always present. This tracing from receiver to thief is an effective theft investigative technique. It is the only method to use when a thief does not leave any fingerprints or "signature" (modus operandi) at the crime scene, when the thief is not observed or apprehended while the crime is in progress, or while the thief is in possession of recently stolen property.

When the stolen property is purchased by an individual seeking a bargain, such tracing is relatively easy. The receiver is informed of the possible criminal implications of possessing stolen property. Usually, the price and the circumstances of purchase create a reasonably probable cause to assume the purchaser knew the property was stolen. In disclaiming any criminal responsibility, this type of receiver either identifies the seller-thief or provides sufficient information about the purchase for the investigator to identify the thief.

When the stolen property is purchased by a professional receiver (a fence), tracing from receiver to thief becomes a problem. Fences with long-standing business dealings with a thief are unlikely to reveal the circumstances of how they received the stolen property.

Fences are the intermediaries of larceny. They buy and sell stolen property regularly. They are in direct contact with thieves and with possible purchasers. Most of them have acquired a reputation on both sides of this business loop and depend on this "goodwill" for third-party referrals of new business. This "rep" means that the fence will not, under any circumstances, inform police of the identity of a thief or a purchaser of stolen property.[10]

The **sting**, or **storefront technique**, is an investigative technique aimed at the wholesale identification and apprehension of thieves involved in property crimes. Police investigators pose as fences for the purpose of "buying" stolen property.[11] Since the prices paid to thieves by a real fence are copied by the police, the cost of this technique is not a real problem. The problem is whether such police activity may encourage local thieves to take more and more—as long as they have a readily available market.

Auto Theft

The theft of passenger cars, trucks, and motorcycles is common throughout the United States. **Auto theft** is the term police generally use to describe this form of larceny. The universe of auto thieves comprises both amateurs and professionals, such as the following six:

1. *The Joyriding Juvenile.* The joyriding juvenile is usually host to several other juveniles. They abandon the vehicle when it runs out of gas or they tire of it.
2. *The Transportation Thief.* The transportation thief is the person who "borrows" a car for transportation, sometimes to cross state lines or for a lengthy period. The vehicle is abandoned when it has served the thief's purpose.
3. *The Use-In-Crime Thief.* Some thieves steal a car for the sole purpose of using it in the commission of another crime, such as a robbery. Again, the vehicle is abandoned when it has served its purpose.

4. ***Insurance Fraud Swindlers.***   An insurance fraud swindler abandons his or her automobile in a ghetto area where the owner knows it will be stripped promptly for its parts, or the owner will have it dismantled or "squished" in a junkyard or arrange for its burning. The owner claims—and usually receives—the current blue-book value of the vehicle from the insurance company.

   In a spin-off of this fraud, the swindler registers and insures a "paper" car (forged title to a nonexistent vehicle), reports it stolen, and puts in a claim to the insurance carrier for the current blue-book value of the phantom car.

5. ***Strippers and Dismantlers.***   **Strippers** usually attack a parked car, taking a variety of parts readily disposed of on the local black market. Stereos, CDs, batteries, bucket seats, transmissions, rear ends, generators, wheels and tires, and even motors have been stripped from automobiles in public places. **Dismantlers** steal a car, tow or drive it to a "chop shop," and cut it up for most of its parts. The body of the stolen car (sometimes even minus fenders, doors, headlights, front grill, and motor hood) is abandoned some distance from the shop, usually in a remote area. These thieves work fast. A parked car can be stripped in place in less than an hour, and dismantlers can chop up a car, dispose of the leftover body, and move the parts to be sold to another location all within an hour or so.

6. ***Professional Auto Thieves.***   The "pro" auto thief steals late-model automobiles and resells them. Sometimes the stolen car is transported to another state and registered in that state with forged or fraudulent papers prior to resale. A contemporary practice is to ship the stolen car out of the country (Mexico and South America are favorite areas) and sell it on arrival. Some of these professional thieves have developed a new trade: stealing cars to order for "chop shops."

Many of these auto thieves now use weapons to gain possession of a car. *Carjacking* is the armed robbery of a person in possession of an automobile or another motor vehicle. One or more thieves confront a car's driver with a gun, a knife, or another weapon and demand the car keys, then drive off.

While amateur car thieves (joyriders and transportation thieves) sometimes seek automobiles with the keys in the lock or the car doors unlocked, the pro uses tools such as a "dent puller" and "slide hammer" or a set of master keys to enter a locked car and to defeat the ignition lock. Many amateur thieves are as skilled at hot-wiring the ignition of a car as the professionals are.

An auto theft investigation has the following five stages:

1. ***Preliminary Investigation.***   The preliminary investigator accepts the report of a stolen vehicle from the owner or his or her representative. The report must contain the owner's name, address, and telephone number; a full description of the vehicle, including registration number and public and other identification numbers; the time and place of the theft and the location of the vehicle when stolen; and assurance that the vehicle was not repossessed

by a finance company or another legal owner. Anything distinctive about the stolen vehicle (e.g., design, color, damage) is entered on this report to aid in its location as promptly as possible.

2. ***Alarm.***   Information from the preliminary investigative report—particularly distinctive characteristics of the stolen vehicle—is transmitted to all members of the police agency, sent to cooperating agencies by Teletype or other means, and reported to state and national computerized records systems.

3. ***Recovery.***   Auto thefts for convenience or joyriding are usually identified by prompt recovery of the stolen auto without any evidence of stripping. The same is also true of the use-in-crime theft, with the recovery time usually within a short time after the crime. Citizens often notice these parked vehicles and assist the patrol force in locating them. The recovery of a stripped or "chopped" vehicle identifies the work of strippers and dismantlers. The non-recovery of the stolen vehicle tends to identify the other types of auto thieves.

4. ***Continuing Investigation.***   Probing into the circumstances of an auto theft is usually reactive to the arrest of an auto thief who is in possession of the stolen vehicle or to its recovery. The probing is proactive when the vehicle is not recovered within a reasonable time; investigators prowl auto accessory and salvage yards and body-and-fender shops to locate stolen vehicles. Local laws usually require the proprietors to allow police inspection.

5. ***Case Preparation.***   Cases involving the theft of a *single* vehicle that are closed by arrest require simple evidence: the appropriation of another's property to the thief's use without the owner's permission. Cases involving *multivehicle* thefts require extensive evidence not only to show the larceny, but also to possibly assemble a conspiracy case against all offenders involved. In either event, inquiries along the basic leads common in property crimes give initial direction to any continuing investigation of auto theft.

The reality of auto theft is that the current high prices for vehicle accessories and components contribute to the growth of "hot parts" dealers. This ready market for the proceeds of their crime assures strippers and dismantlers of better-than-average prices compared with those obtained by thieves stealing other goods and merchandise. In fact, the "growth market" factor in this area has attracted many segments of the national crime syndicate to this lucrative field.

In preliminary or continuing investigations of auto theft, primary identification of a stolen vehicle is made by the public vehicle identification number (PVIN), motor number, and confidential vehicle identification number (CVIN) at various hidden locations on the vehicle. (Vehicle manufacturers and the National Automobile Theft Bureau supply police agencies with information about the location of such numbers on passenger cars, trucks, and motorcycles.)

Theft by Employees

U.S. businesses lose billions of dollars annually as a result of employee theft. **Shrinkage** is the term business uses for the loss of inventory from employee theft. The resulting loss is transferred to the consumer in the form of higher costs for products and services. Many large firms have security personnel who are trained in employee theft investigations. However, the criminal investigator may be involved when the loss is extensive and criminal prosecution is desired or when the business does not have an investigative staff. A thorough investigation is required in these cases because the suspected employee may lose his or her employment and be prosecuted criminally. Generally, employee theft falls within three categories: incidental, situational, and continual theft.

Incidental theft involves instances when employees consume the employer's product while on the job or take items such as pens and pencils home at the end of the day. The cost to the employer is relatively minor, and most businesses deal with this type of employee theft through disciplinary measures and assume the loss as the price of doing business.

Situational theft involves instances when the employee is presented with an opportunity for theft, which, in the employee's mind, must be acted on. Truck drivers, for instance, who at the end of their route have extra merchandise that has not been charged out to them, have an excellent opportunity to take the merchandise. The restaurant manager who is called away to handle an emergency while counting the previous day's receipts inadvertently leaves the office door open. An employee acts on the opportunity and the manager returns to find that some or all of the money is missing. In both instances, the criminal investigator may become involved and presented with the challenge of having a number of potential suspects. The missing merchandise could have been put on any one of a number of trucks, and any of the restaurant's employees could have entered the manager's office while he or she was gone.

The initial goal for the investigator is to reduce to a manageable total the number of possible suspects who will ultimately be interrogated or asked to submit to a polygraph examination. Accomplishing this task requires each suspect to be interviewed individually. Each suspect is asked a predetermined set of questions designed to evaluate his or her reaction to each question. An example of the type of questions the investigator might ask includes the following:

> Do you know why I am talking to you?
> Do you have any idea of who may be responsible for the loss?
> Would you eliminate anyone as a suspect?

Guilty and innocent employees have different motivations concerning the responses to these questions. The innocent employee wants to aid the investigation and knows he or she is there to help the investigator. The innocent employee wants the responsible person caught so that the innocent employee will no longer be a suspect and life will return to normal at work. The innocent person, therefore, will identify the most likely suspects for the investigator and will eliminate those above suspicion. In contrast, the guilty person will want to expand the list of possible suspects as much as possible. The missing merchandise could have been put on anyone's truck or been a clerical error; anyone in the area at the time could have access to the manager's office and the missing money. The guilty would not eliminate anyone from suspicion; after all, everyone could use some extra cash. Guilty individuals will say they do not know why the investigator is talking to them, because they do not want to be considered suspects. When the employee's reactions indicate guilt, the investigator may switch to an interrogation mode or possibly schedule the suspect for a voluntary polygraph examination.

Continual theft involves ongoing, constant acts of theft by an employee. This type of theft is usually motivated by the need to support a vice such as gambling, drugs, or alcohol. In California, the theft of money, labor, or real or personal property valued at more than $400 in any consecutive 12-month period is a felony.

The investigator usually starts the investigation by charting the known dates and times of the losses and comparing this information with employee attendance records. A reasonable match, during a sufficient amount of time, of a specific employee who was on the job when the losses occurred would qualify him or her for closer scrutiny. Trusted supervisors and managers should also be consulted to determine whether any reason exists to believe the suspected employee may be responsible for the losses. Finally, the suspected employee is subjected to surveillance, by either a visual or a contact method, until another loss occurs. Once the surveillance confirms that the employee is the responsible party, he or she should be confronted while still in possession of the money or merchandise and then questioned.

FRAUD

Fraud is not a new offense. It is defined as a nonviolent crime involving elements of intentional deceit, concealment, corruption, misrepresentation, and abuse of trust to gain the property of another, and it is often facilitated by the willing cooperation of unaware or unknowing victims.

The guile, deception, and trickery common to frauds often silence the victim. Either the victim does not realize a theft has occurred or is unwilling to report it because of fear of being involved in a crime or of publicly admitting to having been duped. In addition, police frequently fail to discover unreported frauds because fraud is a covert scheme with a lower profile than that of overt thefts or violent crimes.

Fraud is on the increase in the United States. Swindlers use simple bunco schemes or complex **confidence (con) games** to rip off unknowing victims. Fraudulent check writers menace the integrity of banks. White-collar criminals operating in both the marketplace and the workplace abuse the trust common to merchant-customer and employee-employer relations.

Fraud investigations usually begin with a citizen's complaint or a police probe. A preliminary investigation should disclose whether the act or acts done to further the objective of the fraud are a crime under state laws. Such investigation should spell out the time, place, and modus operandi of the fraud, along with data on the victim, property lost, witnesses, and suspects.

Continuing investigations are the action phase in which suspects are identified, pursued, and apprehended, and the case is prepared for criminal prosecution. When a fraud case reveals substantial economic loss to a victim but cannot be developed for criminal prosecution, it is best referred to state or federal regulatory agencies for possible civil action, a cease-and-desist order, or other appropriate remedial action (Figure 14–3).

Fraud auditing is a new occupational specialty in commercial and industrial employment. Fraud "auditors" are assigned the task of detecting and preventing frauds in commercial transactions. Job descriptions in this role call for the skills of a well-trained auditor and an experienced criminal investigator. Fraud auditors examine the covert aspect of employee behavior and the barriers established to prevent fraud. Can the barriers be breached? When? How? By whom?[12]

Elements of Fraud

Investigators must seek evidence of four common characteristics of fraud:

1. Criminal intent (mens rea)
2. Wrongful objective (deprive true owner of property)
3. Disguise or concealment of objective (wrongful)
4. Reliance on victim's cupidity (greed), carelessness, or compassion

The criminal intent is to achieve the wrongful objective of the scheme. The act or acts done to implement the scheme spell out the disguise or concealment of this unlawful objective. Thieves who profit from fraudulent schemes must induce the victim to part voluntarily with his or her property by signing a contract, paying money, or transferring property ownership.

Bunco Schemes and Con Games

Bunco schemes and con games are frauds based on promises of unusual returns: something for nothing, double your money, or income for life. The victim's false hopes are fostered by assurances that the risk is minimal. The scheme is usually described as a "sure thing."

Some of the more common swindles classed as bunco schemes or con games are the pigeon drop, the payoff, and carnival bunco. The **pigeon drop**, or **pocketbook drop** (Figure 14–4), is street bunco that requires a minimum number of props: a pocketbook or an envelope and a sizable amount of cash. The **pigeon** is the victim, and no more than two or three swindlers participate

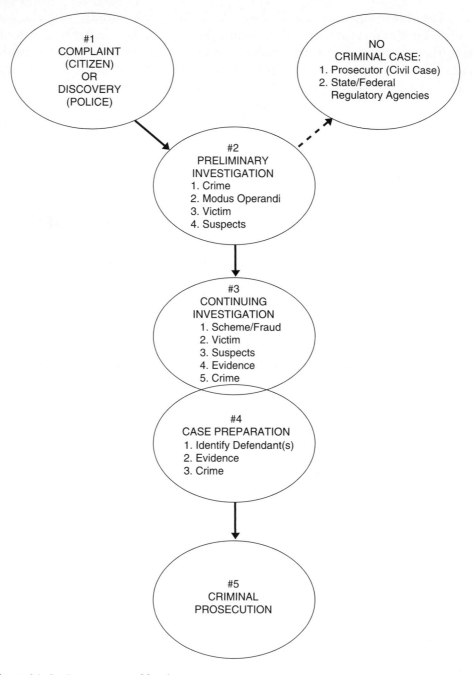

FIGURE 14-3 Investigation of fraud.

487 PC PIGEON DROP

Date: 6/22/2005

Case #:   01-6956 / 01-7010

Name: **UNKNOWN**

Height: **5 Feet 8 Inches**

Weight: **180**

Age: **40**

Sex: **M**

Eyes: **BROWN**

Hair: **BLACK**

Complexion:**CLEAR**

Race: **BLACK**

OTHER INFORMATION BELOW

On 6-20-2005 at 1400 hours, (S) took up conversation with Asian (V) at Valley Shopping Center. (S) told victim he was new in the U.S. and stated he was not trusted since he was black. (S) asked (V) to withdraw money ($6,700) from (V)'s bank account to prove his point. The (V) withdrew the money. The (S) then asked (V) to trust him to walk around the block with the (V)'s money. (S) told (V) that if he did that and if the (S) returned, the (S) would give the (V) double his money. The (V) agreed and the (S) left with the money and never came back.

On 6-21-2005 at 1446 hours, the same (S) made another attempt at the Cheapcost Store. In that crime, a second suspect (BMA) was used. Police were called by the (V) while he was in the bank conducting the withdrawal. (S)s fled the area prior to police arrival.

Please BOL and contact me with any similars.

Officer John Smith   Valley Department of Public Safety
(555) 555-5555

TRAK (59 -> 131:1.70.66) This flyer produced on a TRAK System. For more information about TRAK see www.trak.org

FIGURE 14-4   Pigeon drop con game wanted notice.

in this crime. In this scheme, a victim is conned into withdrawing a large sum of money from a bank account to show financial responsibility. In the presence of the potential victim, one of the swindlers apparently "finds" a pocketbook or an envelope filled with money (usually $500 to $2,500). The approach to the victim is disarming, combining happiness at finding the money along with the query, "What do I do now?" As the victim starts to discuss the swindler's apparent good fortune, the second swindler appears. Assuming the role of a stranger who just happened to witness the "find" and wants to be part of it, the second swindler joins in the "spiel" that makes the victim a partner in a plan to withhold the money from its owner until the origin of this amount of cash can be determined. Since doing so will take time, the two swindlers team up to convince the victim that he or she should hold the find, but to assure them of the victim's "good faith," they ask the victim to "show" cash equal to the amount found (or close to it). Faced with the possible loss of one-third of the found money, the gullible victim goes to a bank, gets the cash, and reveals it to the swindlers. They go through the motions of counting it, advising the victim of their satisfaction, and bundling the found money with the victim's cash and arranging to meet again with the victim the next day. Sometime after this parting, the victim's natural curiosity leads to an examination of the bundle of money. It turns out to be paper cut to size. The swindlers switched the bundle just before they parted from the victim.[13]

The **charity switch** is a variation of the pigeon drop used by swindlers who have a potential victim unlikely to be motivated by greed. The "pitch" in the charity switch is to a victim's compassion. The swindlers convince the victim (often clergy or a nurse) to hold money ($500 to $2,500) for a sick or dying person. If the owner of the money does not recover, the victim can use the money for his or her favorite charity. However, to show "good faith," the victim is asked to show financial responsibility. At this point, the pigeon drop routine is implemented and the swindlers take off with all the money.[14]

The **payoff** is a swindle in which the swindler claims to have access to information about fixed horse races. In its simple street bunco form, the swindler acts out the role of **tout**. Three or four bettor-victims place large bets on horses that the swindler believes will win a selected race. If one of the swindler's horses wins, the winning bettor shares the winnings with the swindler. In its more elaborate form, victims are identified by "ropers" and are put in contact with an "inside person" who poses as representatives of the fixed-race conspiracy. Another "inside person" is the manager of the bogus horse room used in this swindle. In a carefully orchestrated scheme, the "sucker," or "mark," is allowed to win at first, but he or she loses the final large bet. In breaking away with their loot, the swindlers "cool" the victim by implying that he or she is equally guilty of violating federal or state communications laws or participating in a criminal conspiracy.[15]

Carnival bunco is street bunco in which each victim may be "taken" for only small amounts of money, but the overall profit to these swindlers is huge.

Customers pay a ten- to fifty-cent fee to play these games, hoping to win one or more of the better-quality prizes exhibited. However, they cannot win the better prizes. Customers are encouraged to try and try again by allowing them to win minor prizes (cheap merchandise) and fast counting their scores: operators total a customer's score above what has been achieved to convince the victim that he or she is actually close to winning a better prize. The games are rigged so that these scores can never be attained. Trick balls, weighted dolls, underinflated balloons, and oversized marbles are some of the mechanical aids used to defraud gullible carnival goers.

The Bank Examiner Fraud

The **bank examiner fraud** is an ego-building swindle based on many people's hidden desire to serve as a secret agent for the police. Victims are located through telephone books or pseudosurveys. The first telephone call to the victim is double-talk, in which some problem with the victim's account at the local bank is alleged. The next call is supposedly from an officer of the bank. The "spiel" is that one of the bank's employees has been tampering with depositors' accounts, the bank officer wants to catch the employee, and the bank officer needs the victim's help to do so. Cooperative victims are then informed that they should go to the bank, withdraw a specific sum (usually just short of the victim's total deposited funds), and bring it home. The victim is assured that the withdrawal will be secretly watched by an armed agent who will follow the victim home to ensure the money is safe. A few moments after arrival at home with the money, the victim is visited by the swindler posing as the "armed agent." After some double-talk, the swindler counts the victim's money, gives him or her a signed deposit slip, and takes the money. Hours, days, and even weeks later, the victim discovers that the name on the deposit slip is fictitious, the bank knows nothing of a dishonest employee, and the money given to the swindler is a total loss.

Fraudulent Checks

"Passers" of forged checks have always been the concern of police forgery squads. However, only the unusual fraudulent check writer attempts to pass off a signature as genuine. Such forgers do sign names other than their own, but this step is just the first in a fraud that also involves false or stolen identification cards, a spiel that overcomes a merchant's reluctance to cash a check upon minimal identification, and a bunco or a con artist's sense of the right time, place, and victim to conclude this fraud successfully. Fortunately, the modus operandi of these check passers identifies them to investigators. Sometimes, a victim will assist in identification, but since the identification documents are spurious and the contact at the time of check cashing is short, victims have recall problems.

NSF (not sufficient funds) check writers are overt thieves, signing their name to a worthless check and cashing it. Willingness to repay the loss to the victim and an active checking account can overcome the perception of fraud. So-called occasional fraudulent check writers can postpone criminal prosecution on a promise of restitution. The true fraud investigation in this area is of the chronic fraudulent check writer and the extent of his or her theft when more than one NSF check has been cashed.

Credit Card Frauds

Credit card fraud is emerging as a popular form of theft. Fraudulent use of credit cards provides the thief with various goods and services, and credit cards can easily be converted into cash by sale "in the street"—the illegal marketplace. Thieves obtain credit cards by theft (from mail, the person to whom the card belongs, a residence, an auto, a place of business, a hotel, or another location); by fraudulent application to the issuing firm; or by counterfeiting. Credit cards stolen from the mail, intercepted en route to the legitimate receivers, are sought on the illegal market because they have not been reported as lost or stolen. If it is a card requiring a signature, the illegal owner can sign the card in the name of the legitimate card owner and in a style he or she can readily replicate (despite disguising the handwriting).

Credit card thieves may be discovered upon the complaint of merchants who call for an authorization because of the amount of a purchase and discover that the card is on the "hot card list," or those who become suspicious because of alterations on the card, during legal searches, or during other investigations.

Consumer and Business Frauds

Consumer and business frauds are marketplace swindles in which the buyer or investor is defrauded by the swindler's misrepresentations.[16] Three types of common consumer frauds are perpetrated:

1. *Bait and Switch.*   In **bait and switch**, advertised merchandise bargains lure customers into a merchant's place of business. Sales personnel then bad-mouth the advertised merchandise and switch the customer to a higher-priced item of allegedly better quality.
2. *Repair Fraud.*   In **repair fraud**, the swindler overcharges for services performed; charges for services not performed or parts not replaced; fails to provide labor and materials as agreed; and charges for labor or materials not needed, not discussed with the customer, or not within the scope of the customer's agreement.
3. *Misrepresentation.*   **Misrepresentation** is failing to provide the facts about product performance, warranties, credit charges, or other hidden costs.

Other types of consumer and business frauds are as follows: the Ponzi scheme is the base of all investment frauds; securities frauds are get-rich-quick schemes; land-sales frauds have a similar scheme along with the promise of a future home in a desirable climate; and advance-fee swindles offer poor-risk credit applicants assistance in securing huge loans. Home-improvement frauds are consumer frauds that victimize homeowners, bankruptcy frauds are business frauds in which creditors are swindled, and insurance swindles defraud insurance companies.

In a **Ponzi scheme** (named after its originator and also known as **kiting**), the swindler uses money invested by new victims to pay high interest on the investments of earlier victims—whose money the swindler has appropriated to his or her own use instead of investing it as claimed in the spiel given the victim. A Ponzi scheme collapses when the swindler runs out of victims.

Securities frauds are based on promises to victims of rapid capital growth, a high and quick rate of returns on dividends, or special advantages such as tax shelters. Victims are selected on the basis of their liquid or convertible assets. High-income professionals and persons approaching the threshold of retirement are common victims.

Land-sales frauds are based on the swindler's misrepresentations about the value and future development of worthless, unimproved land. Fraudulent land sales have involved the sale of property at inflated prices in which the swindler had no existing title or interest. Undeveloped property owned by the swindler, but without roads, water, or other improvements, is sold because of false statements of current or future development (e.g., roads, water) that does not exist or will not occur and that the swindler has no intention of providing.

Advance-fee frauds victimize businessmen and -women who are having problems securing loans from local banks or other lending institutions. The swindler claims to have access to loan officers, out-of-town banks, or the mortgage loan officials of a labor union pension fund. The advance fee is money upfront to motivate the loan arranger (swindler) to arrange the loan. The swindler has no intention of performing as promised but will make any misrepresentation to secure the victim's money. This swindle is common in the United States because the reality for poor-risk applicants trying to secure loans has been that money upfront has been used to influence bank loan officers and officials of union pension funds.

Home-improvement frauds victimize homeowners with false claims that the work is necessary or that the cost of the proposed work is much below its real worth and will add to the homeowner's basic investment. These frauds include one or more of the following six characteristics:

1. Misrepresentation of the need for labor or materials
2. Poor work

3. Substandard materials
4. Gross overpricing
5. Failure to provide paid-for labor and material
6. Concealment of the cost of credit, as well as the fact that failure to pay will result in a lien on the victim's home

Gangs of home-improvement swindlers move from town to town, transferring their accounts payable to a local bank at a discount and moving to new areas.

Bankruptcy frauds involve false claims of insolvency. Organized crime personnel have used the planned bankruptcy or scam to loot the assets of a business. In bankruptcy fraud, the swindler conceals or diverts to friends and associates the major assets of a business so that they cannot be sold to pay off creditors, or he or she uses previously established credit to secure huge amounts of merchandise and then conceals or converts such merchandise to his or her own use just prior to the bankruptcy—without paying the supplier's bills.

Insurance frauds are common in the world of commerce and business. They are in a class by themselves because the swindler must be the insured, and the victim is the insurer. The swindler may have crime partners, but only the insured can profit from defrauding an insurance company. Filing false claims is the fraud. In some fraudulent fire cases, "sham" mortgages are used to raise the value of a building fraudulently. As a result, insurance policies are issued in amounts far in excess of the true value of the insured building. An arson investigation into a series of fires in an urban ghetto area revealed that the insured owner had engaged in selling to friends and business associates a number of times, with little or no cash involved in the transfer of ownership. Each time, the seller took a new second mortgage to artificially inflate the building's value.[17]

Workplace Frauds

Major frauds in the workplace are embezzlement and computer frauds. Investigations are usually initiated upon discovery of the fraud, and investigators follow leads as to the identity of employees having the necessary access to the funds or the computer.

Embezzlement is the conversion of another person's property over which the thief has custody or control. Victims are the employers of these dishonest employees, with the scope of the theft depending on the position held by the employee and his or her ability to conceal the theft or thefts. Investigators should be alert for money losses reported as armed robberies to cover up embezzlement.

The newest fraud in the workplace involves computers and has frightening potential for victimization. The Equity Funding Insurance Company fraud is an example of using a computer as an essential tool for accomplishing a theft that totaled a $100 million loss to customers, stockholders, and others. To sustain its image as a successful insurance company, the Equity Funding firm produced fake insurance policies, which were recorded in the computer as new business and sold for cash to reinsurance firms. In this case, the computer was also programmed to conceal the fraud: a special code was used to skip the usual premium procedures on the fake policies. At least 75 employees were accomplices and participants in this crime. So-called creative accounting covered up this fraud for many years until a fired employee talked about it.[18]

ATM Frauds

Thieves find ATM cards in their victims' wallets and pocketbooks. They also find a driver's license, sometimes a checkbook, and, often, photographs or papers with the names of family members. In past years, all this material was worthless; today, it has become the "kit" for finding the personal identification number (PIN) that validates the ATM card. ATM cardholders seem to have a subliminal fear of forgetting their "secret" PIN numbers and use easily remembered numbers such as a birth date or an anniversary date, a fore-and-aft series of numbers from their bank account or driver's license number, a simple 1-2-3-4 code based on their name or the names of children or grandchildren, or a transposition of a home or an office telephone number.

Now in possession of the ATM card and the correct PIN number, the thief tries to get to the machine before the rightful owner of the card contacts the bank and cancels the card. Withdrawing whatever the cash limit is for a single transaction, the thief hits an ATM, walks away, comes back for another withdrawal, and continues until the account is empty or the card is reported stolen and the machine retains the card.

Thieves are aware of the surveillance cameras at these machines but knowingly discount any in-court identification at trial and openly scoff at the possibility of arrest. Police and bank fraud investigators deal with the "gotcha" problem in these cases in the following five ways:

1. They move fast upon a stolen card cancellation notice, study the rhythm of the withdrawals by the thief from the ATM transaction record, and, as long as funds remain in the account, wait until the thief arrives to hit the machine again.
2. When credit cards from the same source have been used successfully, they interview the salesclerks who write up the sale, asking for a good physical description and knowledge of the suspect. They also request the cooperation of one or two of these individuals in producing a composite sketch.
3. When forged checks begin to appear, they interview the endorser for help with identifying the suspect.

4. They send cards and checks to the crime lab for latent fingerprint lifting.
5. If they have partial identity, they seek out ex-lovers, ex-spouses, and former friends or crime partners for help in making a full identification from the photos or composite sketch.

If any one of these individuals is in jail awaiting trial, the investigator may have the classic leverage to secure cooperation.

Identity Theft

The **identity thief** is an imposter who uses another person's identifiers to apply for and receive credit cards under the assumed identity. These credit cards are then used to purchase merchandise and services until the theft is discovered. Identifiers are driver's licenses, motor vehicle registrations, and other proofs of identity.

Identity theft is new, and as stolen identifiers become readily available to thieves in an area, it is bound to increase. Such proofs of identity are now being used to buy houses and open bank accounts, all under the assumed identity used by the identity thief. Victims of this scam are expected to report their losses to the issuing credit card company (see Appendix C, Identity Theft).

Computer Fraud

CEOs of large corporations and managers and owners of smaller businesses have accepted responsibility for denying unauthorized persons access to their computer systems. Access codes are guarded zealously to prevent **hackers** from entering their computer system. Ongoing sales talk from both hardware and software computer representatives is about "super safety" that not only blocks access but also sets up an alarm mode when attempts at unauthorized access are made—closing down any entry and promptly triggering a trace program to locate and identify the source of the attempted entry.

When someone does break into a system, the response is fast and oriented toward damage control. Computer security personnel of the victim company react to this crisis by joining forces with computer industry "reps," who fear unfavorable publicity.

When personnel determine who did it, how it was done, and the identity of crime partners, they will terminate with prejudice if an employee of the victim firm is guilty. They may also report the crime to the police.

When a computer fraud is reported to the police, the person reporting should be considered the victim or an identified representative of the victim (corporation, firm), and a standard crime report should be filled out with the interviewing investigator as the reporting officer. In addition to the called-for information, the narrative of this form should include what was taken without permission, an estimated amount of the loss, how this successful "attack" on the victim's computer system was accomplished, and background information on any person listed on the crime report as a suspect. The investigator will likely need legal assistance (what crime has been committed or attempted; what are its essential elements) and a computer expert (e.g., agency or contract employee) who can help in the here-and-now of an investigation and later testify in court as an expert witness.

Then, if the case develops well, the investigator should go to the prosecutor's office and seek help with case preparation. To build a case against clever cyberthieves, the investigator will need a large support group headed by a cybersleuth. Tsutomu Shimomura, a computational physicist and computer security expert, was a leader of a support group comprising Federal Bureau of Investigation (FBI) agents, local police, and telephone experts from the network world. Their charge and mission was to identify, arrest, and assist in the prosecution of a world-class hacker who had outwitted authorities for more than 2 years. After his arrest, both parties negotiated a deal that lowered the severe sentence likely on twenty-three counts of computer fraud and related crimes to less than a year in a county jail and gained the cooperation of this offender as a willing witness in the trials of his former crime partners, an important prosecutorial advantage.[19]

Investigation of Frauds

Since crime scenes are usually nonexistent in fraud cases, the investigator must concentrate on securing facts about the crime from the victim and witnesses and from the records or other documents prepared and used by one or more of the participants. Collected evidence should be organized under the following five major headings:

1. *Description of the Offense.*   How was the scheme conceived, what was its nature, where was it placed in operation, and during what dates was it in operation?
2. *Victim.*   How was the initial contact made? Subsequent contacts? Where? Who was involved? Who made what representations? What was the victim's reliance on such representations? What was the extent of the loss? How was the money paid to the swindlers?
3. *Suspect-Defendant.*   Name, address, occupation, date and place of birth, physical description, associates, and criminal history when available. Identification of a suspect-defendant who may cooperate with the investigation, possibly serving as an accomplice-witness in a criminal trial.
4. *Evidence.*   Data about witnesses, victim, documentary and other physical evidence, and how it was obtained.
5. *Crime.*   A review of the essential elements of the crime or crimes that might be charged, along with the major misrepresentations, false pretenses, or false promises used by the suspect-defendant to obtain the victim's money; and presentation of evidence supporting the investigator's conclusion that the evidence found indicates the suspect-defendant's criminal intent and sets out the fraud involved.

Identification should not be a major problem in fraud investigations once a suspect is located and apprehended. The pursuit and apprehension of swindlers is often handicapped by the inability of victims to properly describe the swindler and others involved. Once the swindler is apprehended, however, the victim can usually identify him or her.

The investigation of credit card frauds provides a splendid opportunity to uncover more-serious crimes and to apprehend crime partners. A credit card is unusual in that the issuing firm (the theft victim in extensive frauds) will aid the investigation by tracing and reporting the activities associated with the illegal use of the credit card. As a result, investigators may secure the following:

- Samples of handwriting in the form of signed sales drafts and applications
- License plate numbers recorded on gasoline sales drafts at service stations
- Drivers' license numbers on car rental contracts or on sales drafts where further identification is requested
- The credit card imprint on copies of sales drafts, airline tickets, hotel bills, or car rental contracts
- The description of a rented motor vehicle that the subject had in his or her possession at any particular time
- The description of merchandise on a sales slip, which could reveal the purchase of guns, knives, or items identifiable by serial numbers, as well as distinctive clothing and wigs

"Decoy" vehicles and appliances have opened up new horizons for proactive, as well as reactive, investigations of consumer frauds. The decoy vehicle or appliance is in good working order except for some minor or easily discovered and repaired fault. When the repair personnel entrusted with the decoy vehicle or appliance lie about needed repairs, or charge for repairs not done or for parts not supplied, the investigator can begin developing a fraud case.

CHAPTER REVIEW

CASE STUDY

The Year My Life Was Stolen

It started in February. I came home about midnight after an evening out with friends, only to see a sight that made my heart drop: there was the front door, wide open.

Someone had ransacked my house, strange hands pawing through my most private possessions. They stole jewelry, crystal, some electronics. They even took the oak nightstand from beside my bed. A nightstand!?

Then, 2 months after the burglary, things went from bad to horrific. It was 5:00 p.m., and I'd just gotten off work. There's a bar and restaurant on Broadway that I usually go to, and I was just pulling up on a nearby side street when it happened.

As I turned off the ignition and started to open my door, I looked up to see a man—I couldn't tell if he was an African American or Hispanic—in a knit cap blocking my way. The first thing I noticed were his eyes. They were absolutely black. Black and cruel.

I started to tell him to back off, but he stopped me cold.

"I want your f***ing car," he hissed. "If you say another f***ing word, I'm going to blow your f***ing brains out."

Then he pulled back his coat to reveal a pistol tucked in the waistband of his pants.

I got the message.

Just then, two friends pulled up in front of us and started walking toward me. I was thinking "No, no, no," because from the look in the guy's eyes, I think he would have blown us all away and not thought twice.

So I jumped out and ran, yelling to my friends, "Get away, get away; he's got a gun."

Were they just looking for the right victim in the right car to come along, or were they waiting especially for me? The thought sent a chill through me.

It was the worst thing that had ever happened in my life, but as I was soon to learn, my problems were just beginning. Part of it was emotional. I was scared all the time. There were the nightmares, too—the carjacker's face, with those black, evil eyes filling my dreams night after night.

But it wasn't only at night that the incident came back to haunt me. Pretty soon, stores all over town were having checks from my account returned to my bank. Someone else, using my driver's license—yeah, that was in my purse, too—was writing checks like crazy. Hardware stores. Grocery stores. Clothing stores. Auto parts stores.

I wasn't held responsible—it was the store's fault for not properly checking identification. But every time it happened, I had to deal with the store, provide them with police reports and things like that so that my credit wouldn't be affected. It was one hassle after another.

This was around Memorial Day, and by then I was getting pretty irritated by the police department, because as far as I could tell, it had done absolutely nothing. It wasn't like they didn't have some leads to work with. There was my cellular phone bill, for example. Even though I'd canceled within a half hour of my car's being stolen, the carjacker still made a few phone calls. When the bills came, those numbers were listed, but I don't know if the police ever did anything with the information.

They did find the car about 3 days after it was stolen. It had been abandoned alongside the road somewhere, the stereo and dashboard ripped out, the clutch blown, and the body all banged up.

It cost about $7,000 to fix, and I never drove it again. Maybe if it had been stolen from my driveway or something, it wouldn't have been a problem. But the way it was, I was just too scared to ever get back in it. I was just about to make my very last payment on it, too, and I sure wasn't looking forward to all those new monthly payments. But I just couldn't get in my old car again, so I traded it in.

Source: Mari Brendel, "The Year My Life Was Stolen," *Sacramento News & Review,* August 3, 1995. Reprinted by permission of *Sacramento News & Review.*

DISCUSSION QUESTIONS

1. What skills or "technology" should be taken into account in classifying burglars?

2. What are the characteristics of semiskilled burglars?

3. List and describe five means of entry common to burglars.

4. Describe the behavior cycle in burglaries.

5. List and describe five means of entry used by burglars to open and enter safes.

6. Why does motive offer little promise as a basic lead in thefts?

7. Why do the proceeds of thefts offer substantial promise as a basic lead?

8. Because a study of modus operandi and a search of police modus operandi files cannot be used in the same manner in thefts as in investigations of crimes of violence, cite the potential of such a study and search in the area of thefts.

9. Explain the "Achilles' heel" of stealing and the bland acceptance of this occupational hazard by thieves.

10. What circumstances may induce a receiver of stolen property to reveal the true circumstances of its purchase?

11. What are the advantages of a sting, or storefront technique, for recovering stolen property? The disadvantages?

12. What is a *chop shop*?

13. What are the four elements of fraud?

14. Describe *the bank examiner fraud*.

15. Describe two consumer frauds and five business frauds.

16. Define *embezzlement*.

17. What are *decoy vehicles*? *Appliances*?

18. Cite the modus operandi of each theft or loss in the case study and the most likely suspects.

19. Consider the victim's feelings in the case study and focus on the police response.

LIBRARY ASSIGNMENT

Review the available literature on criminal investigation and develop a 500- to 1,000-word profile of burglars, thieves and con artists. Conclude this paper with a selected bibliography of references used in its preparation.

WORKBOOK PROJECT

Prepare a list naming and describing the most common consumer and business frauds. Determine which investigative agency in your community is responsible for investigating each of these various types of frauds.

RELATED WEB SITES

For charts and tables about burglary trends in the United States, see this Web site: *www.ojp.usdoj.gov/bjs/glance/burg.htm*.

For information about mail fraud, mail theft, identity theft, and becoming a U.S. Postal Inspector, see the Postal Inspection Service Web site: *www.usps.com/postalinspectors/welcome2.htm*.

To learn more about Internet fraud involving charity scams, online auctions, and pyramid and other schemes, check out this Web site: *www.fraud.org/internet/intinfo.htm*.

NOTES

1. *State v. Wiley*, 173. Md. 119 (1937).
2. *California Penal Code*, sec. 459.
3. Ibid., sec. 461.
4. Ibid., sec. 459.
5. GEORGE RENGERT and JOHN WASILCHICK, *Surburban Burglary—A Time and a Place for Everything* (Springfield, IL: Charles C Thomas, 1985), 53–75.
6. MAURICE J. FITZGERALD, *Handbook of Criminal Investigation* (New York: Arco, 1960), 131.
7. HARRY A. SCARR et al., *Patterns of Burglary* (Washington, DC: U.S. Department of Justice, Law Enforcement Assistance Administration, National Institute of Law Enforcement and Criminal Justice, 1972), 4–5.
8. U.S. DEPARTMENT OF JUSTICE, *Criminal Victimization in the United States, 1992*, (Washington, DC: U.S. Department of Justice, 1994), 154–55.
9. M. A. P. WILMER, "Criminal Investigation from the Small Town to the Large Urban Conurbation," *British Journal of Criminology* 8, no. 3 (July 1968), 259–74.
10. DARREL J. STEFENSMEIER, *The Fence—In the Shadow of Two Worlds* (Totowa, NJ: Rowman & Littlefield, 1986), 13–35, 157–86.
11. *Strategies for Combating the Criminal Receiver of Stolen Goods: An Antifencing Manual for Law Enforcement Agencies* (Washington, DC: U.S. Department of Justice, Law Enforcement Assistance Administration, 1976), 89–97. See Ron Shaffer and Kevin Kloss, *Surprise! Surprise! How the Lawmen Conned the Thieves*, with Alfred R. Lewis (New York: Viking Press, 1977).
12. G. JACK BOLONGNA and ROBERT J. LINDQUIST, *Fraud Auditing and Forensic Accounting—New Tools and Techniques* (New York: Wiley, 1987), 27–42.
13. MARY CAREY and GEORGE SHERMAN, *A Compendium of Bunk: Or, How to Spot a Con Artist: A Handbook for Fraud Investigators, Bankers, and Other Custodians of the Public Trust* (Springfield, IL: Charles C Thomas, 1976), 9–20.
14. Ibid., 28–38.
15. DAVID W. MAURER, *The American Confidence Man* (Springfield, IL: Charles C Thomas, 1974), 30–47.
16. HERBERT EDELHERTZ et al., *The Investigation of White-Collar Crime: A Manual for Law Enforcement Agencies* (Washington, DC: U.S. Department of Justice, Law Enforcement Assistance Administration, 1977).

17. Brendan P. Battle and Paul B. Weston, *Arson: Detection and Investigation* (New York: Arco, 1979), 108.

18. Edelhertz et al., *The Investigation of White-Collar Crime*, 200; Lee J. Seidler, Fredrick Andrews, and Marc J. Epstein, *The Equity Funding Papers: The Anatomy of a Fraud* (New York: Wiley, 1977), 3–19.

19. Tsutomu Shimomura, *Takedown* (New York: Hyperion/New York Times Company, 1996), 313–14.

15

DANGEROUS DRUGS

In the United States, possession of dangerous and restricted drugs or narcotics is illegal. Exceptions are made when such dangerous drugs or narcotics are possessed through a lawful medical prescription. Previous conviction for one or more offenses related to possession of dangerous drugs or narcotics generally adds to the basic penalty imposed on conviction. In many jurisdictions, a convicted offender may not be eligible for parole or release on any other basis until he or she has served a stated minimum number of years in prison. The basic law prohibits unlawfully possessing drugs and narcotics, and transporting, importing, selling, furnishing, administering, or giving away a dangerous drug or narcotic.

The word *possession*, in statutes forbidding the possession of drugs and narcotics, means "an immediate and exclusive possession under dominion and control with intent to exercise control."[1] Persons having such control must have knowledge of the presence of drugs or narcotics, and such knowledge must precede the intent to exercise, or the exercise of, such control. Knowledge is a basic element of crimes related to illegal drugs and narcotics, which also means that a knowledge of the character of the substance is essential to the offense of narcotics possession.

In a prosecution for possession of dangerous drugs and narcotics, the burden is on the prosecution to prove knowledge of the presence of the drugs or narcotics. The prosecution must also show that the defendant knew that the objects in his or her possession were drugs and narcotics. However, the burden of proof may be satisfied by facts that infer such knowledge (circumstantial evidence).

The events leading to a suspect's arrest should show a state of facts amply sufficient to constitute reasonable cause for arrest (Figure 15–1). Reasonable and probable cause for an arrest without warrant, on justified belief that a suspect has committed a violation of illegal drugs and narcotics laws, can be based on an officer's past experience, knowledge of the suspect, and observation of suspicious and furtive conduct. The following two instances illustrate evidence sufficient for arrest:

1. Investigators knew of a suspect's previous arrest and conviction for possession of narcotics; learned from the manager of the suspect's apartment building that a good deal of suspicious traffic had been going in and out of

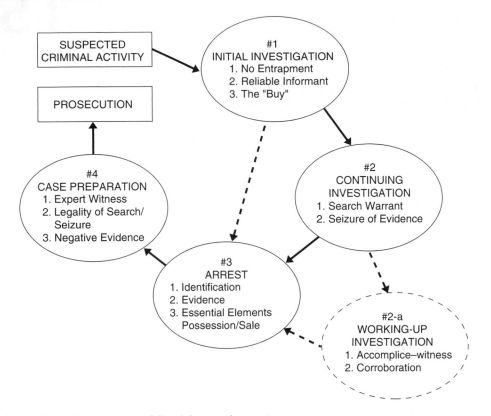

FIGURE 15–1   Investigation of illegal drugs and narcotics.

the suspect's apartment; and overheard occupants' references to "funnels" (used in preparation of narcotics) and "balloons" (commonly used as containers for narcotics). The officers had reasonable cause to believe occupants were committing a felony, and an arrest without a warrant was proper.

2. In a prosecution for possession of heroin, the evidence—including evidence that the arresting officer had known the informant for approximately 1 year, that the informant had given detailed information and a complete description of the defendant and his or her modus operandi, and that such information had been independently verified in substantial part—was reasonable cause to arrest the defendant without a warrant.

The fact that a person is a drug addict, a "user" of drugs, does not justify arresting him or her. In *Robinson v. California*, the U.S. Supreme Court ruled that drug addiction is an illness, drug addicts are sick people, and their capacity to form the necessary criminal intent is diminished.[2] Before this case, California had a law that allowed police to arrest drug addicts just for being addicted—for a condition rather than commission of an act. In *Robinson*, the Court ruled the California law to be unconstitutional.

ENTRAPMENT

Any conviction for the possession (or sale or transport) of illegal drugs should be for a wrongful act voluntarily committed and not for an act induced by the investigator or his or her "special employee" that would not have occurred without such urging. Determining whether, in a particular case, facts suggest the unlawful **entrapment** of an individual who might otherwise have gone through life without an arrest is not simple.

For instance, one defendant charged with narcotics possession for the purpose of sale was not a user.[3] No evidence indicated that he was regularly engaged in trafficking narcotics, and he did not have previous arrests of any kind. The sale of illegal narcotics, which was admitted, was consummated only after constant urging by a police agent for a certain time period.

To avoid a defense claim of entrapment, the investigator can exert no more pressure or persuasion than that ordinarily occurring between a willing buyer and a willing seller. However, a defense of entrapment was not available to a person charged with heroin possession when the suspect suggested to the police investigator that he could obtain illegal drugs or narcotics, and when no persuasion or allurement had been used by the officer, who had merely furnished an opportunity for the suspect to acquire illegal drugs or narcotics to sell to the undercover investigator.[4] The purpose of the law is not to prevent the unwary criminal from being trapped in a crime; instead, it is to prevent the police officer from manufacturing crime—that is, from seducing the unwary, innocent person into a career of crime.

THE DRUG SCENE

Numerous restricted drugs and narcotics, from marijuana to heroin, are being used by millions of people. The most common drugs that can lead to drug dependence or addiction fall into four major groups:

1. *Narcotics.*   **Narcotics** are drugs that depress the central nervous system. They usually lead quickly to both psychological and physical dependence.
2. *Sedatives.*   Like narcotics, **sedatives** cause both psychological and physical dependence, but the dependence develops more slowly. They are also central nervous system depressants.
3. *Stimulants.*   Amphetamines and methamphetamines are **stimulants**. These drugs cause a rapid buildup of tolerance so that additional quantities are needed to achieve the same stimulating effects. Stimulant use quickly leads to psychological dependence.
4. *Hallucinogens.*   **Hallucinogens** cause sensory distortions and result in illusions and delusions. They are the psychedelic, or "mind-expanding," drugs.

Eight types of drugs are commonly encountered on the "drug scene." Each is described next.

Heroin

Heroin is derived from a morphine base to produce diacetylmorphine (the chemical name for heroin), which, when blended with hydrochloric acid, forms into a salt (heroin hydrochloride) that is easily soluble in water. It usually consists of crystals so small as to resemble powdered sugar or flour. Heroin ranges in color from white to ivory, through dull or brownish gray, to tan or brown. Heroin is usually administered intravenously. Narcotics have four main characteristics: First, they kill pain—that is, they have an **analgesic** effect. Second, they are **soporific agents**, which means they induce drowsiness, lethargy, and sleep. Third, used with time, they produce physical and psychological dependency, and, fourth, they generate a sense of **euphoria**—a feeling of well-being and tranquility.

Cocaine

Cocaine is a stimulant, usually derived from the leaves of the South American coca bush, and sometimes from bushes grown in the West Indies, Java, India, and Ceylon. The alkaloid is extracted from the leaves and treated with hydrochloric acid to form cocaine hydrochloride, a salt easily soluble in water. It is encountered as fine, fluffy white crystalline powder, and (depending on the degree of refinement) may resemble snowflakes, camphor, sugar, or Epsom salts. It is sometimes found in tablet form. Cocaine produces feelings of exhilaration and euphoria, and it increases the user's energy level and suppresses fatigue. Cocaine is usually administered by snorting through the nose and produces a psychological dependency. Cocaine is also smoked in two forms:

1. *Freebase.*   When cocaine is freebased, it is dissolved in ether and then heated to boil off the impurities. What remains is a pure form of cocaine, which is then ground up and smoked. Because smoking is a more effective means of administration, the user feels a more intense "rush," which often leads to heavy chronic use.
2. *Crack.*   Also known as **hubba** or **rock**, **crack** is made by soaking cocaine in baking soda and water. The mixture is then heated until the water is driven off. During the heating process, the mixture makes a crackling sound, hence the name. The resulting crystals—or pea-sized "rocks"—are crushed, heated, and smoked in a crack pipe. This smokable form of cocaine gives the user a "rush" that lasts as long as 2 minutes, followed by an afterglow that lasts 10 to 20 minutes.

Marijuana

Marijuana, or **pot**, consists of the leaves and flowering tops of the female hemp plant (*Cannabis sativa*, *C. indica*) cultivated in many temperate zones of the world. Crude marijuana contains parts of the leaves, tops, stems, and seeds (fruit) of the plant; "manicured" marijuana consists of smaller particles of the leaves and tops, from which almost all the stems and seeds have been removed. Fresh marijuana is dark green and turns brown with age and exposure. It may be packaged in tobacco tins, cellophane, paper bags, tissue paper, or cigarettes. Bricks of crude marijuana are about 3 inches by 5 inches by 10 inches and weigh about 2 pounds. The psychoactive agent in marijuana is delta-9-tetrahydrocannabinal, or **THC**. Wild, or uncultivated, marijuana may have a 1 percent THC level. Proper cultivation will raise the THC level to 3 percent. Marijuana grown in Colombia or Hawaii may have a THC level between 4 and 6 percent. Sinsemilla, a hybrid without seeds, may have an 8 to 14 percent THC content. Two derivatives of marijuana are hashish and hash oil:

1. *Hashish.*   The resin of the marijuana flower is dried and compressed to make hashish, which has a THC level of 8 to 14 percent.
2. *Hash oil.*   Amber to dark brown, hash oil is produced by boiling hashish in alcohol. It is sold as a viscous liquid with a THC level between 15 and 50 percent.

Amphetamine and Methamphetamine

Amphetamine and Methamphetamine are synthetic substances usually produced in clandestine labs. The most common form of these substances is **methamphetamine**, also known as **speed**, **crank**, and **meth**. It has the same effects as cocaine and is often referred to as **poor man's cocaine**. Injected meth usually produces a "flash" or "rush" and is taken every 4 to 8 hours, which leads to a "run"—a period of wakefulness lasting 2 to 5 days, followed by a long period of sleep. A chronic user is known as a **tweaker.**

Phencyclidine

Phencyclidine has the street names **angel dust**, **dust**, and **PCP**. It was originally developed as a general anesthetic for surgical procedures. However, its use for this purpose was abandoned because of the ability of the drug to produce hallucinogenic side effects. For a while, it was used in veterinary medicine to tranquilize large animals but was removed from the market in 1978 and is now made in clandestine labs. PCP is a white, crystalline powder that readily dissolves in water. It is commonly applied to tobacco or marijuana cigarettes and smoked. In the right dose, PCP will produce hallucinations and in some users will evoke violent suicidal impulses. Because of the anesthetic effect of this drug, the user may display a total disregard for personal safety coupled with a lack of sensation.

This clandestine methamphetamine lab was found in the kitchen of this suspect's home. From Robert Pennal, Special Agent Supervisor, California Department of Justice, Bureau of Narcotic Enforcement.

Lysergic Acid Diethylamide (LSD)

LSD is a semisynthetic drug derived from a fungus that contaminates rye bread. Although LSD was first synthesized in 1938, its psychoactive properties were not discovered until 1943. LSD is usually swallowed in the form of impregnated paper, tablets, or thin squares of gelatin. A dose equal to a few grains of salt can produce hallucinations lasting 10 to 12 hours. The drug is ambivalent, in that the users experience both good and bad sensations.

Ecstasy

Ecstasy is methylenedioxymethamphetamine (MDMA). First developed in 1912 as an appetite suppressant, it is a stimulant like meth and a hallucinogenic similar to LSD. It produces a warm, fuzzy sense of well-being and the manic energy to dance all night. Most of the drug is produced in Europe, although it can be made in clandestine U.S. labs. It is usually consumed at "raves," where the user spends the night dancing to music.

Rohypnol

A sleeping pill not licensed in the United States, Rohypnol is legal in Europe, South America, and Asia. It is also known as **roofies**. In the United States, the drug is most frequently used with alcohol—the synergistic effect produces disinhibition and amnesia. Because of these effects, Rohypnol is known as the **date rape drug**.

DRUG–SELLING ORGANIZATIONS

Knowledge of the organizational setup of criminals engaged in selling illicit drugs is important to investigators working on the drug scene. The traditional sales-marketing pyramid of manufacturer, importer (source of supply), distributors, wholesalers and jobbers, and retailers (peddling mobs, "pushers") has not changed much since the 1950s.[5] "The boss" is still at the top of the pyramid, whether he or she is a major dealer or importer, or both. However, a few more levels have been added to the distribution network. The formerly lowest level—street dealers—has been augmented by lookouts and runners. **Lookouts** inform about any police presence; **runners** transport small quantities of drugs from the dealer's **stash** to wherever the drugs are being sold (Figure 15–2).

Originally, most of these sales-marketing pyramids were headed by the leaders of Italian crime "families" or their "underbosses," and importation of drugs into the United States was mainly in the hands of Europeans (French, Corsicans, Italians). Criminal organizations have since expanded, and importation routes originate in South America, Central America, and Mexico. Cocaine and its derivative crack are immensely popular in the United States, and both are readily sold at high profits. In addition, the pyramid networks have become more sophisticated in their sales marketing as well as in avoiding police interference with their daily sales. Currently, known criminal organizations engaged in major dealings in illicit drugs are as follows:

- Mafia (La Cosa Nostra) crime families
- Colombians

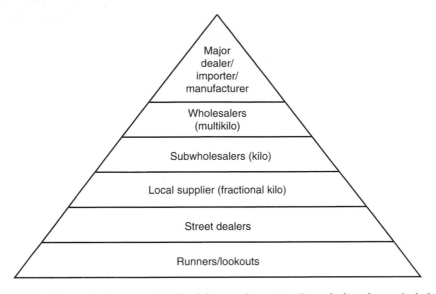

FIGURE 15-2   The marketing pyramid—illegal drugs and narcotics. Drug dealers, from subwholesaler levels up, depend on their anonymity to avoid arrest.

- Jamaican gangs ("posses")
- Asian gangs (Chinese, Vietnamese, Korean)
- Bikers
- Prison gangs
- Street gangs (Crips, Bloods)

Both the Mafia and the Colombians are generally organized along "family" lines; roles in the sales-marketing pyramid result from recommendations from internal sources. The Jamaican "posses" are sophisticated crime mobs dealing primarily in crack in major cities across the United States. Personnel are recruited from Jamaica and other countries in the Caribbean basin. Posses are hardball organizations characterized by ruthless and extensive violence.[6]

Asian criminal organizations have kept a low profile. Not much is known about the extent of their operations, but a great deal is suspected. Because they operate in their own ethnic neighborhoods, investigators have had little success in developing informants or making buys. Youth gangs are often the source of personnel for these networks.

Motorcycle gangs have been involved in general misbehavior and traffic in firearms for some time. Since the late 1980s, they have developed tightly organized drug-selling networks.[7] These nationwide groups have major dealers in most large urban centers. They are disciplined groups, and murder is a common form of punishment for violations of gang rules.

Prison gangs originate in prisons and sell drugs to inmates. Released members of these gangs are soon employed as street dealers in illicit drugs. In the Southwest, the Mexican Mafia is a major prison gang selling drugs both in-side prison walls and on the outside. Various prison gangs (neo-Nazis, Aryan Brotherhood, etc.) operate in other areas of the United States.

Street gangs do not usually buy as a gang, but as individual members or small groups of gang members. They "sling dope," but their manner of pur-chasing drugs and selling them usually reflects the loose organizational struc-ture of these gangs.[8]

All these drug-selling gangs commit murder as a business technique to eliminate competition, protect their territory from the competition of rival gangs, discipline suspected informants, and protect their cash and illicit drugs from rip-offs by armed robbers.

DRUG INVESTIGATIONS

Pickup Arrests

In warrantless arrests for the possession of dangerous drugs or narcotics or both, the investigator must act within the legal bounds of a "reasonable man." The test is this: Would the facts on which the arresting officer acted warrant a man (or woman) of reasonable caution to believe that a crime had been committed? When determining whether an arrest was reasonable, the court usually takes into consideration police expertise gained from training or experience.

An important case in the area of pickup arrests is *Draper v. United States.*[9] In *Draper*, a federal narcotics agent of considerable experience (Marsh) had been informed by a special employee (Hereford, an informant who had always been found to be accurate and reliable) that Draper was peddling narcotics and that he had gone to Chicago and would return by train with 3 ounces of heroin on the morning of September 8 or 9. The informant gave a physical description of Draper and said that he would be carrying a "tan zipper bag" and that he ha-bitually "walked real fast." The agent kept the incoming trains from Chicago under surveillance, and on the morning of September 9 observed a person fit-ting the description given by the informant walking "fast" toward an exit and carrying a tan zipper bag. This person was Draper, and the officer arrested him.

The information given to narcotics agent Marsh by special employee Hereford about Draper may have been hearsay to Marsh, but because it came from a person employed to inform and whose information had always been found accurate and reliable, Marsh would have been derelict in his duties had he not pursued this lead. When pursuing the lead, he saw a man—having the exact physical attributes and wearing the precise clothing and carrying the tan zipper bag that Hereford had described—alight from one of the very trains from the very place stated by Hereford and start to walk away at a "fast" pace toward the station. At that point, Marsh had personally verified every facet of the in-formation Hereford gave him except whether the petitioner had accomplished his mission and had the 3 ounces of heroin on his person or in his bag. With every other bit of Hereford's information personally verified, Marsh had "reasonable grounds" to believe that the remaining unverified bit of Hereford's information—that Draper would have heroin on or with him—was likewise true.

In some instances, officers discover contraband in the form of illegal drugs or narcotics in searches incidental to an arrest or while executing a search warrant. In such cases, the legality of the basic arrest and search or the search under the authority of a warrant must be demonstrated and supported by evidence before the illegal drugs or narcotics case can be developed for prosecution.

Arrests Based on "Buys"

Cases involving the possession or sale of dangerous drugs or narcotics are usually developed by making one or more "buys" of these illegal substances. An undercover police investigator (sworn officer) or an informant (special employee) buys a quantity of dangerous drugs or narcotics from a suspect; the transaction is often witnessed by officers conducting a surveillance of the undercover agent or special employee and of the suspect. The integrity of the informant's buy is preserved by a pretransaction and posttransaction search of the informant, and investigators often secure compelling evidence by registering the serial numbers of the money used for the buy before the transaction. The substance purchased is marked for identification and transported to a local police (or state) narcotics laboratory for examination and identification and is retained as evidence of the sale of drugs or a narcotic substance to the informant or employee.

The informant, under supervision, sets up the buy. The suspect may be identified by police and the informant asked to develop a case, or the informant may identify to the police a suspect known to him or her as a drug seller. After the buy, the informant details the circumstances of the transaction to his or her police associates, turns over the substance purchased, and returns any unused money advanced for the buy.

The usual ten-step procedure for making a buy is as follows:

1. The informant is advised to avoid any taint of entrapment.
2. The informant, under police supervision, makes contact with the subject and arranges the buy.
3. The police arrange a surveillance of the informant and possibly of the suspect.
4. The police search the informant to ensure he or she is not carrying any drugs or any substantial amount of money and provide him or her with "state" money (serial numbers recorded) for the buy.
5. The police maintain contact with the informant to the transaction scene.
6. The police watch the transaction as closely as possible.
7. When the informant returns to his or her police associates, he or she informs them of the transaction, turns over the purchase and any unspent funds, and is again searched (to allow police investigators to testify that the informant had none of the funds given him or her or any other drugs).

8. The purchased substance is marked as evidence and transported to a laboratory.
9. A laboratory analysis is undertaken to confirm the illegal nature of the substance as drugs or narcotics, the type of drug, and the amount.
10. The case is prepared for an arrest warrant, an arrest (with or without warrant) during a subsequent buy, or an application for a search warrant.

When an undercover police agent participates in a buy, he or she conceals his or her identity as a police officer. In a few weeks, a crewcut police recruit can become a long-haired participant in the search for drug sellers. The ability to act out his or her new identity without revealing police employment ensures continuation in this undercover role until the officer must reveal his or her identity as the investigation is terminated.

Successful undercover police operations in the drug scene usually require that an informant introduce and vouch for the undercover agent. The undercover agent's identity is revealed only when the agent has developed cases against a number of sellers of narcotics and the department decides to make all the appropriate arrests simultaneously.

Search Warrants

A buy is a normal prelude to an application for a search warrant in illegal drug and narcotics cases. The purpose of the search warrant is to gain judicial authorization to enter a place in which the suspect from whom the buy was made has his or her stash of drugs, to seize these drugs, and to arrest the suspect.

The past criminal record of a suspected person, his or her association with known narcotics users, and the fact that another person (usually the informant) was found to possess a narcotic after leaving a suspected drug seller's premises may be taken into account in determining whether probable cause exists for issuance of a search warrant (Figure 15–3).

In many instances, an informant's report on his or her drug purchase will identify a specific room, or portion of a room, from which the drug seller procured the drugs. This information allows the application for the search warrant to have the necessary particularity about the place or places to be searched.

To be constitutionally sufficient, an affidavit (accompanying an application for a search warrant) based solely on an unnamed informant's tip must set forth some underlying circumstances, which reveal the source of the informant's information pertaining to the criminal activity, and must present sufficient objective evidence to enable the magistrate to conclude that the unnamed informant is credible or that his or her information is reliable.[10] The report of the chemist examining the substance purchased can be used to establish that the suspect had possessed illegal drugs or narcotics before the transaction or transactions (buys).

··· NO. _____

STATE OF CALIFORNIA – COUNTY OF SACRAMENTO

SEARCH WARRANT AND AFFIDAVIT

(AFFIDAVIT)

JIMMY ▇▇▇▇, being sworn, says that on the basis of the information contained within this Search Warrant and Affidavit and the attached and incorporated Statement of Probable Cause, comprising a total of __14__ pages, he/she has probable cause to believe and does believe that the property described below is lawfully seizable pursuant to Penal Code Section 1524, as indicated below, and is now located at the location(s) set forth below. Wherefore, affiant requests that this Search Warrant be issued.

Night Search Requested YES: _XX_ NO [ ] (Justification on page(s) (9)

Reviewed by _____ *Michael G. Nev*_____

(Deputy District Attorney)

_____
(Signature of Affiant – after having been sworn)

(SEARCH WARRANT)

THE PEOPLE OF THE STATE OF CALIFORNIA TO ANY SHERIFF, POLICEMAN OR PEACE OFFICER IN THE COUNTY OF SACRAMENTO:

proof by affidavit having been made before me by JIMMY ▇▇▇▇, that there is probable cause to believe that the property described herein may be found at the locations set forth herein and that it is lawfully seizable pursuant to Penal Code Section 1524 as indicated below by "x" (s) in that it:

```
_____  was stolen or embezzled
__x__  was used as the means of committing a felony
__x__  is possessed by a person with the intent to use it as means of committing a public offense or is possessed by another to
       whom he or she may have delivered it for the purpose of concealing it or preventing its discovery.
__x__  tends to show that a felony has been committed or that a particular person has committed a felony.
```

YOU ARE THEREFORE COMMANDED TO SEARCH:

▇▇▇ Arcade Boulevard located in the City and County of Sacramento. It is a single story, single family residence, beige in color with brown trim and a brown composition roof. The numbers ▇▇▇ are affixed to the front of the residence and are visible from the street. The single car attached garage is to the right (west) of the residence and the house is on the south side of Arcade Boulevard, between Colfax Street and Edgewater Road. Also to include all attics, basements, rooms, garages, outbuildings, storage sheds, inoperative vehicles, garbage cans and containers located with in the property boundaries.

FOR THE PERSON(S) OF:

▇▇, Dennis Michael aka Dennis Michael ▇▇▇, DOB: 10-4-54.

FOR THE FOLLOWING VEHICLE(S):

A white with blue trim motor home, California license ███████ and also request authorization to search the 1978 Datsun Pickup, California license ███████, registered to ███████.

FOR THE FOLLOWING PROPERTY:

Methamphetamine and paraphernalia associated with its use, sales, transportation and manufacture, including; measuring and weighing devices, milk sugar, baggies, paper bindles, funnels, syringes, bent spoons, chemical formulas, phenylacetic acid, phenyl-2-propanone, methylamine, benzyl chloride, acetaldehyde, formamide, ephedrine, ether, acetone, lye, mercuric chloride, magnesium filings, sulfuric and hydrochloric acid, sodium acetate, chloroform, methanol, ethanol, red phosphorus, palladium black, and acetic anhydride, funnels, flasks, distillation flasks, various types of heaters and heating mantles, hot plates, various types of crystallizing dishes, desiccators, distilling apparatuses, extractors, vacuum dryers, beakers, jars, condensers, graduated cylinders, vacuum pumps, shakers and stirrers, thermometers, transformers, ovens, regulators, glass tubing, hoses, scales, filter papers, PH papers, plastic containers, gloves, masks, fans, air conditioners, generators. bills, receipts, ledgers, maps, charts, buyers lists, seller lists and recordation of sales, personal telephone books, address books, telephone bills, papers and documents containing lists of names, addresses and phone numbers, utility company receipts, rent receipts, addressed envelopes, keys and photographs. Searching officers are directed to answer the phone and converse with callers who appear to be calling in regard to drug/narcotic sales and note and record the conversation without revealing their true identity. They are also directed to note and record phone numbers or other messages received on telephonic pagers for the purpose of calling those persons paging the suspect(s) to determine if the page was regarding an intended purchase or delivery of drugs/narcotics.

AND TO SEIZE IT IF FOUND and bring it forthwith before me, or this court, at the courthouse of this court. This Search Warrant and Incorporated Affidavit was sworn to and subscribed before me this ___5___ day of _January_, 1989, at

_____ P.M./A.M., wherefore, I find probable cause for the issuance of this Search Warrant and do issue it.

Night Search Approved YES [█] NO [__]
(Magistrates Initials)

_____
(Signature of Magistrate)

Judge of the Superior Court [ ] Municipal Court-Sacramento Judicial District [X].

Executed by _____   Date ___1-5-89___   Hr. ___10:45 P.M.___

FIGURE 15–3   Search warrant issued by a California court in an illegal drug case. The request for this warrant totaled fourteen pages. Magistrates are aware of their responsibility for this prior approval of police action and scan these requests with great care. If they do not understand it or believe it is inaccurate, they will deny the request.

317

Unlike an application for search warrants in burglary and theft cases, in which specific articles of stolen property must be identified in the application, an application for search warrants in drug cases can be less specific: drugs may be described in general terms as contraband and by common names. Although "returns" to the issuing magistrate must contain a specific inventory of the drugs and narcotics seized under the authority of the search warrant, the drugs or narcotics seized need not match the drugs or narcotics in the application for the warrant.

A six-step outline of the usual procedure in this major type of investigation is as follows:

1. The case against the suspect is developed by making one or more buys and obtaining information from a reliable informant.
2. The investigator makes observations supporting the transactions and information as evidence of the suspect's criminal behavior and is prepared to prove the informant's reliability.
3. Application is made to the magistrate for a search warrant; in the application, the suspect and the place or places to be searched are named, and dangerous drugs or narcotics, or both, are cited as the object of the search.
4. A warrant is executed, the suspect is arrested, and the return is made to the magistrate.
5. The substances are seized and analyzed, and the fact that the substances are illegal drugs or narcotics, or both, is revealed and reported to the magistrate in a supplementary return.
6. The case is prepared against the arrestee for presentation to the prosecutor.

In the investigation of a major drug seller, the buy is the preliminary investigation. With this transaction, and any subsequent buys, accumulating evidence is likely to support an application for a search warrant. In preparing and executing the search warrant, investigators are conducting a continuing investigation, which will identify the drug seller as the person possessing a quantity of drugs or narcotics.

Warrantless Searches

Reasonableness is the constitutional test of any warrantless search. Exigent circumstances are often present in drug cases. Drug possession for the purpose of sale is an ongoing crime; drug sellers do not suspend their activity while police do the necessary paperwork involved in obtaining a search warrant. Evidence that might be sufficient to convict them may be destroyed if police do not take prompt action.

An example of this reasonableness is a case in which a police officer observed a crime in progress inside a building (a narcotics "cutting" and packaging operation—a "factory") and contraband (drugs) in plain view.[11] An appellate court ruled that, under these circumstances, the police were fully authorized to enter the premises, make arrests, and seek out contraband. The police officer in this case, acting on an anonymous tip, went to a certain address, looked through a basement window, and saw the major narcotics-packaging operation in progress. He then sought the aid of other police officers. With this additional help, the officer subsequently (within 30 to 40 minutes) entered and searched the premises without a warrant. Searching officers found the cutting mirror (used for mixing the illegal drugs with cheaper adulterants) on a table, along with plastic bags and measuring spoons and pans. Nearby, the officers found a large quantity of narcotics packaged for distribution. Four persons found on the premises were arrested.

"Working Up" Investigations

"Working up" the sales-marketing pyramid necessitates both buy-and-bust arrests and arrests and seizures under the authority of a search warrant. First, a person near the base of the pyramid (Figure 15–2)—the street dealer of illicit drugs—is arrested. Second, the supplier of this dealer is arrested, and onward and upward until a major supplier or an importer is arrested. Informants in these working-up investigations are arrestees who have agreed to reveal their suppliers in return for leniency in the indictment or at the time of sentencing.

This snitching is often termed **working off a beef**. However, investigators must be cautious in these cases because many arrestees make a deal with the arresting officer (and prosecutor) but have no intention of informing on their true supplier. They engage in **lateral snitching**; that is, they inform on only drug sellers who are on an equal or lower level than theirs in the drug-marketing pyramid. In this fashion, an arrestee manipulates an investigator, informing primarily on his or her competition.[12]

Lengthy investigations probing upward in a drug-marketing network can develop a case against a manufacturer, a major dealer, or an importer. To be successful, such investigations require a criminal associate of the "targeted" major manufacturer, dealer, or importer; and evidence corroborating the expected testimony of the accomplice-witness.

Arrestees situated above the street-dealer level in a drug-marketing pyramid are more difficult to "turn" than are lesser network members. When a man or woman close to a major manufacturer, dealer, or importer is arrested, the "boss" commonly provides legal counsel, bail, and other assistance pending trial. In addition, the knowledge that informants have, in the past, been murdered while in prison or out on bail is an ongoing deterrent to cooperating with the police. As a result, an investigator needs a strong case against an arrestee to entertain any hope of turning him or her into an accomplice-witness.[13]

When an accomplice-witness can provide data on the date and time of a future delivery of drugs, an arrest and seizure based on this information and involving the major dealer, or importer, provide the most compelling corroboration of the accomplice-witness's information. However, usually, corroboration results from an investigator's collecting bits and pieces of information by using techniques such as the following:

- Physical and electronic surveillance
- Tally analysis of telephone records of outgoing calls from a "suspect" telephone
- A survey of car rental contracts, credit card purchases, hotel and motel registrations, and major cash purchases
- Tracing of "laundered" cash

Corroborating the expected testimony of an accomplice-witness against a major manufacturer, dealer, or importer is more or less a "paper chase." Ideally, the investigators' observations of the suspect's activities will reveal the linkage between others in the drug-marketing network. The observations are supported by these persons' contacting the suspect from time to time by telephone. Renting cars, registering in hotels, and buying items, from gasoline to mansions, place the suspect in various locations on specific dates. Finally, money can be traced. The Bank Records and Foreign Transactions Act (1970) requires bank officials to report deposits and withdrawals of more than $10,000. Thus, concealing millions of dollars in drug-selling profits is extremely difficult.

When a major manufacturer, dealer, or importer is targeted for arrest and prosecution, the investigation is long and difficult. Suspected informants are often quickly murdered, both to negate their services to the police and to reinforce the long-time creed of organized crime: "death to the informer." Public employees may be bribed so that they reveal how much and what evidence the police have to date, as well as the scope of the police's existing plans. Such revelations compromise confidential police files and operations.[14]

The drug trade is all about money, lots of money. From Robert Pennal, Special Agent Supervisor, California Department of Justice, Bureau of Narcotic Enforcement.

Raids

A **raid** in drug law enforcement is entering a building to seize illicit drugs and arrest one or more drug dealers and associates. Entry may be gained by subterfuge (a "tale" to gain entry without force) or by the use of force (sledgehammer, battering ram, kicking).

Commonly, raids are no longer the combined effort of several investigators. They are now a major action of the investigating unit, with a superior officer designated as the overall commanding officer. Most departments now require all members of a raiding party to wear bulletproof vests. In fact, the expectation of a shoot-out during a raid is integrated with raid planning. Special weapons teams are frequently assigned to back up the investigators, particularly when the place to be raided is a "rock house" (from which crack is sold). These premises are heavily armored, and automatic weapons fire from the premises being raided is more than a possibility.

The leadership of a raid on a drug scene has a heavy burden of responsibility. Possible problems include "hitting the wrong door," having a member of the raiding party injured or killed, failing to identify the major suspect among the occupants, not finding any drugs (or only a small amount), and not finding the **trap** (built-in hiding place usually constructed by a skilled carpenter) containing the major stash.

Legally, the authority for a raid is a search warrant authorizing police officers to enter a specific premises to seize illicit drugs believed to be in the described premises. These warrants or local laws will provide for a "no-knock" entry. In past years, the notice-and-demand factor slowed the raiding party to such an extent that drug sellers and associates had time to dispose of the incriminating evidence, usually by flushing the illicit drugs down the toilet. Aware jurists and legislators recognized the police need for a speedy entry and remedied the law.

Armoring the place from which drugs are sold is the drug seller's response to the ability of police to gain speedy entry and to seize drugs before they can be destroyed. Sheet steel panels are screwed or bolted to entry doors, and windows are covered with steel panels and heavy iron gratings. Drug sellers claim that this armoring is necessary to protect them from rip-offs, but it has the additional benefit of preventing speedy entry by police.

Once entry is made and the occupants have been placed under control (and disarmed, if carrying weapons), the commanding officer of the raiding party supervises a methodical search for illicit drugs and weapons and oversees a thorough scanning of the occupants' identity.

PROBLEMS OF PROOF

The classic defense claim in drug-selling cases is entrapment: the investigator or police agent (special employee, informant) urged and persuaded the defendant to sell the drugs and the sale was solely to recover the cost of the drugs to the defendant. Many variations of this entrapment defense are used, and it has been successful in many jury trials. It is likely to continue to be a successful defense unless prosecutors can affirmatively show that no coercive persuasion or allurement was used on the defendant.

In cases involving only a small quantity of illicit drugs, a defendant may claim that he or she was **flaked** by the police investigator or his informant partner, which means the informant or the arresting officer planted the illicit drugs. Unfortunately for the prosecution in these trials, one or more jurors may have heard of the police practice of flaking and are willing to give greater credence to the claim than to the denial.

The compulsion of an accomplice-witness to give immunized testimony presents an in-court problem of credibility. This person is not a sympathetic witness to whom jurors might relate, but rather a person who has turned state's evidence for self-preservation. Many jurors are ready to believe that such a witness will lie, and the defense counsel repeatedly tells them this.

Undercover investigators appear to many jurors as individuals who have used friendship, deceit, and persuasion in making arrests. Defense attorneys' allegations of entrapment—that their client did no more than "accommodate" a friend by getting him or her illicit drugs—cater to this conscious or subliminal belief. The legal significance of most of the evidence may rest on the prosecutor's ability to somehow insert a "victim" into the case—but doing so is difficult. Drug selling is one of the so-called victimless crimes.

CHAPTER REVIEW

CASE STUDY

Dangerous Drugs Law Enforcement—Roles and Story Lines

SCENE: Extracts from the testimony of police investigators tell the story of a major investigation into drug selling.

The first witness was a state chemist who testified that the substances he examined (a bottle of orange tablets and balloons containing a white powder) were dangerous drugs—amphetamines—and a quantity of narcotics—heroin.

The next witness was one of the police investigators, Sergeant Charles Nekola of the City Police.

Direct Examination by the Assistant District Attorney (ADA)

Q: Sergeant Nekola, directing your attention to last April 13, did you have or were you present at an address, 150 "E" Street, here in the city on that date?

A: Yes, sir. I was.

Q: What was the purpose of being out there?

A: We went out there to serve a warrant of arrest on Robert Rodriquez at his residence at 150 "E" Street and a search warrant for the premises.

Q: Was the arrest warrant in relation to the recent grand jury indictment of the defendant?

A: Yes, sir.

Q: Who were you in company with?

A: I was in company with Sergeant James Larson.

Q: Did you approach the door of the residence?

A: Yes, I did.

Q: What did you do, if anything, at that time?

A: I knocked on the front door and waited approximately 15 seconds. A female I later identified as Alice Rodriquez came to the window just north of the door.

Q: Did you observe her through the window?

A: Yes, sir. I did.

Q: What, if anything, occurred at that time?

A: I told her to open the door and she said, "What for?" I told her we were police officers, and we had a search warrant for the house.

Q: Did you in any way identify yourself other than say you were police officers?

A: Yes, sir. I had my badge in my right hand.

Q: Could you hear her through the window?

A: Yes, sir. I could.

Q: And what occurred, if anything, at that time?

A: I waited a short moment, and then she turned and appeared to run toward the back of the house.

Q: Could you hear noise coming from inside the house?

A: Yes, sir. I could.

Q: What, if anything, happened at that time?

A: Sergeant Larson started kicking the door, and he forced the door open with his foot.

Q: You have been a police officer for approximately 13 years?

A: Yes, sir.

Q: Did you feel it was necessary to force the door open?

A: Yes, sir. I did.

Q: Would you explain why?

A: Usually, in a case when we are serving a search warrant on a residence, and we know that the residents are people involved in the sale of drugs, they will recognize the agents and will flush the drugs down the toilet.

Q: Have you ever had this personally happen to you?

A: Yes, sir.

Q: Approximately how many times?

A: Oh, I'd say more than twenty times.

Q: Did you later enter this residence?

A: Yes, I did.

Q: And this young lady you indicated, whom you observed in the window, was she present inside the residence?

A: Yes, sir. She was.

Q: After you entered?

A: Yes, sir.

ADA: No further questions, Your Honor. (Witness was excused.)

Direct Examination of Sergeant James Larson by the ADA

Q: Sergeant Larson, where are you employed?

A: The City Police Department.

Q: How long have you been so employed?

A: Nine and a half years.

Q: Where do you work within the City Police?

A: I'm on assignment to the narcotics detail.

Q: Direct your attention to last April 13. Did you have occasion to be at a residence in the city, specifically 150 "E" Street?

A: I did.

Q: What was your purpose in being there?

A: We were going to make a warrant arrest and execute a search warrant on the residence.

Q: Were you present when a forced entry was made?

A: I was.

Q: Were you through the door first or were you the second one or—

A: (Interposing) I believe I was the first officer through the door.

Q: What did you observe immediately upon entry?

A: There was no one in the front room or in the kitchen, that I could see. I went to the hallway and turned left. As we were entering, I had heard some doors closing in this direction. The door to the bathroom was closed; it opens off this hallway.

Q: Had you ever been in that house before?

A: I had been in it in February.

Q: What, if anything, did you do at this time?

A: I tried to open the bathroom door and I couldn't get it open. I then knocked on it and pounded on it. I said, "Police officer. Open up." They didn't open up, so I then kicked in the door of the bathroom.

Q: You kicked in the door of the bathroom?

A: I did.

Q: After you kicked in the door, what did you find, if anything?

A: Rodriquez was against the wall in the bathroom. He had a bag in one hand, which he dropped to the floor.

Q: Now, let me show you an item marked previously, marked no. 1 for identification. It is a brown manila envelope and contained within there appears to be a brown leather bag. Does that in any way resemble the bag that you saw Mr. Rodriquez holding?

A: Yes, it does.

Q: When you entered the bathroom, did he have it in his hand?
A: He had it in his right hand.

Q: Then what happened?
A: He dropped it to the floor as I entered.

Q: Then what occurred?
A: I then turned him against the wall, searched him, and placed him under arrest.

Q: Had you seen Mr. Rodriquez on previous occasions?
A: I had.

Q: You knew him?
A: I did.

Q: And what was your purpose for being there—in this house at this time?
A: To place Rodriquez under arrest on an arrest warrant we had in our possession, and also to serve a search warrant.

Q: What was the arrest warrant based on?
A: It was two counts of sales of narcotics. We made "buys."

Q: Grand jury indictments?
A: That's correct.

Q: Let me show you this brown leather purse—it is marked no. 1-A for identification. Would you examine the contents contained therein?
A: Yes, sir.

Q: Do you recognize the contents contained therein?
A: Yes, sir. This is the brown leather purse which was on the floor in the bathroom when I arrested Robert Rodriquez, and I seized it as evidence.

Q: How about the other items contained therein; do you recognize any of those?
A: All of these items were contained inside the purse.

Q: Specifically, would you elaborate for the record what items we are talking about?
A: Yes, sir. This is a bottle of orange tablets.

Q: How about the brown paper bag; do you recognize this item?
A: Yes, sir.

Q: Let me open up the contents of the brown paper bag. By the way, does it bear your initials?
A: Yes, sir. It has the initials J.L. on it for my name.

Q: How about any of the contents contained within the brown paper bag?
A: All the items have my initials, J.L., written on them.

Q: Just briefly describe what was contained in this brown paper bag.
A: There were thirteen green balloons containing a powdery substance.

Q: What did you do with these items?
A: I retained them in my possession until such time as marked and submitted to the state chemist's locker.

Q: How long have you been an agent with this special squad?
A: A little over 1 year.

Q: Approximately how many arrests and investigations involving narcotics or restricted dangerous drugs have you participated in?
A: I would have to estimate over a hundred.

Q: Have you personally made "buys" of heroin?
A: Yes, sir. I have.

Q: On more than one occasion?
A: Numerous occasions.

Q: Assuming these items, that is the thirteen balloons, do contain heroin, do you have an opinion as to whether that is an amount sufficient to constitute a possession for sale?
A: Yes, it is.

Q: What do you base that opinion on?
A: On the method of packaging, the quantity contained inside, and the number of balloons.

Q: Have you ever seen heroin packaged in balloons before?
A: Yes, sir. I have.

Q: On numerous occasions?
A: Yes, sir.

DISCUSSION QUESTIONS

1. What drugs are common on the drug scene?
2. Briefly describe the drug-marketing pyramid (network).
3. Under what investigative circumstances is a pickup arrest justified?
4. Name and describe the participants in a "buy" of illegal drugs.
5. In working-up investigations, what investigative techniques have proved useful in discovering evidence to corroborate an accomplice-witness's testimony?
6. What are the story lines of each witness in the case study?

LIBRARY ASSIGNMENT

Secure and list at least five references to writings describing drugs, their appearance, and their effects.

WORKBOOK PROJECT

Prepare a chart or diagram of the procedure for making buys.

RELATED WEB SITES

Want to know what U.S. drug control policy is? If so, visit the Office of National Drug Control Policy Web site. This site contains information on drug facts, enforcement, prevention, and treatment programs: *www. whitehousedrugpolicy.gov.*

To learn more about dangerous drugs as a global problem, visit the United Nations Office on Drugs and Crime Web site: *www.unodc.org.*

NOTES

1. *People v. Martinez*, 256 P.2d 1028 (Dist. Ct. App. 1953).
2. *Robinson v. California*, 370 U.S. 660 (1962).
3. *People v. Monteverde*, 46 Cal.Rptr. 206 (1965).
4. *People v. Munoz*, 18 Cal.Rptr. 82 (1962).
5. PAUL B. WESTON, "The Illicit Traffic in Drugs," in *Narcotics, U.S.A.* (New York: Greenberg, 1952), 127–40.
6. PHILLIP C. McGUIRE, "Jamaican Posses: A Call for Cooperation Among Law Enforcement Agencies," *Police Chief* 55, no. 1 (1988): 20–27.
7. WILLIAM D. HYATT, "Investigation of Major Drug Distribution Cartels," in *Critical Issues in Criminal Investigation*, 2nd ed., ed. Michael J. Palmiotto, 113–39 (Cincinnati, OH: Anderson, 1988).
8. SCOTT H. DECKER and BARRIK VAN WINKLE, "Sling Dope: The Role of Gang Members in Drug Sales," *Justice Quarterly* 11, no. 4 (December 1994): 583–604.
9. *Draper v. United States*, 358 U.S. 307 (1959).
10. *Aguilar v. Texas*, 378 U.S. 108 (1964); *Spinelli v. United States*, 393 U.S. 410 (1969); *United States v. Garrett*, 565 F.2d 1065 (1977).
11. *United States v. Johnson*, 561 F.2d 832 (1977).
12. PETER K. MANNING, *The Narcs' Game—Organizational and Informational Limits on Drug Law Enforcement* (Cambridge, MA: MIT Press, 1980), 161.
13. MARK HARRISON MOORE, *Buy and Bust* (Lexington, MA: Heath, 1977), 135.
14. JAMES MILLS, *The Underground Empire—Where Crime and Government Embrace* (New York: Doubleday, 1986), 72–113, 283–394, 520–618.

16

SPECIAL INVESTIGATIONS

Many times during an investigator's career, he or she will be involved in cases outside or beyond his or her field of expertise. Even so, the investigator will be expected to contribute to the investigative efforts of these cases. This scenario is often played out in the area of the highly specialized investigations involving vice, organized crime, terrorist acts, computer crime, and hit-and-run accidents. Investigators should have a basic understanding of the underlying concepts involved in these investigations to be a contributing member of the investigative team.

VICE

Vice, or public morals, laws are not usually aggressively enforced unless someone is offended and lodges a complaint or the activity is occurring publicly. As an example, most efforts of vice cops are directed toward the highly visible street-level prostitute. Prostitution that has gone underground, or become invisible, generates little attention. The same is true with gambling and other forms of immoral conduct. The degree to which these laws are enforced can easily bring forth criticism. A department that aggressively enforces public morals laws may be criticized for squandering resources that could be used to control far more serious forms of crime. In contrast, critics often cite too little effort in this area as a graphic example of the corrupt nature of the local law enforcement agency. Somewhere between these two extremes is the fine line that most agencies follow in an effort to control vice in their community.

Gambling

The social harm of gambling has diminished with the added convenience of legal betting and a public awareness of the "fairness" of state-run lotteries and horse betting at tracks with a parimutuel setting system—even at "ghost" tracks (without horses but using video systems linked to other tracks; betting is hooked to a central computer system and the payoff is the same as if the races were being run locally). Some states offer off-track betting, which affords a similar advantage of convenience and track odds.

In sports gambling, the main event is both National Basketball Association (NBA) and college basketball games. Baseball is a poor second. Soccer games are currently receiving new interest among fans at local sports taverns. All are aided by the local press, which gives the daily "line" for such events. Boxing is a suspect sport since it lacks the basic fairness of basketball and similar team sports.

Some "boss bookies" will be quick to take a game "off the board" with the knowledge that a "fix" is in action and refuse to lay off bets to even a local betting syndicate. Doing so is only good business—no morality involved.

Casino gambling by American Indian tribal enterprises not under the control of crime bosses brings Las Vegas–type "table games" to the local level. These gambling establishments present a new horizon to the question of fairness: Is it better for the local compulsive gambler to be able to satisfy his or her needs at the local tables than at the hands of the local crime boss?

Illegal gambling is big business, often with interstate connections to organized crime. Investigators need to think big and be proactive in their investigative actions. Once they have probable cause to believe that illegal gambling is occurring, investigators need to gather information and evidence—often by using court-ordered eavesdropping techniques. A task-force approach is an excellent way to gather the necessary personnel and resources to address this problem.

Prostitution

Most cities are large enough to support a variety of prostitutes. They are either call girls, hotel and tavern pickups, "escorts" or alleged massage technicians. In addition, the local **stroll**, is when the girls use the client's car as the place to perform the sex act.

So long as the client names an act the prostitute is willing to perform for a specified price and denies being a police officer, and the prostitute acts in furtherance of committing the sex act (such as getting into the client's car), the crime of solicitation for purposes of prostitution has been committed. Typically, male undercover police officers are used to arrest a prostitute once the crime of solicitation has been committed. The prostitute, who is now in the officer's car, is driven to a staging area where transportation to the local jail facility awaits. Female undercover officers, or volunteer decoys, are used to arrest **johns**, who solicit females for prostitution.

Pimps—men living off the proceeds of one or more prostitutes—are a sign that someone is testing any no-tolerance rule of local law enforcement. Prompt action to arrest these men for their hustling sends a clear message that this behavior will not be tolerated. Similar prompt action should be taken against the so-called part-time pimp—hotel or motel and tavern employees who act out the role of a pimp.[1]

ORGANIZED CRIME

Fighting regional organized crime involves more than solving a single murder case, raiding a house of prostitution, or exposing an illegal bankruptcy ring. The investigation must be pursued beyond the operational level of the local crime overlords to their allies in local government who have been well bribed.

The first characteristic that most distinguishes the crime syndicate (organized crime) is *unity of action*. Criminal actions are dictated by executive and management personnel and performed by subordinates in the organization. Little freelancing occurs; crime is almost a franchise operation.

The hierarchy of command (the lines of authority) begins with the regional boss or chief, then extends to the underbosses, who exercise a functional supervision over a group of activities, and then to the "owner" of an activity, such as a bookmaking enterprise, a ring of prostitutes, or another such activity. Authority is clearly delineated, and orders and suggestions are obeyed without question. The severity of supervision creates a response to executives' direction that is difficult to attain otherwise.

A second major characteristic of syndicate operations is the *corruption* of weak and foolish public officials to secure immunity from arrest and successful prosecution. This protection allows the open and notorious operation of both criminal and quasi-legal enterprises.

A third major characteristic of syndicate operations is the extension of the *death creed* to the informer to justify killing anyone who interferes with organized crime operations. As a business technique, this creed may have originated as the only feasible means of settling disputes and silencing witnesses. Witnesses connected with the syndicate do not talk to police investigators and are unlikely to talk even under the threat of legal action because other witnesses who have talked have died—usually unpleasantly.

Nature of Operations

An emerging characteristic of considerable importance to investigators is the "wraparound" nature of syndicate operations. Organized crime members involved in prostitution have expanded from the traditional role of madam or pimp—enjoying a profit from a prostitute's earnings—to also controlling booking prostitutes from one area to another (a change of merchandise for local customers) and providing them with medical and legal talent as necessary. In labor racketeering, the labor unions are infiltrated for the basic enterprise, but operation of nonunion shops and control of employee associations provide fringe profits. In the infiltration of legitimate business, in addition to a planned bankruptcy or monopolistic activity is in-plant gambling and assignment of all freight business to syndicate trucking firms. A trade-off is made in every business of organized crime, until the operation is wrapped around every possible means of making money.

Characteristic Activity

Unity of action, immunity from governmental action, murder as a technique of business, and expansionistic methods sum up the characteristics that have made the crime syndicate a successful business in which large regional groups operate with nationwide unity.

A significant factor in syndicate activity is whether an enterprise can be operated without interference from law enforcement agencies. The syndicate does not dislike sharing its profits with its allies in government, but corrupt politicians and police officers often make distinctions among different types of corruption. Syndicate members know that they must operate in areas like their initial business of bootlegging (i.e., in activities having a modicum of public approval). Such business is a black market of consumer services and sales in which the fixers and hookers of the crime syndicate corrupt politicians and police with the plea that nothing is wrong with a little prostitution, gambling, money lending at high interest rates, or manufacturing and selling a good grade of untaxed alcohol. The enterprise must be illegal to ensure a lack of competition by legitimate business groups, but it cannot be "too illegal" because immunity then not only is costly but may not be purchasable.[2]

The syndicate also operates in other areas of crime, such as selling narcotics, receiving and selling stolen goods, labor racketeering, infiltrating legitimate business, and having hidden ownerships in casinos in Nevada and other areas in which gambling is legalized by state or local law.

Investigative Alerts

A lead alerting an investigator to local activity by members of an organized crime syndicate may originate in a federal or local agency. Personnel of the U.S. Drug Enforcement Agency (DEA) alert the local police when they believe the syndicate has started a new operation—and these men and women work closely with informants who have in-depth knowledge of the lower-echelon members of the syndicate. The Federal Bureau of Investigation (FBI) continuously inventories the operations of organized crime and their allies in government. The work of FBI agents in clearing cases involving interstate transportation of stolen goods has made this bureau extremely knowledgeable about the massive fencing operation of the syndicate. Local police intelligence units collect and interpret all incoming information from their own and the foregoing sources and compile their own files on the resident representatives of organized crime and the transients who display interest locally.[3]

Investigators, in their work on other cases, often encounter facts indicating organized crime is developing a local interest—the changeover of a cabaret or roadhouse to a "strip joint," the opening of an after-hours "club," or the expansion of the local sales of pornographic material. A little probing may indicate that these places of business are employing persons with police records or that ex-convicts are involved in their management through a hidden ownership shield if licenses are required. The investigator has a lead to some of the initial operations of the syndicate when a restaurant owner complains he or she is being pressured into buying meat from one firm or leasing linens from a particular concern, or when a bartender mentions that he or she and the owner of the bar were "asked" to use a certain vending machine firm. These danger signals are probable cause to inquire into the pressure and its origin. The inquiry may reveal the monopolistic control of a legitimate business and isolate and identify some of the resident members of the syndicate.

Arrests for illegal gambling, prostitution, and violations of state laws regulating the sale of alcoholic beverages can be audited by supervisors of the criminal investigation unit for traces that indicate syndicate takeover. Such traces include a new pattern of arrests (mere increase or decrease is not significant) marked by continuing operations and the use of a small group of bail bonding agencies and attorneys after arrests. Patrol force reports about suspicious persons and premises—whether increasing or diminishing—should be integrated to see what patterns emerge.

Because syndicate members are now closely involved with business, the initial alert may originate with the rank and file of a union, a trade association, or the Better Business Bureau. Such an alert may be little more than an allegation of unfair treatment or competition or a complaint of in-plant gambling.

Frequently, syndicate activity can be detected because of a killing, a suspicious fire, or an aggravated assault. Because of the massive fencing operation developed by organized crime, the presence of organized crime in an area may be noted from the activities of burglars and thieves who appear to operate without selling their loot. The alert may result from some suspicion that the police agency has been penetrated (for information) or infiltrated (for protection) if evidence indicates that suspected personnel are living above their wage levels or engaging in other suspicious behavior.

Gang Activity

"Biker" gangs have an organization similar to that of regional organized crime syndicates (La Cosa Nostra, the Mafia) but often specialize in peddling firearms and illicit drugs.[4] The bikers flaunt their crimes rather than attempt to conceal them or secure approval for their commission. Police surveillance can easily revealed the bikers' lifestyle.

Asian criminal organizations, made up primarily of Chinese and Vietnamese persons, are ethnic crime groups that closely resemble other "families" of organized crime in terms of their possible relationship to other social business groups of the same ethnic composition, in this case called **tongs**. These group's crimes are concentrated on extortion of local illegal gambling groups and legitimate business owners.[5]

Prison gangs operating outside prisons are similar to organized crime groups, although they also have a limited range of criminal activities—primarily drug selling. Other drug-selling organizations, such as those composed of Colombians and Jamaicans, are likewise similar to organized crime syndicates.

Ideally, the person to lead a comprehensive investigation into the operations of organized crime is the local prosecutor or U.S. Attorney. These public officials can develop a special investigation that combines the interrogation of witnesses with the examination of subpoenaed or seized records. Witnesses can be called before grand juries by prosecutors and placed under oath when they are questioned. Witnesses fearful of the syndicate may talk when granted immunity or threatened with jail for contempt if they refuse to testify, or for perjury if they lie when they do testify. Even though members of the hierarchy of organized crime rarely become informants, the dilemma of cooperation versus jail for contempt or perjury can persuade otherwise mute witnesses to talk. Police investigators do not wield this power, but prosecutors can do so in their role as legal adviser to a public investigative body.

Problems of Proof

Witnesses are the major source of evidence in a case. They are commonly available when none of the defendants have links to organized crime or other crime groups such as bikers, prison gangs, and similar organizations. However, any time a defendant has a link to a crime group, witnesses will usually be threatened and intimidated—if they have not previously been conditioned by the "death to the informer" stance of most of these groups. Usually, all coconspirators know of potential witnesses who have been killed or so intimidated that they moved out of town without leaving a forwarding address. This disposal of witnesses by death or intimidation tends to silence anyone thinking of becoming a witness for the prosecution.

TERRORISM

Terrorist violence aimed at achieving radical changes in society, causing capitulation to specific demands, or weakening an established government gives a new dimension to violent crimes such as arson, bombing, robbery, kidnapping, and murder. The major role of criminal investigation into such violence is continuing investigation, either as the criminal conspiracy is being organized or subsequent to a criminal act by one or more members of a terrorist group. Police intelligence is the first line of defense against terrorism—trying to stop it before it starts, and police operations units have the major

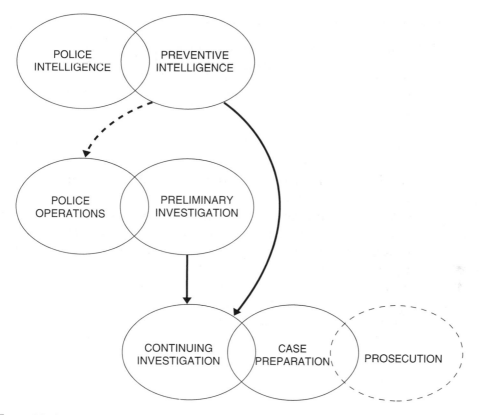

FIGURE 16-1   Investigation of terrorist activity.

responsibility for containing either threatened or in-progress acts of terrorists (Figure 16–1).

The political terrorist differs from other individuals who commit violent crimes. Persons who endanger life and property by fire, explosives, weapons, and other violent means are usually motivated (a) by profit; (b) by the anger-hate-revenge complex; (c) by the need to eliminate or silence competitors, associates, or witnesses for the state; or (d) by some irrational motivation common to persons with psychosis and other disturbed individuals. In contrast, political terrorists are motivated by their ideological convictions. This rationale for crimes of violence is the major reason to modify basic investigative techniques, to track down and prosecute these "convictional" criminals. The basic techniques for investigating violent crimes remain unchanged. The modified methods reflect the characteristics of political terrorists as members of a group believing in the philosophy that power comes out of the barrel of a gun, as persons who are trained and schooled to act in furtherance of group objectives, and as persons who are monitored closely by other group members and subjected to severe disciplinary measures for any breach of the group's code of conduct.

Terrorist Groups

Carlos Marighella, author of a how-to text on urban guerilla warfare, the broad goals of political terrorists summed up:

- To show the general public that police and military authorities are impotent to protect themselves from political terrorists, and thus powerless to protect the public
- To provide, by acts of terror, an overreaction by police or military authorities to "radicalize" many members of the general public and develop sympathizers for the political (revolutionary) aims of the terrorist group
- Ultimately, to overthrow the established government

"Blind date" bombings are acts committed by terrorist groups to gain publicity and public recognition. Any act of frightening violence is an attention getter, particularly when the human victims are individuals who just happen to be in the vicinity when a bomb explodes.

"Target blue" ambush slayings of police officers are in the same category of mindless violence. The police victims are also randomly selected, not because of who they are, but because of what they represent. The attention getter is the willingness of the terrorist group to kill the armed representatives of law and order.[6]

Hostage taking is another theatrical way of gaining attention. If the terrorists' demands are not met, hostages may be killed. Although the hostages are the on-site victims, this type of terrorism is aimed at the people who learn of the event through the news media. A dramatic hostage situation forces the police (government, military authorities) into a confrontation in which they must bring all the hostages out alive and terminate the situation by obtaining the hostage takers' surrender.

Terrorism committed to punish is a carefully structured three-act play, presented to the public, in which the terrorist group casts itself as the "good guys" and some representative of government or corporate life as the "bad guy." The first act involves a kidnapping and is frequently highlighted by the brutality of the seizure: for instance, bodyguards or a casual passerby is killed. The second act is devoted to identifying the terrorist group and delineating its role as representative of the "people" or the "revolution." Act three begins with discovery of the victim's body. The terrorist group also gives the news media reports that it has "executed" the victim after an alleged fair trial. The third act ends with the police hue-and-cry alarm for pursuit of the terrorists.

Variations of this punishment theme are assassination of political or corporate leaders—or **kneecapping** (a technique developed by the Irish Republican Army to cripple rather than kill informers)—and execution of a disloyal member of the terrorist group or of a person who has infiltrated the group (police informant, police undercover agent). In these deliberate dramas, the news media detail not only the event and its circumstances, but also the terrorists' assignment of guilt to the victims and the terrorists' belief in the righteousness of their cause.

Armed robbery by terrorists is a basic means of gaining funds to support the terrorist group's activities. To avoid total public rejection of the group and this activity, the terrorists attempt to put a Robin Hood twist on this crime of violence by concentrating their attacks on banks and other lending institutions: taking money from those who have a great deal of it, rather than robbing the poor.

Kidnapping for **ransom** has become a profitable activity for terrorists. Primarily aimed at executives of multinational corporations, it is characterized by ransom demands in the millions of dollars. Although this crime is not common in the United States, it could occur. When terrorists attack in kidnappings, the assault on a chosen target is planned, and unless rescued or ransomed, the victim is usually killed.[7]

Any contemporary terrorist group has its hard-core "operations" personnel and a larger group of people who aid and abet their activities by providing moral, political, and financial support. The operations personnel are usually divided into small "cells" of six to ten individuals for internal security. Membership identity is a closely guarded secret. Cell members are aware of only the identity of one another and possibly that of one or two liaisons whose function is to provide communications among cells or with supporters.

The terrorist attacks on the World Trade Center, the Pentagon, and Flight 93 on September 11, 2001, clearly demonstrated the capabilities of these groups. Immediately after the attacks, intelligence agencies actively rounded up suspected terrorists in Yemen, Germany, France, Great Britain, Belgium, Peru, Paraguay, and the United States with the hope of preventing another strike. These suspected terrorists were believed to have ties with Osama bin Laden and his Al Qaeda network.

The nineteen suicidal terrorists identified as responsible for turning four jetliners into guided missiles came from terrorist cells located in the United States. Many of the terrorists who participated in these attacks were in the United States on student visas. The terrorists were also able to raise money and obtain flight training in the United States to accomplish their mission.

Because of the U.S. open-borders policy, tracking terrorists is extremely difficult. As many as 1,000 foreign nationals with ties to terrorists are estimated to be currently living in the United States. Such people could include **sleepers**, who live normal lives for years and are activated only for a specific operation.

Terrorist cells are clannish and secretive and extremely difficult to penetrate. Even the most persuasive interrogation may not crack a suspect who is willing to die for a cause.[8]

The damaged Pentagon building in Virginia surrounded by fire trucks and ambulances in the aftermath of the terrorist hijacking and airliner crash of September 11, 2001.

Preventive Intelligence

Preventive intelligence is an indispensable element in the investigation of terrorist activity. Federal, state, and urban area police agencies usually provide local police agencies with intelligence data on persons and groups having a serious potential for future criminal involvement in acts of terrorism. Current intelligence material on political terrorism at local levels is the local police agency's responsibility.

Preventive intelligence is focused inquiry. Intelligence operations may include informants (paid and unpaid), police undercover agents, and various surveillance techniques.

Legal standards must be considered before preventive intelligence operations can be initiated. The nature of the existing grounds for suspicion must be examined in relation to the anticipated or past terrorist activity. Any secret agent (informant or undercover police agent) has an "agency" relationship to the employing police agency. Once the police encourage an agent to collect information, they assume some responsibility for the agent's actions.

The U.S. Supreme Court is reluctant to place constitutional barriers on the police's use of informants or infiltrating agents. In 1966, the U.S. Supreme Court dealt with this question:[9]

> Whether evidence obtained by the government by means of deceptively placing a secret informer in the quarters and councils of a defendant during one criminal trial so violates the defendant's Fourth, Fifth, and Sixth Amendment rights that suppression of such evidence is required at a subsequent trial of the same defendant on a different charge. (p. 296)

The Court answered this question with the opinion that no legitimate interest protected by the Constitution protected[10]

> [a]wrongdoer's misplaced belief that a person to whom he voluntarily confides his wrongdoing will not reveal it. . . . The use of secret informers is not per se unconstitutional . . . nor does it follow that his [secret informant, confidant] testimony was constitutionally inadmissible. (p. 296)

Preventive intelligence is not counterterrorism. It is an awareness that any war on terrorism is difficult, but it involves collecting intelligence, not interrogating individuals. Therefore, police investigators are not confronted with the need to supplant intelligence gathering for the immediacy of interrogation and the dilemma that a breach of law is required to avert a greater harm—the "necessity defense."

Using police deception to gather evidence for a criminal prosecution is not yet hindered by constitutional barriers. For instance, police investigators purchasing narcotics (a buy) from drug sellers must conceal their true identity and occupation.

For the present, a defendant cannot claim constitutional privacy if he or she voluntarily reveals his or her criminal plans to someone believed to be a confederate or a confidant. Even the use of electronic recording equipment by the pseudoconfederate or -confidant has not yet been constitutionally criticized. The U.S. Supreme Court has even praised the use of recording equipment in these "misplaced confidence" situations, because of its accuracy and reliability over human memory, and has allowed the recording as evidence in the absence of the informer or agent as a witness at the trial.

Role of Police Operations Units

Operations units of a police agency are responsible for controlling the acts of terrorists once such acts are threatened or in progress. Patrol units are the first line of defense in these instances, and specialists are available to them. Specialists in threat analysis will pass on the credibility and potential of the threat. Bomb detection and disposal specialists will direct the search for explosives and incendiary devices and effect their disposal if such items are found. Hostage negotiators will establish communications with terrorists in hostage-kidnapping cases and conduct negotiations leading to termination of the event.

The commanding officer of the operational units is also responsible for the preliminary investigation:

   I. Threats
      A. Date and time of threat, how received, and who received it
      B. Nature of act threatened, including target, time element, and weapon (e.g., fire, bomb)
      C. Demands or grievances accompanying threat
      D. Stated political or organizational affiliation of threat maker, including any claims of responsibility for prior terrorist threats or acts
      E. Other data, such as background noises (telephone threat, speech characteristics, and apparent personal characteristics of threat maker)
  II. Events
      A. Arrest of any terrorist at the scene; identification; collection of data and preparation of "alarm" for terrorists who have fled the scene
      B. Assignment of personnel to interview victims and witnesses and to search the scene for evidence likely to identify the terrorists and their modus operandi
      C. Assignment of personnel to protect the scene until qualified personnel can assist in the search for physical evidence
      D. Assignment of a sworn officer or supervisor to collate all collected information and evidence and to prepare the preliminary report

The Criminal Investigator's Role

The role of a criminal investigator in relation to terrorist acts can be summed up as follows:

- Identify the responsible parties—coconspirators.
- Reinterview victims and witnesses, get statements, and check stories; follow up on physical evidence and laboratory examinations.
- Identify alders and abettors—individuals on the fringes of the crime or criminal conspiracy.
- Pursue unapprehended terrorists, coconspirators, and alders and abettors.
- In kidnapping cases, immediately organize a pursuit to attempt to locate the victim and terrorists, immediately take action to reveal the terrorists' identity

and the hideout in which their captive is held, participate in rescue planning, and, if ransom is paid, probe for clues to the kidnappers during ransom negotiations and the ransom payment and on release of the person kidnapped.

- Apprehend all persons wanted in connection with the terrorist act or conspiracy.
- Investigate all arrestees to disclose their associations, past history, and potential for cooperation: to serve as an accomplice-witness and to provide information.
- Upgrade preventive intelligence surveillance to secure more information on suspects.
- Prepare the case, highlighting the relevancy and probative value of various items of evidence in relation to prosecution for a specific crime or crimes.

An investigation should be considered incomplete until evidence, direct or circumstantial, has been secured of an overt act that constitutes a "substantial step" in furtherance of the conspiracy. Forming or planning a conspiracy is not a true overt act, nor are acts done merely to cement the agreement.

A social network analysis is useful in investigating terrorism. This analysis is a linking of known members of a group (or cell) with suspected members, or just a linking of suspects believed to be joined in a group. The individual suspects are linked to one another, then to the group, and then to incidents and their scenes.[11]

Another network analysis is how the terrorists secured reliable information about the targets of their attacks, particularly the targets to be killed or kidnapped. In this case, the linkup relates to the source of information: members, sympathizers, collaborators, dissidents, or whomever. The names of these individuals should be worked into the social network analysis for development of connections between known members of a group and sources of information.[12]

Investigators assigned to cases of terrorist activity require all the standard skills of criminal investigators plus a high level of integrity and an appreciation for the legal significance of collected evidence. Integrity guarantees against illegal shortcuts that may ruin evidence; an appreciation for the legal significance of evidence is a safeguard against building a case on evidence of little relevance or probative value.

Problems of Proof

Most trials of terrorists in the United States have survived or perished on the issue of the legality or illegality of the means investigators used to gather evidence. Electronic eavesdropping evidence has been attacked as an unreasonable and broad invasion of privacy; undercover agents have been described as partisan witnesses, unworthy of belief; and informants (and the rare accomplice-witness) are perceived as persons of no credibility, intent on getting some benefit from the prosecution for their testimony. Unless the police-prosecutor team can overcome the damage wrought by these attacks, many jurors will downgrade the legal significance of the prosecution's evidence in these areas and conclude a reasonable doubt of guilt exists.

COMPUTER CRIME

Computer crime, or **cybercrime**, is distinguishable from other forms of crime in that a computer was either the target of the crime or the means of committing the crime. Computer crimes were originally limited to theft or vandalism by employees of businesses using computer applications. With the advent of the Internet in 1993, new opportunities were presented to criminals to expand their activities to a larger scale—even worldwide. Cybercrime now includes the crimes of theft, vandalism, counterfeiting, fraud, child pornography, child molestation, and terrorism.

Hackers and Their Tools

Hackers are, in essence, trespassers—intruders who enter into another person's computer system without authorization. In one study, 85 percent of the businesses and government agencies surveyed detected security breaches during the previous year. Businesses have suffered more than $250 million in losses at the hands of hackers—a figure that will continue to grow.[13] Three types of hackers are recognized: crackers, computer criminals, and computer vandals. **Crackers** are often antisocial misfits who are more comfortable online in front of a computer than with other people. They are usually intelligent, curious, and experts with computers. They rarely have a specific goal in mind beyond exploring another person's system. Their ultimate challenge is to get around the system firewalls or security protections, such as user names and passwords. The tougher the task, the better. The cracker is into hacking for the challenge—a test to determine whether his or her computer skills are better than those of the person who designed the system security protections. One "cyberpunk" was caught after he hacked his way into a computer security firm's Web site, the computer systems of four U.S. military bases, and the antidrug site of the Los Angeles Police Department, where he added a cartoon of Donald Duck with a hypodermic needle in his arm.[14]

Computer criminals engage in fraud, sabotage, industrial sabotage, and theft. They are the mercenaries of cyberspace. Like cat burglars, they hope to gain access, commit their crime, and leave without being detected. The primary threat comes from full- and part-time employees, a secondary threat comes from contract employees, and outside hackers are a close third. These thieves most frequently target intellectual property, including such items as new product plans, new product descriptions, research marketing plans, prospective customer lists, and similar information, which they then sell to a competitor. The criminal may also sabotage a system to destroy databases or conduct terrorist activity such as taking over a nation's power grid or air traffic control system. Most computer criminals' objective is money.

Computer vandals are motivated by revenge as a result of some real or imagined wrong. Vandals seek to destroy databases and wreak havoc, to shut down another person's system or the entire Internet. Vandals may be employees who, when notified of being laid off or fired, strike back against the employer by destroying the employer's databases. Vandals may also be outsiders who use the Internet to get even—such as an animal rights activist who targets companies who deal in fur coats and destroys their databases as a means of striking a blow for the cause.[15]

The tools of the vandal include viruses, Trojan horses, worms, and logic bombs. A **computer virus** is a type of malicious code that replicates and inserts copies or versions of itself into other programs. A virus may be as simple as letting the user know that it exists or as malicious as destroying the entire contents of computer memory. The 1999 "Melissa" virus was unleashed by a 31-year-old New Jersey man and was designed to infect the e-mail of the first 50 e-mail addresses on the users' mailing lists. Because each infected computer could infect 50 additional computers, which in turn could infect another 50 computers, the virus proliferated rapidly and exponentially, which overloaded e-mail servers. The result was shutdown networks and significant costs to repair or cleanse computer systems. More than 1 million personal computers in North America were affected by Melissa—a virus that caused damage exceeding $80 million in costs.[16] More than 10,000 viruses are known worldwide.

Trojan horses are stand-alone programs disguised as other programs that innocent users pass to one another, usually in the form of e-mail attachments. When the program is opened or executed, the malicious instructions are executed as well.

Worms are like viruses, but they do not replicate. Instead, they make duplicates of themselves—stealing system resources in the process. Most worms are designed to bring the user's system down.

Logic bombs are programs within programs that perform destructive acts on the basis of a trigger event. The trigger event might be a significant future date or an act such as the removal of a person's name from the payroll database, which would indicate that he or she has been either fired or laid off.[17]

Computer Fraud

The cybercriminal can forge business and government documents and create counterfeit documents of reasonable quality at a relatively low cost. Documents such as checks, entertainment and transportation tickets, and stock certificates are relatively easy to produce with a computer by using graphic software, scanners, color printers, and the appropriate paper stock. The U.S. government recently redesigned its currency to include security features that would make counterfeiting it by using advanced computer technologies more difficult. Ticketless travel and the electronic transfer of funds are available to eliminate the need for paper documents and may lessen the threat of counterfeiting in the future.[18]

The Internet provides the perfect means for committing basic to complex frauds. Simple business frauds include offering items for sale and either supplying worthless goods or not sending the merchandise. For anyone making purchases over the Internet, the old adage "Buyer beware" is still sound advice. A more complex type of scheme is the **salami fraud**, which refers to the technique of taking small "slices" to deceptively acquire the whole "salami." For example, an enterprising programmer in a bank was asked to write a program that would refund excessive interest collections from credit card holders. The program was written as requested, with one important distinction. It reduced the refunds to randomly selected cardholders by 25 cents each and forwarded these amounts to the programmer's account. Because the cardholders did not know exactly what they were supposed to receive as a refund, they were unable to detect the discrepancy. Fortunately, an alert bank auditor noticed the programmer's upscale lifestyle, and the programmer was successfully convicted of bank fraud.[19]

Child Pornography and Exploitation

The Internet, with its ability to transmit information around the world, is also a mecca for persons distributing sexually explicit material. While pornography is not illegal in the United States, information and pictures depicting sex with children—child pornography—is prohibited by law. This material often originates from Russia or Indonesia, where it is legal, and is then distributed in the United States. In one case, a 37-year-old man who ran the largest child pornography distribution company in the United States was arrested and received a record 1,335-year prison term for trafficking in child pornography. Hundreds of the company's customers were also arrested. To meet the standards for effective prosecution, federal agents sold and mailed child pornography videos, CDs, and floppy disks to the company's former customers. The agents then arrested the customers as they received the deliveries of the pornographic material. The names of another 30,000 alleged buyers of child pornography from this company have been offered to local police for investigation. The goal of these investigations, according to former Attorney General John Ashcroft, is "to help make the Internet a safe place for children to play and learn."[20] While all crimes committed by computer are a concern to law enforcement, perhaps the gravest concern is the use of a computer to harass and molest children. Approximately 77 million kids are currently online.[21] Computers and the Internet have made the predator's job easier. Historically, child predators found their victims in public places where children tend to gather—schoolyards, playgrounds, and shopping malls. With so many children now online, the Internet provides predators a new place—cyberspace—to target children for criminal acts.

Young children and teenagers are perfect targets for criminal acts because they are often trusting, naive, curious, adventuresome, and eager for attention and affection. However, the most attractive factor to predators is that children and teenagers historically have not been viewed as credible witnesses. The danger to children is currently even greater because the Internet provides predators anonymity. Whether the victimization occurs in person or over the Internet, the process is the same: the perpetrator uses information to target a child victim. For example, the predator may initiate an online friendship with a young person by sharing hobbies and interests. This friendship may lead to the exchange of gifts and pictures. Just like the traditional predator who targets children in person, the online predator is usually willing to spend considerable time befriending and grooming a child. The predator wants to build the child's trust, which will allow the predator to get what he or she ultimately wants from the child.

Predators contact teenagers and children over the Internet and victimize them by enticing them through online contacts to engage in sexual acts. These Internet contacts are also used for producing, manufacturing, and distributing child pornography and for exploiting children for the purpose of **sexual tourism**—travel with the intent to engage in sexual behavior—for commercial gain or personal gratification.[22]

Investigation into the exploitation of children requires a proactive response. Investigators, pretending to be children, go online and enter chat rooms that might be attractive to the predator. When approached, the investigator communicates with the predator as a child would, to determine the predator's intent. Such contact may provide sufficient grounds to obtain a search warrant for the predator's computer or lead to an arrest when the predator shows up at a predetermined location with the intent of molesting the child.

Cybercrime Investigation and Prevention

The foundation of dealing with computer crime is prevention. Antivirus programs are available that offer firewall software useful in preventing unwanted intrusions into personal computers. These programs also track the Internet address of any person who launches an attack on the protected computer. This address provides information useful in any subsequent criminal investigation. Computer forensic lab personnel, using data-mining and tracking programs such as SilentRunner (Computer Associates International, Inc., Islandia, NY), which captures and analyzes all activity on a computer network, aid the investigation of computer crime. These programs are so powerful that they were at one time classified as government secrets. With such programs, cybersleuths can pinpoint internal sources of misstated earnings, nab thieves of trade secrets, track down hackers, and uncover improper Internet use.

The FBI is well on its way to addressing many issues that challenge the new world of fighting computer crime. Most of the larger populated states now have full-time investigators dedicated to computer crime. Smaller jurisdictions should consider the creation of regional cybercrime investigative divisions.

Police academies should start offering training on the basics of assisting fully trained cybercrime investigation personnel in the proper methods of legally seizing and protecting computer criminal evidence. Every college and university that offers a curriculum in criminal justice should be offering training on the subject of computer-crime investigation. In addition, all companies connected to a network should employ the services of a professional information system security officer as a cost of doing business in the cyberworld.[23]

HIT AND RUN

Investigators have difficulty avoiding personal involvement when they are attempting to solve a crime without motive and usually without any witnesses—such as hit and run. Standard police procedure calls for the issuance of a prompt alarm for the fleeing vehicle, an extensive crime scene search, and assignment of police investigators to the accident-and-crime scene around the time of occurrence and on days following the accident to search for witnesses.

The Hit-and-Run Operator

Hit-and-run drivers have been grouped into three categories according to possible psychological explanations for their motivation for flight:

1. The apprehensive, panic-driven, fearful driver
2. The projectionist—projects guilt
3. The sneak—minor property damage accidents

The **apprehensive driver** has a greater sin to hide, either morally or criminally. This individual typically flees the scene for one or more of the following reasons: driving while intoxicated, operating without a license, having no insurance, having a companion in the car who is not the driver's mate or who is another person's mate, driving a stolen car, having stolen goods in the car, leaving the scene of another accident, fleeing a crime scene, or being wanted for another crime.

The **projectionist driver** tries the case in his or her mind. Sitting as judge and jury, he or she finds the other driver at fault, refuses to be a party to the accident, and drives off as the offended person.

The **sneak operator** crushes a fender and smashes grillwork as daily occupational activities. He or she chalks up the action as the calculated risk shared by all vehicle owners who place their vehicles on the roadway.

Fortunately, hit-and-run operators do not have the attitudes of professional criminals, nor are these operators skilled at concealing the damage to the vehicles. These persons will usually be cooperative when found, and traces of vehicle damage can easily be located, even if it was recently repaired.

The Alarm

The basic line of investigation in hit-and-run cases must relate to opportunity: What car was at the scene, and who operated it?

(a)

(b)

(a) This vehicle was involved in a hit and run. (b) Note the victim's eyeglasses in the door frame of the suspect's vehicle.

The ideal time of apprehension is while the hit-and-run driver is still operating the fugitive car. For this reason, time is of the essence in determining that the accident was a hit and run and in getting a broadcast on the air.

When investigators find the scene of an accident to be a hit-and-run case, their first effort should be to obtain from available witnesses a full description of the car involved. This description should include all odd or unusual details. Even noises are sometimes useful. Descriptive items that may prove extremely valuable in locating the vehicle are stickers on the windows or the windshield, dented fenders, fancy wheel covers, broken radio aerials, distinctive ornaments and fixtures, broken window glass, unusual colors and body styles, and out-of-state license plates.

These data, together with a description of the occupants and the direction of the vehicle when it was last seen, should be immediately broadcast in a police radio alarm to all department members and to nearby police units. The alarm alerts police on patrol to look for abandoned vehicles or vehicles in transit with such damage and as described. Particular attention is usually directed along the possible escape routes of the fleeing vehicle.

Police should promptly check garages, parking lots, used car lots, and other places where a vehicle might be stored or taken for repairs. Generally, if a car is not located within a reasonable time after the accident, the assumption is made that the driver removed it from the streets and placed it in a private garage. A prearranged list of all public garages and other likely storage places will facilitate the assignment of police to conduct preliminary inquiries. Prearranged contacts with garages may result in immediate reporting of a damaged vehicle.

Officers at the accident scene should also check suspicious persons at the scene or an inquisitive passerby. Sometimes hit-and-run drivers return to the scene, curious to find out how much evidence the police have discovered. In many cases, the hit-and-run driver stops from habit, examines the victim's injuries, stays a few minutes, and then flees. Officers should keep this habit in mind when questioning witnesses about information on persons who were at the scene but drove away.

Police officers should be alert for a vehicle that fits the description of the fugitive car and is reported stolen after the hit and run. When no description of the vehicle is available, all cases of reported car theft should be investigated for possible involvement. The reason for such investigation is that hit-and-run drivers often flee the scene, park the vehicle in some out-of-the-way area, and report it stolen so that they can explain any vehicle damage and the presence of the vehicle at the scene without implicating themselves.

The Scene Search

Transfer evidence is important in hit-and-run investigations. Since the only investigative leads are along the line of opportunity, searching for evidence at the accident scene that will identify the vehicle and the driver involved is vital. Such evidence should not be limited to prime identification that will lead to prompt recognition of either the vehicle or the operator, but should extend to any evidence that will connect the vehicle and its driver to the scene when the suspect vehicle is located or the fleeing operator is apprehended.

The search for physical evidence at the scene should be thorough. It should be planned so that every part of the area is carefully and methodically searched. A haphazard search procedure may frustrate the entire investigation by failing to reveal evidence or by destroying or impairing the value of evidence. This step is the most important in the investigation. The scene must be protected and safeguarded, then the search must be pointed toward broken headlight glass, door handles, hubcaps, paint marks or scrapings, soil and mud fallen from cars on impact, and any other debris. Objects carried in or on a hit-and-run vehicle are also of value. Damage to fixed objects can be studied for traces of paint and indications of damage to the vehicle.

Whenever the scene search reveals the nature of the damage to the car or the probable make or model of the car, this information should be immediately added to the alarm and broadcast to all units aiding in the search. Several police agencies use an artist or a special-effects photographer to prepare a graphic illustration of the wanted car on the basis of known information secured in the investigation. This illustration also shows probable damage, on the basis of damage sustained by vehicles involved in previous accidents of a similar nature.

Experienced hit-and-run investigators attempt to identify the hit-and-run driver's original purpose. What brought the driver into the neighborhood of the accident scene? What brought him or her into this area at the time of the accident, on the day of the week on which the accident happened? This assumption of purposefulness, coupled with the habits of motorists who use the same routes to and from work or for leisure activity, forms the basis for returning to the accident scene on stakeout duty to locate witnesses.

Stakeouts

Investigators should regularly return to the scene to look for new witnesses. The return should be at the same time of day and day of the week as that of the accident. The neighborhood of the accident, the route of travel, and other possible areas should be canvassed thoroughly for new witnesses. Perseverance is the rule, not the exception. For example, in several New York hit-and-run cases, the author (P.W.) was about to quit looking when patient police work turned up witnesses who did not realize they were the object of our extensive police search as the only eyewitnesses.

Transfer Evidence

Science has provided the police with one of their most effective weapons against hit-and-run drivers. Scientific analysis of evidence found at an accident scene sometimes identifies the make and model of the wanted car. Comparison analysis of such evidence with that recovered from a suspect's automobile provides data placing the vehicle at the crime scene. Some of the most common types of evidence found in hit-and-run accident investigations are amenable to scientific analysis.

Glass fragments found at accident scenes are excellent evidence for proving that a suspect car, when located, was at the accident scene. Broken automobile parts, paint, soil, hairs and fibers, bloodstains, and tire marks all lend themselves not only to identification of the type and make of a car in the first phase of searching for the vehicle, but also to later comparison analysis when the suspect vehicle is located.

When a suspected car is located, it should be impounded for an immediate search for evidence. All exterior parts of the vehicle should be carefully examined. Special attention should be given to all protruding parts where hair or fibers might have been caught. All damaged parts should be noted and inspected for traces of blood or signs of contact with other objects. No foreign material should be discarded from consideration until its source is determined. Evidence of recent damage, repair, new painting, or a wash job should be carefully noted. If damaged parts have been replaced, attempts should be made to obtain the original parts.

The undercarriage of the vehicle should receive special attention. The car should be placed over a mechanic's pit or up on a grease rack for a proper search. Spots that appear to have been brushed by an object and all protruding parts should be thoroughly examined for hairs, fibers, and blood spots.

The investigator must always attempt to develop latent fingerprints to use to identify the driver of the vehicle. Frequently, a suspect denies having driven the vehicle, and it may in fact have been driven by a thief. Fingerprints may tell the story.

All evidence should be properly preserved and compared with evidence found at the scene of the accident so the investigating officer can prove that the suspect's vehicle was at the accident scene and was involved in the accident. The vehicle is the key to the criminal in these cases. If transfer evidence connects the vehicle with the accident scene, police can look to its owner for honest answers in a fact-finding inquiry about the operator.

One explanation the owner of a vehicle often offers is that his or her car may have been involved, but he or she denies having driven it at the time and claims to have loaned it to a friend or recent acquaintance known only as "Joe." Until "Joe" is identified, found, and confesses, investigators should not believe this claim.

Accountability

Apprehension of a hit-and-run driver is difficult because information can be secured only from victims and witnesses and from physical evidence found at the scene. Informers are of little use in these cases, and the criminal usually has no modus operandi: a suspect does not usually have a record of previous offenses and could be any member of the community.

The motive for the crime is not a potential line of inquiry in these cases because the criminal did not desire to kill or injure the victim. The only motive that may be ascertained is that for flight from the scene, and it has no connection with the victim. Therefore, the line of inquiry about who wanted to kill the deceased, which frequently leads to the criminal in homicide cases, is useless in hit-and-run cases.

Car dealers and motor vehicle license authorities can supply the names and addresses of persons recently purchasing a car similar to the wanted vehicle or having a license plate number close to that of the wanted car. Apprehension can be effected from such information, but a great deal depends on chance.

Legislation has been proposed that would require body-and-fender repair shops to be licensed so that the shops and their records could undergo regular checks. However, not much progress has been made because effectively administering such licensing would be unwieldy.

Hit-and-run investigations should be conducted by accident investigators. When this work is assigned to detective units, a detective working on criminal homicides, felonious assaults, kidnappings, and bank robberies will naturally consider hit-and-run cases to be less important. Yet, in this field of traffic safety, the people of a community can be won over to the police's side by the quick solution of these cases and prompt apprehension and trial of the offenders. Much of this work can be accomplished by accident investigators working in uniform, but permission should be granted to assigned investigators to work out of uniform when necessary. Accident investigators are key personnel in getting these investigations started without delay. A prompt alarm and search will result in an apprehension before a car can be hidden and the damage repaired. It will also cause an emotional shock to the fleeing driver, which may result in the offender's waiving his or her right to silence and legal counsel and making a prompt and full admission of fleeing the scene and the reasons for such flight.

Possible Murder

Infrequently, a pedestrian, walking or jogging on a sidewalk or along the side of a road, is struck by a fast-moving vehicle and is dead on arrival at the local hospital before police arrive. Local homicide detectives should be notified when the slightest evidence of murder is indicated and should be asked to run a regular homicide check on who might "profit from or want the victim dead." In the meantime, the hit-and-run investigator should concentrate on finding the damaged car and witnesses.

CHAPTER REVIEW

CASE STUDY

Hit and Run

June 8

2045 Hours. The city police dispatch center receives a 911 call of a pedestrian versus vehicle accident at 21st and Jay Streets. Patrol and medical units are dispatched to the scene.

2052 Hours. The first police unit arrives on the scene and confirms that a pedestrian has been struck by a vehicle and that the victim is critically injured. According to witnesses, the vehicle involved has left the scene. The vehicle is described as a tan four-door sedan, last seen heading west on 21st Street. All available units are updated with this information and requested to search the area for the suspect vehicle.

2054 Hours. An ambulance arrives on the scene and begins emergency medical treatment. The victim is transported to the nearest hospital, code 3: red lights and siren.

2105 Hours. The highway patrol transfers a cellular 911 call to the city dispatch center. A young woman advises that she and her boyfriend are following a tan sedan that was just involved in an accident at 21st and Jay streets in the city. The caller states that they were in light traffic when they observed the car in front of them run the light at the intersection and hit a pedestrian. The force of the impact caused the pedestrian to strike the windshield and be thrown over the roof of the vehicle and land in the street. As other drivers stopped to aid the victim, the couple decided to follow the suspect as he fled from the scene. The couple is now a few car lengths behind the suspect vehicle, headed east on the freeway toward the suburbs. The dispatcher asks the caller to stay on the line and to continue to follow the suspect at a discreet distance. The dispatcher obtains the suspect's license plat number from the caller and runs the number through the Department of Motor Vehicles (DMV) database.

2110 Hours. Patrol units are advised of the suspect's location and possible destination. The DMV inquiry discloses that the suspect's vehicle is registered to a location in the eastern part of the county. As the suspect's residence is located in the jurisdiction of the sheriff's department, this department is advised.

2117 Hours. The couple following the suspect advises that the vehicle has stopped at a residence and that the suspect has parked the vehicle and gone inside. The address given by the couple matches the address supplied by DMV records.

2120 Hours. Police and sheriff's units arrive at the suspect's residence and secure the area to prevent escape. Officers knock at the suspect's door, but no one responds to open the door.

2135 Hours. The telephone number for the residence is obtained from the reverse directory, and the dispatcher places a call to the suspect's residence. After a few minutes, a male answers the telephone and is advised to step outside to talk to the officers. When he opens the door and steps outside, he is taken into custody.

2215 Hours. Crime scene technicians arrive at the suspect's residence and begin to photograph and process the vehicle for evidence. The victim's eyeglasses are recovered from the door frame of the vehicle.

2230 Hours. The officer at the hospital advises that the victim was just pronounced dead as a result of the injuries sustained in the accident. The suspect is subsequently booked at the county jail for vehicular homicide.

September 12

During a formal ceremony at City Hall, the young people are presented with a citation from the chief of police commending their actions leading to the apprehension of this hit-and-run driver.

DISCUSSION QUESTIONS

1. Describe how a police agency can be criticized for actively enforcing vice laws in the community.
2. Explain how an agency can be criticized for not actively enforcing the same laws.
3. Define *organized crime*.
4. What is an *accomplice-witness*? Why do accomplice-witnesses agree to cooperate with the police investigator? Do they require protection? Why?
5. What is the major difference between political terrorists and other violent criminals?
6. What are *"blind date" bombings*? *"Target blue" ambush killings*?
7. Describe *terrorism to punish*.
8. Define *preventive intelligence*. Define *misplaced confidence situations*.
9. Describe *social network analysis*. What is its basic utility in criminal investigation?
10. What information should be contained in the preliminary investigative report of a bomb threat? An actual bombing?
11. Discuss how, in the case study, the witnesses' use of a cell phone facilitated the suspect's identification and arrest.
12. Discuss how investigators can use other technology, such as security cameras, in solving hit-and-run cases.

LIBRARY ASSIGNMENT

Search available literature for at least five references to the organizational structure of terrorist groups or the psychosocial characteristics of members.

WORKBOOK PROJECT

Prepare a to-do list for an investigator who is assigned to (a) a bomb-threat case, (b) a bombing case, and (c) a case involving a bombing followed by a fire.

RELATED WEB SITES

To get up-to-date information about organized crime, visit this Web site: *www.ganglandnews.com.*

For the history of organized crime, including biographies, pictures, mug shots, and more, see this site: *www.gangrule.com.*

For information about the U.S. government's response to cybercrime, visit the Computer Crime and Intellectual Property Section of the U.S. Department of Justice *www.usdoj.gov/criminal/cybercrime/compcrime.html.*

NOTES

1. FREDERICK W. EGEN, *Plainclothesman: A Handbook of Vice and Gambling Investigation* (New York: Arco, 1968), 3–104.
2. DONALD R. CRESSEY, *Theft of the Nation* (New York: Harper & Row, 1969), 248–89.
3. DREXEL GODFREY, JR., and DON R. HARRIS, *Basic Elements of Intelligence: A Manual of Theory, Structure and Procedures for Use by Law Enforcement Agencies Against Organized Crime* (Washington, DC: U.S. Department of Justice, Technical Assistance Division, Law Enforcement Assistance Administration, 1971), 11–35.
4. JAMES BUBRO, *Mob Rule—Inside the Canadian Mafia* (Toronto: Macmillan, 1985), 256–58.
5. FRANCIS M. ROACHE, "Organized Crime in Boston's Chinatown," *Police Chief* 45, no. 1 (1988): 48–51.
6. See ROBERT DALEY, *Target Blue* (New York: Delacorte Press, 1973), and International Association of Chiefs of Police, *Ambush Attacks: A Risk Reduction Manual for Police* (Gaithersburg, MD: International Association of Chiefs of Police, 1974).
7. CHARLES A. RUSSELL, "Businesses Becoming Increasing Targets," in *Managing Terrorism: Strategies for the Corporate Executive*, ed. Patrick J. Montana and George S. Roukis, 55–71 (Westport, CT: Quorum Books, 1983).
8. EVAN THOMAS, "The 10-Year Hunt for bin Laden," *Newsweek*, October 1, 2001, 38–49.
9. *Hoffa v. United States*, 385 U.S. 293 (1966).
10. Ibid.
11. CHRISTOPHER A. HERTIG, "The Investigation of Terrorist Activity," in *Critical Issues in Criminal Investigation*, ed. Michael J. Palmiotto, 235–45 (Cincinnati, OH: Anderson, 1988).

12. WALTER LAQUEUR, *The Age of Terrorism* (Boston: Little, Brown, 1987), 109–11.

13. GANNETT NEWS SERVICE, "Computer Security Lacking, Experts Warn," *Sacramento Bee*, March 23, 2001, A6.

14. STEPHEN FROTHINGHAM, "Jailed Hacker Builds Firm," *Sacramento Bee*, September 4, 2001, D1.

15. PETER STEPHENSON, *Investigating Computer-Related Crime* (Boca Raton, FL: CRC Press, 2000), 31–38.

16. U.S. DEPARTMENT OF JUSTICE, UNITED STATES ATTORNEY FOR THE DISTRICT OF NEW JERSEY, "Creator of 'Melissa' Computer Virus Pleads Guilty to State and Federal Charges," press release, December 9, 1999, 1–3.

17. STEPHENSON, *Investigating Computer-Related Crime*, 81–88.

18. DONN B. PARKER, *Fighting Computer Crime* (New York: Wiley, 1998), 98.

19. Ibid., 126.

20. LENNY SAVINO, "Web Child Porn: A Test For Police," *Sacramento Bee*, August 15, 2001, A7.

21. U.S. DEPARTMENT OF JUSTICE OFFICE OF JUSTICE PROGRAMS, OFFICE FOR VICTIMS OF CRIME, OVC *Bulletin: Internet Crimes Against Children* (Washington, DC: U.S. Department of Justice Office of Justice Programs, Office for Victims of Crime, 2001), 1.

22. Ibid., 2–5.

23. JIM E. REAMES, "Computer Crimes, Hacking and Cybernetic Warfare" *Journal of California Law Enforcement* 34, no. 1 (2000): 22–25.

17

The Investigator as Witness and Ethical Awareness

THE INVESTIGATOR AS WITNESS

At the conclusion of an investigation, an investigator knows the victim, the circumstances of the crime, and the offender's identity and sometimes has data on the motive for the crime. He or she has collected facts, linked them, and mentally shaped a pattern of the crime and a narrative of the event with form and order. However, the events and incidents of a crime are known to the investigator only indirectly, through interviewing witnesses and other investigative techniques. No matter how much intelligence and honesty went into the many decisions common to any investigation, the sum is a subjective impression in the investigator's mind.

Therefore, the investigator as a witness is confined to the same narrow band of personal knowledge as any other witness. He or she is under the same requirement to establish a proper foundation for sharing personal knowledge before giving any oral evidence.

Criminal investigators have a basic obligation to court and community when testifying as a witness in a criminal case; to tell the truth as they found it. They also have a basic obligation to themselves and their employing agency not to allow any part of their appearance or any act done within the courtroom to adversely affect their testimony on the witness stand. The legal significance of an investigator's testimony can be damaged by behavior not in harmony with his or her role as impartial fact finder and reporter. Men and women serving as trial jurors evaluate witnesses by what they say, how they say it, and their overt behavior while saying it.

Action Prior to Court Appearance

Investigators should review the substance of their testimony before the defendant's trial. They can easily review areas of likely inquiry with a friendly associate—the prosecutor. Unfortunately, investigators can never fully prepare for cross-examination. This portion of the trial usually involves hostile questioning by the defense counsel. Five major areas of self-analysis are as follows:

1. Is the possible testimony arrayed in a manner that allows me to relate it simply and convincingly so that the triers of fact will both understand it and believe it?
2. Am I willing to state that I do not know or cannot recall certain facts?
3. Am I ready to acknowledge mistakes made in the investigation when I am questioned, and am I prepared to answer questions truthfully and directly, without hedging?
4. Am I prepared to refute and rebut any allegation of "improving" the case against the defendant?
5. Will I prepare for being a witness by refreshing my memory immediately prior to trial?

The legal significance of evidence demands a pretesting for credibility. Self-analysis is often difficult, but it is vital to the integrity of an investigator's testimony. The facts told by the investigator as a witness will be tested in court against standard bases of credibility.

A short time before the court appearance date, the investigator should confer with the assigned prosecutor for a last-minute check. The prosecutor should be well informed about the expected testimony and possible areas of difficult cross-examination. A brief review just before a court appearance can be helpful. Ethical prosecutors will make certain that any conference with witnesses does not degenerate into a "coaching" session, and under questioning, an investigator-witness should promptly admit to any such meetings because they are part of normal case-preparation procedure.

On the date that an investigator is scheduled for a court appearance, he or she should allow a generous amount of time for the trip to the courthouse. This allowance is a safeguard against unexpected traffic delays or other events that may make the trip longer than anticipated. In court appearances, being early is better than rushing in at the last minute.

On arrival at the courthouse and prior to opening of court, the investigator should sign in or check in as required by local regulations and make contact with the assigned prosecutor. If witnesses are excluded from the courtroom until they have testified and been excused, the investigator must wait outside the courtroom until a bailiff calls his or her name. If witnesses have not been excluded, the investigator should take a seat within the courtroom and await his or her call.

This point is an excellent time to quell the "stage fright" common among witnesses about to testify. This fear is nebulous, often based on no more than a reluctance to talk in front of a group of people. With investigator-witnesses, it may be complicated by knowledge that the presiding judge has a short-fuse temper or by an unpleasant memory of the last experience with an aggressive cross-examiner.[1]

Stage fright is often cumulative. Initially, the witness's blood pressure and respiration rate increase, which results in a feeling of being "charged up." This feeling is accompanied by a noticeable dryness of the mouth and sometimes shaking hands. These feelings are unusual and uncomfortable, and the common reaction is increased anxiety.

However, stage fright can be controlled. Planning ahead is the first step. Therefore, the investigator should quickly review the substance of the case and possible questions. Second, he or she should mentally scan past experiences that can be considered satisfactory or better and relax in the thought that such experience will be helpful in successfully concluding the forthcoming session as a witness. Finally, the investigator should remember that anxiety at this time is nothing more than the body's way of preparing him or her to do his or her best.[2]

General Behavior

Upon being called as a witness, the investigator should walk promptly to the front of the courtroom. He or she should stop in the "well" of the court, usually in front of the witness stand, to take the oath to tell the truth. This stop is an important waypoint. A court officer proffers a Bible. The witness-to-be places his or her hand on it. The court officer then administers the oath (usually slowly and clearly) and the witness-to-be replies in the affirmative. The investigator's behavior during this portal ceremony should reflect a deep and sincere belief in the oath.

The first questioning of a witness is the **direct examination**, which is conducted by the party calling the witness. In the case of investigator-witnesses, this party is most often the prosecutor. This questioner guides the witness to prevent deviation from relevant facts. This stage of the examination is followed by **cross-examination** by defense counsel. Cross-examiners are likely to be aggressive. In either stage of this examination, a witness is expected to respond to questions.

Cross-examiners often prefer to limit a witness's responsiveness by phrasing questions to call for a yes-or-no answer. A "yes" means that the witness accepts the idea expressed in the question; a "no" indicates that the witness rejects the idea. If a cross-examiner does not use simple language in his or her query, then "yes" or "no" is not a simple response. Therefore, if a witness does not fully agree with the idea expressed in the question, he or she should give a negative response: "no." A "qualified yes" is often a responsive answer, but it is not usually allowed because the scope of the question may be extended when the witness explains the need to qualify the answer. As a general rule, the investigator-witness is not alone at this time. The prosecutor will usually speak out and ask the court to have the question withdrawn, reworded, or thrown out. Any witness who does not understand a question has the right to ask that the question be repeated—usually read by the court reporter. Sometimes, when this request is made, the questioner will withdraw the question and rephrase it.

The best way to answer questions is to speak loudly and clearly enough for everyone in the courtroom to hear all the testimony, and to use simple language in responses. Simple language is plain talk. It helps people understand what each answer means. Beyond the limits of a yes-or-no answer, an investigator-witness should speak in complete sentences rather than use sentence fragments. Normally, each sentence should express no more than one idea. Short sentences space out ideas. When the investigator-witness uses short sentences, jurors, and other individuals in the courtroom, get a break between ideas that allows them to digest what they heard.[3]

Open-ended questions are often asked of investigator-witnesses during direct examination. These queries detail one segment of the investigation and ask the witness to respond "in your own words." The key to a responsive answer, and one that will usually be understood by all listeners, is to use short sentences arranged in chronological order.

The time element in responding to questions is also important in any evaluation of a witness by in-court listeners. A short pause before responding is good behavior. It allows the prosecutor to interpose an objection to the question if he or she wants. It also indicates a thoughtful reflection on the substance of the question and the response.

Investigator-witnesses should avoid using underworld slang and police lingo. Jurors are unfamiliar with such language and will not understand it—and possibly a good portion of the witness's response in which this language is used. To many jurors, a "hit" does not mean to kill, a "piece" does not indicate a pistol or revolver, and a "scam" does not describe a criminal conspiracy. Similarly, jurors have little understanding of words common among police personnel—for instance, *pinch* (arrest), *frisk* (search), *DOA* (dead on arrival), and *FOA* (for other authority).

An investigator-witness must be courteous to questioners. This rule is imperative, even with difficult defense attorneys. Questioners should be carefully addressed. The prefix "Mister" should be avoided because it may be viewed as sarcasm. "Madam" not only means a lady, but also is the title given to a woman in charge of a brothel. "Counselor" seems to be fairly safe as a general term for either the prosecutor or defense counsel, man or woman.

The apogee of discourtesy is to interrupt a questioner when he or she is phrasing a question. An interruption usually damages the jurors' ability to understand the question and any response made by the witness when the question is finally completed. Jurors, as well as others in the courtroom, view this conduct as argumentative. Such an evaluation can be harmful to the prosecution's goals.

Another caution for any investigator-witness is this: do not argue with the defense counsel. Arguing destroys the image of the witness as an impartial fact finder and reporter. Jurors do not expect investigators to be "friendly with" the defendant or his or her counsel, but any argument during cross-examination can antagonize many jurors. It projects a hostility toward the defense beyond the expectations of these men and women. *Remember*: Defendants are innocent until proved guilty.

A final caution is not to lie or misrecollect on the witness stand. Unfortunately, many investigator-witnesses are sensitive about one or more areas of the investigation in which they failed to perform up to standard or were overzealous in their performance. No circumstance of this area of the investigation will be left unexplored when a cross-examiner detects this sensitivity. Any attempt to "stonewall" or "cover up" can be disastrous to the witness's credibility.

If any sensitive areas do exist, the best procedure is to discuss them with the assigned prosecutor prior to trial and obtain his or her guidance. These guidelines will probably be to admit to any substandard practice, inefficiency, or incompetency if questioning begins to exploit one or more of these areas. Having the jurors think of a witness as a bungler (a common human condition) is better than having them think of him or her as a perjurer (an unacceptable human condition).

One survival technique for withstanding the most aggressive and belligerent cross-examination is to constantly think and rethink the fact that cross-examination of a witness is a constitutional right of all defendants—an absolute right.

Nonverbal Communication

Nonverbal communication is anything someone does that another person finds meaningful. It is the process of a person's transmitting unspoken cues that have potential meaning to one or more observers.[4] Nonverbal communication is "body language." Body movement and eye behavior send signals to observers.

In the drama of witness and questioner as it is staged in U.S. courtrooms during criminal trials, the observers and listeners are jurors. These men and women are alert to what the witness is saying, and they are also alert to any body language signs that will help them to better understand the witness's testimony and evaluate his or her credibility. Many jurors mentally note what they do not hear to fully evaluate the net worth of what they do hear from a witness.

Communication without speech is transmitted through body movements and eye behavior. Facial expressions (smiles to frowns), head nods and shoulder shrugs, gestures (clenched fists to folded arms), leg crossing, and toe tapping are all body movements. Common eye behavior includes the direction of eye movement and the frequency and duration of eye contact.

A good portion of body language is involuntary and difficult or impossible to control. Nevertheless, anyone can learn to mask some basic emotions.

The investigator-witness can easily learn the rudiments of masking nonverbal communication that indicates to observers that he or she is bored, impatient, anxious, surprised, angry, or fearful. Then, a conscious effort to avoid these indicators while testifying should not interfere with the investigator-witness's testimony.

As far as any body movement is concerned, most basic police academy lectures on being a witness have long emphasized "Don't fidget." In other words, the investigator-witness should sit still.

Eye behavior is a nebulous area. "Do what comes naturally" is generally good advice. During initial eye contact, the eyes should move casually to the presiding judge, the jury, prosecutor, defense counsel, defendant, and spectators. When the investigator is asked a question, eye contact should be made with the questioner. When answering, the investigator should move his or her eye contact from the questioner toward the jury and scan the jury box as he or she responds. If reading from notes or exhibits, the investigator-witness should look up toward the jury box now and then and briefly make eye contact with one or two jurors. When extensive answers are called for by questions, the witness may pick out jurors who he or she believes to be more attentive than others and make less-than-staring eye contact.

Clothing is also nonverbal communication, but investigator-witnesses are usually police officers, and most police departments have established rules for the appearance of their members in court. If a man or woman is working in uniform, these rules usually require court appearance in uniform. For members working as investigators in an out-of-uniform assignment, a dress code is usually specified—or stylized by custom—for appearance in so-called plain clothes. So that the latter group can be identified as police officers, most departments require that badges or identification cards be pinned to the witness's outer garment. Many badge cases are designed so that one-half of the case slips into the breast pocket of a coat and the other half hangs out and over the pocket, displaying the badge or ID card as if pinned to the coat.

To be identified as a police investigator by uniform or badge is acceptable. After being sworn in, a police witness must give his or her name and assignment and the name of his or her employing agency. A negative nonverbal communication would be to stress this class membership by displaying a holstered revolver or pistol through an open jacket.

Conduct After Testifying

After testifying, the investigator-witness should make a graceful exit from the courtroom. Stopping to shake hands or chat with the prosecutor on the way out is definitely taboo. If the witness has not been excused by the court, he or she should wait in the hallway until the next recess before speaking to the prosecutor in a low-key conversation. Recess is also the time for the witness to speak to the prosecutor about segments of his or her testimony that are of concern.

Many prosecutors want the investigator-witness to be available for recall to the witness stand, and they will make whatever arrangements are necessary. While in or near the courtroom during this period, the investigator should not discuss his or her testimony with anyone except the prosecutor assigned to the case or a person designated by this official.

At this time, or shortly thereafter, the investigator should review, in his or her mind, as much of the testimony given as possible. These periods are self-teaching sessions in which the investigator impartially examines his or her performance on the witness stand. Thus, every minute spent on the witness stand can be educational and serve as a means of improving future performance in court.

ETHICAL AWARENESS

Law enforcement ethics includes two distinguishable topics: corruption and noncorrupt misconduct. The term **corruption**, as used in its traditional sense, involves an officer's misuse of police authority for personal gain; police **misconduct** may involve issues such as excessive use of force, violation of a suspect's constitutional rights, and a variety of other misdeeds.[5]

Dealing with these concerns can be called **ethical awareness**. Ethical awareness, even at average levels, warns a person that criminal behavior is wrong and unlawful and warns that misconduct on the job is improper, substandard conduct. Similarly, criminal investigators usually have inner indications that using the wrong means to gain a desired result, using the right means to achieve a wrong end, or doing anything immoral or unprincipled is not proper.

Crime and Outrageous Conduct

The U.S. police establishment has a rich history of corrupt conduct. Years ago, the locus of this corruption was vice. Madams, bookmakers, and other gambling-game operators paid police officers on vice squads for "protection" each month to avoid arrests. Currently, the "money tree" includes narcotics and drug dealers, and the thing of value is money—big money—and drugs.

Corrupt narcotics officers do not receive a monthly "pad" similar to vice payments for so-called protection. Instead, these agents depend on "scores," or deals, made at the time of the arrest or another threat to a drug dealer's business. "Scoring" has the essential element of armed robbery.[6] Outrageous behavior is detailed in the complaints of citizens against police officers and the litigation and settlements made based on these claims.

Impact of Misconduct on Criminal Investigation

Disclosures of outrageous behavior and police misconduct have three ramifications. First, the major result is that the labor pool of men and women who want to become police officers decreases and the most desirable candidates do not apply to the police academy. Recruiting working police officers from other agencies also becomes more difficult because many applicants may have records of prior misconduct.

Second, investigators have become aware of a change from times past, when witnesses were not reluctant or unwilling to talk to investigating officers. Investigators have identified this unfriendliness as a general mistrust of police, which indicates that simply blaming "a few bad apples" in a department cannot erase all the recent transgressions.

Third, and finally, **jury nullification** is becoming more common in U.S. courthouses. The jury's not-guilty verdict is influenced by mistrust of police witnesses.

Standards for Criminal Investigators

Investigators have obligations that derive from common membership in the community of investigators, including a basic responsibility to conform to prevailing practices and an accountability when behavior is strange and unusual. In general, the behavior expected is that of a reasonable person exercising care, prudence, self-discipline, and judgment in his or her work.

Reasonable care—in its legal definition—is care fairly and properly taken in response to the circumstances of a situation, such care as an ordinary prudent person would take in the same time frame, under the same conditions, and when performing the same act or acts. *Self-discipline* and *judgment* mean jump-starting and heeding an inner moral sense when decisions are made on the moral quality of actions, and discriminating between right and wrong.

A person conforming to professional standards of conduct and having an appreciation of the ethical viewpoint of a reasonable person is a profile of an investigator who is conscientious, reliable, and responsible, regardless of varying situations. Such a person can justify, warrant, or excuse his or her conduct.

Prevention of Misconduct

Officers live and work in a constantly changing and dynamically social context in which they are exposed to myriad ethical conflicts. Officers who are unprepared to meet these challenges are more likely to go with the flow and become compromised. The progression is predictable and for the most part preventable. If officers are going to survive ethical dilemmas, they need to be as mentally prepared as they would be for tactical encounters.

To be mentally prepared requires credible ethical instruction, proactive supervision, and continual ethical awareness. Ethical instruction begins at the academy and should continue throughout an officer's career. Ethical training taught in the academy should be reinforced by field training officers who have been selected as ethical role models and who have been provided with specific ethical awareness training. Ethical training should continue through ongoing professional training sessions and should be relevant job-specific training on ethics rather than a result of, or knee-jerk reaction to, a recent event.

Proactive supervision involves an acknowledgment of the existence of the "continuum of compromise" and the need to be ever vigilant for even the most minor unethical acts. Supervisors must be committed to acting quickly and be held responsible for the unethical conduct of the officers under their command. Supervisors should strive to prevent small infractions of unethical conduct from becoming major problems. Proactive supervision also includes "walking the talk" by setting the example of ethical professional conduct.[7]

CHAPTER REVIEW

CASE STUDY

The Special Crime Squad

Cast of Characters

Judge	Anonymous
Defense Counsel	Anonymous
Assistant District Attorney	Anonymous
Defendant	Bob (not otherwise identified)
Prosecution Witness	Detective Sergeant Daniel Costello

SCENE: A courtroom. There is a high judicial bench, an adjacent witness stand and chair, and a table and two chairs in front of the bench and witness stand. As the scene opens, the judge is seated on the bench, the two chairs are occupied by the defendant and his counsel, the witness chair is empty, and the Assistant District Attorney is standing in front of it.

ASSISTANT DISTRICT ATTORNEY: I would like to call my first witness: Detective Sergeant Daniel Costello. (Sergeant Costello appears, is sworn in, and sits down in witness chair.)

ASSISTANT DISTRICT ATTORNEY: What is your name and occupation?

DETECTVE COSTELLO: Daniel Costello. I am a sergeant of detectives—all detectives are sergeants—and I work for the police force of this city.

ASSISTANT DISTRICT ATTORNEY: How long have you been in this occupation and rank?

DETECTIVE COSTELLO: Ten years in the police department, 4 years in the rank.

ASSISTANT DISTRICT ATTORNEY: About 2 years ago, I understand you were assigned to this new unit, the Organized Crime Suppression Squad, and that within a few days of working in your new job you visited a high official of your police force. Do you recall this event?

DETECTIVE COSTELLO: Yes, I do.

ASSISTANT DISTRICT ATTORNEY: When was it and who was involved?

DETECTIVE COSTELLO: It was just after St. Patrick's Day, March 18th, of this year. It was about ten in the morning, and the person involved was Captain Richard Jones of the Police Academy.

ASSISTANT DISTRICT ATTORNEY: Tell us in your own words what happened on this occasion.

DETECTIVE COSTELLO: I knew Captain Jones from the Academy— he was my instructor. He was a lieutenant, and I was a recruit. I told him I thought the OCSS, the whole group, was infiltrated or penetrated by the mob, the hoodlums, and drug pushers. He listened— I talked. His advice was to take it up with higher authorities in the department. He made a phone call arranging a meeting for me, and I thanked him, and left the office.

ASSISTANT DISTRICT ATTORNEY: What happened next in direct relation to this talk?

DETECTIVE COSTELLO: I met a captain from the Internal Security Division that night, at a few minutes after ten, in the parking lot of the golf course—the city one.

ASSISTANT DISTRICT ATTORNEY: Would you please identify this man and tell us, again in your own words, what happened at this meeting.

DETECTIVE COSTELLO: His name is Captain John Behan. He works directly under the chief. He came over to my car, and I told him substantially what I had told Captain Jones. He told me that I had no specific evidence that he could use, but that if I was willing to work with him, I could get the evidence. Captain Behan gave me his home phone number, and told me to call him. He said we would meet again where we were, in the golf course parking lot. That was for when I had something to tell him. We shook hands and split.

ASSISTANT DISTRICT ATTORNEY: Did you meet the captain again in this golf course parking lot? That is, Captain Behan?

DETECTIVE COSTELLO: Yes, I did. All told, I met with him about seven or eight times.

ASSISTANT DISTRICT ATTORNEY: At any of these meetings did Captain Behan spell out in any way what your job was in this new arrangement with him?

DETECTIVE COSTELLO: Yes, he did. Thoroughly. I was to work undercover, for him and the chief. I was to act as if nothing was out of order, and to come up with some specific evidence of what I had said about dishonesty.

ASSISTANT DISTRICT ATTORNEY: In this new role, did you know the defendant?

DETECTIVE COSTELLO: Yes, he was one of my associates, another detective sergeant—a member of OCSS.

ASSISTANT DISTRICT ATTORNEY: During this time of your association with the defendant, did you at any time participate with the defendant in any event which led you to make a report about him to Captain Behan?

DETECTIVE COSTELLO: Yes, and it was on the Monday after I first met Captain Behan. That would be March 21st of this year.

ASSISTANT DISTRICT ATTORNEY: Tell us, in your own words, what happened at this time—on this occasion.

DETECTIVE COSTELLO: I met the defendant, Bob, in the Nitro Bar and Grill on Seventh and Main Streets. It was about 11:00 a.m. He had a hoodlum with him that I knew as Big

Bart, Bart Nino, and he introduced us. Nino took some money from his pocket right away and handed some bills to me. I said, "What's that for?" Nino said, "Get yourself a hat." I said, "I don't wear a hat," and gave him back the money.

ASSISTANT DISTRICT ATTORNEY: Do you know the amount of money?

DETECTIVE COSTELLO: No, I don't. Several bills, folded up. No, I do not.

ASSISTANT DISTRICT ATTORNEY: What happened next?

DETECTIVE COSTELLO: Nino shrugged his shoulders and gave the money to Bob, the defendant. Then, Nino talked a little bit about nothing much, ball games and girls, and he left. I asked Bob, "What's he buying?" He said, "Not much." Then I said something like, "Why me?" He said, "Why not, you don't use money?" Then he told me that Nino wanted to get some records taken out of our squad files about his brother—his younger brother. Bob said the kid was trying to go legit, and our records were bugging him in getting a job. I heard him out, then left and went back to the office.

ASSISTANT DISTRICT ATTORNEY: Did you do anything in relation to this conversation?

DETECTIVE COSTELLO: Yes, I did. I went to our files. Everyone went out to lunch. I got young Nino's file folder out, looked at it, found he was wanted for suspicion of receiving stolen property and for suspicion of homicide in another case. I Xeroxed the file papers, and I put the Xerox copies in my desk drawer—which I locked—put the record file back in our filing cabinet, and then I went out to lunch myself.

ASSISTANT DISTRICT ATTORNEY: Now, at any future date, did you have anything to do with this record again?

DETECTIVE COSTELLO: Yes. It was the following Saturday—that's March 26th, this year. I went into the office early, went to our files, and looked for young Nino's record. I took it out and examined it, and I found that the photo had been changed. Big Bart's photo was substituted for his brother's picture, and the wanted cards were missing.

ASSISTANT DISTRICT ATTORNEY: I show you folder marked "Nino, Alberto," and I ask you, do you recognize it?

DETECTIVE COSTELLO: (Reading) Yes, it's the fixed-up, tampered-with folder.

ASSISTANT DISTRICT ATTORNEY: In relation to this Xerox copy of the original folder in your squad files about this young Nino—what happened to that?

DETECTIVE COSTELLO: I have that here (showing file folder) with me now.

ASSISTANT DISTRICT ATTORNEY: Your Honor, can I have both these files marked for identification? Thank you. Your witness (to Defense Counsel), Counselor. (Defense Counsel stands and begins cross-examination.)

DEFENSE COUNSEL: Are most of your fellow police officers honest?

DETECTIVE COSTELLO: Yes. Most of them are honest—and hard working.

DEFENSE COUNSEL: How many officers, in your knowledge, entered the police department for the purpose of becoming dishonest?

DETECTIVE COSTELLO: None, to my knowledge—not to my knowledge.

DEFENSE COUNSEL: I gather from your prompt answers that you know a great deal about your fellow police officers; is that true?

DETECTIVE COSTELLO: Well—I guess I do. They're my co-workers. Why not?

DEFENSE COUNSEL: Now—Tell the court if any conduct of yours has bothered or upset your fellow co-workers.

DETECTIVE COSTELLO: I don't—I don't understand the question.

DEFENSE COUNSEL: It's a simple question, but let me withdraw it, and phrase it in this fashion: To your knowledge has any of your conduct upset your fellow police officers?

DETECTIVE COSTELLO: Oh sure! That's a different thing. Sure, yes.

DEFENSE COUNSEL: Tell us of such an incident that you consider important.

DETECTIVE COSTELLO: Well—When I was transferred out of uniform, from patrol to the OCSS in plainclothes, I grew a beard (puts hands to face, indicating beard) and wore some clothes; well, the kind of clothes I only used to wear on my day off, kind of sharp, I suppose. The guys in the squad used to tell me, "What a disguise!"

DEFENSE COUNSEL: And that upset you, bothered you—emotionally disturbed you?

DETECTIVE COSTELLO: Well, I don't know all that. You asked the question. Say it bugged me a bit.

DEFENSE COUNSEL: Why? Why would this remark bother you—this "Quite a disguise"?

DETECTIVE COSTELLO: It wasn't any makeup, really a disguise. It was just the clothes I liked. That's why it bothered me.

DEFENSE COUNSEL: Oh, I'm beginning to understand. Now— Tell me this: In relation to the charges of dishonesty against my client, your fellow police officer, did you ever get any feedback from him about yourself as a person, or as a police officer?

DETECTIVE COSTELLO: Yes, a few times, mostly about—or along the lines of—something like: "Why don't you go along with the guys?" or "Why do you have to be different?"

DEFENSE COUNSEL: This was in relation to your manner of dress, your appearance?

DETECTIVE COSTELLO: No, it wasn't. It was in relation to the money he was making, and that I didn't want to take—like from Nino.

DEFENSE COUNSEL: Your Honor, would you direct the witness just to answer the question?

JUDGE: No, I don't think I will. You asked the question, and it was open ended. Let it stand along with its answer.

DEFENSE COUNSEL: Thank you, Your Honor.

DEFENSE COUNSEL: Did the defendant or any of your co-workers in this Organized Crime Squad ever actually do anything to indicate any dislike for you?

DETECTIVE COSTELLO: They— They sure did. All of them did. They stopped talking to me. Except when they had to, like a phone call for me, then it was a "Here, you—" Real brief. And they would stop talking to one another when I came in the room, or walked up to them on the street.

DEFENSE COUNSEL: This animosity resulted from your dirty work, the role of informer, or spying on your fellow workers?

DETECTIVE COSTELLO: No, Counselor. At that time, no one knew of what you term "dirty work." All they knew was that I wouldn't do any business with the hoodlums—that I wanted to do my job just like I get paid for it.

DEFENSE COUNSEL: There is entrapment in your role, is there not?

ASSISTANT DISTRICT ATTORNEY: Your Honor, I object. The question—

JUDGE: (Interrupting) Sustained.

DEFENSE COUNSEL: (Resuming questioning) Since you place such a premium on doing what you get paid for, did you ever counsel or advise my client to do the same thing?

DETECTIVE COSTELLO: You sure you want to hear this?

DEFENSE COUNSEL: I asked the question.

DETECTIVE COSTELLO: Just before I left the Nitro Bar on the day we met Big Bart Nino, I said to Bob, the defendant: "My God, you're making good money as a police detective. You could never make this kind of money on the outside doing any other kind of work. You know you have a family, kids. Don't be stupid. Think about it." That was how it ended.

DEFENSE COUNSEL: Was there any response to these words of yours—any words said at all by my client?

DETECTIVE COSTELLO: No, not much. Something like, "If I really did think about it, I'd blow my brains out."

Source: Paul B. Weston, *Criminal Justice and Law Enforcement: Cases* (Upper Saddle River, NJ: Prentice Hall, 1972), 83–88. Reprinted by permission of Prentice Hall.

DISCUSSION QUESTIONS

1. Can stage fright be controlled? How?
2. Why are investigator-witnesses advised not to argue with a cross-examiner?
3. Define *nonverbal communication*.
4. What body movements indicate boredom, impatience, anxiety?
5. Do you believe eye contact between an investigator-witness and jurors in a criminal trial is important? Why?
6. Sum up the recommended behavior for investigator-witnesses following their appearance on the witness stand.
7. Do the facts of the case study justify a conclusion that police dishonesty is an inescapable part of the "system"?
8. Is the "thing of value" in this attempt to corrupt Detective Costello the money that would be given to him or the approval of his associates?
9. If you were a member of the jury in this case, would you consider Detective Costello to be a credible witness and his testimony truthful?

LIBRARY ASSIGNMENT

Review available material and prepare a short bibliography on police corruption and criminal behavior.

WORKBOOK PROJECT

Prepare an outline of major body movements. List what you believe is the likely message transmitted to jurors when a witness makes each movement during his or her testimony.

RELATED WEB SITES

The U.S. Department of Justice, Civil Rights Division, Special Litigation Section seeks court orders to address systemic cases of police misconduct. To review the types of complaints addressed by this agency, consult its Web site at *www.usdoj.gov/crt/split/police.htm.*

The FBI's Civil Rights Division is responsible for investigating citizens' allegations of police misconduct, known as "color of law" violations. Its Web site can be accessed at *www.fbi.gov/hq/cid/civilrights/color.htm.*

NOTES

1. JOHN J. BURKE, "Testifying in Court," *FBI Law Enforcement Bulletin* 44, no. 9 (1975): 8–13.
2. JOHN F. WILSON and CARROLL C. ARNOLD, *Dimensions of Public Communication* (Boston: Allyn & Bacon, 1976), 34–36.
3. RUDOLF FLESCH, *The Art of Plain Talk* (New York: Harper & Brothers, 1946), 31–56.
4. LORETTA A. MALANDRO and LARRY BARKER, *Nonverbal Communication* (Reading, MA: Addison-Wesley, 1983), 4–28.
5. WILLIAM GELLER, ed., *Local Government Police Management* (Washington, DC: International City Management Association, 1991), 239.
6. JAMES LARDNER and THOMAS REPPETTO, *NYPD: A City and Its Police* (New York: Holt, 2000), 276–77.
7. KEVIN GILMARTIN and JOHN HARRIS, "The Continuum of Compromise," *Police Chief*, January 1998, 25–28.

CASE BRIEFS

A. SEARCH AND SEIZURE

FOURTH AMENDMENT OF U.S. CONSTITUTION

Mapp v. Ohio, 367 U.S. 643 (1961)

Facts: Miss Dolly Mapp was convicted of possession of lewd and lascivious books, pictures, and photographs. At her trial, evidence seized during a forcible search of her home without a warrant was admitted into evidence and was the primary evidence leading to her conviction.

Issue: Can evidence seized during an illegal search be admitted as evidence to convict a defendant?

Decision: No evidence seized illegally may be admitted as evidence in any case. It must be excluded as evidence in any state or federal court. The exclusionary sanction is to deter the police from unlawful acts and to preserve the integrity of the court.

Katz v. United States, 389 U.S. 347 (1967)

Facts: In a U.S. district court, Charles Katz was convicted of transmitting wagering information by telephone. At his trial, the prosecution was permitted to introduce evidence of Katz's portion of telephone conversations, despite defense counsel's objection. Federal Bureau of Investigation (FBI) agents had attached an electronic eavesdropping and recording device to the outside of the public telephone booth Katz used.

Issue: Was the evidence obtained through a legal surveillance (electronic eavesdropping)?

Decision: Admitting such evidence was a reversible error, in view of the lack of prior judicial authorization (search warrant).

Dalia v. United States, 441 U.S. 238 (1979)

Facts: Pursuant to Title III of the Omnibus Crime Control and Safe Streets Act of 1968, the federal district court found probable cause and authorized the government to intercept all oral conversations taking place in the suspect's business office. Even though the court order did not specifically authorize entry of the suspect's business office by government agents, FBI agents did secretly enter the business office at midnight and install an electronic bug.

Issue: Was the secret entry of the specified office a violation of the Fourth Amendment or the federal statute?

Decision: Secret entry to install an electronic device pursuant to a lawful search warrant is not a violation of the U.S. Constitution or the statute.

Terry v. Ohio, 392 U.S. 1 (1968)

Facts: A revolver was introduced as evidence at the trial of John W. Terry for carrying a concealed weapon unlawfully (after failure of a pretrial motion to suppress). A police officer had observed unusual conduct by Terry and two other men, and—concluding that they were contemplating a robbery—he stopped and frisked them, discovering the weapon carried by Terry and seizing it.

Issue: Is the police stop-and-frisk procedure constitutional?

Decision: The police stop-and-frisk procedure does not violate the Fourth Amendment rights of Terry (under the circumstances of the case), and the revolver seized from Terry was property admissible at his trial for carrying a concealed weapon unlawfully.

Chimel v. California, 395 U.S. 752 (1969)

Facts: Police officers armed with an arrest warrant but not a search warrant were admitted to Chimel's home by his wife in his absence. The officers awaited Chimel's arrival and then arrested him when he entered his home. Chimel refused to consent to the officers' search of his home (to "look around"). Despite this refusal, officers searched the entire home on a claim that the lawful arrest justified the search. Chimel was convicted on burglary charges, and items taken from his home during the police search were admitted into evidence despite counsel's objection on constitutional grounds.

Issue: What is the scope of a search incidental to a lawful arrest?

Decision: Under the circumstances of this case, the scope of the police search was unreasonable under the Fourth and Fourteenth Amendments.

Gustafson v. Florida, 414 U.S. 260 (1973)

Facts: James F. Gustafson was convicted for unlawful possession of marijuana. The state introduced into evidence several marijuana cigarettes found in a box in his coat pocket when a municipal police officer conducted a full body search of Gustafson after a lawful arrest for driving an automobile without having his driver's license in his possession.

Issue: Was the scope of this search connected with a lawful traffic arrest reasonable?

Decision: The scope of the search was reasonable under the Fourth and Fourteenth Amendments of the Constitution.

Rochin v. California, 342 U.S. 165 (1952)

Facts: Having "some information" that Rochin was selling narcotics, officers went to his home and found the defendant in bed. On the nightstand were some capsules and when the officers asked what they were, Rochin put them in his mouth and swallowed them. He was taken to the hospital, where his stomach was pumped against his will. Two capsules were recovered that contained morphine, and he was convicted of possession of narcotics.

Issue: Was the scope of this search—stomach pumping—unreasonable?

Decision: The court found that this search was unreasonable because it runs counter to the decencies of civilized conduct and, as such, shocks the conscience of the court and society.

B.   INTERROGATION

Payne v. Arkansas, 356 U.S. 560 (1958)

Facts: The suspect confessed to murder, was convicted by this and other evidence of murder in the first degree, and was sentenced to death. Undisputed evidence in this case showed that Payne, a mentally dull 19-year-old youth, (a) was arrested without a warrant; (b) was denied a hearing before a magistrate, at which he would have been advised of his right to remain silent and of his right to counsel, as required by Arkansas statutes; (c) was not advised of his right to remain silent or of his right to counsel; (d) was held incommunicado for 3 days, without counsel, adviser, or friend, during which time his family members tried to see him but were turned away and he was refused permission to make even one telephone call; (e) was denied food for long periods; and, finally, (f) was told by the chief of police "that there would be 30 or 40 people there in a few minutes that wanted to get him."

Issue: Did the acts and statements of the police deprive the suspect of due process of law?

Decision: The use in a state criminal trial of a defendant's confession obtained by coercion—whether physical or mental—is forbidden by the Fourteenth Amendment.

Lego v. Toomey, 404 U.S. 477 (1972)

Facts: The suspect was arrested and made a confession to the police. Evidence on the issue of voluntariness (coercion) of the confession was conflicting. The trial court admitted the confession into evidence.

Issue: What is the burden of proof necessary to admit a confession into evidence? Who determines the admissibility of the confession?

Decision: "By a preponderance of the evidence" is a constitutionally permissible burden of proof. Admissibility of evidence is a determination for the court, not the jury.

Miranda v. Arizona, 384 U.S. 436 (1966)

Facts: Ernesto A. Miranda was arrested by police for kidnapping and rape and taken to an interrogation room in a police building. In response to police questioning, Miranda signed a confession containing a typed paragraph stating that the confession was made voluntarily with full knowledge of his legal rights and with the understanding that any statement he made therein might be used against him. This confession was admitted into evidence at his trial on kidnapping and rape charges, and Miranda was convicted as charged.

Issue: Were Miranda's constitutional rights to counsel and against self-incrimination violated?

Decision: In the absence of an intelligent waiver of the constitutional rights involved, confessions and other statements obtained by custodial police interrogation are inadmissible as evidence, when the suspect (as Miranda) was not informed of his right to counsel, or of his right to be silent, or of the possible use of his statements as evidence against him.

C.   RIGHT TO AN ATTORNEY

Gideon v. Wainwright, 372 U.S. 335 (1963)

Facts: The defendant was charged and convicted of the felony of breaking and entering a poolroom with the intent to commit a misdemeanor. The trial court denied the defendant's request for an appointed attorney pursuant to Florida law, which allowed appointed attorneys for indigent defendants in capital cases only. The defendant proceeded to trial and was convicted without an attorney to represent him.

Issue: Does the Constitution require the appointment of an attorney for indigent defendants accused of crime?

Decision: The Sixth Amendment requires appointment of counsel, unless waived, for indigents accused of crime. The provision is obligatory on the states by the Fourteenth Amendment.

United States v. Wade, 388 U.S. 218 (1967)

Facts: Several weeks after Wade's indictment for robbery of a federally insured bank and for conspiracy, he was, without notice to his appointed counsel, placed in a lineup in which each person wore strips of tape on his face, as the robber had allegedly done, and on direction, repeated words like those the robber had allegedly used. Two bank employees identified Wade as the robber. At the trial, when asked if the robber was in the courtroom, they identified Wade. The prior lineup identifications were elicited on cross-examination. Urging that the conduct of the lineup violated his Fifth Amendment privilege against self-incrimination and his Sixth Amendment right to counsel, Wade filed a motion for a judgment of acquittal or, alternatively, for a ruling to strike the courtroom identifications. The trial court denied the motions and Wade was convicted.

Issue: Are courtroom identifications of an accused at trial to be excluded from evidence because the accused was exhibited to the witnesses before trial at a postindictment lineup conducted for identification purposes without notice to and in the absence of the accused's appointed counsel?

Decision: In-court identification by a witness to whom the accused was exhibited before trial in the absence of counsel must be excluded, unless proof can be shown that such evidence had an independent origin or that error in its admission was harmless beyond a reasonable doubt.

Appendix B

Federally Controlled Substances Law*

TITLE 21, USC *SECTION 812*

Controlled substances are placed into any one of five schedules as follows:

Schedule I

A. The drug has a high potential for abuse.
B. The drug has no currently accepted medical use in treatment in the United States.
C. There is a lack of accepted safety for use of the drug under medical supervision.

Schedule I Controlled Substances

Heroin
Lysergic acid diethylamide (LSD)
Marijuana
Mescaline
Peyote
Psilocybin

Schedule II

A. The drug has a high potential for abuse.
B. The drug has a currently accepted medical use in treatment in the United States or a currently accepted medical use with severe restrictions.
C. Abuse of the drug may lead to severe psychological or physical dependence.

---

*This appendix was edited. For a full understanding of the law on this topic, see Title 21 of the *United States Code*, Sections 812–844. See *http://uscode.house.gov/* to search for specific sections.

Schedule II Controlled Substances

Cocaine
Opium
Fentanyl
Methadone
Injectable methamphetamine

Schedule III

A. The drug has a potential for abuse less than that for the drugs in Schedules I and II.
B. The drug has a currently accepted medical use in treatment in the United States.
C. Abuse of the drug may lead to moderate or low physical dependence or high psychological dependence.

Schedule III Controlled Substances

Amphetamine
Methamphetamine (not injectable)
Barbituric acid
Phencyclidine (PCP)
Codeine
Anabolic steroids

Schedule IV

A. The drug has a low potential for abuse relative to that of the drugs in Schedule III.
B. The drug has a currently accepted medical use in treatment in the United States.
C. Abuse of the drug may lead to limited physical dependence or psychological dependence relative to the drugs in Schedule III.

Schedule IV Controlled Substances

Barbital
Chloral hydrate

Schedule V

Any compound, mixture, or preparation containing limited quantities of narcotic drugs, such as the following:

Codeine
Dihydrocodeine
Ethylmorphine
Opium

TITLE 21, USC   *SECTION 841.*   *PROHIBITED ACTS*

It shall be unlawful for any person knowingly or intentionally to manufacture, distribute, or dispense, or possess 1 kilogram or more of heroin; 5 kilograms or more of cocaine; 100 grams or more of phencyclidine (PCP); 10 grams or more of lysergic acid diethylamide (LSD); 1,000 kilograms or more of marijuana, or 1,000 marijuana plants; 50 grams or more of methamphetamine or cocaine base (crack cocaine). Such person shall be sentenced to a term of imprisonment which may not be less than 10 years or more than life and if death or serious bodily injury results from the use of such substances shall be not less than 20 years or more than life, a fine not to exceed $4,000,000 if the defendant is an individual or $10,000,000 if the defendant is other than an individual.

After a prior conviction for a felony drug offense, such person shall be sentenced to a term of imprisonment which may not be less than 20 years and not more than life imprisonment and if death or serious bodily injury results from the use of such substances shall be sentenced to life imprisonment, a fine not to exceed $8,000,000 if the defendant is an individual or $20,000,000 if the defendant is other than an individual, or both.

TITLE 21, USC   *SECTION 844.*   *PENALTIES FOR SIMPLE POSSESSION*

It shall be unlawful for any person knowingly or intentionally to possess a controlled substance unless such substance was obtained directly, or pursuant to, a valid prescription or order, from a practitioner, while acting in the course of his or her professional practice. Any person who violates this subsection may be sentenced to a term of imprisonment of not more than 1 year, and shall be fined a minimum of $1,000, or both. A person with a prior conviction shall be imprisoned for not less than 15 days but not more than 2 years, and shall be fined a minimum of $2,500. After two prior convictions, the person shall be imprisoned for not less than 90 days but not more than 3 years, and shall be fined a minimum of $5,000. Notwithstanding the preceding sentence, a person convicted under this subsection for the possession of a mixture or substance which contains cocaine base shall be imprisoned not less than 5 years and not more than 20 years, and fined a minimum of $1,000.

IDENTITY THEFT: WHAT TO DO
IF IT HAPPENS TO YOU

Unfortunately, victims of identity theft are burdened with resolving the problem. Acting quickly and assertively is imperative if you are to minimize the damage.

When dealing with authorities and financial institutions, keep a log of all conversations, including dates, names, and telephone numbers. Note the amount of time spent and any expenses incurred. Confirm conversations in writing. Send correspondence by certified mail (return receipt requested). Keep copies of all letters and documents.

WHAT TO DO*

Once you discover you are a victim of identity theft, you should do the following:

1. ***Credit Bureaus.*** Immediately call the fraud departments of the three major credit-reporting companies—Experian (formerly TRW), Equifax, and Trans Union. Report the theft of your credit cards or numbers. Ask that your account be flagged. Also, add a victim's statement of as many as 100 words to your report. (*Example*: "My ID has been used to apply for credit fraudulently. Contact me to verify all applications.") Be sure to ask how long the fraud alert will be posted on your account, and how you can extend it if necessary. Be aware that these measures may not entirely stop new fraudulent accounts from being opened by the impostor. Ask the credit bureaus, in writing, to provide you with free copies every few months so that you can monitor your credit reports.

    Ask the credit bureaus for names and phone numbers of credit grantors with whom fraudulent accounts have been opened. Ask the credit bureaus to remove inquiries that have been generated as a result of the fraudulent access. You may also ask the credit bureaus to notify people

---

*Adapted from State of California, Department of Justice, Office of the Attorney General, *Tips for Victims* (Sacramento: State of California, Department of Justice, Office of the Attorney General, n.d.): *http://caag.state.ca.us/idtheft/tips.htm*.

who have received your credit report in the last 6 months to alert them to the disputed and erroneous information (2 years for employers).

2. ***Creditors.***   Immediately contact by phone and in writing all creditors with whom your name has been used fraudulently. Get replacement cards with new account numbers for your accounts that have been used fraudulently. Ask that old accounts be processed as "account closed at consumer's request." (This type of account closing is better than "card lost or stolen" because when this statement is reported to credit bureaus, you can be blamed for the loss.) Carefully monitor your mail and credit card bills for evidence of new fraudulent activity. Report it immediately to credit grantors.

    Creditors' requirements to verify fraud. You may be asked by banks and credit grantors to fill out and notarize fraud affidavits. Doing so could become costly. The law does not require that a notarized affidavit be provided to creditors. A written statement and supporting documentation should be sufficient (unless the creditor offers to pay for the notary).

3. ***Stolen Checks.***   If you have had checks stolen or bank accounts set up fraudulently, report this fact to the check-verification companies. Put "stop payments" on any outstanding checks about which you are unsure. Cancel your checking and savings accounts and obtain new account numbers. Give the bank a secret password for your account (not your mother's maiden name).

4. ***ATM Cards.***   If your ATM card has been stolen or compromised, get a new card, account number, and personal identification number (PIN). Do not use your old password. When creating a password, don't use common numbers like the last four digits of your Social Security number or your birth date.

5. ***Fraudulent Change of Address.***   Notify the local postal inspector if you suspect an identity thief has filed a change of your address with the post office or has used the mail to commit check or bank fraud. (Call the local postmaster to obtain the phone number.) Find out where the fraudulent credit cards were sent, and request the local postmaster for that address to forward all mail in your name to your own address. You may also need to talk with the mail carrier.

6. ***Social Security Number Misuse.***   Call the Social Security Administration (SSA) to report fraudulent use of your Social Security number. As a last resort, you might want to change your number. The SSA will change it only if you fit their fraud victim criteria. Also order a copy of your Earnings and Benefits Statement and check it for accuracy.

7. ***Passports.***   If you have a passport, notify the passport office, in writing, to be on the lookout for anyone ordering a new passport fraudulently.

8. ***Phone Service.***   If your long distance calling card has been stolen or you discover fraudulent charges on your bill, cancel the account and open a new one. Provide a password that must be used any time the account is changed.

9. ***Driver's License Number Misuse.***   You may need to change your driver's license number if someone is using yours as identification on bad checks. Call the Department of Motor Vehicles (DMV) to determine whether

another license was issued in your name. Put a fraud alert on your license. Go to your local DMV to request a new number. Also, fill out a DMV complaint form to begin the fraud investigation process. Send supporting documents with the complaint form to the nearest DMV investigation office.

10. ***Law Enforcement.***   Report the crime to the law enforcement agency within your jurisdiction in your case. Give them as much documented evidence as possible. Get a copy of the police report. Keep your fraud investigator's phone number handy and give it to creditors and others who require verification of your case. Credit card companies and banks may require you to show the report to verify the crime. Some police departments have been known to refuse to write reports on such crimes. Be persistent.

11. ***False Civil and Criminal Judgments.***   Sometimes victims of identity theft are wrongfully accused of crimes committed by the impostor. If a civil judgment has been entered in your name for actions taken by your impostor, contact the court where the judgment was entered and report that you are a victim of identity theft. If you are wrongfully prosecuted for criminal charges, contact the State Department of Justice and the Federal Bureau of Investigation (FBI). Ask how to clear your name.

12. ***Legal Help.***   You may want to consult an attorney to determine legal action to take against creditors or credit bureaus if they are not cooperative in removing fraudulent entries from your credit report or if negligence is a factor. Call the local bar association to find an attorney who specializes in consumer law and the Fair Credit Reporting Act.

13. ***Emotional Stress.***   Psychological counseling may help you deal with the stress and anxiety victims commonly experience. Know that you are not alone.

Glossary

Accomplice-witness. Person liable to prosecution for the same offense charged against the defendant or defendants in a pending trial. Earns leniency in return for his or her cooperation with the prosecution.

Accusatory pleading. The indictment or information.

Active information. Information that establishes a group of suspects.

Advance-fee frauds. An advance fee is required upfront from a business-person having problems securing a loan from local lending institutions. Swindler absconds with advance fee.

Aggravated arson. Any arson in which explosives are used and people are present or placed in danger at the site.

Aggravated assault. Assault with a deadly weapon or in which serious injury is inflicted with or without a weapon.

Aggravated rape. Rape in which rapist is armed with a dangerous weapon, kidnaps the victim, inflicts bodily injury, or is in a position of trust with regard to the victim.

a.k.a., Aka, A.K.A., AKA. Means "also known as"; alias; nickname; street name.

Algor mortis. The cooling of a body after death.

Alibi. Claim of being elsewhere at the time of the crime.

Alleles. Person-to-person differences within a particular segment of a DNA sequence.

All points bulletin (APB). Alarm issued, when adequate descriptive information is available, to a large area that may extend to neighboring states.

Altercation. Verbal dispute.

Amateur burglars. Persons who commit burglary primarily to obtain money for drugs.

Amber Alert system. Nationwide system that disseminates information to the general public about suspected kidnappers and sexual predators and their vehicles, by means of highway signs, television spots, and radio broadcasts. Named after Amber Hagerman, a 9-year-old girl whose abduction and murder inspired a similar alert system in Texas.

Ambush robbery. Least planned type of robbery, based on the element of surprise.

Analgesic. Pain killer.

Analysis. The conversion of information into intelligence.

Angel dust. See *PCP.*

Anger killing. Extension of the crime of assault, in which a dispute occurs, anger develops, and the victim is attacked—with or without weapons—and fatally injured.

Anger rapist. Someone who commits the crime of rape as a means of expressing and discharging feelings of pent-up anger and rage.

Apprehensive driver. Hit-and-run driver who is apprehensive and panic driven because he or she is driving while under the influence, is operating without a license, has no insurance, has a companion in the car who is not his or her mate or is someone else's mate, is driving a stolen car, has stolen goods in the car, has left the scene of another accident, has fled a crime scene, or is wanted for another crime.

Arson. The burning of property with a malicious intent.

Assault. Unlawful attempt, coupled with the current ability, to commit an injury to the person of another. An attempt to commit a battery.

Audio surveillance. Observation through listening. Wiretapping and electronic eavesdropping are the primary forms.

Autolysis. Chemical breakdown of the body that results in softening and liquefaction of body tissue after death.

Autonomic nervous system. System that governs respiration, heartbeat, and perspiration.

Auto theft. Form of larceny involving the theft of passenger cars, trucks, and motorcycles.

Backup person. A member of a robbery gang who remains in the background unnoticed and, in case of trouble, supports the gang members who are committing the robbery.

Bacterial action. After death, when bacteria produce gases that cause the body to swell and produce an unpleasant odor.

Badger game. Male and female crime partners operate a three-act extortion scam: (1) the victim (sucker) is placed in a compromising position; (2) the offender discovers the situation, claims to be the female's husband or lover, and screams and threatens, demanding money; (3) the offender goes to the bank with the victim to get cash.

Bait and switch. Consumer fraud in which advertised merchandise bargains lure customers into a business where sales personnel bad-mouth the advertised merchandise and convince the customer to buy a higher-priced item of allegedly better quality.

Ballistics. The study and identification of firearms, bullets, cartridges, and shotgun shells.

Bank examiner fraud. Ego-building swindle based on people's hidden desire to serve as a secret agent for the police.

Bankruptcy frauds. When swindlers conceal or divert the major assets of a business to friends or associates so that the assets cannot be sold to pay off creditors, or when swindlers use established credit to buy huge amounts of merchandise and then conceal or convert the merchandise to their own use just prior to bankruptcy proceedings without paying the suppliers' bills.

Base pair. Two of four nucleic acids combined to make a "rung" of the "twisted ladder" of the DNA molecule.

Basic-lead informant. Informant through which one or more basic leads can be developed.

Battered child syndrome. Physical and psychological trauma exhibited by children who have undergone physical abuse.

Battery. An unlawful beating or other wrongful physical harm inflicted on a human being without his or her consent.

Benefit. Basic investigative lead about who might gain by committing the crime in question.

"Better him than me." The philosophy adopted by a crime partner who agrees to testify for the prosecution in return for a reduced charge or a reduced sentence.

Blasting. The use of explosives to open a safe during a burglary.

"Blind date" bombings. Acts of violence against random victims.

Broadcast alarm. Order to be on the lookout for a suspect, a vehicle, or stolen property, usually transmitted first by radio to the local unit and then, if appropriate, by Teletype, fax, or computer to adjacent jurisdictions to alert them to the recent crime.

Bugging. Secret wiring of a suspect's home, office, or car with an electronic eavesdropping device, or "bug."

Bumper beeper. Electronic tracking device hidden on the underside of a suspect vehicle; monitored by a receiver in the police surveillance car. Allows pursuit without fear of discovery.

Burglarizing. The behavior of committing at least one and most likely more burglaries.

Burglary. Entering a structure to commit a theft or a felony therein.

Burning. In a burglary, when the safe is attacked with an oxygen-acetylene torch, and a section of the safe is burned out to allow entry.

Canvass. Systematic inquiry for witnesses in view, shopping, and neighborhood areas.

Cardiograph. Instrument that records changes in pulse rate and blood pressure. Component of a polygraph.

Career criminals. Offenders who have previous arrests, have one or two cases pending in local courts, and are on the street on some form of conditional release at the time if their latest arrest.

Carjacking. When a vehicle is taken or an attempt is made to take a vehicle from a driver by force or fear.

Carnival bunco. Street bunco in which each victim may be swindled of only small amounts of money, but the overall profit is huge. Games at a carnival in which customers have no chance of winning big.

Carrying away. In a burglary, when the burglar removes the safe to a more convenient location to open it.

Celebrity stalker. Person who engages in stalking a victim whom he or she knows on an impersonal level (e.g., actor, sports star).

Chain of possession. Written document accounting for an item of evidence from the time it came into an agency's possession to the time it was presented in court.

Charity switch. Variation of the pigeon drop in which a pitch is made to the victim's compassion.

Chicken hawks. Pedophiles or child molesters who are commonly older men seeking out young boys as sexual partners.

Child abuse. The intentional and deliberate assault on a child in which serious bodily injury is inflicted by a parent, a foster parent, a babysitter, a day-care worker, or a person in a nonparental relationship.

Chromatography. Laboratory method of separating compounds to identify the components.

Circumstantial evidence. Evidence from which an inference may be drawn.

Clue-in. Public plea technique in which a local television station telecasts clues about an unsolved and recent crime so that listeners can call the station if they have information on the crime or the criminals involved. Objective is to locate witnesses.

Clustered crime scene. Crime scene in which most of the activities occur at one location: the confrontation, the attack, the assault, and sexual activity.

CODIS (Combined DNA Index System). National database of DNA data obtained from individuals convicted of sexual assaults or homicides.

Cognitive interviewing. Investigative technique used to enhance a witness's ability to recall events.

Collation. The orderly arrangement, cross-indexing, and filing of evaluated information so that meaningful relationships can be developed between apparently unconnected bits and pieces of information.

Comfort-oriented serial killer. Type of "hedonistic" serial killer. Kills for personal gain. An example is professional assassins.

Community threat group. Organization engaging in hate crimes and their advocacy (e.g., Ku Klux Klan, skinheads, Aryan Nation).

Composite sketch. Drawing of a suspect developed from a victim's or a witness's description or a description given by several witnesses.

Computer criminals. Mercenaries of cyberspace who engage in fraud, sabotage, and theft.

Computer vandals. Persons who are motivated by revenge to destroy databases and wreak havoc by shutting down another person's system or the entire Internet.

Computer virus. Malicious code that replicates and inserts copies or versions of itself into other programs.

Confidence (con) games. Frauds, rip-offs, or scams based on the promise of a high profit in a "sure thing."

Contact burns. Burns caused by flames or hot, solid objects. Examples are cigarette and iron burns.

Contact surveillance. Certain tracer preparations are used to stain an object likely to come in contact with a suspect or suspects. Such staining transfers to the person and becomes visible on the person's hands, or his or her clothes, usually under exposure to fluorescent light.

Contaminated fingerprints. Prints observable by the naked eye, such as bloody fingerprints.

Continual theft. Ongoing, constant acts of theft by an employee.

Corpus delicti. Body, or essential elements, of a crime.

Corruption. Misuse of police authority for personal gain.

Covert collection. When information is obtained from sources such as undercover police agents and confidential informants, or from various types of surveillance of unaware targets.

Covert informants. Men and women who report information to a police investigator about a terrorist or another criminal organization from a position of trust and confidence within the group.

Crack. A smokable form of cocaine.

Crackers. Computer hackers who are interested in exploring another person's system only for the challenge.

Crank. See *Methamphetamine*.

Credit card fraud. The use of another person's credit card or cards to purchase various goods and services. Often the stolen cards are sold on the black market.

Crime laboratory. Facility equipped for the scientific examination of evidentiary material submitted by police evidence gatherers, staffed by qualified forensic scientists or criminalists; can provide reports explaining what was discovered in the lab, by whom, relevancy to the issue of guilt or innocence, and whether the examiner is qualified as an expert witness in court in the scientific area of the examination.

Crime scene area diagram. Sketch pinpointing the location of shoe prints, tire tracks, weapons, and similar evidence linked to the crime scene but lying beyond the crime scene.

Criminal agency. A person's unlawful act or omission. The means of the crime.

Criminal agent. Person responsible for the crime.

Criminal homicide. Murder in the first degree, second-degree murder, and manslaughter.

Criminal investigation information center (CIIC). Division within a police agency that can assist investigators in clearing assigned cases.

Criminalistics. The profession and scientific discipline directed toward recognizing, identifying, individualizing, and evaluating physical evidence by applying the natural sciences in matters of law and science. Also referred to as *forensic science*.

Criminalists. Laboratory technicians in a forensic science lab.

Cross-examination. Questioning of the witness by the party who did not call the witness.

Cruising robberies. Robberies committed in above-average residential areas and secluded hotel rooms. Unplanned robberies.

Cryptography. When ciphers and codes (cloak and dagger) are used to protect underworld communications; also decoding such cryptograms.

Cult. An organization, a group, or a sect (not a gang) bound together by a charismatic leader and his or her "spin" on one or more segments of the Bible or areas of religious worship; often accused of child abuse, unorthodox lifestyles, misuse of funds, use of undue influence in recruiting members, and use of mind-bending techniques to retain them.

Cybercrime. Crime in which a computer was either the target of the crime or the means of committing the crime.

Date rape. When the female of a couple (date or acquaintance) is forced to have sexual intercourse by the male.

Date rape drug. Rohypnol. Also called *roofies*.

Deliberate immersion burn. In child abuse cases, when the child has been intentionally held in place in a tub or another container of hot liquid. Depth of burn is uniform. Wound borders are distinct, sharply defined "waterlines" with little tapering of depth at the edges.

Direct evidence. Witness testimony about what he or she saw or heard.

Direct examination. The first questioning of a witness at a trial by the party calling the witness.

Discovery. Before the trial, a request by the defense counsel for the prosecutor to disclose the police case against the defendant. Aids in ensuring a fair trial.

Dismantlers. Auto thieves who steal a car, tow or drive it to a "chop shop," and cut it up for most of its parts.

Disorganized offenders. Killers who are inadequate, experience intense sadistic sexual fantasies, and suddenly act out these fantasies on a victim of opportunity. Usually are of below-average intelligence, are loners, and do not own a vehicle but have access to one. Use "blitz" style of attack, catching victim off guard. Crime scene is disorganized and clustered.

DNA (deoxyribonucleic acid). Genetic code analyzed and identified in crime labs through the study of blood samples and samples of other body fluids. In a growing number of cases, the accuracy, reliability, and validity of such analysis are established by in-court testimony of DNA experts. The primary carrier of genetic information in living organisms.

Domestic stalker. Person who engages in stalking an ex-lover or ex-spouse, using violence to get even.

Drilling. In a burglary, a means of entry involving drilling holes in the door of the safe to expose the lock mechanism.

Drugs, narcotics. See *Narcotics* and Appendix B.

Dust. See *PCP*.

Embezzlement. The conversion of another person's property over which the thief has custody or control.

Emotional offender. Person experiencing feelings of remorse and mental anguish as a result of committing the offense.

Entrapment. A crime or wrongful act induced by the investigator that otherwise would not have occurred.

Ethical awareness. Alertness to behavior that is wrong, immoral, unprincipled, substandard, and criminal.

Euphoria. A feeling of well-being and tranquility.

Evaluation. Screening out useless, incorrect, irrelevant, and unreliable information.

Ever-narrowing circle. A search of the crime scene that starts at the outskirts and works toward its focal point.

Ever-widening circle. A search of the crime scene that starts at its focal point and works outward by circling in a clockwise or counterclockwise direction until the fringes of the protected area are reached.

Exhumation. Court-ordered removal of a deceased person's body from its burial place for a medicolegal examination.

Exothermic reaction. The rapid increase in temperature, followed by a sharp decrease in temperature, of the compounds and elements deposited on a person's hands when he or she fires a weapon, the result of which is a unique spheroidal formation not generally observed in the natural environment.

Exterior ballistics. Study of projectiles in flight.

Factual analysis approach. Best approach to use with a nonemotional offender. Technique in which an attempt is made to persuade the suspect that his or her guilt is established and the intelligent choice is to tell the truth. Appeals to suspect's common sense and reasoning rather than to his or her emotions.

Felony murder. Death that results from injuries inflicted by someone in the act of committing a felony.

Fence. Professional receiver of stolen property.

Field contact reports. Reports of suspicious occurrences not amounting to crimes.

Field notes. Memoranda recorded by the investigator during an investigation, starting upon assignment to the case and continuing until the case is closed.

Firebugs. See *Pyromaniacs*.

Fire sets. Ignition devices used to start fires.

Fixed visual surveillance. Observation of a suspect through windows, doors, roofs, or other fixed locations, usually within a building or vehicle. A stakeout, or plant.

Flaked. When illicit drugs are planted on the suspect by the informant or the arresting officer.

Flashover. A rapid development of a fire that occurs when the volume of active fire becomes a significant portion of the room volume. At this time, all the previously uninvolved combustibles in the room suddenly ignite.

"Flipped." Confronted with evidence of his or her guilt, a suspect agrees to become an accomplice-witness in return for a reduced charge or a lesser sentence.

Floating base. Reference point that may be moved or cannot be located with accuracy. Any distance measurement with a floating base should be avoided.

Forensic science. See *Criminalistics*.

Forensic science laboratory. The crime lab in which physical evidence obtained by police during an investigation is examined.

Forensic scientists. Laboratory technicians in a forensic science lab.

Foul play. When the circumstances of a suspicious death indicate some criminal agency.

Fraud. Nonviolent crime involving elements of intentional deceit, concealment, corruption, misrepresentation, and abuse of trust to gain another person's property. Often facilitated by willing but unaware victims.

Fraud auditing. In the commercial and industrial world, detecting and preventing frauds in commercial transactions.

Galvanic skin response (GSR). Least reliable method of detecting deception. Measured by the resistance of the skin to the passage of a small electric current.

Galvanograph. Instrument that records the electrodermal response (skin electrical resistance changes) of a person. Component of a polygraph.

Gamma-ray spectrometer. Apparatus used to measure the distinctive radioactive gamma-ray emissions and thereby to identify the elements from which the rays originate.

Genome. The full complement of an individual's DNA. Does not vary from cell to cell.

Getaway driver. A driver specialist who remains in the escape vehicle until the robbers have completed the robbery, then picks them up and flees the scene.

Global positioning system (GPS). Device that electronically signals the location of automobiles or other objects to which it is affixed.

Grid search. A search of an outdoor area that starts with a strip search and covers the same area in a similar manner but at right angles to the strip search pattern.

Gunshot residue (GSR) examination. Application of adhesive tapes to a person's hands, then removal of the tapes, which are then sent to the crime lab, where they are examined with a scanning electron microscope for the presence of compounds and elements deposited on a person's hands when he or she fires a weapon.

Habeas corpus. Usually habeas corpus ad subjiciendum, a writ for inquiring into the lawfulness of a person's imprisonment.

Hackers. Intruders who enter into another person's computer system without authorization.

Hallucinogens. Psychedelic, or "mind-expanding," drugs that cause sensory distortions and result in illusions and delusions.

Hate crimes. Vandalism and violent crimes motivated by apparent hate of the victim's religion, race, ethnic heritage, or sexual orientation. May be linked to the offender's membership in a community threat group.

"Hedonistic" serial killer. Murderer who has made a connection between personal violence and sexual gratification. Torture, mutilation, and other fear-instilling activities may be committed by this type of killer. Lust or thrill killers and comfort-oriented serial murderers are examples of this type of killer.

Hit stalker. Professional killer.

Home-improvement frauds. False claims that home-improvement work is necessary or that the cost of proposed work is much less than its real worth and will add to the homeowner's basic investment.

Home invasion (robbery). Vicious and violent robbery of a family in its home. Pistol-whipping and threats to kill force the victims into disclosing their hiding place for cash and jewelry.

Household larceny. The theft or attempted theft of property or cash from a residence or the immediate vicinity of the residence. The thief must have a legal right to be in the house (e.g., guest or maid).

Hubba. See *Crack*.

"Human fly" burglar. Burglar who can progress upward or downward on the sides of a building to a selected point of entry.

Hypnosis. A state resembling normal sleep.

Hypnotist. Person who has studied the science or art of inducing hypnosis.

Identification. The determination of some set to which an object or a substance belongs, or the determination as to whether an object or a substance belongs to a given set.

Identikit system. Means of developing a composite sketch by identifying single portions of a suspect's face from several hundred plastic slides showing one small portion of a human face.

Identity thief. Impostor who uses another person's identity to apply for and receive credit cards under the assumed name. The credit cards are then used to purchase merchandise and services.

Immediate control. Doctrine that indicates the area in which a search is justified (e.g., if the arrest is made on the street when the suspect is walking, his or her person and the immediate public area may be searched, whereas if the arrest occurs in a parked vehicle, the vehicle may be searched).

Impressions. Markings made by a person or an object in a material softer than the item of evidence making the impressions (e.g., tire tracks or footprints left in snow or soft dirt).

Imprints. Markings on a surface left by protruding parts of a person or vehicle (e.g., bloody handprints, tire tread marks).

Incest. Crime committed by a person who has sexual intercourse with a person known to be his or her parent or child, brother or sister, uncle or aunt, or nephew or niece.

Incidental theft. When employees use the employer's product while on the job or take items such as office supplies home at the end of the day.

Insurance frauds. Frauds in which the swindler is the insured person and the victim is the insurer.

Intelligence. The information about crime and criminals not normally available to investigators through overt sources that is secretly or clandestinely collected and evaluated.

Interior ballistics. Study of the functioning of firearms through the firing cycle.

Interpretation. Development of a hypothesis and a tentative statement about the meaning of the information involved.

Interrogation. The adversarial questioning of a suspect with the goal of soliciting an admission or a confession of guilt.

Interview. Person-to-person conversation engaged in to obtain information about a crime or its circumstances.

Investigative phase. "Cold" portion of the crime-solving process.

Jimmy. Pry bar.

Johns. Men who solicit females for prostitution.

Jury nullification. Jury verdict apparently influenced by mistrust of police witnesses or testimony.

Kiting. See *Ponzi scheme*.

Kneecapping. Technique developed by the Irish Republican Army to maim an informer's knees (by gunshot) rather than to kill him or her.

Knowledge. Basic investigative lead about the identification of the person who had the knowledge, skill, or capacity to commit the crime in question.

Known identity. When the perpetrator is known and has been named by the victim or witnesses.

Known standard of evidence. Evidence collected from a known source.

Land-sales frauds. Misrepresentations about the value and future development of worthless, unimproved land.

Larceny. The unlawful taking or stealing of property or articles without the use of force or violence, including shoplifting, pocket picking, purse snatching without strong-arm tactics, thefts of and from vehicles, and property or cash taken from a home.

Latent fingerprints. Fingerprints that must be developed or dusted because they cannot be seen by the naked eye.

Lateral snitching. Informing on only drug sellers who are on an equal or a lower level than the snitch in the drug-marketing pyramid.

Linkages. Relationships formed between persons engaged in criminal activity.

Link analysis. Tool used in proactive investigation that visually shows the relationships among a number of people and organizations.

Lividity. Postmortem irreversible process in which blood settles to the lowest part of the body.

Locard's exchange principle. The idea that suspects will bring items of trace evidence into the crime scene and will take items with them when they leave (e.g., hairs, fibers, dirt, blood, dust, skin cells, body fluids, dust).

Logic bombs. Computer programs within programs that perform destructive acts on the basis of a trigger event.

Lookouts. Persons who inform drug dealers about any police presence.

Love-scorned stalker. Person who intends violence against a known victim who has rejected the stalker in some way.

Lust stalker. Person who stalks a victim with the intent of engaging in predatory sex that escalates to murder.

Lust or thrill killer. Type of "hedonistic" serial killer. Kills because he or she derives pleasure from the act: it is an eroticized experience.

Malice. An offender's inexcusable, unjustified, unmitigated, person-endangering state of mind.

Manslaughter. Any criminal homicide that cannot be legally classified as murder.

Marijuana. Leaves and flowering tops of *Cannabis sativa* or *C. indica*, which are dried and usually smoked. Most popular illegal drug in the United States and usually the most available and least expensive.

Mass murder. Homicide of four or more victims during a single event at one location.

Match (matching). Most favorable term in a crime lab report of a comparison analysis of evidence submitted by police investigators.

Meth. See *Methamphetamine*.

Methamphetamine. An illegal drug that is sold in powdered form that is injected, snorted or smoked by the user. Usually made in clandestine labs in the U.S. and Mexico. Also known as *crank, meth, speed, or the poor man's cocaine*.

Mind control. Use of undue influence and unethical means to recruit and retain members in a cult.

Misconduct. Police conduct involving issues such as the excessive use of force, violation of a suspect's constitutional rights, and various other misdeeds.

Misrepresentation. Failing to provide the facts about product performance, warranties, credit charges, or other hidden costs.

"Mission" serial killer. Murderer who feels a need to eradicate a certain group of people (e.g., prostitutes, racial members). Not psychotic.

Modus operandi. Choice of a particular crime to commit and selection of a method for committing it.

Moles. In international espionage cases, covert informants that often remain "buried" for years before being activated.

Moving visual surveillance. Observation of a suspect by following him or her on foot, in a vehicle, or by both walking and riding. A tail, or shadow.

Mug shots. Photographs of suspects taken at the time of a previous arrest.

Multicide. Killing of a number of victims by one or more persons working in concert. Examples are mass murder, spree murder, and serial murder.

Munchausen syndrome. Psychological disorder in which the patient fabricates the symptoms of a disease or an injury in order to undergo medical tests, hospitalization, or even medical or surgical treatment.

Munchausen syndrome by proxy. Psychological disorder in which a parent or caretaker suffering from Munchausen syndrome attempts to bring medical attention to him- or herself by injuring or inducing illness in his or her children.

Murder in the first degree. Is the unlawful and intentional killing of a human being by another person with premeditation.

Murder for profit. Elimination of another person because the murderer would gain some benefit.

Murder-suicide. Pattern of criminal homicide in which the killer self-destructs shortly after the fatal assault on the victim and takes his or her own life.

Mushroom factor. When the diligent investigation of a child molester leads to exposure of a network of these offenders.

Narcotics. Drugs that depress the central nervous system and lead quickly to psychological and physical dependence. See also *Drugs, narcotics.*

National Integrated Ballistic Information Network (NIBIN). National computer database containing ballistic images for comparison with gun evidence found at crime scenes to solve open firearms cases. Maintained by the Bureau of Alcohol, Tobacco, Firearms and Explosives (ATF).

Neighborhood canvass. Method of contacting people in the area of a crime scene to locate potential witnesses.

Neutron activation analysis (NAA). Laboratory technique used to detect the presence of antimony and barium, common gunshot residues, on a subject's hands.

Nonemotional offender. Person who does not ordinarily experience a troubled conscience as a result of committing a crime.

Omission. Failure to act when such action is required by law.

Opportunity. Basic investigative lead that places the suspect at the crime scene at or around the time of its occurrence.

Organized offenders. Killers who have above-average intelligence, are methodical and cunning, own a car in good condition, travel many more miles than the average person, are socially adept, and commit the crimes out of their area of residence or place of work. They engage in fantasy and ritual and use verbal skills to manipulate and gain control over a selected victim. They plan the crimes carefully and often take "souvenirs" from their victims as reminders. Victims are usually strangers who share some traits.

Overhauling. The examination and search by firefighters for hidden flames or sparks that might rekindle the fire.

Overt collection. When information is obtained from public sources or from nonintelligence police personnel.

Participant informant. The go-between who identifies the drug seller and introduces the undercover agent as a potential buyer.

Participant monitoring. Consensual electronic surveillance.

Passive headspace concentration method. Way of separating flammable and combustible liquid residues from fire debris when a low concentration of ignitable liquid residues is in the sample. An adsorbent material such as activated charcoal is used to extract the residue from the static headspace above the sample, then the adsorbent is eluted with a solvent.

Passive information. Data useful when a group of suspects is developed in a crime investigation.

Payoff. Swindle in which the swindler claims to have access to information about fixed horse races.

PCP. Phencyclidine: angel dust or dust.

Pedigree. Complete information about a person.

Pedophile. Someone who "loves" children.

Pedophilia. Sexual perversion in which children are the preferred sexual object.

Peeling. In a burglary, a means of entry involving prying off the outer surface of the safe door so that the locking mechanism is exposed and can be pried open.

Perception management. Attempting to influence a target of deception by verbal and nonverbal behavior designed to demonstrate the implausibility of a person's involvement in a crime. Examples include yawning to indicate boredom with the police interview, stretching out to indicate ease, and making manipulative statements.

Personal larceny. The theft or attempted theft of property or cash by stealth, either with contact but not force or threat of force, or without direct contact between the victim and the offender.

Personal larceny with contact. The theft or attempted theft of property or cash directly from the victim by stealth, but with no force or threat of force.

Physical assaults. Attacks on the person that produce death or serious bodily injury.

Physical evidence. Liquid to solid material amenable to scientific analysis by forensic science technicians in a crime lab.

Pigeon. Victim.

Pigeon drop. Street bunco that requires a minimum number of props and in which the victim is conned into withdrawing a large sum of money from a bank account to show financial responsibility to the con artist, who then absconds with the money.

Pimps. Men living off the proceeds of one or more prostitutes.

Planned-operation robbery. Carefully structured robbery in which the robbery group examines all aspects of the situation and plans for all foreseeable contingencies.

Plant. In arson, the fire-boosting material used to spread the fire.

Plastic fingerprints. Prints left in soft material such as tar or tacky paint.

Pneumograph. Instrument that records respiration (breathing rate and depth). Component of a polygraph.

Pocketbook drop. See *Pigeon drop*.

Point-to-point movement. A search that follows a chain of objects that are obviously evidence.

Political stalker. Person who engages in stalking a victim who is a stranger but who has a known political or religious view.

Polymerase chain reaction (PCR) analysis. Extraction of DNA from a small evidence sample, then repeated replication to obtain a sufficient quantity of DNA to locate alleles.

Ponzi scheme. A con in which the swindler uses money invested by new victims to pay high interest on the investments of earlier victims whose money the swindler has appropriated for his or her personal use.

Poor man's cocaine. See *Methamphetamine*.

Postmortem. Means "after death."

Pot. See *Marijuana*.

"Power and control" serial killer. Murderer who experiences sexual gratification from complete domination of the victim. Sociopath.

Power rapist. Rapist who uses sex as a means of compensating for underlying feelings of inadequacy and of expressing mastery, strength, authority, and control over another person.

Preferential child molester. Person who prefers children to adults as providers of sexual satisfaction.

Preliminary investigative report. Report containing data obtained at the crime scene during the initial investigation.

Proactive investigation. Technique that moves into attack mode long before an arrest is made. Begins with "quiet" investigation, then moves into "hustle" mode.

Professional burglars. Persons who work at burglary as a trade, making their living by burglary and larceny alone and having no other means of income.

Projectionist driver. Hit-and-run driver who tries the case in his or her mind and finds the other driver at fault, refuses to be a party to the accident, and drives off as the offended person.

Proof marks. Emblems or symbols that indicate tests performed to prove the chamber strength of a firearm by actually firing it with maximum loads.

Property crimes. Burglary, theft, and fraud committed for the perpetrator's personal gain.

Psychological incest. Sexual activity between a child and a stepparent, foster parent, or live-in boyfriend of the child's mother. Includes nonrelated family members such as stepbrothers and stepuncles.

Pulling. In a burglary, a means of entry in which a device similar to a gear or wheel puller is used to pull the dial or spindle completely out of the safe door.

Punching. In a burglary, a means of entry in which a sledgehammer and a drift punch are used to knock the combination dial from the safe and drive the spindle back into the safe to make the release mechanism of the lock accessible.

Putrefaction. Decomposition of a body after death, as a result of autolysis and bacterial action.

Pyromania. Obsessive impulse to start fires. A "pyro" is a firebug, or a pyromaniac.

Pyromaniacs. Pathological fire setters. Irrationally motivated.

Questioned document. Document that is an important item of evidence (e.g., check, suicide note, charred paper).

Raid. Entering a building to seize illicit drugs and arrest one or more drug dealers and associates.

Random killing. The killing of a complete stranger. Considered an unmotivated killing because the motive is obscure or unknown until the suspect is discovered.

Ransom. Money or other consideration paid or demanded for a kidnapped victim's release.

Rape. Having sexual intercourse with a woman by force and without her consent. Sexual assault of a man is not usually considered rape, but crimes of sodomy, forcible oral copulation, or both.

Rape trauma syndrome. State of shock a victim may be in after a rape.

Rapport. Harmonious relationship with another person.

Rapport building. Bonding process between the witness and the interviewer.

Rap sheet. The report of a records search indicating arrests and imprisonments of a person with a criminal record.

Reasonable care. Care fairly and properly taken in response to the circumstances of a situation. Such care as an ordinary, prudent person would take in the same time frame, under the same conditions, and when performing the same act or acts.

Repair fraud. Overcharging for services performed; charging for services not performed or parts not replaced; failing to provide labor and materials as agreed; or charging for labor or materials not needed, not discussed with the customer, or not within the scope of the customer's agreement.

Retinal hemorrhage. Bleeding in back of the eyeballs. A classic medical symptom of shaken baby syndrome.

Retroactive interference. Also known as reverse transference. When a witness discusses the crime or overhears other individuals talking about the crime and unconsciously incorporates some of this information as his or hers or alters recollection to fit with those of the other witnesses.

Revenge or jealousy killing. Murder of a person who was involved with the suspect, who became jealous or vengeful and killed the victim.

Reversal transposition. Cipher in which the digits of a number, most commonly a telephone number, are used in reverse order (e.g., 445-1769 becomes 967-1544).

Rigor mortis. Stiffening of the body muscles after death. Factor in determining the time of death in criminal homicides.

Ripping. In a burglary, a means of entry involving battering the top, bottom, or sides of a safe with a chisel or another metal cutter.

Robbery. Taking personal property away from a person or the presence of a possessor against the possessor's will by using force or fear.

Rock. See *Crack*.

Roofies. See *Date rape drug*.

Runaway. Any unemancipated young person under the legal adult age who, without a parent's or guardian's permission, remains away from his or her home for 24 hours or more.

Runners. Persons who transport small quantities of drugs from the dealer's stash to wherever the drugs are being sold.

Sadistic rapist. Rapist who finds the intentional maltreatment of his victim intensely gratifying and takes pleasure in her torment, anguish, distress, helplessness, and suffering.

Salami fraud. Technique of taking small "slices" to deceptively acquire the whole "salami."

Santa Ana winds. Wind condition in Southern California in which the strong airflow is associated with low humidity and quickly dries out forest fuels. When such winds are blowing and a fire is started, it can spread quickly and violently in any direction.

Scam. See *Con (confidence) games*.

Search warrant. Judicial authorization to enter a specified place to gather evidence or arrest a suspect.

Second-degree murder. Any murder that is not first-degree murder.

Securities frauds. High-income victims are falsely promised rapid capital growth, high and quick rates of return on dividends, or special advantages such as tax shelters.

Sedatives. Similar to narcotics but the dependence develops more slowly.

Selective-raid robbery. Minimally planned robbery that involves some "casing" of the robbery scene.

Serial killers. Killers who commit serial murder. May make special efforts to elude detection.

Serial murder. Two or more separate murders when an individual, acting alone or with another, commits multiple homicides during a period of time, with time breaks between each murder.

Serious bodily injury. Battery or physical abuse of a person. A standard that excludes police intervention in cases involving only minor assaults that could be described as corporal punishment incidental to disciplining a child. Injury involving a substantial risk of death, extreme physical pain, obvious disfigurement, or loss of impairment of the function of a body member, an organ, or a mental faculty.

Set theory. Theory that all objects can be divided and subdivided into various sets on the basis of their properties.

Sex and sadism murder. Murder that may follow child molestation, acts of perversion, or sadistic acts. Marked by unusual violence and often bizarre overtones.

Sexual tourism. In cases of child pornography or exploitation, travel for the purpose of engaging in sexual behavior for commercial gain or personal gratification.

Shaken baby syndrome. Injuries caused by a violent, sustained shaking action in which the infant's head is violently whipped forward and backward so that it hits the chest and shoulders. Primarily occurs in children 18 months old or younger because at that age the neck lacks muscle control and the head is heavier than the rest of the body.

Shills. Decoys.

Shopping area canvass. Canvass encompassing the geographic area in which witnesses (not the perpetrator) travel to and from the crime scene.

Short tandem repeat (STR). Short sequence of DNA, normally two to five base pairs long, that is repeated a different number of times in different people.

Shrinkage. Loss of inventory from employee theft.

Signature. So-called trademark that is part of the modus operandi of a crime and distinguishes it as the work of a specific criminal or group of criminals who have committed previous crimes in which the same identifying circumstances occurred.

Single-officer search. Associates of an officer assist in locating evidence but do not disturb or collect it. Objective is to limit the number of officers in possession of crime scene evidence to only one officer searching the scene.

Single-teller bank robbery. Person armed with a note and some threat of force victimizes only one teller. Often unplanned.

Situational child molester. Person who does not have a true sexual interest in children but will experiment with them when the opportunity arises. Will do likewise with other vulnerable persons such as those who are elderly or mentally impaired.

Situational theft. When an employee is presented with an opportunity for theft, which, in the employee's mind, must be acted on.

Sleepers. Terrorists who live normal lives for years and are activated only for a specific operation.

Sneak operator. Hit-and-run driver who crushes a fender and smashes grillwork as daily occupational activities, chalking up the action as the calculated risk of all vehicle owners who put their vehicles on the roadway.

Snitching. In the criminal world, the social felony of revealing other people's secrets.

Soporific agents. Drugs that induce drowsiness, lethargy, and sleep.

Spectrum. Unique and characteristic pattern of wavelengths.

Speed. See *Methamphetamine*.

Split combination. Cipher in which groups of digits of a number, often a telephone number, are scrambled (e.g., 445-1769 becomes 176-4459 or 769-4451).

Spontaneous "play" groups. Persons who live in or frequent the same neighborhood, who purchase drugs from the same source, or who have served sentences in juvenile or adult institutions together.

Spree murder. Killing of three or more persons within a relatively short time frame. Victims are often randomly selected.

Stakeout (plant). See *Fixed visual surveillance*.

Stalking. Aggressive and threatening pursuit of a victim selected because of his or her celebrity status, a past relationship, or some irrational motive. Initial harassing letters and telephone calls escalate to threats and demands and then to serious injury or even a fatal attack.

Stash. Hiding place of a drug seller's inventory of drugs. Generally, hiding place of cash, weapons, or stolen property.

"Stepover" burglar. Burglar who is an aerialist, stepping from a fire escape, a balcony, or another building to a nearby window.

Stimulants. Speed up the signals passing through the central nervous system. These drugs inhibit fatigue, stimulate physical and mental activity, and produce euphoria and a sense of well being. These drugs are highly psychologically addictive.

Sting. Police-operated "fencing" operation to trap thieves as they sell their stolen property to undercover police. The thieves are videotaped and identified for future arrest at completion of the operation. Also modified and used to trap graft-taking public officials and others.

Storefront technique. See *Sting*.

Strippers. Auto thieves who usually attack a parked car, taking a variety of parts and accessories that can be readily disposed of on the local black market.

Strip search. A search of an outdoor area that is plotted like a football field. Search starts at a sideline and moves across the field to the other sideline. Searchers work back and forth across the field until the entire area is searched.

Stroll. When a prostitute performs the sex act in the client's car.

Substitution cipher. A cipher in which a symbol, letter, or digit stands for another symbol, letter, or digit.

Sudden infant death syndrome (SIDS). Not a positive finding; rather, a diagnosis made when no other medical explanation exists for the abrupt death of an apparently healthy infant.

Surveillance. Observation of people and places by investigators to develop investigative leads.

Suspicious death. Case in which the circumstances of the death indicate violence or foul play; when death occurs in a place other than the deceased's residence; or when the deceased was not under a physician's care at the time of death.

Synchrony. When the tone of each party in an interview mirrors that of the other's with time. Synchrony should occur between what is being said and the events of the moment.

Taggants. Coded microparticles added to explosives during manufacture. These particles survive detonation, can be recovered at the bombing scene, and can be decoded by the crime laboratory to indicate where and when the explosives were made.

Tail (shadow). See *Moving visual surveillance*.

"Target blue" ambush slayings. Killings of police officers by terrorist groups. Victims killed not because of who they are, but because of what they represent. The attention getter is the willingness of the terrorist group to kill the armed representatives of law and order.

THC. Delta-9-tetrahydrocannabinal; psychoactive agent in marijuana.

Tongs. Asian criminal organizations.

Tout. In a payoff swindle, the swindler, who gives tips or solicits bets on a racehorse.

Trace metal detection technique (TMDT). Process by which the "signature" patterns of handguns, tools, and other metal objects are made visible on the suspect's skin or clothing when it is treated with a test solution and examined under ultraviolet light.

Trailers. Objects used by arsonists to spread fires from a point of ignition to other parts of a room or a building. May be nothing more than a rope or ropelike string, toilet paper, newspaper, or rags soaked in a fire accelerant.

Transposition ciphers. Ciphers characterized by a change in the order of the enciphered material.

Trap. Built-in hiding place for drugs, usually constructed by a skilled carpenter.

Triangle killing. When a romance involves a person other than a married person's spouse, the married person may decide to rid him- or herself of the spouse.

Trojan horses. Malicious stand-alone computer programs disguised as other programs that innocent users pass to one another in the form of e-mail attachments.

Tweaker. Chronic user of methamphetamine.

Ultrasonic cavitation. Etching method for restoring obliterated serial numbers on firearms and other metal objects.

Unknown identity. All cases other than those of known identity.

Unwilling witness. Witness who usually disappears from the crime scene because he or she dislikes authority, has an outstanding warrant, is a crime suspect, or does not want to get involved.

Venue. Territorial jurisdiction in which a crime happened.

Vice. Immoral conduct such as gambling and prostitution.

View area. In an attempt to locate witnesses to a crime investigators contact potential witnesses not only at the crime scene but include those areas of entry or flight from the crime scene as well.

Violent injury. Application of physical force, even if such force entails no pain or bodily harm and leaves no marks on the victim.

"Visionary" serial killer. Murderer compelled to kill by voices he or she hears or visions he or she sees. Psychotic.

Visual surveillance. Keeping a watch on a particular suspect, vehicle, or place.

Voiceprinting. Graphic identification of voices.

Wanted notice. Printed version of a pickup order that follows a short time after the initial broadcast alarm. Contains information about the crime and possible suspect and any additional information. Provides probable cause for a stop-and-arrest.

Willing witness. Witness who may wait at the crime scene until police arrive or contact police with information. Motivation is a sense of civic duty, a way to eliminate competition, or revenge.

Window of death. Time frame during which death is likely to have occurred. Determined through a process of discerning the time the body was found, then working backward by interviewing witnesses who talked with the deceased prior to the fatal assault and by examining the activities in which the victim was engaged prior to death.

Working off a beef. Process in which an arrestee makes a deal with the arresting officers and prosecutor to exchange information and cooperation in an investigation for leniency in drafting the indictment or at the time of sentencing.

Worms. Malicious computer codes that duplicate—stealing system resources—until the user's system shuts down.

X-ray crystallography. Laboratory process used for the identification of any crystalline solid or compound from which a crystalline-solid derivative can be made.

Zone or sector search. When the crime scene is divided into segments and each zone or sector is searched as a unit.

SELECTED BIBLIOGRAPHY

ABRAHAMS, PETER. *The Fan*. New York: McGraw-Hill, 1990.

ADLER, MORTIMORE J. *Desires: Right and Wrong—The Ethics of Enough*. New York: Macmillan, 1991.

ALLEN, BUD, and DIANA BOSTA. *Games Criminals Play—How You Can Profit by Knowing Them*. Sacramento, CA: Rae John, 1981.

BATTLE, BRENDON P., and PAUL B. WESTON. *Arson Detection and Investigation*. New York: Arco, 1979.

BING, LEON. *Do or Die*. New York: Harper Perennial (HarperCollins), 1993.

BIONDI, RAY, and WALT HECOX. *All His Fathers Sins*. New York: Pocket Books, 1988.

BOLOGNA, G. JACK, and ROBERT J. LINDQUIST. *Fraud Auditing and Forensic Accounting— New Tools and Techniques*. New York: Wiley, 1987.

BUBRO, JAMES. *Mob Rule—Inside the Canadian Mafia*. Toronto: Macmillan, 1985.

CAREY, MARY, and GEORGE SHERMAN. *Compendium of Bunk, or How to Spot a Con Artist: A Handbook for Fraud Investigators, Bankers and Other Custodians of the Public Trust*. Springfield, IL: Charles C Thomas, 1976.

CLARKE, MICHAEL. *Business Crime: Its Nature and Control*. New York: St. Martin's Press, 1990.

CONWAY, JAMES P. *Evidential Documents*. Springfield, IL: Charles C Thomas, 1959.

COOK, CLAUDE W. *A Practical Guide to the Basics of Physical Evidence*. Springfield, IL: Charles C Thomas, 1984.

COUNT, E. W. *Cop Talk—True Detective Stories from the NYPD*. New York: Pocket Books, 1994.

CUOMO, GEORGE. *A Couple of Cops—On the Street, in the Crime Lab*. New York: Random House, 1995.

DALY, ROBERT. *Prince of the City—The True Story of a Cop Who Knew Too Much*. Boston: Houghton Mifflin, 1978.

DELATTRE, EDWIN J. *Character and Cops: Ethics in Policing*. Washington, DC: American Enterprise Institute for Public Policy Research, 1989.

DILNOT, GEORGE. *Great Detectives and Their Methods*. Boston: Houghton Mifflin, 1928.

ECK, JOHN E. *Solving Crime—The Investigation of Burglary and Robbery*. Washington, DC: U.S. Department of Justice, National Institute of Justice, 1983.

ESTRICK, SUSAN. *Real Rape*. Cambridge, MA: Harvard University Press, 1987.

FARR, ROBERT. *The Electronic Criminals*. New York: McGraw-Hill, 1975.

FISHER, BARRY. *Techniques of Crime Scene Investigation*. New York: CRC Press, 2000.

GARBARINO, JAMES, EDNA GUTTMAN, and JANIS WILSON-SEELEY. *The Psychologically Battered Child—Strategies for Identification, Assessment, and Intervention*. San Francisco: Jossey-Bass, 1986.

GEBERTH, VERNON J. *Practical Homicide Investigation: Tactics, Procedures, and Forensic Techniques*. New York: CRC Press, 1996.

GODDARD, DONALD. *Undercover—The Secret Lives of a Federal Agent*. New York: New York Times Books, 1988.

GRAYSMITH, ROBERT. *The Sleeping Lady—The Trailside Murders Above the Golden Gate Bridge*. New York: Onyx (Penguin Books), 1990.

GREEN, GARY S. *Occupational Crime*. Chicago: Nelson-Hall, 1990.

GROSS, HANS G. A. *Criminal Investigation*. Translated by John Adam and J. Collyer Adam. 5th ed., revised by R. L. Jackson. London: Sweet & Maxwell, 1962.

GROTH, A. NICHOLAS, *Men Who Rape: The Psychology of the Offender*. New York: Plenum Press, 1979.

HAMMER, RICHARD. *The CBS Murders*. New York: Morrow, 1987.

HAZELWOOD, ROBERT R., and ANN WOLBERT BURGESS. *Practical Aspects of Rape Investigation—A Multidisciplinary Approach*. New York: Elsevier Science, 1987.

HIBBARD, WHITNEY S., and RAYMOND W. WORRING. *Forensic Hypnosis in Criminal Investigations*. Springfield, IL: Charles C Thomas, 1987.

HICKEY, ERIC W. *Serial Murderers and Their Victims*. Pacific Grove, CA: Brooks/Cole, 1991.

HOLMES, RONALD M., and STEPHEN T. HOLMES. *Profiling Violent Crimes*. 2nd ed. Thousand Oaks, CA: Sage, 1996.

KESSLER, WILLIAM F., and PAUL B. WESTON. *The Detection of Murder*. New York: Arco, 1961.

KIRK, PAUL. *Fire Investigation*. New York: Wiley, 1969.

LAQUEUR, WALTER. *The Age of Terrorism*. Boston: Little, Brown, 1987.

LARSEN, RICHARD W. *Bundy—The Deliberate Stranger*. Upper Saddle River, NJ: Prentice Hall, 1980.

LARSON, ERIK. *Lethal Passage*. New York: Viking Books, 1995.

LEVIN, JACK, and JACK MCDEVITT. *Hate Crimes—The Rising Tide of Bigotry and Bloodshed*. New York: Plenum Press, 1993.

LEVINE, MICHAEL. *Deep Cover—The Inside Story of How DEA Infighting, Incompetence, and Subterfuge Lost Us the Biggest Battle of the Drug War*. New York: Delacorte Press, 1990.

LOFTUS, ELIZABETH, and KATHERINE KETCHAM. *Witness for the Defense—The Accused, the Eyewitness, and the Expert Who Puts Memory on Trial*. New York: St. Martin's Press, 1991.

MAAS, PETER. *Serpico*. New York: Viking Press, 1973.

MANNING, PETER K. *The Narcs' Game—Organizational and Informational Limits on Drug Law Enforcement*. Cambridge, MA: MIT Press, 1980.

MAURER, DAVID W. *Language of the Underworld*. Lexington: University Press of Kentucky, 1981.
———. *The American Confidence Man*. Springfield, IL: Charles C Thomas, 1974.

MCALARY, MIKE. *Buddy Boys—When Good Cops Turn Bad*. New York: Putnam, 1987.

MCCARTHY, BILL, and MIKE MALLOWE. *Vice Cop—My Twenty-Year Battle with New York's Dark Side*. New York: Morrow, 1991.

MCDONALD, PETER. *Tire Imprint Evidence*. New York: Elsevier, 1989.

MCGINNISS, JOE. *Cruel Doubts*. New York: Pocket Star Books (Simon & Schuster), 1991.

MILLER, LARRY. *Human Evidence in Criminal Justice*. Cincinnati, OH: Anderson, 1983.

MILLS, JAMES. *The Underground Empire—Where Crime and Government Embrace*. New York: Doubleday, 1986.

MOORE, MARK HARRISON. *Buy and Bust*. Lexington, MA: Heath, 1977.

MURPHY, HARRY J. *Where's What: Sources of Information for Federal Investigators*. Washington, DC: Brookings Institution, 1975.

NEFF, JAMES. *Mobbed Up—Jackie Presser's High-Wire Life in the Teamsters, the Mafia, and the FBI*. New York: Dell, 1989.

O'BRIEN, DARCY. *Two of a Kind—The Hillside Stranglers*. New York: New American Library, 1985.

O'CONNOR, JOHN J. *Practical Fire and Arson Investigation*. New York: Elsevier, 1987.

PALMIOTTO, MICHAEL J., ed. *Critical Issues in Criminal Investigation*. Cincinnati, OH: Anderson, 1988.

PARKER, DONN B. *Fighting Computer Crime*. New York: Wiley, 1998.

PERRY, NANCY, and LAWRENCE WRIGHTSMAN. *The Child Witness: Legal Issues and Dilemmas*. Newbury Park, CA: Sage, 1991.

POLAND, JAMES M. *Understanding Terrorism—Groups, Strategies, and Responses*. Upper Saddle River, NJ: Prentice Hall, 1988.

POLLOCK-BYRNE, JOCELYN. *Ethics in Crime and Justice—Dilemmas and Decisions*. Pacific Grove, CA: Brooks/Cole, 1988.

RENGERT, GEORGE, and JOHN WASILCHICK. *Suburban Burglary—A Time and Place for Everything*. Springfield, IL: Charles C Thomas, 1985.

ROBBINS, LOUISE M. *Footprints—Collection, Analysis, and Interpretation*. Springfield, IL: Charles C Thomas, 1985.

SAFERSTEIN, RICHARD. *Criminalistics: An Introduction to Forensic Science*. 5th ed. Upper Saddle River, NJ: Prentice Hall, 1975.

SCHMALLEGER, FRANK. *Ethics in Criminal Justice*. Bristol, IN: Wyndham Hall Press, 1990.

SHIMOMURA, TSUTOMU. *Takedown*. New York: Hyperion, 1996.

SIMON, DAVID. *Homicide—A Year on the Killing Streets*. Boston: Houghton Mifflin, 1991.

SLOAN, STEPHEN. *Simulating Terrorism*. Norman: University of Oklahoma Press, 1981.

STEFFENSMEIER, DARREL J. *The Fence—In the Shadow of Two Worlds*. Totowa, NJ: Rowman & Littlefield, 1986.

STEPHENSON, PETER. *Investigating Computer-Related Crime*. Boca Raton, FL: CRC Press, 2000.

TABOR, HAMES D., and EUGENE V. GALLAGHER. *Why Waco? Cults and the Battle for Religious Freedom in America*. Los Angeles: University of California Press, 1995.

THORNWALD, JURGEN. *Century of the Detective*. Translated by Richard Winston and Clara Winston. New York: Harcourt Brace Jovanovich, 1965.

TOSI, OSCAR. *Voice Identification: Theory and Practice*. Baltimore: University Park Press, 1979.

VOLKMAN, ERNEST, and JOHN CUMMINGS. *The Heist—How a Gang Stole $8,000,000 at Kennedy Airport and Lived to Regret It*. New York: Franklin Watts, 1986.

WAKEFIELD, HOLLIDA, and RALPH UNDERWAGER. *Accusations of Child Sexual Abuse*. Springfield, IL: Charles C Thomas, 1988.

WALLS, H. J. *Forensic Science*. 2nd ed. New York: Praeger, 1974.

WAMBAUGH, JOSEPH. *The Blooding*. New York: Perigord Press (Bantam Books), 1989.

WARNER, CARMEN GERMAINE, ed. *Rape and Sexual Assault: Management and Intervention*. Rockville, MD: Aspen Systems, 1980.

WELLS, KENNETH M., and PAUL B. WESTON. *Criminal Procedure and Trial Practice*. Upper Saddle River, NJ: Prentice Hall, 1977.

WESTON, PAUL B., and KENNETH M. WELLS. *Criminal Law*. Santa Monica, CA: Goodyear, 1978.

WESTON, PAUL B., KENNETH M. WELLS, and MARLENE HERTOGHE. *Criminal Evidence for Police*. 4th ed. Upper Saddle River, NJ: Prentice Hall, 1995.

WHITED, CHARLES. *The Decoy Man—The Extraordinary Adventures of an Undercover Cop*. Chicago: Playboy Press, 1973.

WILSON, JAMES Q. *The Moral Sense*. New York: Free Press, 1993.

INDEX